THE
NETANYAHU
YEARS

THE NETANYAHU YEARS

✡

BEN CASPIT

Translated by Ora Cummings

THOMAS DUNNE BOOKS
St. Martin's Press
New York

To those who dared to speak

THOMAS DUNNE BOOKS.
An imprint of St. Martin's Press.

THE NETANYAHU YEARS. Copyright © 2017 by Ben Caspit. Translation © 2017 by
Ora Cummings. All rights reserved. Printed in the United States of America. For information,
address St. Martin's Press, 175 Fifth Avenue, New York, N.Y. 10010.

www.thomasdunnebooks.com
www.stmartins.com

The Library of Congress Cataloging-in-Publication Data is available upon request.

ISBN 978-1-250-08705-8 (hardcover)
ISBN 978-1-250-08706-5 (ebook)

Our books may be purchased in bulk for promotional, educational, or business use.
Please contact your local bookseller or the Macmillan Corporate and Premium Sales
Department at 1-800-221-7945, extension 5442, or by email at
MacmillanSpecialMarkets@macmillan.com.

First Edition: July 2017

10 9 8 7 6 5 4 3 2 1

Contents

PART ONE

✡

BIOGRAPHY

1

Return of the "Bibi Spirit"

March 2015

On Wednesday, March 11, 2015, six days before the general election, Benjamin Netanyahu summoned a few leaders of the settler movement to an urgent meeting at the prime minister's Jerusalem residence. It wasn't the ordinary forum of Judea and Samaria leaders, those who have ties with the media and regularly leak the contents of their meetings with the PM to the press. This was to be a key meeting; historic, even. Netanyahu required complete secrecy. He had invited only people in whom he had absolute faith: those closest to him, the most experienced and reliable activists on the ground, the people who could tell Netanyahu what he needed to know.

What he most wanted on that day were voters. The last weeks of the campaign had turned into a catastrophe for Netanyahu. Everything that could go wrong had gone wrong. After unilaterally calling the election to score an easy victory, he suddenly found himself slipping behind his enemy, Yitzhak Herzog, in all the polls. From a sure winner and eternal prime minister, Netanyahu turned into a lame duck waiting to be put out of its misery. Herzog was leading by a steady two to four points. The street was controlled by left-wing NGOs funded by American billionaires supporting the peace process. Those parts of the media that could not yet be controlled by Netanyahu filled the headlines with derogatory stories about his wife and him. A constant stream of former generals called for Netanyahu's ouster and replacement, claiming he was jeopardizing Israel's security. According to most pollsters the gap between Netanyahu and Herzog was even greater, and the wider it became, the sooner Netanyahu's imminent collapse. Herzog's campaign managers spoke of a double-digit victory. It had happened before to Netanyahu in 1999 when he was pushed from office by Ehud Barak. Bibi had opened that campaign with a lead of 1 or 2 percent and ended it with total failure.

During the final weeks of the 2015 campaign, Netanyahu was subjected to a seemingly endless series of electoral catastrophes. The media were full of stories of his wife's obsession with collecting empty bottles for recycling and pocketing the deposit on bottles bought with public funds. There was the state comptroller's report on greedy and wasteful spending in the PM's residences (both official and private); a failed broadcast campaign comparing the country's larger trade unions with Hamas in Gaza; and there was the ongoing housing and real estate crisis in Israel, most of the responsibility for which fell on Netanyahu's shoulders. All this added to the fact that less than a year earlier, Tel Aviv had been bombed by Hamas nonstop for two months. There was more. In short, Bibi was everyone's scapegoat. Led by the free daily *Israel Today*, financed by a staunch supporter, the American casino mogul Sheldon Adelson, he tried to fight back, but by this time Netanyahu was drowning in a flood of bad news that threatened his tenure in the prime minister's office.

Netanyahu was under siege. He was surrounded by political adversaries aspiring to replace him, or at least to kick him out of office. Moshe Kahlon, a former minister in his government, resigned and established a rival party, "Kulanu." Kahlon had already closed a coalition deal with Labor's Herzog. Kahlon intended to go with Herzog even in the event of a draw with Netanyahu. Kahlon's wish to depose Netanyahu was an ambition shared by others: Avigdor Lieberman, who had sworn to depose Bibi, was in on it, as was Yair Lapid, who seemed to feel that getting rid of Netanyahu was his mission in life. Even Shas leader Aryeh Machluf Deri was sick of Netanyahu saying behind closed doors that he would do everything he could to rid the country of his leadership, even if this meant sitting in the same coalition as Yair Lapid.

In Likud, too, things were looking bad: Netanyahu had virtually no strongholds within his own party, except for that devoted stalwart, cabinet minister Yuval Steinitz. Many Likud MKs had already begun deploying for the "day after." Some of them held secret meetings with former minister Gideon Sa'ar, who had resigned several months earlier and swore to do everything in his power to remove Netanyahu from the prime minister's office. The knives were unsheathed and honed for Bibi's downfall, which was meant to take place the day after his election defeat. Senior Likud members vowed to learn their lesson from the 2006 defeat, when the party, under Netanyahu's leadership, won only twelve Knesset seats, an unprecedented political low, but at that time none of them had had the power to overthrow him. This time, the Likud leaders would not let that happen. They would not grant him a single minute of grace. According to the plan, Netanyahu would be overthrown immediately after his defeat.

Benjamin Netanyahu heard it all and saw it all. He was alone against the world. From Washington to the European capitals down to the city of Tel Aviv, everybody wanted to be rid of him. Yitzhak Herzog took wing and nested in Jerusalem, Likud's stronghold and Bibi's city.

It was during these days that, against all odds, he was infused yet again with the "Bibi Spirit" made famous in his first campaign. Call it the spirit of resolve, the refusal to quit, the code of the last man standing. Suddenly, Netanyahu had gone back twenty years to the days when he was young and full of energy, the great white hope of the Israeli right. Then he had managed to achieve the unbelievable: to defeat Shimon Peres only six months after the assassination of Yitzhak Rabin. Then, too, no one believed he stood a chance. The day after the Rabin assassination, he was sure the right didn't have a hope of winning an election for the next twenty years at least. But he won.

Netanyahu's wife, Sara, was also present at the meeting in the PM's residence on the Wednesday before the elections. Bibi and Sara are two people completely united in personality and spirit. Several of the campaign leaders were also present at that meeting, including Shlomo "Momo" Filber, a long-standing Netanyahu associate and a successful operations officer in everything concerning the Judea and Samaria regional council. Filber was the campaign's operations officer, responsible, too, for the program devised at that meeting. Netanyahu looked at the assembled settlement activists before him before embarking on the speech of his life. As far as he was concerned, at that moment this speech was even more important than the one he had delivered to the U.S. Congress.

"I suggest you start packing," Netanyahu told his guests. "I am facing defeat. The left is about to win the election. I will be ousted from the PM's office, but it's you who'll be paying the real price. You will be ousted from your homes. Remember the disengagement from Gaza? It's back. The left will form a government that will dry out the entire settlement enterprise. Some of you will have to leave the House; others will simply be dried out. But it's not too late. It all depends on us and, especially, you. You have to understand the gravity of the situation. It's a war of to be or not to be, a war for our home, for the Land of Israel. First you need to know that a vote for Naftali Bennett and Jewish Home is tantamount to a vote for the left. So maybe Bennett will get three to four more seats, but Herzog will form the government. The minute you understand this, you have to pass it on. To your family, your friends, everyone who is part of this huge settlement enterprise. They all have to understand the repercussions of a vote for Bennett in this election.

"I need one more thing from you," Netanyahu added. "I need you in the field. I want every regional council in Judea and Samaria to take responsibility for one or two towns with a strong Likud support base and act there, starting today and until Election Day; especially on Election Day. Our voting public is apathetic, doesn't understand how important it is, and I want you working in these towns, 24-7. We have lists; all you need is to go to the people and bring them to the voting stations and explain what they have to do. It's not impossible. It's not too late."

Netanyahu made a huge impression on his guests, some of whom having known him for years and having heard him speak dozens of times. But this time, they said, it was completely different. There was an apocalyptic air in the room. Netanyahu sounded like a prophet of doom and spoke from the heart. This time he did not make do with words; this time he would translate his words into deeds. Modern technology reveals voting trends in real time, which made it possible to pinpoint the reserves of potential Likud voters to the tiniest resolution. Databases and digitization make possible an organized and efficient campaign to reach every potential voter, in record time and with good chance of success. Filber quickly divided Likud's traditional voting strongholds among the settler activists. Electronic databases were updated. The system was activated. The pollsters intensified their pace. Netanyahu meant to fight to the end, not to lose a single vote. If he had to go, he wouldn't go without a struggle.

It was Benjamin Netanyahu's finest hour. The past year had seen a steady increase in the number of his eulogizers. The sixty-six-year-old leader looked tired, burned out, and sounded monotonous. There were no more rabbits to pull out of the hat. His slogan "Strong Against Hamas" had bankrupted itself during the month of rocket attacks on Tel Aviv. Most of his allies in Likud loathed him. Almost all the other party leaders, from right and left, prayed for him to leave. At one point, the most desperate moment in the campaign, a far-reaching proposal was raised in Bibi's inner circle: Netanyahu could announce on the eve of the election that this would be his final attempt to be elected prime minister, and if elected, his last term in office. The proposal garnered considerable support. Netanyahu himself was in favor of it. It may have softened the intense anti-Netanyahu sentiment that prevailed both within and outside his camp. Just give him one more chance, and then he'll go. It was his wife, Sara, who rejected the idea out of hand. And it was Mrs. Netanyahu's word that prevailed. The prime minister was not often one to disobey his wife, and certainly not over something like this.

As the campaign drew to a close, Netanyahu worked around the clock, gripped by a manic frenzy. Netanyahu is remarkable, sleeping a mere three to four hours a night. His dreams are no doubt work-related—how to bring home the votes he needs to prevail. When his adversaries rest, Netanyahu forges forward. An obsessive, relentless fighter, failure is not a legitimate option for him. He tries to be the justification for the victory. In the 2015 campaign, Netanyahu raised all these attributes to unprecedented heights, eclipsing his own previous performances.

The fight was not only for the post of prime minister, but for his very life, or at least quality of life. At that time, there was talk of a possible criminal investigation into irregularities in the prime minister's residence. The press and the state comptroller's report painted a problematic, some said sick, picture of hedonistic behavior in the Netanyahu household, and excessive misuse of public funds. Bibi had already been there back in 2000 after he was ousted from office the first time. Then, too, his wife was under criminal investigation regarding gifts that her husband had received as prime minister, and exorbitant expenses. Netanyahu and his wife were interrogated countless times by the National Fraud Unit. He had been thoroughly humiliated, but evaded an indictment. He would later say of his accusers that the police investigation and his public humiliation were responsible for the untimely death in 2000 of his mother, Cela Netanyahu. In the end, and after much hesitation, the attorney general decided to close the case without indictment, but leaving Netanyahu emotionally scarred. Ever since, he has been terrified of the possibility of once again having to face a similar experience.

Bibi knew that if he lost the election and was ousted from office, he'd be vulnerable to another series of interrogations, and was not willing to go through that humiliation. So, in March 2015, he was fighting not only for his political life, but also for his honor, and quite possibly for his personal freedom as well. He knew that as soon as he vacated the prime minister's office, he would lose the immunity granted him by the state's law enforcers. He knew all those who wished to collect a bounty on him, to be rid of him, who sought revenge.

During the final days of the campaign he pulled out all the stops. He gave interviews to every available television and radio channel, blatantly defying Israeli election laws that forbid political propaganda during the final two weeks before Election Day. Television networks played along. Netanyahu's objective was simple: Spread fear. He created a deliberate front against the media, banished a television crew from his official Jerusalem residence on Election Day, refused interviews to specific journalists, and presented a version of reality in which the left-wing media were trying to oust him from office by cooperating with the extreme left and the Arabs. He knew that this was the way to bring home traditional Likud voters and to rake in as many of the Jewish Home voters as possible. He wanted this community to vote for him, to identify with the siege he had been under, to feel indebted to him for his political sacrifices on their behalf, and to rally round the incumbent prime minister. He made his by now famous announcement that "hordes of Arabs are flocking to the voting stations," claiming that "buses funded by left-wing NGOs are driving them in." This was untrue, but on Election Day truth was the last thing that concerned Netanyahu. He knew how to stir the most basic instincts of right-wing voters, and had succeeded in awakening them. Throughout his campaign, his HQ distributed untrue video clips and beeper messages via social media claiming that Hamas and its military arm, Izz ad-Din al-Qassam, were calling all Israeli Arabs to vote against Netanyahu. It worked.

On Election Day, Moshe Kahlon, ex-Likud MK and now head of his own political party, toured the voting stations. Toward evening, he visited towns with a heavy Likud electorate, where his own potential voters were lurking. An experienced political fox who could sniff a Likudnik from a mile away, he noticed an extraordinary phenomenon that evening: large numbers of Likud voters flocking to the voting stations. Dozens of them greeted him warmly. We want you to be the next finance minister, they told him; you are one of ours; we love you. "So you'll be voting for me?" he asked. They were not and they said so.

"We are voting Bibi."

And so they did. During the last days of the campaign, Netanyahu managed to bite off four to five seats from Jewish Home, around four from Kahlon, two to three from Avigdor Lieberman, and a similar number from Shas party. Even Eli Yishai, who had established a party to rival Shas from the right, lost all his support and remained out of the Knesset. Netanyahu's campaign caused the right-wing ultra-Orthodox camp to lose much of its power, but it didn't matter. Netanyahu won.

Netanyahu himself could not believe what he had achieved. Just four days before Election Day, he was telegraphing defeat. "It's the end of an era," he said to his supporters. "We've lost." An internal poll gave Herzog a three-point advantage. It was the same on Sunday and Monday. But Netanyahu didn't despair. He fought to the end, getting louder and pushing harder those final forty-eight hours. The fact that he had become the underdog actually helped him. At the start of the two previous campaigns he was considered the man to beat for premiership, a certain winner. And in the course of those campaigns he lost five to eight Knesset seats. This time he was heading for defeat. At the last moment, the Likudniks rallied around him, which gave him the election. An idea of Bibi as a man under siege by all of Israel's enemies, starting with the media and the left all the way to the Arabs, succeeded beyond all expectations. Add to this mix President Barack Obama, one of Netanyahu's most valuable electoral assets. For Israel's right, Obama has been an enemy who wanted to see Bibi deposed, and that fact was a major boost for Bibi's campaign. Taken together with the massive get-out-the-vote effort of the West Bank settlers on Election Day, something unprecedented happened: Netanyahu's party won thirty Knesset seats, twelve more than predicted only a week earlier.

The first rumors of a possible draw spread during the afternoon of Election Day. As the stations closed, the gossip became reality. The television analysts were reporting a draw. Netanyahu, ensconced with his close supporters and waiting to deliver a defeat speech, was happy. A draw was all he wanted. Netanyahu headquarters had already sent out a group of Likud activists to demonstrate outside Kahlon's headquarters, to pressure him against joining a coalition that was forming under Yitzhak Herzog. By morning, it was no longer relevant. During the night, the draw had turned into a sweeping victory for Netanyahu. Earlier, in the late evening and into the night, Herzog had been trying to form a coalition. He spoke with Kahlon, Lieberman, Lapid, and others. They all gave the impression there was something to discuss. But by morning, it was all over. Netanyahu had thirty seats and Herzog only twenty-four. As far as Netanyahu was concerned, this was only the beginning, but even he couldn't believe it. The Bibi Spirit had done it again. The magic was back. Netanyahu had reinvented himself.

What was he going to do next?

2

The Pussycat That Became a Lion

May 2009–August 2015

Bibi vs. Obama

On Saturday night, May 16, 2009, Israel's prime minister, Benjamin Netanyahu, set out for Washington for his first meeting with President Barack Hussein Obama. Both men were new to their jobs. Netanyahu was apprehensive and downcast about meeting the new president. En route, he read the latest edition of the popular Israeli daily *Yediot Ahronot*, which carried the ominous headline "Bushar in Return for Yizhar," an article by veteran Israeli journalists Nahum Barnea and Shimon Shiffer. It was based on American sources. The story was simple: If you, Netanyahu, want American aid for everything connected to the Iran nuclear program (Bushar), you must meet Obama halfway on everything relating to the peace process with the Palestinians, both in general and in particular with regard to the settlements (Yizhar).

Netanyahu was unprepared for such a deal, so the headline only served to ignite the paranoia and fear that he already harbored for the new president. During the flight he talked with some of the journalists in his entourage, one of whom was myself. "What do they want from me?"

Netanyahu asked me. He was pale, worried, unsure about how he should act. He kept asking, "Do they want to overthrow me?" In secret, Netanyahu had prayed for the Republican candidate to win, war hero John McCain. With McCain, Bibi knew, he would be all right.

By definition Netanyahu is a classic republican, both in his world view and in his values. Had he not returned to Israel after completing his studies, the young Netanyahu—who went by the name of Ben Nitai—would have stayed on in the United States, and would almost certainly have become a successful, conservative Republican politician. But reality didn't cooperate with Netanyahu's aspirations for U.S.-Israeli relations. Instead of McCain, he got Obama. And, as if this wasn't enough, Obama appointed Hillary Rodham Clinton to the post of secretary of state in his administration. Netanyahu remembered Hillary well. In his opinion, her husband had played a significant role in Netanyahu's 1999 defeat, after serving only one traumatic and tumultuous term in office. At that time, Netanyahu swore an oath that he would never again allow an American president to push him out of office, no matter how powerful and outspoken. Obama wasn't going to make that oath easy. Netanyahu was consumed with fear as he flew to Washington. Obama and his chief of staff, Rahm Emanuel, awaited him the way a mohel awaits the arrival of an eight-day-old baby boy.

Three Years Later

President Obama is running for a second term in office. The Republicans are working through a list of opponents and in the end settle on former governor Mitt Romney. He's supposed to be the candidate who will make Obama a one-term president, and a historic failure in the bargain. Benjamin Netanyahu decides to do what no other Israeli leader has done before him: comes out in support of Romney, actively campaigning to defeat Obama. He does this with some reservations, but his actions speak for themselves. On the eve of the U.S. elections, Netanyahu hosts Romney at a fund-raising dinner in Jerusalem. His people, including his close associate Ron Dermer, are active in Romney's headquarters; Bibi adopts

Romney's messages, openly using them. And then there is the money: Netanyahu's patron billionaire Sheldon Adelson invests almost $100 million in Romney's campaign. Netanyahu encourages this investment. Ron Dermer has convinced him that Obama is a one-term president. A little push and over he goes, a job that falls to Netanyahu. They all agree that another Obama term in office would be a catastrophe for Israel, to Zionism, and to the Jewish nation.

In Obama's HQ They See, Hear, and Take Note

Obama defeated Romney and was elected to another term. Under normal circumstances, Netanyahu should have been shocked, remorseful, and considered a new tactic like repentance. He does none of these. On the contrary, Netanyahu deliberately weakens his relations with Washington. There were attempts to improve relations with Obama that culminated with his visit to Jerusalem beginning March 20, 2013, but in the main Netanyahu reverted to type and declared war on the president. In December he appointed Dermer to the very sensitive post of Israel's ambassador to the United States.

The Americans protest, but decide ultimately not to torpedo the appointment. They soon regret it. Dermer becomes Israel's ambassador in Las Vegas. He is refused entry to the White House, and so tours the country working against the president's policies. Things peaked during 2014, when Netanyahu turned Obama into a personal punching bag; and in early 2015, when he delivered a speech to Congress against the president's will. Netanyahu regularly preached against the president's foreign policy and remained steadfast in his opposition of the nuclear agreement with Iran to the very last moment.

In the summer of 2015, Netanyahu rejected all offers from the U.S. administration to embark upon strategic dialogue and to receive a large, generous, and important American "compensation package." Netanyahu relinquished whatever chance there was to reach a strategic understanding on Iran's nuclear program and Middle East policy. He refused all contact with Obama's administration, in the process defying the Israeli security establishment's wishes to take advantage of the deal between Iran and superpower stakeholders in order to upgrade Israel's military abilities. Netanyahu disavowed Obama, turning him into an electoral asset of the first order. He lost his fear of the most powerful man in the world, and adopted in its place a loathing and genuine disdain for the one person with whom an alliance constituted the most important strategic asset to Israel's security.

What happened to Netanyahu between May 2009 and August 2015? Did he undergo a personality transplant? At times he appears to be in a trance, totally detached from the world around him. He waged a lengthy war against President Obama, going for the grand prize. The strangest part of it is that he was fighting Obama as an equal.

This process that Netanyahu underwent over a period of three to four years during the second decade of the twenty-first century is at the crux of things.

3

Grandfather Nathan Mileikowsky

1880–1935

Rabbi Nathan Mileikowsky was born in Lithuania in 1880. According to the Netanyahu family tree, Mileikowsky was a distant descendant of the Gaon of Vilna. At eighteen he was ordained into the rabbinate, and he was an observant Jew all his life. As such, Grandfather Mileikowsky became a genuinely valuable political asset to his ambitious grandson, Benjamin Netanyahu. During Netanyahu's meetings with his coalition partners from the religious parties, he rarely skips an opportunity to mention his "grandfather, who was a rabbi in Lithuania," thus elegantly disregarding the fact that the distinguished rabbi's son, Benzion Mileikowsky, was completely secular. Like Bibi himself.

The young Nathan Mileikowsky admired Theodor Herzl, but when the debate turned to the "Uganda Plan," he attached himself to Ze'ev Jabotinsky, leader of the Jewish Revisionist movement, and changed alliances. Mileikowsky vehemently opposed Herzl's plan to find a temporary national homeland for the Jews in Uganda, instead adopting the Revisionists' right-wing ideology, according to which all necessary means should be used to achieve a renaissance of the Jewish people in the Land of Israel. Moreover, he approved the use of force against Diaspora Jews who were more concerned with "what would the gentiles say" than with "what's best for the Jews."

He wandered the length and breadth of Europe and many thousands of Jews flocked to hear his emotional speeches. The media defined Mileikowsky as "a brilliant grass-roots tribune, reminiscent, in his speeches, of Homer." His rhetoric was legendary and he became famous for his ability to hypnotize the masses.

Mileikowsky's first son, Benzion, was born in March 1910. Thirty-nine years later, Benzion would produce his second son, Benjamin, who was destined to become Bibi Netanyahu, prime minister of Israel. In the meantime, Nathan and Sara Mileikowsky continued to reside in Poland where they raised nine children—eight sons and one daughter—in a fiercely Zionist home. Nathan instilled in his family a powerful Hebrew spirit. They all spoke fluent Hebrew and yearned for the return to the Jewish homeland in the Holy Land. The family intended to move to the Land of Israel in 1914, but World War I thwarted their plans. In the course of the war, Mileikowsky, by now a well-known Jewish leader, negotiated an extraordinary deal with Germany that would take him and his family to the United States, where he would manipulate the American Jewish community into lobbying the Wilson administration. The goal was to keep the United States from joining the Allied forces in their war against Germany. Mileikowsky was willing to do this, but demanded in return that Kaiser Wilhelm pressure the Turkish sultan into granting a Jewish national homeland in the Land of Israel. Although nothing materialized from this plan, it is indicative of the family's general attitude. Thirty years later, Nathan's son Benzion would exercise a similarly principled move and, seventy years after him, so would his grandson, Benjamin.

In 1920, the Mileikowsky family uprooted and moved to the Land of Israel: Nathan and his wife Sara, who was descended from the family of the great biblical commentator Rashi; and their nine children, Benzion, Sa'adia, Elisha, Matthew, Amos, Miriam, Ezra, Hovav, and Zacharia. Five of the eight sons were named after the prophets of Israel, and the daughter named for a female prophet. The family took a tourist ship from Trieste to Alexandria and from there to the coastline of the Jewish homeland. After the exhausting crossing, they were transferred to rowboats that took them to Jaffa where they were shocked by the meagerness, poverty, and filth of the Arab-Jewish town. They spent several days in nearby Tel Aviv, the first Jewish town, only nine years old at the time and no more than a cluster of white houses in the middle of a sandy beach. From there the family made its way overland to Zemah, on the banks of the Sea of Galilee. After that they took a boat to Tiberius, and thence to Rosh Pina and Safed. Today, the journey from Jaffa to Safed takes less than three hours; it took them four full days and nights.

In 1922, following two years in Safed, a singularly neglected town lacking running water and electricity, the family moved to Jerusalem, where Nathan secured a job that suited his talents as director of the Jewish National Fund in Europe. At around the same time, Mileikowsky decided to change the name that his family had borne for hundreds of years in the Diaspora for one he chose himself, Netanyahu. He started traveling and spent much time in the United States and Europe. He was a talented public speaker and was considered the ultimate fund-raiser.

When it came to family, however, Mileikowsky was less successful. Years later his son Sa'adia published his childhood journal in which he described the beatings he and his siblings suffered at their father's hands every time he returned from his travels abroad.

Mileikowsky died in 1935, at age fifty-five. Most of his children did not follow in his footsteps. Five sons became businessmen, and eventually left Israel. Sa'adia, Zacharia, Matthew, Amos, Ezra, and Hovav became metal magnates, and settled in North America. Benjamin Netanyahu tends not to discuss the delicate, too-close-to-home issue of Jews who chose to leave Israel and make their fortunes abroad. The one daughter, Miriam, became a successful sculptor. Elisha and Benzion entered academia, but the only one to choose a political career was Benzion Netanyahu, Bibi's father.

4

Benzion Netanyahu

1910–1948

Nathan and Sara Mileikowsky's oldest son, Benzion, was sent to a boarding school in Jerusalem at the age of twelve. He took with him the fiery revisionism and admiration for Ze'ev Jabotinsky that he inherited from his father. From the beginning, it was clear that the diligent and intelligent Benzion would turn to academia. In 1929, he enrolled at the Hebrew University of Jerusalem, on Mount Scopus, to study history, literature, and philosophy. Like his father, Benzion believed that Jabotinsky would bring salvation and rebirth to the Jewish people. From an early age he harbored a belief in Jewish supremacy, armed struggle, and the refusal to surrender to another sovereign power. No one else could be trusted, no one else could be believed; the credo that burned in the heart of the young Benzion was that Jews could rely only on themselves. He began his studies the first year of the Arab riots, when Muslim mobs attacked Jewish neighborhoods in Jerusalem, Hebron, Tel Aviv, and elsewhere. One hundred thirty-three Jews perished in those riots and many hundreds were wounded. The riots intensified nineteen-year-old Benzion's belief that Jewish power was the only thing that would bring renewal. The time had come to stop talking and start acting.

In 1933, the leader of the Jewish community in Palestine (the *yishuv*) and one of the leaders of the Labor Zionist movement, Haim Arlozorov, was assassinated in Tel Aviv. To this day, no one knows who did it. But the Revisionist right was singled out as the culprit. This accusation infuriated the Mileikowsky/Netanyahu family: Benzion, like his father Nathan, considered it an attack on Revisionist ideology. To become a mouthpiece who would balance out the media's influence on mainstream *yishuv* society, he became involved some years later in establishing the Revisionist daily *Hayarden*, and was its first editor. The British Mandatory authorities, considering this paper to be a tool for incitement, would periodically close it down. Young Benzion Mileikowsky Netanyahu used the paper to publish attacks on the "defeatist" policies of the *yishuv*'s leaders, David Ben-Gurion and Chaim Weizmann, and to call for much firmer political action.

Benzion's rightist theories drove him to the very fringe of society. In those days the *yishuv* in the Land of Israel was governed by the Labor movement. When Benzion did not succeed in establishing a suitable academic career at the Hebrew University, he uprooted in 1939 and left for New York, disappointed, frustrated, and convinced that left-wing Mapai Party activists were trying to torpedo his political aspirations. There he grew ever closer to Ze'ev Jabotinsky and eventually became his personal assistant. Jabotinsky's sudden death in 1940 left Benzion in shock and pain. In Jabotinsky he had seen the greatest Zionist leader of all time. He decided to remain in New York and promote the Revisionist movement's agenda.

In New York, Benzion Netanyahu became familiar with the Bergson Group, led by Revisionist Zionist activist Hillel Kook, who subsequently changed his name to Peter Bergson. The group placed pressure on the American establishment, the Roosevelt administration, and Congress to raise public awareness of the plight of Jews in Europe, and to influence British policies on Jewish immigration to the *yishuv* in Mandatory Palestine. Bergson and Netanyahu confronted American Jewish leaders who gravitated traditionally toward the Democratic Party to take action against the administration. They applied public pressure, got people to sign petitions, plowed America from coast to coast in mass rallies, and even organized a "March of Rabbis" on the White House.

According to Israeli historian Avner Ben-Zaken, "It was at this time that the personal historical consciousness of Benzion Netanyahu was forged. For him, history became a movement through the dimension of time, one of profound and contradictory trends, of cosmic good and cosmic evil, tussling with one another. They rise up and hover above the surface, expressing themselves at refined moments of political catastrophes."

American historian Rafael Medoff conducted a series of interviews with Professor Benzion Netanyahu in Jerusalem—when his son, Bibi, was already prime minister of Israel—and subsequently published posthumous transcripts. In one interview, Netanyahu describes Rabbi Stephen Wise, the prominent leader of American Jewry in the 1940s, as a servant of President Franklin D. Roosevelt. According to Netanyahu, Wise was like all the other Jewish leaders in America, afraid of causing a fuss or making waves. All he wanted was a little attention from the president.

This, according to the elder Netanyahu, was the reason American Jewry avoided all effort on behalf of their murdered brethren in Europe. With his colleagues in the Bergson Group, Benzion Netanyahu decided to change the rules of the game. No longer would Jews cower in fear, waiting for some kindness from the squire; from now on Jews would be proud, vigorous, and active, uninhibited in their dealing with authority. They even tried to draft the Republican Party into the effort, get it to persuade President Roosevelt to change his attitude toward the Jews.

Netanyahu had told Medoff his theory about Roosevelt, essentially that he hadn't cared what happened to the Jews of Europe. They decided to drill some concern into him by exerting political pressure. The hope was that Roosevelt would then urge Britain to bring about policy change vis-à-vis the Jews in the Land of Israel.

Seventy-five years after his father, Benjamin Netanyahu would take an almost identical approach. The way the two events track is fascinating, son following in his father's footsteps under remarkably similar circumstances. "Roosevelt understood only the language of political power," said Benzion Netanyahu to Medoff. "The Jewish American leaders should have done what my friends and I did; we simply went to the Republicans. Only then did Roosevelt understand. We built a coalition with members of Congress and

Republican leaders, such as former president Herbert Hoover and presidential candidate Alf Landon, and we lobbied the 1944 Republican convention."

Seventy years later, Benzion's son would become the closest thing to a Republican senator, without even being an American citizen. At that event, at the height of World War II, the term "Jewish voice" was born. For the first time ever, American Jewish leaders and activists dared step out publicly against the administration and the president. Right-wing Revisionist Jewish political activists succeeded in setting the Republican Party against the Democrats on behalf of Zionist interests.

In both cases, father and son garnered political support in the United States to pressure a presidential administration about a Jewish Zionist objective. The first time it took place was during the Holocaust in Europe. The second came amid apocalyptic prophecies of a "second Holocaust." These prophecies were promulgated by Benjamin Netanyahu, mainly about the Iranian nuclear program. Netanyahu exercised all the considerable powers of rhetoric and alarmism at his disposal. This time it would happen in their homeland, Israel. As far as he was concerned, there wasn't a big difference between 1944 and 2014. He equated the 2015 agreement with Iran to the Munich Pact on the eve of World War II, and compared its nuclear threat to the lives of nearly seven million Jews in Israel to the fate of the slaughtered six million Jews in Europe as the world stood by in silence. Then as now, neither political restraint nor integrity could be allowed to get in the way. Benjamin Netanyahu's world view, in a nutshell, was "Never again." Catastrophic history was repeating itself within the same family.

The problem with this world view is that not all catastrophes actually take place, and not all prophecies of doom come to pass. On September 12, 1947, Benzion Netanyahu signed an announcement that was published in America, opposing the partition of the Land of Israel between Jews and Arabs. For the proposal to pass in the United Nations General Assembly, a 75 percent majority vote was necessary. Approval of the proposal would allow the Jews, on the one hand, to declare the establishment of a new Jewish national homeland, while being forced to compromise on modest territory and extremely problematic boundaries. As a fiery Revisionist,

Benzion was one of the most vehement ideological opponents of the Partition Plan, which granted most of the land to the Arabs and left the Jews with three separate territories with tenuous territorial contiguity and indefensible boundaries. To the Revisionist right this proposal was a nonstarter and they demanded its total rejection, but the Mapai establishment, under Ben-Gurion, was enthusiastic and supported it by a broad margin. With this accomplished, Ben-Gurion had to decide whether to declare the establishment of a Jewish state then, or postpone the declaration to a later date. Although he didn't have a majority in the temporary Jewish National Council, Ben-Gurion understood the historic meaning of the moment. He obtained a majority and on May 14, 1948, he led the declaration of statehood for Israel. It was the last day of the British Mandate in Palestine, and Ben-Gurion's declaration was preemptive in the face of the anticipated flood of Arab armies into the territories about to be evacuated. It is hard to imagine what would have happened to the Zionist dream and the fate of the Jews in Israel if Ben-Gurion had not chosen to disregard the alarmist prophecies of doom and make do with the little allocated to Israel. The state of Israel came into being with Ben-Gurion's declaration, the War of Independence broke out the following day, and the rest is history. Indecision, prevarication, postponement, or insistence on waiting for a "better option" could have changed everything. Shortly after the establishment of the state, Benzion Netanyahu returned to Israel with his wife, Cela, whom he had met in New York, and their oldest son, Yonatan ("Yoni"). A year later their second son, Benjamin, was born in Tel Aviv.

Catastrophes don't always happen, but with every perceived risk comes an opportunity. As Ben-Gurion proved, it is sometimes worthwhile to focus on the opportunity and take the risk.

5

A Young Family

1949–1967

Benzion Netanyahu's prophecies of doom for the future of the state evaporated with Israel's victory in the 1948 War of Independence. Israel expanded the boundaries of the Partition Plan and settled on the "Green Line," the boundary recognized by the international community to this day. After two thousand years in exile the third Jewish sovereignty was established in the Land of Israel.

After returning to Israel at the end of the war, Benzion was less successful. The stern-faced scholar from Jerusalem was exposed to daily existential hardships; he was unable to find suitable employment and suffered exclusion because of his affinity to the political opposition. At that time, Mapai, the governing predecessor to the Labor Party, made it virtually impossible for opponents to become involved in the young state's economic and academic life. Israel was a one-party country so, in order to obtain a reasonable job, it was necessary to be part of it. Having the right connections, or a recommendation from one of the *yishuv*'s bigwigs, was a prerequisite to advancement. Benzion Netanyahu had neither connections nor recommendations. Even in his own camp he was considered an odd duck. His exclusion was twofold: as far as the Mapai establishment was concerned, he was a member of the hated opposition; on the other, his fellow opposition-ists in the right-wing Herut Party refused to accept him. He was different, didn't speak their language. To make matters worse, all his efforts at ob-taining a position in academia failed. He grew increasingly bitter and frus-trated.

Fortunately, Professor Joseph Klausner, one of the greatest historians of the time, and a personal friend, offered Benzion the post of editor in chief of *Encyclopedia Hebraica*, which was seen at the time as the Jewish/Israeli equivalent of *Encyclopedia Britannica*. Netanyahu accepted the position and began editing volumes. Still, his time there had its potholes. During the midfifties, activists in the governing party began to complain that Net-anyahu was trying to disrupt and understate the Labor movement's role in important events, while highlighting the contributions of the Revi-sionists. Several years later Netanyahu had a falling-out with publishers of the encyclopedia, and resigned.

The atmosphere was heavy in the Netanyahu home. Benzion was an in-troverted and difficult man, an ascetic and a scholar, a man with no sense of humor who had devoted his life to books. His wife defended her husband by placing him in a kind of sterile bubble. Childish laughter and noisy games were anathema in the Netanyahu household, and Cela allowed no one to invade the somber and heavily fortified quiet surrounding the husband she worshipped. Discipline was unyielding and any child who violated it was punished, at times physically. A few of Bibi's friends recall that as a child, he was beaten on several occasions by his mother. According to some of those friends, the scar on his upper lip was caused by one of these beatings. It should be noted that in 1950s Israel, it was quite common for parents to administer physical punishment. "Spare the rod and spoil the child" was an accepted method of discipline. So although the conduct in the Netanyahu household was not commonplace, nor was it out of the ordinary. The awe in which the Netanyahu brothers held their parents was definitely unusual. Traces of his early years were apparent even in the adult Benjamin Netan-yahu. Whenever his elderly father entered a room, any room, Bibi would spring to his feet. When his father opened his mouth to say something, Bibi fell silent. And so it was until his father's death in 2012, at the age of 102.

In the meantime, the political and economic isolation gnawed at Benzion and exacerbated his inherent, unyielding pessimism. Even among his right-wing counterparts he was uncomfortable. He hadn't been in Israel during the war; he was barely there when the *yishuv* was struggling against the yoke of the British Mandate; he traveled the world, spent time huddled with Jabotinsky, wandered through America, and thus lacked the shared experiences of the underground fighters. During the most definitive moments in the history of the Revisionist struggle, Benzion Netanyahu was elsewhere. He was an outsider almost all his life, both in America and in Israel. And he instilled this in his sons. Decades later, when Ehud Barak was asked, in private conversations, to describe Bibi Netanyahu, he said simply, "He is not from here." Like his father, Bibi, too, spent many of his formative years abroad. His early childhood was spent in Philadelphia, then in New York and, after his military service in Israel, Boston and elsewhere.

A sense of gloom hung over the stone house in Jerusalem where the Netanyahu family lived. The moment the young Yoni and Bibi stepped out onto the Jerusalem streets, it was as if they were entering an altogether different world. Outside their home they grew up in a young, vibrant, enlightened, open, and uninhibited Israeli environment. On the surface, theirs was a happy Israeli childhood, at first in a small house in the Talpiot neighborhood and later in a more elegant building in Katamon. Yoni used to lead Bibi across the length and breadth of Jerusalem, which was at that time a city dotted with fields, hills, and nature reserves, as well as dangerous outlying regions on the seam between Israel and Jordan's Arab Legion. Together they accumulated experiences, kilometers, and adventures. A unique fraternity developed between the two; Bibi looked up to his handsome and inspiring older brother, who was the perfect role model. During those childhood years, Bibi's only aspiration was to be like Yoni. This, too, is commonplace among brothers (Bibi was a middle child, between firstborn Yoni and Iddo, born when his parents were older), but in the case of Bibi and Yoni, the relationship was intense. Jerusalem in the 1950s was a fun place to be in, and Yoni and Bibi were a familiar and popular, virtually inseparable, pair. They spent a lot of time together, sometimes involving themselves in squabbles where they stood their ground and refused to budge. The fact that most of their friends were from families deeply rooted in the Labor movement did not particularly impinge on the Netanyahu brothers' integration into the city's teen life. But when it was time to go home, they at once entered a totally different galaxy. They had to lower their voices, improve their appearance, tread silently, not slam doors, and not disturb their father, who was closeted "with books."

Yoni and Bibi were excellent sportsmen and joined the Scouts movement, where Yoni soon became a highly admired Jerusalem brand name. Bibi was mainly "Yoni's brother," following him everywhere and trying hard to keep up. Their youngest brother, Iddo, was quite different, more introverted, less of a sportsman, preferring his piano lessons to the Scouts.

Left-handed Bibi discovered a talent for drawing and devoted considerable time to it, when he wasn't out with Yoni scouring the area around Jerusalem. Often they would defy their mother by venturing dangerously close to the no-man's land between the eastern and western parts of the city, crawling up a hill and observing the activity of the Arab Legion beyond in Jordan. These areas were subject to sniper fire that resulted in significant loss of life, but Yoni and Bibi were unafraid. They were young, strong, and self-confident. Together they overlooked the "promised land" on the other side of the border, convinced that one day Israel would return to the Old City of Jerusalem. Yoni pointed out the region's important strategic points, and they would return home hyped on adrenaline. On one occasion, their mother discovered where they had been and gave them both a thorough hiding. They took their punishment in silence. Their thirst for adventure didn't fade, and they were happy.

A serious threat to this happiness came in 1957 when their parents decided to move to New York, where Benzion had secured the position of guest lecturer at a local college. Life in Manhattan's Upper West Side was urban and noisy and didn't agree with the two boys, especially eleven-year-old Yoni, who found it hard to exchange his Jerusalem school for the crowded New York streets. Eight-year-old Bibi was quicker to adapt. When the family returned to Israel two years later, the three brothers enthusiastically resumed their lost Jerusalem childhood. Bibi, a hardworking, determined, and serious student, excelled in school. More focused than his peers, he had a well-developed political awareness inherited from his father, and he stood out in ideological arguments that ranged long into the night with friends who did not really connect with his fervor. A right-wing ideologist, he believed in "Two Banks to the Jordan," the legendary anthem of the Revisionist movement, and never gave up an argument until he felt he'd defeated his adversaries.

Three years later, the family was packing up once again. Benzion and Cela had been less successful than their children in their attempts to integrate into Israeli life. Again, Benzion accused Mapai of being behind his personal persecution and, in 1962, he accepted a tempting offer from Dropsie College in Philadelphia to study the Jews of Spain at the time of the Inquisition, and to edit *Encyclopedia Judaica*. It was an offer he couldn't refuse, even if Benzion had had reasons to do so at that time. Since he didn't, it was left to his wife, Cela, to inform their sons that the family was moving once again to the United States. The boys were deeply saddened by the news, especially sixteen-year-old Yoni. Yoni tried to dissuade his parents from making the move and, when he realized he couldn't, begged them to allow him to stay behind with relatives. The parents would hear nothing of it. Bibi saw the brother he worshipped at his tear-stained worst and identified wholeheartedly with Yoni's budding rebellion.

One of Yoni's hopes in those days lay in his upcoming military service, less than two years off. In those days, the state made it hard for youths approaching military service to travel abroad. Benzion turned to his old friend Deputy Minister of Defense Shimon Peres, who solved the problem. Benzion, Cela, Yoni, Benjamin, and Iddo took off for America, trailing complex emotions of bitterness and lost happiness. Benzion never understood the extent of pain he'd inflicted on his children by these frequent moves to the United States. The souls of all three were torn. They were in Philadelphia, their hearts yearning for Jerusalem. They were Israeli sabras (Yoni was the only one born in the United States, but considered himself in every way an Israeli), trapped in their exile, longing for home and the streets of Jerusalem.

The boys' deep respect for their father never wavered. If anything, it became increasingly engraved in them until it was a part of their DNA. In years to come, a debate would rise among historians and pundits over Ben-zion Netanyahu's real value as a historian and as a thinker. Had the stern professor really been pushed to the sidelines by the Mapai establishment in Israel only because of his politics? The leading perception in Israeli academia was that Benzion Netanyahu's advance had been halted not for political reasons, but because he was not the genius he thought he was, and his problematic personality contributed to his career not moving ahead in Israel. To reinforce this hypothesis there are the examples of Israeli academics, such as Professor Joseph Klausner, whose opinions and ideologies were similar to Netanyahu's, yet who rose to the very pinnacle of academic life; there was also Professor Elisha Netanyahu, Benzion's brother, who achieved a glorious career in prestigious Technion's faculty of mathematics. It had nothing to do with politics.

Right-wingers such as Netanyahu, indeed blocked during those early days of Israel's statehood, were forced to equip themselves with weird and wonderful reinforcements to overcome those hurdles. Professor Benzion Netanyahu dealt with those challenges alone and without resources. His reclusive personality and social limitations, coupled with his not having played a role in the physical struggle for the establishment of the state, were his undoing. The debate over his professional stature may be disputed, but the narrative in the Netanyahu household was clear: Benzion Netanyahu was one of the greatest scholars and thinkers of his generation, and his genius failed to be recognized by the establishment for political reasons. The family was united around him. They learned to loathe the Mapai establishment and its leader, Ben-Gurion, whose regime was responsible for restricting their father's movement and choking his career. The Netanyahu boys were underdogs—adherents to the ideology of their parents, suspicious of everything outside the family, jeering at the establishment, and advocating the right wing's causes. Decades later, when Bibi was elected to a fourth term as prime minister of Israel, he faced an incredible political challenge: to break Ben-Gurion's record in office. This will happen in 2018, if Bibi manages to reach it as prime minister of Israel. If it happens, his family will have finally defeated the old guard.

In 1964, a tearful Yoni Netanyahu took leave of his family and flew home to Israel to enlist in the Defense Forces. He was especially sad about departing from his brother Bibi. Yoni sent long letters to Bibi, full of lyrical, even romantic descriptions of his love for Israel. Bibi committed his brother's letters to memory, and studied them day and night. As a youth, Bibi was reserved, never revealing to his friends in Israel how deeply hurt he was by his parents' decision to move yet again to America. Years later, a friend recalled Bibi telling him that the two boys wandered around their new environs weeping. Bibi was determined to stay in Israel and not become an American. His double life in Jerusalem continued in Philadelphia. At school, Bibi was a diligent student, serious and conscientious; consistent; competitive; and his performance was excellent. This did not change the feeling that he was an Israeli in exile. Throughout the year he worked in restaurants in Philadelphia to finance air travel to Israel. Every summer he arrived alone, and left again at the beginning of the school year. In Jerusalem he behaved like a local. He didn't talk about America, didn't boast, he just picked up his life where he'd left off the year before. He stayed with relatives and friends, wore sandals, and concealed his perfect English, allowing it to show only when he howled with laughter at the American movies that he and his friends went to see. (He was the only one who really understood the jokes.) He joined his friends at work camps, always the hardest-working one, the guy who got up before everyone else and labored without complaint. With knees aching, he would do physiotherapy at night and work through the day, lips pursed in pain. He finished his work quota before everyone else, ahead of the others in the number of flower beds he'd dug, or the rows of plants he'd picked. Always competitive, making a challenge out of every simple assignment, always having to come first.

And indeed, he did come first. Bibi had no sense of humor and never played practical jokes, nor did he ever dance or sing in public. His specialty was his ability to win. Even when his friends jumped into the swimming pool in Kibbutz Shoresh, Bibi would turn it into a tournament. Who can swim quickest, who can stay longest underwater? It exhausted them all, except him. His friends remember him being an obsessive winner. In everything, every sphere, whether it was swimming, working in the fields, or study, he was always competing, humorless. There was no alternative, according to his friends. He had to win. This was probably what was required of him at home, but it was also a deeply embedded trait. As some of his friends understood, a person who grew up feeling like an underdog couldn't avoid the aspiration to come first.

Even then, in his mid-teens, Bibi used to spout his economic theories and his belief in a free economy, and his deep dislike for communism. He brought this with him every summer from America; his right-wing ideologies came from home. He discussed it all endlessly, delivering his theories in the form of speeches. He barely listened to his friends' opinions and ridiculed their ignorance. He was a man of the world. His rhetorical talents were leagues above those of his peers in Jerusalem. His arguments were aggressive; he would sum up debates by declaring his own victory; anyone who didn't agree with him was inevitably wrong. It could be quite unpleasant. Still, Bibi continued to be popular among his friends, who eagerly awaited his return every summer.

In the summer of 1965, Bibi was introduced by his friend Uzi Beller (now a distinguished professor of medicine in Jerusalem) to Miriam "Micki" Weissman. They were both sixteen. "The prettiest girl in our year" was how Beller described her to Bibi, accurately. The chemistry between the two youngsters was immediate. Their love was ignited instantly. Micki was tall, beautiful, charismatic, and talented. She was a student of sciences at the prestigious Rehavia High School, which spawned numerous professors, scientists, economists, and even well-known military officers. Like Bibi, Micki also held right-wing opinions (albeit more moderate than his). She, too, loved challenges, and was a perfectionist and very ambitious. Both of them wanted to succeed in life and to prove themselves. At the beginning of each academic year when Bibi returned to America, Micki would sink into a deep melancholy. She was passionately faithful to him; everyone knew that she was Bibi's girl. He, too, on the other side of the ocean, was faithful to her and poured his heart out in long letters.

In his other life, the one that lasted ten months each year, Bibi was an introverted, serious young man. With Yoni he attended Cheltenham High School, located in a Philadelphia suburb. His parents chose to send their sons to a secular American school rather than a "Jewish" school. The family was awarded American citizenship, which Bibi relinquished years later when he was given his first diplomatic appointment in Israel's foreign service.

At school, Bibi was hardworking and diligent, sitting in the front row to the left, known to everyone as "Ben." Apart from football and chess, Bibi kept to himself, spending little time with his peers. He was thirsty for knowledge about Israel and ended all his letters with a plea to keep him updated. In the absence of the Internet and with telephone calls being very expensive, communications were limited to the postal services. He took no interest in American current events, and virtually ignored the war in Vietnam. Fashion, too, passed him by without a trace. He didn't grow his hair long like everyone else, didn't listen to pop music; his look was restrained. He had lost his Hebrew accent. He exhibited a keen interest in American history and learned to love it. He had a short fuse when he encountered anti-Semitism. Once he and some Jewish friends happened upon a group of local youths who made anti-Semitic remarks. Bibi and his friends gave them a thorough beating. Later, he reported the incident proudly to his friends in Israel, especially to Yoni, who reminded him that the winner is the guy who deals the first blow.

Bibi graduated fourth in his year from high school. In the psychometric tests he was among the top twenty. But he did not attend the June 7, 1967, graduation ceremony, usually a definitive event when all American youths are supposed to receive a diploma in person from the school's principal.

In May 1967, Israel was threatened by the gravest security crisis in its history. The Egyptian army crossed the Suez Canal and advanced into the Sinai desert; the Syrian army was deploying in the Golan Heights. Egypt's leader, Gamal Abdel Nasser, blocked the Straits of Tiran, and Arab mobs protested in the streets of Cairo, Damascus, and Amman, saying it was time to throw the Jews into the sea and put an end to the Zionist experiment. Bibi realized that his place was not in Philadelphia and informed his shocked parents that he was leaving early to meet Yoni before the outbreak of war. He arrived in Israel on June 2 and managed to find Yoni, now a reserve paratroop officer, in one of the troop deployment areas. War broke out on June 5. Bibi spent it at Jerusalem bomb shelters, hand in hand with Micki, filling sandbags and preparing shelters with his friends. At the entrance to one of these shelters, near Uzi Beller's home, they wrote their names on the wall: Uzi Beller and Bibi Netanyahu, so they'd be remembered. Deeply concerned, he followed the movements of his brother the paratrooper, who was on the front line, and was wounded by a round of fire that caught his elbow.

In the meantime, Bibi received the news he'd been waiting for from Philadelphia: he'd graduated in the top ten. It had been his objective. A couple of months after the Six-Day War, Bibi kissed Micki and set off to enlist in the Israel Defense Forces.

6

Brave Soldier Bibi

1967–1972

Within six days, the June 1967 war replaced Israel's existential melancholy with near-manic jubilation. Almost overnight, the state of Israel—only nineteen years of age—changed from a country whose tenuous existence was constantly imperiled to an empire that defeated the armies of three Arab countries, burst through the siege, and conquered territories several times larger than its original size, including the Golan Heights, the Sinai desert, the West Bank of the Jordan, and east Jerusalem. In Bibi's eyes, the real hero of that war was his brother, Yoni, who was wounded in battle. As usual, Bibi wanted to follow in his brother's footsteps and joined the paratroop brigade. He arrived at the recruitment camp together with his childhood friend Uzi Beller. To their surprise, they both passed the tests for pilot training and had to decide if they were willing to volunteer for a pilot course in the Israeli Air Force. Bibi's discovery that the IAF demanded a commitment of five years' professional service, in addition to the mandatory three-year regular service, decided it for him; eight years was too long. Beller agreed. The two signed a waiver and moved on—Beller to the Seventh Armored Brigade; and Bibi to the paratroops.

On his way to the paratroops recruitment tent, Bibi encountered a tall,

mysterious-looking sergeant. When he heard that Bibi was planning to volunteer for the paratroops, the sergeant told him about another, more interesting unit, undercover and prestigious. Bibi's interest was piqued. Within
an hour he was being interviewed for the IDF elite force known as Sayeret
Matkal, which was affiliated with the Directorate of Military Intelligence.
Bibi was interviewed by Danny Yatom, a tall, bespectacled officer, who
subsequently rose to the rank of major general, Mossad chief, and Ehud
Barak's chief of staff. Yatom asked the young Bibi if he was ready to invest
superior and constant effort and endure considerable hardship in the course
of his military service. Bibi was game. In the meantime, Yoni, a wounded
paratrooper in IDF uniform, came to visit Bibi at the induction center.
Bibi told him that he was trying to get admitted into Sayeret. "Go for it,"
Yoni told him. "It's the best."

The following morning, Bibi received the news that he'd been accepted.
He was pleased; for the first time in his life, he would be starting from a
point higher than his adored brother. Yoni was "only" in the paratroops,
whereas he, Bibi, was joining Sayeret. In Sayeret's induction tent, everybody was exchanging opinions on the tall, mysterious sergeant who'd head-
hunted them out of the queue for the paratroops. The soldiers Bibi shared
a tent with in those days remember him well as a tall, strong, serious young
man who was constantly reading books in English, didn't participate in
small talk or improvised games, but was always sure to go on long lonely
jogs, after which he would torture himself with a series of tough workouts,
push-ups and the various other physical hardships he imposed on himself.
He would return from his jogging session dripping with sweat and continue with exercises to build up muscle and improve strength. People
around him looked on in wonder. Diligent, persistent, withdrawn. He had
discovered that the basic training that awaited them, followed by the training for Sayeret, was tantamount to a form of physical hell. There, too, Bibi
had no doubt: he had to be first.

"Bibi Netanyahu from Jerusalem" is how he would introduce himself.
Later, they learned that he was what's called a "lone soldier" (i.e., he had no
close family in Israel). The commander of Sayeret at that time was Lieutenant General Uzi Yairi, the legendary officer who was killed eight years

later in the attack on Tel Aviv's Savoy Hotel, when Palestinian terrorists holed up there with Israeli hostages. The name of the military unit was one that no one dared utter in those days. The military censor forbade all use of the term *Sayeret*, so most Israelis were unaware of its existence. Its soldiers referred to it as *hayehida* ("the unit"). Bibi had landed himself in the most highly classified place in the IDF. He loved every minute.

Sayeret Matkal soldiers undergo basic training together with paratroop rookies, and only afterward do they go through the more rigorous training required by the elite force. Bibi was an outstanding rookie once again, awake before everyone else, demanding more of himself than anyone else, always doing his utmost, and trying harder, as usual, to be first. During his first parachute drop, he was first to go, not only because he always liked to be first, but also because he'd been advised by Yoni that it's more fun to be first out of the plane. The wild burst of wind slammed into his face; he was blinded by the fabulous checkered landscape below. He later described this moment in a letter to his parents in Philadelphia, adding that the second drop is actually more frightening. His letters to his parents were typically shorter than Yoni's. At times they were no more than polite notes. But in this particular letter he outdid himself.

In November 1967, Bibi completed his basic paratroop training and joined his colleagues to meet their new commanding officer. It was an especially stormy evening when they arrived at the central bus station in Haifa and met their commander, who divided them into teams. "We're off to camp," they announced, which meant "on foot," not "in trucks." Their camp was in the center of the country, some seventy-five miles from Haifa. In pouring rain the teams of young soldiers set off on their strenuous journey. It was a test of leadership, tenacity, and ability, the first in a long series that awaited them—twenty hours of strenuous marching that none of them would ever forget. Bibi, of course, turned it into a competition, and his team was the first to walk through the camp gates. The hardship was not merely physical; it was also, and especially, mental. That came as a huge surprise; they were unprepared for it. Another surprise awaited them at the camp gates: the people were exhausted but the team commander, Amiram Levin, later an IDF general and deputy Mossad chief, didn't stop. He continued to march his men across the camp and dragged them into the camp's training area, where he sent them through an obstacle course and various exercises until they were near collapse. Welcome to Sayeret, where anyone who shows signs of breaking will be dismissed immediately. Even when the body is depleted, the soul is supposed to remain strong. Bibi withstood all those hardships in a way that was almost perfect, without complaint. And finished first.

He was an outstanding soldier. During the long, exhausting stretcher marches, he was the only one who never asked to be replaced when the heavy stretcher was placed on his shoulders; on the contrary, he would sometimes tell the soldier who came to take over from him that it was too early, that he could go on. His fantastic physical condition made him the best MAG handler in the company.

His MAG general-purpose heavy machine gun was always pristine and highly polished, and Bibi could reload at phenomenal speed. Bibi's competitor for first place on the team was Avi Feder from Haifa, later a senior officer in the Israel Police. The competition was fiercest during the twenty-four-mile night patrols, when the soldiers carried no maps or navigational guides to help them and had only the North Star and the constellations to go by.

Bibi's baptism by fire took place in the Jordanian township of Karameh, a place riddled with terrorist cells belonging to the Palestine Liberation Organization. It was a time when Israel was suffering multiple attacks by terrorists who originated mainly in Karameh, and the IDF invaded the township in hope of capturing the number-one man, Yasser Arafat. The operation turned into a tragedy, with the IDF suffering twenty-eight losses and the Jordanian army more than a hundred. The terrorist command posts were blown up by an IDF force under the command of a young officer named Yitzhak Mordechai (who reached the rank of major general in the IDF and subsequently served as defense minister in Netanyahu's first government). A paratroop unit commanded by Matan Vilnai (later a major general, deputy chief of staff, and government minister in various administrations) tried to capture Arafat, who got away on a motorcycle, dressed as a woman. In 1996, almost thirty years later, when Bibi was prime minister of

Israel, he and Arafat met in the White House after the bloody uprising that followed the opening of Jerusalem's Western Wall Tunnel exit. They embraced. "In the White House I found a friend," Netanyahu is reported as saying. He spent the next years doing everything he could to live it down.

In the meantime, Yoni was released from the IDF with the rank of captain, and spent an academic year at Harvard before returning to study mathematics and philosophy at the Hebrew University of Jerusalem. Contrary to expectations, the Six-Day War did not bring peace to Israel. Security concerns intensified. In the south a war of attrition raged between Egypt and Israel, and Palestinian terrorists who repeatedly penetrated the country from Jordan carried out attacks at a dizzying rate.

Yoni was unable to find his place in civilian life. Bibi, who was nearing the end of his combat training, was being pressured to embark on an officer training course. He hesitated and suggested to Sayeret Matkal commander Uzi Yairi that Yoni should go on the course instead of him. Yoni Netanyahu, the legendary paratrooper, would fit Sayeret like a glove, Bibi told his friends. He spent long nights with Yoni trying to persuade him to return to the army, until Yoni was convinced. The two planned it all out in secret, behind their parents' backs. Even Yoni's new wife, Tutti, knew nothing. When Iddo, their younger brother, caught them quietly planning their moves, they stopped talking immediately, but he understood. Yoni did not remain a civilian for long afterward.

All that time, Israel was facing a new kind of threat. Terrorism in the air was beginning, including many attacks on planes belonging to El Al, Israel's national airline. One plane was hijacked to Algiers; another was attacked in the course of a layover in Greece. Israel decided to respond. On Saturday evening, December 28, 1968, helicopters crossed the coast north of Rosh Hanikra and flew at low altitude over the sea, skirting the land border between Israel and Lebanon. North of Sidon, the helicopters cut toward Beirut's international airport and landed there. Israeli commandos blew up fourteen passenger planes belonging to Arab airline companies on the runway. It was a complicated operation that included blocking a highway joining Beirut to the airport, in order to prevent the arrival of backup troops. The operation was commanded by Lieutenant Colonel

Rafael "Raful" Eitan, one of the most courageous officers in Israel's history, who subsequently became the IDF's chief of staff. Sayeret troops participated in the operation alongside paratroop forces, who walked around on the runways of the airport, red berets on their heads, as if strolling around Ben Gurion International Airport. Bibi and his team took part in the operation and blew up a plane belonging to the Lebanese national airline. A different team took control of the terminal. No passengers were hurt and the forces returned to Israel.

Then the ongoing War of Attrition between Israel and Egypt on both sides of the Suez Canal escalated. A decision was made to send the young Sayeret troops to the canal to carry out mainly commando operations on its western, Egyptian side.

On May 11, 1969, Bibi's team crossed the canal in rubber dinghies and laid an ambush for an Egyptian military truck.

The unit's attack came in response to traps laid by Egyptians for Israeli patrols and their attacks on commando units in Israeli strongholds along the Bar-Lev Line, a defensive line along the Suez Canal. The IDF was concerned about Egyptian successes and the Southern Command wanted to respond in kind. Sayeret, along with the paratroop unit, was sent to carry out special operations in the canal region. The paratroopers laid ambushes in regions vulnerable to Egyptian invasion, while the Sayeret and the Shaked elite commando forces carried out activity on the canal's west bank.

On that May 11 night, Sayeret's holding force, of which Bibi was a member, opened fire at close range on an Egyptian truck. The truck went up in flames. The unit's safe retreat to the canal's eastern bank was illuminated by Egyptian star shells.

Two days later, on May 13, when they were a short distance from the canal, the two young teams comprising Sayeret were called by their commanding officers for a briefing. Shortly before, the unit's commander had been replaced by Lieutenant Colonel Menachem Digli. The team commanders were briefed on a planned ambush of Egyptian commando forces west of the canal.

Bibi prepared a special sling on which he laid four boxes of ammunition for his MAG machine gun. The sling weighed almost two hundred pounds and Bibi was supposed to carry it on his back, in addition to his usual equipment. He arranged the straps of his ammunition belt to keep them from pressing on his shoulders or making any noise when he was moving quickly. The additional ammunition would increase his firepower.

His comrades recall that he was uneasy about the operation. Under the command of Amiram Levin, the force set off in a truck in the direction of the canal, a few miles before the waterline. They disembarked and continued on foot. Israeli Navy SEALs awaited them at the bank of the canal with three rubber dinghies. They boarded the dinghies and started moving toward the Egyptian bank of the canal. Halfway there, they were spotted. Egyptian star shells lit up the sky and the Egyptians opened heavy fire on the Israeli dinghies, which were several dozen yards from the Egyptian bank. They were taken by surprise. Haim Ben Yona, commander of the first dinghy, where Bibi was, was shot in the head and dropped into the black waters of the canal. The boat was riddled with bullets and started to lose air. Several of the fighters jumped into the water, Bibi among them. He forgot the excruciatingly heavy sling on his back, remembering only when he touched water, but it was too late by then. He started sinking. His strength and physical condition didn't matter. He was unable to float while bearing the huge weight of metal on his shoulders.

Fortunately for him, Israel Assaf, the SEAL in charge of the boat, noticed the disappearance of one of the Sayeret fighters. The water was disturbed when Bibi sank, and Assaf understood. He pushed his hand in and felt a head, grabbed the hair on that head, and pulled with all his might. Bibi gulped for air, on the verge of death as Assaf helped him release the heavy load from his shoulders and inflated Bibi's life belt. Bibi was exhausted. One of his comrades swam up to support him, helping him keep his head above water. In an effort to return to the Israeli side of the canal, Israel Assaf changed the direction of the boat, which continued to lose air. "Hold on," he called to the Sayeret fighters grasping the swiftly deflating dinghies. Bibi did not reply. He was unable to speak, occasionally losing his grip and sinking into the water, his comrades supporting him to keep him afloat. The boat made it to the Israeli side. The waiting fighters dragged it a few yards to shore and continued to support the sinking Bibi, who arrived at the bank with his last breath and lay there, depleted, physically destroyed at the water's edge, his chest heaving up and down like bellows. An Egyptian shell exploded a few yards away. The fighters rushed for shelter. Only Bibi didn't move. He didn't react. The body of Sayeret's commander, Haim Ben Yona, was not found despite the numerous attempts of commando divers. Some weeks later it surfaced near Port Said, a dozen miles from the spot where he had died.

Bibi's team took the death of Haim Ben Yona badly. He had been the first of Bibi's peers to leave for officer training and return to the unit. For Bibi, Ben Yona was the epitome of an Israeli soldier and officer, the kind of man he himself would have wanted to emulate. He was the first member of the team to fall in action. In his book *A Place Among the Nations*, Netanyahu described his meeting with Ben Yona's mother Shlomit at her son's funeral in Kibbutz Yehiam in the Western Galilee. She told Bibi that Haim had been born shortly after she and his father had been liberated from the death camps in Europe. Had he been born two years earlier, she said, he would surely have been thrown in the ovens, together with the million nameless Jewish babies who perished in the Holocaust.

Sayeret's training regimen continued, and Bibi excelled at almost everything. He did, however, have two significant weaknesses: a total lack of technical ability and an inherent inability to navigate. When it came to technical abilities, there was nothing to be done. Bibi is left-handed, and he is clumsy. He is incapable of assembling or disassembling anything. But the other issue he found difficult to master, navigation, is much more important. Sayeret fighters are expected to have an inherent ability to navigate with ease alone on dark nights in enemy territory. Bibi had no natural talent for navigation. His team commander, Amiram Levin, identified the problem and, liking Bibi's determination to conquer every obstacle, decided to help. The two spent many nights poring over maps, using a classroom ruler to measure out azimuth directions. They set out together on navigation tours.

Levin's personal project succeeded: a few weeks later Bibi was a master navigator. His test came during an exercise in the Negev, in which the entire unit took part covered in dust and sand. Bibi was in the last half-track in the row, and Ehud Barak and Yoni were navigating in the first half-track. Although Bibi had great respect for the two men—the unit's commander and his deputy—they appeared to be lost. First Lieutenant Bibi Netanyahu told them, "Gentlemen, you seem to have missed the point." The entire convoy turned back in the opposite direction. If anyone had had any doubts as to Bibi's navigational talents, here was proof that he had no problem.

Throughout his military service, Bibi never got used to the sloppy dress code of his kibbutz counterparts. One of the perks of being in an elite IDF unit was the license to be unkempt, the strict rules relating to dress uniform and fatigues not applying to Sayeret fighters, who improvised their dress and carried their scruffiness with pride. Bibi, on the other hand, was always neatly groomed and smartly dressed. Even his fatigues were tidy, while the kibbutzniks looked as if they had just come back from a stint in the barn. His speech was different from theirs, too. Bibi's language was cultured and he used American expressions, unlike his counterparts, who were unreserved about using vulgar sabra expressions that were alien to him.

He started to open up to his comrades, even on political issues, revealing for the first time his right-wing views and admiration for Ze'ev Jabotinsky. In those years, Sayeret Matkal consisted mainly of people from the Labor movement, from kibbutzim and moshavim. In that atmosphere it wasn't easy to be a fan of Jabotinsky. Bibi was undeterred. He had to be constantly involved, so he often found himself embroiled in political conversations and even arguments far into the night. And he always had to have the last word.

In March 1969, the Netanyahu brothers' plans shifted from the planning stage to the operative model: Yoni returned to the army, straight into Sayeret Matkal, and was appointed commander of the unit's younger platoon. Bibi's joy knew no bounds when his beloved brother had come to serve with him in the same unit. At the same time, Bibi gave in to the pressure to undergo officer training. He returned as a freshly appointed lieutenant and was given a team of his own, "Team Bibi." Now, too, he gave his utmost to ensure that his team was the best of the best. Training under Bibi was harsher, the objectives more difficult, the motivation higher. He had very few real friends. His fellow officers were put off by his extreme motivation, his obsessive competiveness. He maintained a distance from his men and was considered a good, but not excellent, officer. He was too square and lacked creative imagination, sticking rigidly to the rule book. Once at the final stages of an arduous navigation trek in the desert, long after Team Bibi's water supply had run out and any fighter would have given anything for a sip of fresh water, they came across an IDF command car towing a water wagon. It turned out that the water wagon belonged to another of the unit's teams. Bibi forbade his men to drink water from the wagon. "It's not our water," he told them. It took a lot of effort to persuade him to turn a blind eye.

At that time, the commander of Sayeret Matkal was Lieutenant Colonel Ehud Barak, one of the most creative and astute officers in the history of the IDF. Bibi worshipped him, almost as much as he worshipped Yoni. Barak, for his part, was enamored of the two Netanyahu brothers, although his real love was Yoni. A unique relationship evolved between Barak and Yoni Netanyahu. Barak was considered one of the people closest to Yoni, whose relations with Bibi were also close, but on a different level. Bibi admired Barak as a junior officer admires a legendary commanding officer. Only someone who served in this unit can understand the intensity of that admiration. In time, when Netanyahu was prime minister and Barak was minister of defense in his government, Bibi drew enormous pleasure from the fact that Barak was now working for him, and not vice versa.

"As far as Bibi is concerned this is an ongoing orgasm, the fact that he's approving Barak's operations and not the other way round," recalled one of his confidants.

As the date of Bibi's release from the IDF approached, the unit trained for one of its most complex and challenging operations. Preparations lasted nine months. The operation was to be carried out deep behind enemy lines by two of the unit's teams, and Bibi's team was one of them. Barak found it hard to decide whom to entrust command of the operation, Bibi or the second team leader. Barak's indecision deeply disappointed Bibi. So sure was he about being chosen, and so upset, that it occasioned him filing his release papers and making final arrangements for his return to civilian life. Barak, realizing he was losing Netanyahu, called him and informed him that he was giving him command of the operation. Bibi postponed his release. But just them, Prime Minister Golda Meir decided not to approve the operation. This was extremely painful for Sayeret, especially for Netanyahu, who had signed on for another year's military service but did not get the command he so wanted.

This disappointment did not diminish Bibi's unreserved admiration for his commanding officer. Barak possessed qualities that Bibi lacked, in particular a sense of humor, imagination, and creativity, which, as commander of Sayeret Matkal, he made much use of. Ehud Barak was a brilliant, original, and charismatic commanding officer. He was also fond of the occasional joke. Following a complex and daring operation carried out by Bibi's team across the northern border, Barak ordered Bibi to bring back a large granite pole that was less than a mile before Waset Junction on the Golan Heights. It was a simple order, but impossible to carry out. Bibi and his team located the pole, which weighed many tons. It is uncommon to return to base without completing a mission, so Bibi's team circled the pole trying out various ideas and types of levers, but nothing helped move the heavy pole. To move a pole of this size and weight, they needed more than a tank. Netanyahu returned to base without carrying out the order. It was the first time such a thing had happened to him; he was usually considered an excellent executor. But not this time. What began as a joke on the part of his commanding officer turned into a nightmare for the subordinate. To this day, Netanyahu remembers that granite pole from Waset Junction on the Golan Heights.

Years later, after having already entered politics, Bibi would say that his service in Sayeret Matkal had been instrumental and influential in shaping his character and abilities. The perfectionism, thoroughness, and sense of mission all helped prepare him for what the future held in store. Nonetheless, he recognized the limitations of the unit, which was elite, limited in size, and didn't function like the rest of the military. From the perspective of decades of experience, more people criticize the men of Sayeret than come to its defense. Although their personalities are completely different, Bibi and Barak both exemplify perfectly the weaknesses of ex-Sayeret fighters in every aspect of real life outside the IDF. Contrary to commonly held opinions, the job of Sayeret is not to kill the Arab enemy, but to deceive him. It is an intelligence unit whose original task is to use various means to provide quality intelligence from behind enemy lines. Everyone who has completed a stint of service in Sayeret becomes pathologically suspicious, obsessive, and inherently secretive. After the two had already served one term each as prime minister of Israel, it was possible to identify the strong similarity in the ways Barak and Bibi conducted their affairs. Both emerged as oversuspicious leaders, unable to delegate authority, virtually incapable of trusting anyone but themselves and separating the people who worked for them from each other. They habitually carried out simple tasks in the most circuitous and creative manner, which complicated life and resulted in serious fiascos. Not everything that is appropriate for a secret military unit acting behind enemy lines is necessarily right in the political arena. Both, Barak and Bibi are aware of this weakness, but it is stronger than they are. Over years of training and operations behind enemy lines, it intensified and became carved into their flesh, and neither man has been able to shake it off.

On May 8, 1972, members of the terrorist organization Black September hijacked a passenger plane belonging to the Belgian company Sabena on a flight from Brussels to Tel Aviv. The plane landed at Israel's international airport and the terrorists, armed with guns and explosive devices, threatened to blow it up with all its passengers if Israel did not release hundreds of Palestinian terrorists imprisoned in Israeli jails. The government of Israel entered negotiations with the hijackers, while Sayeret devised and began drilling a secret plan of action to burst into the plane and release the hostages.

The operation for the release of the Sabena hostages, named "Isotope," went into action under the command of Ehud Barak on May 9, the day after the hijacking. The fighters were armed with small 22mm handguns and dressed in white El Al flight technicians' overalls so they would look like they were on their way to repair some malfunctions in the plane. The fighters broke into the plane on Barak's signal. The operation was over in ten minutes: two male terrorists were killed, two female terrorists captured, three passengers wounded (one fatally), and two Israeli fighters sustained light injuries. One of these was Bibi, who was hit in the shoulder by a bullet fired by fellow Sayeret fighter Marco Ashkenazi. It happened as he attempted to get information out of the female terrorist about the location of their explosive devices, when Ashkenazi slapped her hard across the face with the hand holding his gun. The intensity of the slap sent a bullet into Bibi's shoulder. Had the bullet landed a few centimeters to the left, Netanyahu often jokes, it would have solved a problem for many of his political rivals.

Bibi Netanyahu was released from the IDF in 1972, after serving five years. With his girlfriend, Micki Weissman, Bibi decided to go abroad to complete his studies. Shortly afterward the couple landed in Boston and Bibi became a student at the prestigious Massachusetts Institute of Technology. His whole life lay ahead of him, but he had no idea what it held in store.

7

Ben Nitai in Boston

1972–1976

It was not common in 1970s Israel for people to go abroad to study in foreign universities, especially not for a bachelor's degree. In those days there was no global village; foreign travel was complex and expensive, and the average Israeli student aspired to be accepted by the Hebrew University of Jerusalem, Tel Aviv University, or Haifa's Technion. Not so for Bibi. By the time of his release from the IDF, his girlfriend, Micki Weissman, already had a bachelor of science in chemistry and physics. Bibi spoke of studying in America. He was familiar with the prestigious American universities, believed in the American education system, and knew that an American degree would open doors to a successful career. He was fluent in English, his parents were still living in Philadelphia, and Micki was happy to go with him.

Armed with impressive letters of recommendation, he first enrolled at Cornell University, and Micki enrolled at Brandeis to study for a graduate degree. Only when he realized that his studies would place him in upstate New York and Micki in Boston did Netanyahu transfer to MIT. His excellent high school grades, perfect English, and American citizenship got him in, but Bibi was in a hurry. He wanted to complete his studies as quickly as possible. His plan was to study architecture and business administration.

Years later, Professor Leon Groisser, then dean of students, recalled a conversation with the young undergraduate, who was registered as Ben Nitai. Bibi had asked to be allowed to complete the course in four years. Groisser tried to explain that this was impossible, but Bibi insisted that he could do it. If he were given the chance he wouldn't let the professor down. Groisser capitulated, and Bibi did it. When Bibi was elected prime minister of Israel for the first time in 1996, Groisser told *Yediot Ahronot* that although Netanyahu wasn't the most brilliant student he'd encountered in his life, he was certainly the most ambitious. He focused on an objective and decided when he wanted something that there was nothing he couldn't achieve.

Some months after arriving in the United States, Bibi and Micki were married in the elegant back garden of his uncle Zackary Milo (Zacharia Mileikowsky), in a Westchester County suburb of New York. His parents, Benzion and Cela, attended. Shortly afterward, the young couple adopted the more American-sounding name that Bibi had adopted at MIT: Nitai. It was Micki's idea; she was tired of having to explain the more cumbersome name Netanyahu, and Bibi went along with it. Nitai was a pseudonym his father sometimes used in his articles, after Nitai Arbeli, a famous sage from the Mishna period. When Yoni arrived at their Boston home some months later and noticed the new name, he was sufficiently impressed to change his own name to Nitai. When he was killed in 1976, Yoni was buried under the name Netanyahu, at the special request of his parents. The tragedy caused Bibi to revert to his childhood name. Thus Yoni, at his death, and Bibi, still in his lifetime, returned to their original name, which was not really original, since Benzion Netanyahu was born Mileikowsky and Hebraized his name.

The years during which he shortened his first name to Ben caused Bibi considerable trouble in the future. When he ran for the premiership, rumors were rife that he was planning to leave Israel and build his life in America. Many official documents still have him registered under the name Ben Nitai, and the naturally suspicious Israelis used this fact against him. Bibi denied everything. The truth, as always, lies somewhere in the middle. Bibi did not plan to emigrate from Israel, but many thousands of Israelis did emigrate without planning to do so. They left to further their studies abroad and find employment, but then assimilated, married, had children, and stayed. Bibi didn't have plans to do that, but it could easily have happened, if other things hadn't occured.

His student years in America were the happiest of Bibi's life. He was free, in love with Micki, and relatively laid-back. Despite a persistant lack of funds, he soon discovered the good life, even developing early signs of hedonism. Micki was an excellent hostess and the couple was as popular on campus as off. Bibi visited museums, exhibitions, and galleries. His penchant for Italian restaurants began during those years and continues to this day. During his long conversations with Micki, he barely mentioned politics. He was at peace with himself and it seems he was enjoying his life.

As a typical middle child, Bibi had to struggle all his life for recognition. His father was remote and his mother worshipped Yoni, so Bibi always knew that he was, at best, number two. In the Netanyahu household, there was only one significant number one, Yoni, who bore the torch for the family. It was he who was revered, the designated, the one singled out for greatness. Yoni was the son who might rise to be the IDF's chief of staff and, later, even prime minister. The task designated for him by his father was to bring his rejected Revisionist family to the position it was destined for, namely the leadership of the Jewish nation. Yoni was born for this role and played the game with all his might. Bibi, too, understood and never shirked his supporting role in this play. It was the reason Bibi relinquished his birthright from the onset and gave it to Yoni. For him nothing could be taken for granted. He had to struggle for each achievement and every bit of popularity outside the family, and for every crumb of recognition meted out by his parents. It was for this reason that Bibi resigned from Sayeret after five years and made room for his brother to become its commander. During those long-ago years in Boston, Bibi tried to plan a different life for himself as a famous architect, or perhaps a successful businessman; to establish a career, maybe even make money, achieve fame in fields where he would not be in the heavy shadow of Yoni.

These plans changed in October 1973, when complacent Israel was surprised by the Egyptian and Syrian armies in the start of the Yom Kippur War. Bibi managed to find a seat on a plane to Israel. While en route he also encountered Uzi Beller, his childhood friend from Jerusalem, who was studying medicine in New York.

Bibi tried unsuccessfully to locate Yoni. Between wars, Sayeret Matkal is the busiest of all the IDF units. In wartime Sayeret fighters find themselves helping the large armored corps units. During the first days of the war, Yoni fought a courageous battle in the Golan Heights against a Syrian commando force that had taken over an IDF command post. After that, Yoni commanded a Sayeret force that rescued armored corps officer Lieutenant Colonel Yossi Ben Hanan, who achieved fame in a *Life* magazine cover from the Six-Day War where he is crossing the Suez Canal waving a Kalashnikov rifle in the air. Bibi, in the meantime, joined an infantry corps, and his Sayeret force made its way to Sinai to defend IDF tanks in nightcaps against Egyptian commandos. He took part in defending tanks under the command of Ehud Barak, who had returned home from his studies in New York and was given command of an armored corps brigade. Later, Bibi was moved to similar tasks on the northern front. Yoni and Bibi, and their younger brother Iddo, all survived the Yom Kippur War.

Bibi did not remain in Israel a single day longer than necessary. As soon as a cease-fire was declared in late October, he returned to Boston and his studies. Sometime later, he met Colette Avital, Israel's local consul general, who identified his exceptional talents for rhetoric and used him in pro-Israel lectures. He was thrilled when he discovered that he was even getting paid (a token $25) for these lectures. In no time at all, he had become a sophisticated lecture beast. On one occasion Avital asked him to represent Israel in a televised debate against Edward Said, one of the most eloquent and impressive speakers the Palestinians have ever had in America. To her surprise, Bibi was happy to accept. She was apprehensive. Said was older than Bibi, much more experienced, had participated in countless such confrontations, and was a veteran television guest. Bibi was a young, unknown student. When she watched the confrontation, Avital's jaw dropped. Bibi was calm and fearless, challenging Said as an equal, time after time managing to surprise the Palestinian professor.

The confrontation was a definitive event, the first meeting between Ben Nitai—aka Benjamin Netanyahu—and a television audience. This meeting sparked a love affair, one that has lasted to this day. Never before had Israel had so effective and impressive a spokesperson as Bibi Netanyahu. The camera loved him, and he loved it in return.

Bibi graduated with honors, quickly studied the American employment market, and decided to go for it big-time by joining the prestigious Boston Consulting Group. For the first time in his life he became financially independent. His days of scrounging off rich American uncles and living in cheap rentals were over. He signed a $100,000-a-year contract (not including bonuses), was assigned a Thunderbird company car and, just like that, he was living the American dream. Bibi and Micki had no idea how short this dream would be, or how traumatic their wake-up call.

8

Handing Over the Torch

Micki and Bibi celebrated the bicentennial, Independence Day on July 4, 1976, with friends in their Boston apartment. They ate and drank, heard the echoes of fireworks, and then the telephone rang. Micki picked it up. On the other end, a woman introduced herself as a member of the diplomatic corps at the Israeli consulate in Boston. She asked to speak with Bibi. Micki asked what was the matter, but the woman was adamant and demanded to talk with Netanyahu. Bibi walked over and picked up the telephone. Within seconds Bibi's face had turned a deathly shade of gray. Micki needed no explanation. She knew at once that Yoni was dead.

The woman from the consulate used no platitudes, wasn't cautious in her words, and showed no sensitivity. She said dryly, "Yoni is dead. He was killed heading Sayeret Matkal in a commando operation in Entebbe." Deeply shocked, Bibi decided to spare his parents the agony of such an announcement and asked her not to call them. Minutes later, their friends had dispersed and Bibi took off on a seven-hour drive through the night to his parents' home in Ithaca. A couple of their friends offered to help with the driving on the long journey.

Bibi wept all the way to Ithaca. It was the hardest thing he'd ever had to do. Pictures of his childhood floated before his eyes, the so-familiar image of Yoni, who was no longer alive. Yoni, his beloved handsome older brother, his idol, who'd held his hand and led him through the hills of Jerusalem. Yoni of the Scouts, of the long emotional letters, of Sayeret. Yoni who was supposed to go as high as was possible, as far as was possible; who had led the family, who was his parents' great hope. The Thunderbird with the four youngsters inside reached Ithaca in the early morning. Bibi got out of the car and approached the front door. Through the window he saw his father striding back and forth in his study, his arms crossed behind his back. It was a regular habit of Professor Netanyahu's in the early morning. Bibi continued to walk toward the front door, his face frozen. Suddenly his father looked up through the window, saw his son on the front path, and his eyes lit up. Within seconds his face froze. He knew. There was no reason in the world for Bibi to be there unless something terrible had happened. The professor said something inside the house. Seconds later, Cela appeared, too. Bibi and Micki arrived at the door as it opened. The elderly couple watched their son and daughter-in-law. Cela met Micki's eyes and asked, "It's Yoni, isn't it?"

"It is," Bibi affirmed.

The flight to Israel was horrendous. The parents' pain was infinite, but they contained it with typical restraint. Bibi, too, swallowed his tears, even though a major part of his world was collapsing around him. He had grown up with Yoni, he worshipped Yoni, he was Yoni's best friend. He didn't know what he would do without him. There is no doubt that the death of his older brother was the hardest and most definitive event in Benjamin Netanyahu's life. He went to his brother's funeral as Ben Nitai and returned from it as Benjamin Netanyahu. Now he was the torchbearer. Bibi transformed overnight into the family's substitute big hope. Now that Yoni was no more, circumstances had turned him into the new "intended," to the one on whom all eyes are turned and in whom all hopes and aspirations are focused.

He was unprepared. He had not planned it, he didn't want it; he'd thought his life would be ordinary, in the shadow of his big brother. This idea would haunt him for a long time to come.

Yoni's death allowed Bibi to be reborn. The second son reignited him-self, but it wasn't an automatic decision on Bibi's part. He was given no choice. It was the "party's ruling." From being a student who dreamed of the good life in America, Bibi was now the man on whose shoulders lay all the history of the Jews as understood by his family. All that was now his mission. He was the one who would have to arrive, to fulfill and repair the injustices of the past. He would turn into a political animal aimed at the highest point possible; this was the fate he was destined for, and he had no intention of arguing.

The tragedy hurt his relations with Micki. Although he was happy with his childhood sweetheart, the lovely, impressive Micki, his good friend, the perfect hostess, Bibi became less available as he set out to find himself. In the university library, he met Fleur Cates, a tall, fascinating Englishwoman. As always with Bibi, it was the woman who made the first move. It was he who found it hard to refuse. A romance sparked between them. It didn't take Micki long to catch him out: one long blond hair on the lapel of Bibi's jacket, muttered excuses, unexplained absences from home. The minute Micki realized her husband had betrayed her, the moment Bibi admitted his infi-delity, it was over. No amount of begging, promises, oaths, or vows were of any use. Micki asked him to pack his bags and leave. She was pregnant with his baby, but she was determined.

A few months later in Boston, Micki gave birth to their daughter, Noa, Benjamin Netanyahu's firstborn child. The ties between the two remained firm. He came to the hospital, had his picture taken with his baby daughter, the proud father. But there was no real happiness there. Micki and her baby daughter returned to Israel when Noa was three months old. Bibi stayed behind in Boston, with Fleur Cates. He was already someone else entirely. He was the torchbearer.

9

Boston, Jerusalem, Washington

1979–1982

Toward the end of 1979, Bibi decided to return to Israel. Life in Boston had been most comfortable, his salary at BCG was high, and his relationship with Fleur moving along nicely, but Bibi was torn between the American dream, which by then was well within his grasp, and his yearnings for Israel. He obtained an appointment as vice president of marketing with the large furniture company RIM and, full of youthful enthusiasm, he attacked the new job. His finances tight, Bibi went back to live with his parents. His divorce from Micki was final and things weren't promising. But he didn't fall into a depression. On the contrary, he had plans. A few months after Yoni's death, he had established the Jonathan Institute for the study of international terrorism. He dreamed of holding a large conference for the institute in Jerusalem, with the participation of leaders, politicians, academics, terror experts, and journalists from around the world. Bibi devoted all his energy, talent, and obstinacy to this dream, which was realized when the Jonathan Institute convened the Jerusalem Conference on International Terrorism in July 1979. The institute's first congress was a huge success, with people like George H. W. Bush, George Shultz, Edwin Meese, William Webster, Jeane Kirkpatrick, Yitzhak Rabin, and Moshe

Arens attending. The conference was given wide coverage by the Western media, and Bibi managed to garner an important international headline. Arab terrorists were receiving military training in dozens of camps in the Soviet Union. Almost overnight, the conference turned Bibi from a complete unknown to "the brother of Yoni, hero of Entebbe," the eloquent and intriguing figure, the leader in the fight against terrorism. Had Google been in existence, Bibi would have instantly found himself at the top of the list of people involved in the "war against terror."

At the same time, he continued to make advances in the RIM company, introducing American management systems and scouring the sales stations and stores countrywide. One day, when he was moving between houses in Jerusalem, he asked one of his coworkers to help him lift furniture. As the two were piling Bibi's old refrigerator on the truck, Bibi suddenly exclaimed, "One day I'm going to be prime minister." His friend looked at him in amazement.

In the meantime, Fleur started visiting Bibi in Israel. Their relationship deepened. She pressed him to marry her, and to live in the United States. Bibi was undecided. His career in RIM was progressing and the Jonathan Institute was a success. At the same time, however, he was drawn to the American market and to Fleur, who was tall and beautiful, intelligent and loving. In May 1981, they got married in a civil ceremony officiated by a New York judge. Later, Fleur underwent a Conservative Jewish conversion.

Bibi's life shuttled between Boston and Tel Aviv. His ambivalence about the two worlds continued until the day he received a phone call from Israel's ambassador in Washington, Moshe Arens, who was seeking a political attaché for the embassy. Arens's proposal was completely unexpected. The relationship between the two was superficial; on his father's orders, Bibi had visited Arens at his Jerusalem home one summer. Arens, a veteran Likudnik, and a member of the "Fighting Family" of Likud, was well acquainted with the Netanyahu family and had been impressed by Bibi during the terror conference in Jerusalem three years earlier. Looking for a brilliant political attaché, he had initially offered the post to veteran diplomat Zvi Rafiah, but Rafiah declined. Arens decided to think out of the box and suddenly remembered the impressive, eloquent, and charismatic young man he'd met. They met again in the capital's Plaza Hotel. Bibi deliberated for half a minute before giving Arens a positive reply. For Bibi, the proposal was a gift from heaven. The position of political attaché was a serious starting point for someone who planned to conquer the summit. Bibi was definitely up for the challenge.

10

A Rising Star in the Embassy

1982

On June 3, 1982, Shlomo Argov, Israel's ambassador to the United Kingdom, was shot as he got into his car after a banquet at the Dorchester Hotel in London. Ambassador Argov sustained wounds from which he never recovered. The peace in Lebanon ended six days later when a large Israeli force invaded Lebanon and quickly advanced on three fronts across the country. The Israel of Menachem Begin and Ariel Sharon did not know at the time that this would lead it to a complicated, bloody, twenty-year presence in this land of the cedar trees. Bibi was busy at the time making the final preparations for his departure to Israel's embassy in Washington. When war broke out in June 1982, he was called to reserve duty in Sayeret Matkal. Unlike previous times, he requested to be released from service, which shocked his comrades. They were used to seeing Bibi volunteer for action, be first to fight in operations, quibbling for the right to be included in every battle, but suddenly, he doesn't turn up? Could Bibi have turned into a peacenik?

He had changed. His agenda was different. Yoni's death had left him thoroughly unsettled. He knew that his parents could not stand losing another son, and he had bigger plans. He quite rightly believed that the IDF and his unit would survive without him. He didn't like the reaction to his decision. He explained that there was political and propaganda work to do. This time he preferred the diplomatic arena to the military front. Ambassador Moshe Arens had placed heavy pressure on him to come to Washington as soon as possible in the wake of the harsh international criticism over Israel's invasion of Lebanon. Sayeret Matkal was now a part of Bibi's past. He was looking forward to his future.

Bibi stormed Washington with guns blazing. Aware of the importance of the media, including television, he soon became a popular talking head. He rented three television cameras and spent his weekends rehearsing interviews in his home, with Fleur playing the interviewer and Bibi the guest. He learned how to condense complex ideas into a few short sentences; studied his best camera angles, the importance of body language, the power of a message conveyed in a catchy or memorably clear and convincing turn of phrase. He became a television-appearance expert, spending hours repeatedly watching recordings of himself being interviewed. He started to adopt certain gestures, as well as poses and confident looks, to express leadership. He learned how to use sharp hand gestures, which he practiced when alone, to raise his level of adrenaline and, with that, vigilance, to get ready for an interview. He became an actor of sorts.

Bibi was hard to ignore. Within a short time he had formed personal friendships with major media personalities including William Safire, George Will, and *Nightline*'s Ted Koppel. At the same time, Bibi had regular meetings with heads of the leading newspapers, always leaving behind a trail of fans. Bill Bradley and *The Washington Post* fell at his feet; the brothers Marvin and Bernard Kalb; Barry Schweid of the Associated Press, Sam Donaldson, and others. Bibi also met George Nader around this time, an American reporter of Syrian ancestry. Years later, Nader would be one of the secret negotiators between Netanyahu and the Syrian regime, during Bibi's first term in the PM's office.

Netanyahu followed a similar ascendency among the large Jewish organizations in America. There it was much easier for him. He was on home ground with an excited audience that admired him. Bibi was the perfect poster boy for the Jewish community, presenting the ultimate Israeli sabra full of confidence, success, and courage, with a distinguished past in the legendary Sayeret, and as the mourning brother of the hero of Operation Entebbe. Add to this his impeccably groomed appearance; his perfect English; his deep, convincing baritone voice; and all the gestures and mannerisms Bibi had learned to affect, and you got an Israeli star in Washington. Bibi studied the corridors and levers of Jewish power in the American capital and became expert at negotiating them. He became the favorite of the Jewish billionaires who supported Israel, and was highly regarded by the Jewish community leaders and elders. In the embassy, he established an efficient propaganda system that operated with military discipline and reacted to any instance of smear propaganda whether blatant or subtle. He became self-confident, even repeating to one of the embassy's secretaries an oath from earlier days: "Just you wait; one day I'll be prime minister." The secretary, of a more liberal bent, was horrified. "I'll commit suicide if that happens," she said. When it did happen fourteen years later, she required an extended vacation.

In the meantime, the Lebanon War intensified. In Washington, Netanyahu was obliged to contend with a daily barrage of terrorist propaganda. Once it was the American diplomat Philip Habib, who was almost killed by IDF cannon fire; another time a small Lebanese child whose arm was severed, allegedly by an IDF bomb. Almost every week he had to deal with a media catastrophe that originated in Lebanon. Israel's public image was badly damaged. Bibi adopted a proactive approach to his messaging. He made no apologies, preferring to attack; the case of the girl with the severed arm being an example of his success. Suspecting that the story was false, Bibi asked for an enlarged picture of the child, passing along all the details to the IDF with a request for in-depth analysis. Bibi was brought up never to believe Arabs, and to always check their version, never accepting anything at face value. The IDF located the girl in Beirut and discovered that she had lost her arm in an accident more than a year before the outbreak of hostilities. Netanyahu rejoiced. But reality cut short this brief euphoria a few days later when Christian Phalange forces burst into the Sabra and Shatila refugee camps in Beirut and slaughtered hundreds of Palestinian refugees.

Pictures of bodies, including women and children, piled up and lining the streets of the camps, horrified the world. Israel was seen at the very least as having enabled its allies to slaughter their enemy. There was an international outcry. This time, even Bibi's rhetoric was unable to help.

Frustrated, Bibi complained to Israel's Foreign Office for neglecting to provide him with the necessary resources. He decried the archaic Israeli propaganda system, which was stuck somewhere in the sixties and dumbfounded by the Arab propaganda machine. Tension intensified between him and Foreign Minister Yitzhak Shamir. Bibi's patron, Ambassador Arens, did his best to minimize the damage. As far as Bibi was concerned, the war against terror was expressed mainly in the propaganda war. It was the only way to recruit the world to Israel's struggle.

The first order of business was to prove to the world that terrorism was not only Israel's problem. In his book *A Place Among the Nations*, Netanyahu wrote that a world accustomed to seeing Israel as an aggressor will clap its hands for every Israeli withdrawal from disputed territories. Israel will be praised and have its back patted so long as it continues to agree to unilateral concessions, but international pressure will still increase. Anyone who believes that Israel's propaganda problems will be overcome with the establishment of a Palestinian state will see that the Arabs focus their efforts on nurturing the national isolation of Arab Israelis.

Netanyahu achieved several significant successes on the topic of terrorism. One day U.S. secretary of state George Shultz summoned him to his office to share with him data on the spread of terror and its effect in the Middle East. Bibi was excited. Shultz spoke of the differences of opinion between himself and Defense Secretary Caspar Weinberger, who refused to use American military force against terror. Bibi voiced his own doctrine. Terror, he said, can be conquered in two ways. The first: never negotiate with terrorists or give in to their demands. That was the key. The second: never recoil from exercising force against countries that support terror and sponsor terror. Shultz agreed. Bibi went on to say that only when America understood the necessity of adopting a firm stance against terrorism, including political and economic sanctions and, where necessary, military force, would there be a chance of eradicating it. He proposed holding an international antiterrorism conference in Washington, under the auspices of the Jonathan Institute. Shultz agreed. When Bibi asked if he would be prepared to speak at such a conference, Shultz promised enthusiastically to be there.

Preparations for the conference were under way. Douglas Feith, special assistant to the deputy secretary of defense and friend of Bibi, suggested engaging the Jewish pianist David Bar-Ilan to host the event. Bibi agreed, beginning a long relationship with Bar-Ilan, who later became Bibi's choice to head the prime minister's propaganda department during Bibi's first term in office. The relationship ended when, in the course of an interview, Bar-Ilan let slip something unflattering about Mrs. Sara Netanyahu, an unforgivable offense in Netanyahu's world.

The Jonathan Institute Conference on International Terrorism, which took place in Washington's prestigious Four Seasons Hotel in June 1984, was a huge success and was attended by members of Congress; experts on terror; experts on Arabs; professors; and leaders of public opinion. Ted Koppel, Bibi's personal friend, hosted a special panel of media personnel. The lecturers included Charles Krauthammer; Daniel Schorr; Paul Johnson; Winston Churchill (the grandson); John Emery; Senators Pat Moynihan and Alan Cranston; Jeane Kirkpatrick; and Paul Lequest. The Israeli delegation included Moshe Arens and Yitzhak Rabin. The key lecturer was, as promised, Secretary of State George Shultz, who spoke about the need for change in America's policy on the dangers of terrorism. Bibi was overjoyed. He had managed to place the terrorism issue at the top of the agenda of a world power. And he became a megastar in the process.

Those were the days when the neoconservatives started to emerge in American politics. Some of them were Jews. All of a sudden you could be a hawkish right-winger, an intellectual, and have a liberal foundation at the same time. Bibi appeared at his conference as the grieving brother of Yoni, hero of Entebbe, and as a promising young Israeli diplomat, but he sounded just like an American neoconservative. He spoke like a neocon, thought like a neocon, and argued like a neocon. Bibi wanted to prove by example that the right can also be intellectual. Reason, based on facts, had a historical perspective, philosophical underpinnings, and a geopolitical outlook. Not for nothing does his third wife, Sara Netanyahu, repeat to anyone willing to hear that Bibi would have become president of the United States had he been born in America.

Following the conference, Netanyahu published his famous book on terrorism, which was actually a collection of the major speeches and debates at that event. At a charity event in which Netanyahu interviewed him, George Shultz recalled how he had showed the book to President Reagan and asked him to read it. Reagan was deeply impressed. A few months later, American fighter planes attacked targets in Libya in response to that country's involvement in an attack on American soldiers in Germany. Hearing this news, the Jewish audience burst into enthusiastic applause. Bibi was barely able to hold back his smile. At private events, he was introduced as "the future prime minister of Israel." If there was any embarrassment, it was not evident. Bibi accepted these announcements naturally and graciously. He was sure it was going to happen.

In the meantime, he had become a well-oiled fund-raising machine. He knew exactly how to excite his audience, to produce a well-timed tear; he pulled on their heartstrings, and they pulled out their wallets. He became an essential participant at charity events, constantly flying from one part of the country to another, and expanding his circle of contacts, acquaintances, and fans. The scope of his influence over the American media was also increasing. At one remove from all this chaos there was an inner circle known as Bibi's "Gang of Four," which consisted of A. M. Rosenthal and William Safire from *The New York Times*, George Will from *Newsweek*, and Charles Krauthammer from *The Washington Post*. They didn't move without hearing Bibi's opinion, and he knew how to instill in them his ideas.

Away from the limelight, away from the aura of the media, Netanyahu was beginning to accumulate enemies, especially inside the Israeli embassy, where many suspected him of being a shallow creature, without any real backbone, far too full of himself and ambitious to be trusted. His lust for power knew no bounds, was the main criticism at the embassy, and that he focused almost entirely on himself.

One ostensibly small thing that took place at the embassy around this time illustrates what Bibi's critics meant. One day Bibi set out for a meeting at the Capitol. He was late, as usual, and asked his driver, Moshe Hanini, to rush. The police stopped them for speeding. The policemen found a licensed gun on Hanini, but since he had been speeding, they decided to arrest him. Hanini was terrified. "What'll happen, Bibi?" he asked, to be answered, "Don't worry, I'll drive myself to the meeting." A shocked Hanini watched his boss get into the car and drive off. Hanini was taken to the police station. Bibi forgot the incident and didn't report to anyone at the embassy that his driver had been arrested. Hanini used his one phone call to contact the embassy's security officer, who pulled some strings and bailed him out. When he returned to the embassy that evening, Netanyahu still didn't bother to report his driver's arrest. Later, when one of the security personnel asked him where Hanini was, Netanyahu raised his head from the pile of papers on his desk and murmured, "Ah, there was some problem this morning. I think he was arrested or something. . . ."

11

Cock of the Roost

1984–1985

Ariel Sharon was forced out of the defense minister's office shortly after the publication of the Kahan Report on the Sabra and Shatila massacre. In Washington, Israel's ambassador and Bibi's patron, Moshe Arens, was summoned urgently to Jerusalem to take over from Sharon, leaving the embassy unattended. Bibi took over temporarily from Arens, and immediately set about imposing heavy pressure in Jerusalem to make the appointment permanent. There was absolutely no doubt in his mind that he would make an excellent ambassador. Bibi exercised all his charm, pulled all the strings at his disposal, and dispatched numerous advocates, including George Shultz, to Prime Minister Yitzhak Shamir to persuade him. But Shamir was resistent. He was too conventional, and the suave, intense young man in Washington disconcerted him. "Bibi is young and in too much of a hurry; he can wait a little longer," said Shamir, who gave the appointment to Meir Rosen, the Foreign Ministry's legal counsel. Rosen was a veteran diplomat, a highly respected and experienced older man.

Those were the hardest few months of Rosen's life. Officially he was Israel's ambassador to Washington, but Netanyahu continued to function in that capacity de facto. Rosen was older, heavier, an old-fashioned diplomat, conservative and restrained. In comparison, Bibi was a firebrand. Energetic and self-confident, he paid no attention to Rosen and acted on his own counsel. He stole political meetings from under Rosen's nose, took advantage of his absences to make appearances on *Nightline*, and did everything in his power to dwarf and undermine the older man. Rosen flooded Jerusalem with telegrams filled with complaints against his deputy, but all to no avail. Netanyahu continued to do as he wished in the embassy, while Rosen grew increasingly frustrated.

In the meantime, Israel went to the polls. The two blocs, Likud and Labor, achieved a political draw, so a national unity government was formed with the two leaders, Shimon Peres and Yitzhak Shamir, taking turns as prime minister. Peres went first, and the first decision taken by his "government of rotation" was to appoint Benjamin Netanyahu to the post of Israel's ambassador to the United Nations.

It wasn't easy. Shamir, the foreign minister, wanted the appointment for the distinguished lawyer Elyakim Rubinstein, who had already begun outfitting himself for the job. This time, too, Moshe Arens interfered by proposing Bibi. Shamir hesitated, but Arens did not capitulate. At the end of a government meeting he approached Prime Minister Peres, who was trying to hurry away, and struck up a conversation as they walked. "I have an idea for a UN appointment," said Arens. "I'm listening," Peres replied. "[I'm thinking of] my number two in Washington, Bibi Netanyahu."

"Excellent idea," said Peres. He would never have imagined that twelve years later this excellent idea would lead to Netanyahu defeating him in the general elections and becoming prime minister of Israel.

Netanyahu suited the UN appointment perfectly. However, he found the Israeli delegation to the United Nations in a state of low morale, even on the verge of clinical depression. Since the outbreak of war with Lebanon, Israel had become an international punching bag, and the delegation experienced disappointment and failure on a weekly basis. This only motivated him further. He stormed the UN hungrily and instilled new life in the delegation. Within a short time, he had become a media star there, too. His winning streak seeped down the ranks and the results were quick to surface. In the United Nations, too, Netanyahu never missed a chance to attack. He established a research department, developed new work patterns, gave his staff a reason to work hard, and created a feeling that there was something to fight for, and no reason to give up in advance. It was a diplomatic war and Israel fought back.

It was during the years he was serving in Washington and New York that Bibi's world view was formed and his opinions, methods, and outlook on America were defined. It was then that he established his extensive network of contacts among the centers of Jewish power and financial and political nerve centers of the strongest country in the world. He focused mainly on the Republican Party, which had been his party almost from the first moment. Benzion Netanyahu had instilled the basis for that in his sons from the very start. Back in the 1940s, over the course of World War II, it was Benzion who had tried to set the Republicans against President Roosevelt. Now, forty years later, his son Benjamin was collaborating with the Republicans at the height of their power. This was Reagan's America, which had thrown Jimmy Carter's Democrats under the bus. The neoconservatives appeared on the scene, Ronald Reagan's revolution was a huge success, and Bibi looked on with eyes wide open. He saw Reagan, an aging ex–Hollywood actor, transformed from a common joke into a successful and very popular president. Bibi noted Reagan's every movement, expression, step, and speech. He was especially intrigued by Reagan's ambivalent relationship with the media: sometimes ignoring or teasing it, sometimes flirting with and flattering it. Reagan was a superb orator, so his public appearances were always the best show in town. He had risen not from among America's elite classes, but from the country's obscure backyard. Being an outsider, he had no fear of the traditional structure of government institutions and power, nor of the trade unions. He conquered America in true Hollywood style, like a cowboy on a white horse taking control of a town from the bad guys. Bibi looked at Reagan and was captivated. It's possible to be an outsider and succeed, he told himself, thinking, "If Reagan did it here in America, I can do it in Israel."

Bibi spent much of those years reading all the histories and biographies he could lay his hands on, as well as collections of the important political and economic essays of the day. His respect for Reagan was great, but there was someone else who captured Bibi's imagination even more, someone who became Bibi's number-one role model: Winston Churchill. Bibi's idolization of Churchill continues to this day. As far as he is concerned, the great British leader is the be-all and end-all of everything. He has no equal. Churchill fired Bibi's imagination so much that he believes himself to be a kind of modern-day Churchill, a man who doesn't go with the flow, is not afraid to speak his mind, identifies the dreadful dangers lurking in wait for his nation, and declares war on them no matter how unpopular it is. Bibi read every work Churchill wrote and every book written about him. The British leader symbolized for him everything a nation requires: courage, originality, sobriety, open-mindedness, and determination. Bibi admired Churchill's ability to identify the danger of Nazism in time, not fall for Hitler's phony plea for peace; to insist on his principles, to fight for them, to not recoil from temporary obstacles and setbacks on the way; and to lead his people toward the final victory. Bibi decided he would be the Israeli Churchill, no matter what.

In the meantime, a loving partnership flourished between Bibi and Fleur, his second wife. She was beautiful, impressive, and articulate, an exceptionally talented Harvard graduate in business administration. Fleur became the editor in chief of all of Bibi's speeches, articles, and books. She complemented him, defended him, and worshipped him, and he worshipped her in return. She had been born in Germany to a Jewish father and a Christian mother. After the family had escaped the Nazis Fleur was raised and educated in the United Kingdom, where she acquired her British accent and mannerisms. Although it wasn't obvious, Fleur was several years older than Bibi, and she took care of him as a mother would. Bibi and Fleur became a leading power couple in New York and she, a classic diplomat's wife, made friends with all of Bibi's milieu and slipped into her position easily. She soon found a unique common language with Ted Koppel, a German-born Jew who had escaped to Britain at an early age. Throughout this time, Bibi continued to wander the length and breadth of America, punctuating his diplomatic chores with fund-raising missions on behalf of the United Jewish Appeal, Israel Bonds, the Jewish National Fund, and various other "scrounge" organizations. He was a fund-raising and propaganda machine, returning from every trip with a new list of fans and followers, most of them warmhearted Jews.

Shortly before Bibi began his term at the UN, the Israeli embassy purchased a small apartment on Fifth Avenue, overlooking Central Park, to serve as an official residence for the ambassador to the United Nations. Fleur furnished the apartment tastefully, while Bibi continued to nurture his relations with the New York media aristocracy. He became a regular guest on CNN's *Larry King Live*, and after every interview there would be a flood of calls. King was shocked to discover that a large proportion of the callers were young women asking about the handsome young ambassador's marital status. King himself liked interviewing Netanyahu, who inevitably delivered the goods. But in a private conversation, he scored him only an eight out of ten: "If he'd only had a sense of humor, he'd have got a full ten." A veteran interviewer with sharp instincts, King had identified one of Netanyahu's greatest failings, a total lack of humor and, even worse, zero self-irony. When it came to questions about his character, Netanyahu lost whatever trace of humor he had. Saving the Jewish nation and the state of Israel was not a joking matter.

Although he was adored by women, Bibi was never a flirtatious man. When it came to women, he was never the one to take the initiative. And he has never left a woman. Micki Weissman left him, as later would Fleur. Even with his third and last wife, Sara Netanyahu, Bibi never considered leaving her, despite numerous people who would urge him to do so. He's just not the type who leaves. In everything concerning women, he is passive. Micki was first introduced to him by Uzi Beller; Fleur hit on him in the university library; Sara Netanyahu was an airline stewardess who left him a note on a flight he was on. In New York, he was surrounded by well-known and wealthy women; flooded with proposals, hints, and winks. But to the best of my knowledge, he has never followed them up. He was faithful to Fleur, and was oblivious to the buzz around him, or pretended to be. Still, he was a social magnet, dripping with charisma, drawing interest and the attention of a considerable number of women. Strong women like Lally Weymouth of *The Washington Post*, Joan Lunden of *Good Morning America*, Jane Pauley, and Judith Miller of *The New York Times* were but a few of a long list of women who enjoyed his company. He continued to be a regular at television studios, regardless of how harsh or unsympathetic his interlocution. For example, he had no qualms about being interviewed by MacNeil/Lehrer on *PBS NewsHour*, or accepting an invitation to be interviewed by Pat Buchanan, or to sit with CNN's Evans and Novak. He rarely missed a television confrontation, always arriving on time equipped with the right card up his sleeve, full of self-confidence and charm. He flourished in the studios, and enjoyed every moment. His social circle expanded at a dizzying rate and was significantly enhanced by the well-known historian Bernard Lewis, who became another one of Bibi's confidants.

In New York Bibi discovered the good life again: expensive restaurants (especially Italian and Indian), fat cigars, and designer suits. In those days, he was unable to afford himself so expensive a lifestyle but, fortunately for him, there was no need, as there was always someone willing to pick up the tab, to provide the cigars, to pay for a suit. Bibi grew accustomed to living well at a low cost. Over the years, this became a way of life and he developed an attitude of entitlement. He suffered no guilt for living ostentatiously at the expense of others, and considered the fact that he chose to serve his people rather than joining the business world to be a kind of self-sacrifice. According to this logic, it seems obvious that the state would know how to reward him. And if not the state, then at least his friends.

12

Ambassador to the United Nations

1985–1988

Despite his success, Bibi never rested on his laurels. Perhaps because he aimed so high, he understood that there was always room for improvement. In 1986, the embassy's permanent spokesperson, Judy Varnai, left, so Bibi replaced her with Eyal Arad, a young, somewhat eccentric and reserved, bearded theology student. A short interview was sufficient for Bibi to know that Arad was perfect for the post. Extremely intelligent with impeccable English, Arad held right-wing opinions but looked just like a left-leaning flower child. Arad was appointed embassy spokesman and became Netanyahu's closest confidant. Until Bibi's 1996 election success, which to a large extent is attributed to Arad, the two became inseparable. Arad used to ride around the country on a large motorcycle, and Bibi enjoyed introducing him to fellow Likudniks as "a lefty with right-wing opinions."

But the two men's successful relationship came to an abrupt end as a result of Sara Netanyahu's meddling and, immediately after the 1996 campaign, Arad joined a long list of disillusioned "casualties of Sara," some of whom became Netanyahu's bitterest enemies, while others turned the page and tried to forget.

Back at the UN and New York, Bibi continued to improve himself. His book *Fighting Terrorism: How the West Can Win*, based on the Jonathan Institute conferences, was published in 1986 and quickly became a best-seller. Already a media megastar, Bibi was now an expert on terror and an especially desirable person to talk to on the subject. But his face had become too familiar, so the Israeli secret service (the Shabak), responsible for securing VIPs abroad, decided it was time to equip him with a bodyguard. After the Americans soon reached a similar conclusion, the man provided by the Shabak was replaced by three American bodyguards.

One day, when Netanyahu and Arad were flying to a lecture in Canada, the American bodyguards accompanied them to the airplane. A Canadian bodyguard was supposed to wait for them at their destination. For the first time in many months, they were unguarded.

By a strange turn of fate, it was on this particular flight that Bibi noticed two suspicious-looking passengers of Middle Eastern appearance. The two had mustaches and seemed to spend a long time huddled together and whispering. Bibi sent Arad to the lavatory to check out the two men on his way. Arad returned with worrying results, reporting that he heard one of them telling the other to write on the immigration form that they are Jordanians. Bibi became tense. He ordered two bottles of wine from the stewardess and asked Arad if he knew how to break a bottle with a single blow. Arad confirmed that he did. Although not a graduate of Sayeret Matkal, he had been a combat officer in the armored corps and knew some Krav Maga. Bibi started to disassemble his seat belt and asked Arad to do the same. "Wrap it around your arm like this," he ordered, "and if anything happens we'll break the bottles and go for them with broken bottles and metal belts around our arms. We can take them," he told Arad, who was beginning to sweat. The flight continued uneventfully—with the exception of two vandalized seat belts.

In addition to Arad, Bibi employed two external advisors: David Garth and Lilyan Wilder. Garth was charged with building Bibi's political image, while Wilder focused on improving his speeches and television appearances, as well as how to dress, what to emphasize, and how to respond to provocations. Bibi was a diligent and disciplined student and continued to improve. He also brought Ralph Swarman to the embassy team. Swarman prepared Netanyahu for his public appearances. He also prepared files of heavy intelligence and background material for each event, including never-before-published material, important points, and reasoned arguments. Nothing was left to chance. Netanyahu became a well-oiled one-man propaganda machine.

Eyal Arad made sure Bibi's exploits were covered by the Israeli media to make him as well known at home as in the United States. He caught the interest of Israeli's leading commentators, who interviewed him via satellite, completely overshadowing Meir Rosen, the luckless ambassador in Washington. In 1986, the Israeli daily *Hadashot* published a famous cover story forecasting that within a decade Ehud Barak and Benjamin Netanyahu would be competing for the post of prime minister of Israel. Barak was at the time an IDF general, and Bibi was of course ambassador to the United Nations. It didn't seem likely at the time, but it came true almost in its entirety. In 1996, Bibi ran against Shimon Peres and in 1999, he faced Ehud Barak.

Those were successful years for Bibi, who continued energetically to nurture the "Netanyahu brand." In his long conversations with Arad he was not yet talking about the premiership as a strategic objective, but it was there, floating in the air. Arad had no doubt that this was the ultimate goal.

Bibi made a habit of taking long walks in New York. Sometimes he was accompanied by his bodyguards, sometimes by Arad, and on occasion he went with others. Recalling his days in Sayeret Matkal, Bibi would walk quickly, taking long steps, usually from the ambassador's residence on Eighty-second Street to the UN building on Forty-second Street. He gulped up the distance, taking a break on the way, sometimes to eat a plate of fresh pasta followed by a fragrant cigar, a habit that migrated back to Israel with him. Bibi likes to walk quickly, to say little and to think, and always managed to turn even these walks into a race, never allowing anyone to finish before him. When he found a fast bodyguard, Bibi avoided taking him on his walks—as always, the obsessive winner.

Success soon went to his head. While he was trying to educate the world not to conduct negotiations with terrorists, in Israel the Peres/Shamir government agreed to a prisoner-exchange deal with the Palestine Liberation

Organization. Israel agreed to release some one thousand prisoners in exchange for three Israeli soldiers. When Bibi learned of this he was furious. Without waiting for official permission, he granted an interview to the Voice of Israel morning show and strongly criticized the deal. Prime Minister Peres heard the interview on his car radio. It was his turn to fume. Bibi anticipated the possibility of facing dismissal and prepared Arad, too. But no letter of dismissal arrived. Peres decided on restraint. It was Bibi's first declaration of independence; it was to be followed by many more. He was the ambassador to the UN, but felt no need to remain tied to government policy.

When Peres and Shamir changed places in 1986 and Peres became Israel's foreign minister (and, as such, Bibi's direct boss), Netanyahu occasionally contradicted Foreign Ministry directives, and had frequent altercations with Deputy Foreign Minister Yossi Beilin, who was very close to Peres. Here, too, Netanyahu was playing a dangerous game, but Shamir backed him up and made it impossible for Peres to hurt his overzealous UN ambassador.

Throughout his term at the United Nations, Bibi maintained close contact with his daughter, Noa. She was ten years old and Bibi missed her badly, stealing every possible moment to spend with her. Any opportunity to pop over to Israel for "consultations" was greeted, and he always made a point of meeting her. Micki was happy to comply. For years on end, Bibi postponed the divorce he ultimately granted her but, when he finally gave in, he was given exceptionally generous visitation rights with the daughter they shared. Micki encouraged the relations between her daughter and her father who was, during those years, the best he could be under the circumstances.

Bibi's relationship with Fleur, on the other hand, gradually waned. Their many attempts at having a baby, which included grueling fertility treatments, proved fruitless, and the relationship started to crack. There was no definitive crisis, no terrible quarrel, and there were no extramarital affairs. The marriage simply declined. The differences between them blurred by their great love for each other started to manifest themselves, and the flame burned out.

13

Coming Home

1988

Bibi took his leave of the United Nations in 1988, after four stormy and successful years, and returned to Israel. Fleur decided to come with him, to give her husband one more chance and to help his career. Bibi sent Eyal Arad back first, with clear directions: meet Moshe Arens and set about establishing a political camp. Israel was facing a general election, so the timing of Bibi's return couldn't have been more perfect. Likud was split into various camps: Prime Minister Shamir and Moshe Arens led one, David Levy led the second, and Ariel Sharon headed a third camp. The generation of "Likud princes," which included Dan Meridor, Roni Milo, Ehud Olmert, and even Benny Begin, was turning its eyes to the leadership and waiting for change. Benny Begin, son of legendary Likud leader Menachem Begin, had returned from abroad a few weeks after Bibi, and considered himself best suited to follow in his father's footsteps. It was clear to all that between the two men lay a potential minefield. Benzion Netanyahu and his colleagues ridiculed Menachem Begin, whom they found to be odd, a simple man devoid of all intellectual qualities. While Netanyahu Sr. was an ideologist of the Revisionist movement, a man who had poured water on the hands of great guru Ze'ev Jabotinsky, Begin was a worthless roughneck. How amazing that several decades later, the Likud princes would see in Bibi exactly what his father saw in Menachem Begin, as these men arrived simultaneously in town to realize their fathers' legacy. This notwithstanding, Bibi tended to cooperate with Benny Begin in their new venture. He even invited Begin to be a guest of honor at several of his campaign meetings. Begin knew little about politics and never rolled up his sleeves to pay the price of admission. He was a prince. Bibi was a fighter.

Bibi was not entirely anonymous to the Likud voters. His name had been mentioned here and there and a positive buzz developed. But he was strange, different from all the other candidates. He spoke another language, and his social codes were completely different. He was a polished American candidate in the heart of the Middle East, a Western politician in the Orient. He walked around in ironed shirts, and usually in matching tailored jackets, while others wore open sandals and shapeless clothes, bleary-eyed and sweating. In a political world where table manners were reminiscent of the jungle, Bibi looked like a million dollars.

The senior Likud members and the second-generation princes prepared for Bibi's arrival. They saw in him a long-term danger. The Likud princes scorned him. At first they didn't take him seriously. They asked, "Who does he think he is?" Whenever his name came up, Olmert, Meridor, and their friends would respond with a dismissive wave of the hand. "The air will soon escape this balloon," they promised. The older leaders tried to get rid of him. David Levy, who wanted Bibi out of the Shamir/Arens camp, offered him the chairmanship of the Jewish Agency. Bibi declined. He received an invitation to join former chief of staff Rafael "Raful" Eitan's new party and rejected that, too. There were many other offers and proposals, but Bibi knew exactly where he was heading. He had a plan; he was reserving the announcement of his decision to try to get elected to Likud for a special interview on the leading (and only) political talk show of the time, *Moked*.

The veteran host, Yoram Ronen, was unprepared for the quality of the guest before him. Giving an elegant and polished performance on *Moked*, Bibi totally stole the show. It couldn't have been easier. After years of experience in the toughest studios in the world, *Moked* was small fry in comparison. Everyone who watched the interview—a huge portion of the population of Israel and most of the senior members of the political establishment—understood that something had happened. A new force had come to town, someone who didn't resemble anyone else, and he was ostensibly Israeli. In actual fact, everything about him was American. With a different quality, a different style, and an execution that was almost inhuman. The Likud princes went into the bunker. Bibi, they realized, was here to conquer.

Like a giant magnet, Bibi's charisma attracted volunteers and activists. Eyal Arad established a small but efficient headquarters that was run mostly by volunteers. Offices were donated by Yitzhak Fisher, owner of a computer company and a personal friend of Bibi. Fisher would later become a wealthy man with control of a large business empire. Then, too, he continued to concentrate on Bibi's overseas patrons and was in charge of funds. In the meantime, volunteers flowed to Bibi's headquarters from across the country. They signed up and were then distributed among the different regions and given tasks to fulfill. The team close to Bibi was small and intimate, in the style of Sayeret Matkal. The budget was minuscule. No one knew that beyond the immediate objective, a place near the top in the Likud primaries, that Bibi had also conceived a "grand plan" while still in New York: namely, to conquer Likud. Bibi's people believed in their man and worked for him around the clock. John Gandel, an Australian millionaire, gave Bibi a comfortable apartment on Hayarkon Street near the Hilton Tel Aviv to use "until he got organized." On Arad's advice, Bibi paid Gandel a token monthly rent to legitimize the arrangement. Fleur lived in the apartment and spent most of her time there while Bibi traveled with his small team, which consisted of Yaffa Motil, a devoted volunteer from Beit Horon (a settlement in the occupied territories), a driver, Eli Biton, and activist Ya'akov Akset from Ariel, an Israeli town in the central West Bank. They traveled the country in rented cars, hundreds of miles a day, going from rallies to house visits to drop-ins at local party branches. Bibi used to talk in those cars, into the small hours. He opened up to his people as he had never done in his life. He described life in his father's home, talked about Yoni, about grandfather Nathan Mileikowsky, and even of his grandmother, Sara Mileikowsky, who was a scion of Rashi. According to tradition, said Bibi, a descendent of Rashi will one day be the messiah. The activists in the car listened, and understood.

Nonetheless, one incident marred those idyllic days. At the end of a particularly arduous day, Bibi invited Yaffa Motil to accompany him on a visit to his parents in Jerusalem. After all the stories she'd heard about the family, Yoni, and the house in the Katamon quarter, it was time to see things for herself; Motil was excited. When they arrived, Yaffa was fascinated by the beautiful colonial house with its mosaic floor, and the treasure trove of books. An atmosphere of study and culture permeated the place. Bibi's mother, Cela, welcomed Yaffa warmly. A door opened; Bibi's father peeped out with a grave expression on his face. He summoned Bibi, who entered his father's room. The door had been shut but Motil could still hear the elder Netanyahu raising his voice. After several minutes of that, Bibi left the room, his face ashen. They left the house almost immediately, and Motil never mentioned the event to Bibi.

Likud continued to prepare for the primaries. The voting system in the ruling party was complex and cumbersome, consisting of two separate rounds of balloting: the first round chose the Likud panel, ranking thirty-five Likud candidates according to their total votes. The Knesset list was determined in the second round, called "the sevens." In this round the Likud members elected the panel list in groups of seven: first seven, second seven, etc. Bibi and Arad's first objective was to get into the first ten on the panel list, which would enable Bibi to aim for a place in the first group of seven on the Knesset list. Such a place, they hoped, would ensure a ministry job in the next government. They knew the chances of this happening were slight, but decided to try. Likud was packed with political superstars: some veterans, including Ariel Sharon, Moshe Arens, David Levy, Dan Meridor, and Roni Milo; and their promising protégés, such as Meir Sheetrit, Benny Begin, and David Magen. Netanyahu was still relatively unknown, lacking political tenure or a proven record, and he'd spent most of his life outside of Israel. He was not a member of the local political swamp; was unfamiliar with its rules and didn't know its ways. His aspirations to reach the top were considered somewhat impertinent.

Bibi's shortcomings in this, his first political baptism by fire, turned out to be advantages. He brought something quite different to Israel's sweaty political scene.

14

A Star Is Born

1988

Netanyahu's "American" election campaign in Likud progressed quickly. Bibi and Eyal Arad brought American methods home with them. Building a database of thousands of Likud Central Committee members, they sorted them all and figured out their affiliations to the various camps. Each potential voter was graded according to his or her affinity to Netanyahu and possible recruitment. No party member was overlooked, however remote. Bibi himself called every single name on the lists. Bibi's headquarters bombarded Likud Central Committee members with letters and pamphlets. The campaign would peak at the large convention planned for a few days before the elections to the panel. Bibi and Arad hoped that the convention would be attended by hundreds of Likud Central Committee members. Thousands turned up. Benny Begin was invited to attend as a guest, which intensified the overall buzz in the hall.

Bibi arrived at the venue with Fleur. It was one of their last public appearances together. She already understood that she had lost her husband to his political ambition. He would not return to America with her, would not be a businessman, and wasn't interested in life outside the world of Israeli politics. Bibi was destined for politics, following in the footsteps of Yoni, the great hope of the Netanyahu dynasty. Fleur played the game to the last.

The convention took place at Tel Aviv's Gan Oranim banquet hall. Everything was carefully planned and executed. Previously, Bibi had sent out 2,500 personal letters to all the members of the Likud Central Committee. Like his speeches, Bibi wrote the letters himself, editing and erasing, rewriting and changing his mind, until he had a final draft. A second reading revealed a word he didn't quite like. The letters were destroyed and printed again despite a very tight schedule. This perfectionism endangered the entire project, but Bibi insisted. To him, the written word is more important than any act. The letters, therefore, were more important than the convention itself. The letters would be placed in archives and survive long after the convention was forgotten. Words, in Bibi's eyes, are of the utmost historic importance. Throughout his career, when anyone else wrote something for him, he would spend hours editing it, changing and improving what was to be said until the last moment. To meet the deadline, Bibi placed another printer on standby, as backup, in case his regular printer was unable to carry out the mission. He brought this way of doing things from his stint in Sayeret Matkal.

Sara Akset was chosen to host the evening. This, too, was preplanned. Akset was a volunteer activist, not a professional one, who added a homey aspect to the glittering American event in the north Tel Aviv conference center. Akset added some softness to the somewhat overpolished Bibi. She carried it off perfectly and, when the time came to call him to the stage, did it with genuine enthusiasm. A spotlight focused on him as he made his way to the stage. The audience rose to their feet and went crazy. Suddenly, a rhythmic cry of "Bi-bi, Bi-bi, Bi-bi" filled the hall. Heard for the first time on that mid-May 1988 evening in Gan Oranim, it would become the war cry that accompanied Benjamin Netanyahu wherever he went through the decades to come. Hundreds of people calling out his name in tom-tom beat let loose an enormous surge of adrenaline in Bibi's veins. He could barely believe it was really happening. A smile spread over his face as he reached the podium, and he looked for a moment at the enthusiastic crowd. He had conquered the Likud Central Committee only a month after diving into Israel's political waters, another victory achieved with almost no battle.

Fifteen hundred activists attended Bibi's convention, more than half of the Central Committee members. Likud leaders David Levy and Moshe Katsav also held conventions that evening. Levy's was attended by 150 members, and Katsav had an even smaller turnout. Bibi and Eyal Arad had been confident of good results, but they couldn't have dreamed how successful they would be.

The panel elections took place on May 19, 1988, at the Herzliya Country Club in the middle of a heat wave. Sweating candidates scurried around among the voters, but Bibi took no part in the commotion. His Election Day passed in a closed caravan, which lent him an aura of mystery. Reporter Nahum Barnea wrote at the time, "It was very crowded at the Herzliya Country Club. It was also terribly hot. Bibi Netanyahu was nowhere to be seen. Someone said that he was not mingling on principle. A woman said she'd seen him at noon, after he'd changed a shirt for the third time. All his shirts are pale blue in color. No one will ever catch Netanyahu perspiring. He'll always ensure that if he does, his perspiration will have a lavender scent from which dreams are made in America. Netanyahu, so it seems, is going to achieve everything he wants to achieve. And he wants a lot. They say, and he has never been heard denying it, that he wants to be prime minister. . . ."

Bibi and Fleur entered the hall as the results were about to be announced. They were met by loud applause and took seats in the front row, opposite the podium, holding hands out of habit. The chairman of the voting committee went to the podium, grasping a thick envelope full of results. "In the first place in the Likud panel, with 1,408 votes, Benjamin Netanyahu," he announced. In second place was Moshe Katsev; third was Moshe Arens; fourth was Ariel Sharon. David Levy, leader of one of the largest camps in Likud and independent candidate for the party leadership, was only sixth.

A current ran through Bibi's body, and he broke out in a cold sweat that hampered his habitually crisp shirt. People were breaking open bottles of champagne and spraying him from every direction. He stood up, surrounded by ecstatic supporters, television cameras, and lights, dripping with perspiration and champagne. For the first time, he wasn't looking for a fresh shirt, but for words to say. He stepped up to the stage, waving his arms in the air, with the generous smile of a winner. Someone handed him a bunch of flowers. He delivered a victory speech, praising Likud's "new team." He was too ecstatic to notice the looks of hate and fury that burned in the eyes of the Likud princes Meridor, Milo, and Olmert, who had completely discounted him, and now saw his back. A hurt and furious David Levy declared, "We'll meet in the sevens."

The sevens were a much harder assignment. He was no longer under the radar. All eyes were on him. The princes swore to destroy him. Veteran leaders, headed by Levy, swore revenge. The lack-of-objections index that worked in his favor the first time was set to give him hell in the second. He had to decide which "seven" he was competing for. After much deliberating, he decided on fifth place in the first seven. It was a daring gamble, and according to some of his advisors he was aiming too high. But he was adamant. The euphoria had its way. Bibi made a few calls to his benefactors in New York, who caught a whiff of victory and opened their wallets. Morad Zamir, a millionaire diamond dealer; Jay Meislis and others; they all stepped forward. This group would expand, develop, and intensify in the future, so Netanyahu would be in the possession of countless lists of millionaires all ready and willing to come to his aid at any given time.

The sevens elections were set for July 6. Bibi was under enormous pressure. This time he was working against everybody, and climbed up the mountain to the slipperiest slope. Almost all the strongest elements in Likud feared him and joined forces to destroy him. David Magen, one of the more promising and younger Likud members who enjoyed the support of many of the different camps, decided to compete with Bibi for the fifth place in the first seven. Magen was promised support and backup from David Levy and most of the party princes, so long as he succeeded in blocking Bibi.

When the time came to announce the results, in the packed country-club hall, Bibi was a bundle of nerves. Was the dream going to dissolve? Would the balloon burst? "Bibi is nothing but a pompous balloon," the princes said of him. "When all that air comes out, all that'll be left is Eyal Arad."

First place in the sevens was taken by David Levy; an enormous personal victory and sweet revenge against the Shamir/Arens camp, and even Netanyahu. He was followed by Ariel Sharon, Moshe Arens, and Moshe Katsav. And in fifth place? Bibi Netanyahu. He had survived. They hadn't managed to destroy him. He was now a fait accompli. Bibi beat Magen by a tiny margin, only six votes, but only Magen will remember this margin in the future. In addition to his charisma, determination, and political talent, Bibi was beginning to reveal another important attribute: luck. It's impossible to know what would have become of his political career were it not for the six Likudniks that preferred him to his competitor. Like Moshe Arens's stubborn insistence on appointing him to the position of ambassador to the United Nations, and Zvi Rafiah's refusal to be number two in the embassy in Washington (which allowed Arens to offer the position to Bibi), every inch of the way, Bibi has enjoyed an extra-large portion of luck. To his credit, he always says that luck goes with the good ones. On May 29, 1988, with a considerable amount of luck, Bibi placed his stake in the top of the Likud hierarchy. He was there to stay. A star was born—again. A new era had begun.

15

Deputy Foreign Minister

1988–1990

In late May 1988, a new life began for Benjamin Netanyahu. The journey on which he had embarked had the single, predetermined objective of becoming prime minister of Israel. At that time, Bibi believed that it would take between ten to twenty years. It was during this major change in his fortune that he took leave of his former life, beginning with his departure from Fleur, which was quiet and dignified. It happened gradually, but was unavoidable. Fleur's telephone calls to Bibi, who spent most of his time on the road, dwindled. One evening, when he arrived home at a reasonable hour—a rare occurrence—she told him she couldn't take it any longer. She was leaving and returning to New York. Bibi was devastated. In his heart he knew that his relationship with Fleur had no future, but still the separation hurt him. Bibi is the ultimate deserted male. His women always leave. Every time, even though it is his fault, he is deeply hurt, surprised, and depressed. Fleur made it clear that the separation was final. Over several weeks she took her leave of her close circle of friends, tried again to find work in Israel, but in the end stuck by her decision to return to New York. The divorce between her and Bibi was settled quickly and without rancor. Fleur promised not to make trouble for Bibi in the future, not to be interviewed, and to maintain a low profile. Bibi committed himself to help her to the best of his ability. Shortly after the divorce, Fleur started working for Ronald Lauder. She faded out of Bibi's life as quietly, and as modestly, as she had entered it.

In the meantime, Likud tried to figure out this new shining star. Bibi was given the responsibility of watching over his party's strategic polls in preparation for the general elections, in an attempt to keep him away from the focus of real decision-making. But Bibi stormed the job with his usual gusto. He called in Frank Luntz, a junior researcher at the time, now considered a guru in his field. Bibi recruited computer experts from America and established a system like no other in Israeli politics. His fellow Likudniks were unimpressed. "This isn't America," they said, and dismissed the data Bibi provided on a daily basis.

Likud did not, however, underestimate Bibi's extraordinary talent for raising funds. He was sent on schnorr missions in the United States and returned with a million and a half dollars. Bibi was an incomparable financial asset, so the funds he contributed were what held together Likud's campaign. Nonetheless, the princes continue to resent him and talk behind his back about his extravagant spending on database management and his exaggerated dependency on opinion polls. The tension between Netanyahu and the three Likud princes Meridor, Milo, and Olmert reached new heights as they tried to trip him up in every way possible. But Netanyahu still managed to get himself into several of Likud's propaganda movies, and it was in the movie studios that the princes noticed a strange phenomenon. "He sat there, in front of the unmanned cameras," recalled one of them years later in a private conversation, "and started to make sharp movements with his arms, as if he was practicing karate. We didn't understand what it was. He sat there in front of the camera and did karate moves with his arms, to the left and to the right. It looked weird. It must have been his way of raising his adrenaline levels before the cameras started rolling." Bibi wasn't aware that as he went through this strange personal ritual in the deserted studio, curious eyes in the control room were watching him. This story quickly spread and only increased the princes' disdain for Bibi, whom they saw as a smooth, narcissistic American, a pompous balloon filled with hot air. But they also understood that this was a stubborn adversary, and a determined professional. They had never encountered anyone quite like him in the Israeli political swamp.

One of his MIT colleagues tells a similar story of how Bibi would stand in front of a mirror making sharp, stylized moves in the air, right and left. Sometimes he would draw an imaginary gun, reminiscent of the wild west. The friend hypothesized that it was Bibi's system for raising his concentration and awareness, or something. It was certainly strange to watch.

Apart from fund-raising, Bibi was also excellent at touring the country. Bibi was Likud's king of the road, a breath of fresh air that lit up every market or town square he arrived in. Bibi's tours of the markets were the closest thing to an American political campaign to be found in Israel in 1988. Unlike most politicians, Bibi appears to have enjoyed them. After a tour of Tel Aviv's Carmel Market, his spirits were exceptionally high. One of the leaders of the market vendors, a man gifted with particularly powerful windpipes, roared at the sight of Bibi approaching his stall, "You'll be prime minister yet, Bibi." The exclamation drew the entire market, which joined the deafening applause. A few moments later, sitting in his car next to Eli the driver, Bibi turned to Yaffa Motil in the backseat, pointed his finger, and repeated over and over that mantra, "You'll be prime minister yet, Bibi," a broad smile plastered across his face.

The man elected prime minister that year was Yitzhak Shamir, who established another national unity government with a small edge in favor of Likud. This time there was no rotation. Shamir was prime minister, Peres was finance minister, Rabin was defense minister, and Arens was appointed foreign minister. The princes Meridor, Milo, and Olmert were given other government ministries. Bibi, the outsider, remained outside. He tried to fight, asked for a private meeting with Shamir and was granted one, but the meeting was stiff and the winds that blew from the elderly leader toward the young superstar were cool. Shamir was a conservative, old-school politician who recoiled from the virtually anonymous young man who'd come from nowhere and challenged the old order. "There's plenty of time," he said to Bibi. "You are still young." Eventually Shamir conceded to Arens's pleas and appointed Bibi deputy foreign minister. The same Arens, Bibi's guardian angel, diverting the course of events at the very last moment and enabling his protégé to continue to rise. But at this stage, even Arens couldn't have imagined how high and how fast this rise would be.

Netanyahu attacked his new position in the Foreign Ministry with his usual gusto. When the first intifada raged, Israel was thrown inadvertently into the role of Goliath, against the Palestinian child with a stone in a sling playing David. The international media ground Israel down daily. Bibi was frustrated. He'd lost all the media credit accumulated in New York. The charm expired. Even CNN, for example, was reluctant to interview him. He was almost a pariah. The international media's coverage of the intifada was completely biased and one-sided. An infuriated Bibi realized that a different approach was necessary. He had no issue with stooping to conquer, and so found his opening in a news item in one of the local dailies. Robert Wind, CNN chief in Jerusalem and a Jew, had demanded that a mezuzah be removed from the entrance of the building where CNN was located. Bibi pounced on the incident, waging a sharp attack, insinuating that anti-Semitism was rife in CNN's Jerusalem office. And it worked. Ted Turner replaced Wind and his staff with a new team, which included people like Peter Arnett and Linda Scherzer, and adopted a new, more moderate line. There was no outspoken support for Israel, but the attacks became less intense, which was a victory of sorts.

Bibi's days and nights became a constant, ongoing, rearguard battle with the propaganda surrounding the intifada. It was a battle that could not be won, but Bibi gave it his best. He criticized the American administration's policies on terror; he created his own weather, dragging American photographers to the sights of terrorist attacks, refusing to give in to the way news in Israel was covered. When a Palestinian terrorist sent by Hamas took control of a bus on its way to Jerusalem and forced it into a wadi, killing sixteen passengers and injuring many more, the U.S. State Department avoided condemning the attack outright before the identities of the terrorist and the organization behind him were ascertained. A furious Netanyahu appeared on CNN, standing at the bedside of one of the wounded, an American woman who died shortly after. "Who do you believe," he asked American viewers, "the victims of the attack who reported it was a Palestinian terrorist shouting *'Allahu akbar'* as he grabbed the steering wheel, or Yasser Arafat's evasive tactics?"

Within two days the Bush administration admitted its mistake and published a condemnation.

Foreign Minister Arens gave responsibility for relations with the U.S. Congress to Bibi, whose strong relationship with Capitol Hill enabled him to take control of the Israel lobby. But then came the retirement of Secretary of State George Shultz, a personal friend of Bibi and an avid supporter of Israel. He was replaced by James Baker, which meant an end to the excellent relations between Israel and the U.S. State Department. Baker was a new broom, not always supportive of Israel's positions and not always easy on Israel. The diplomatic team also changed, now including Dennis Ross, Aaron Miller, and Richard Haass, names that would become familiar in Israel over the next twenty-five years. Bibi identified this as a problem. This change in attitude and atmosphere was first expressed in the dialogue that the United States initiated with the Palestine Liberation Organization.

Bibi considered this dialogue to be a strategic threat to Israel, so he decided to put an end to it. He had no compunctions about using various embarrassment tactics to force the State Department's hand. He succeeded in ending the dialogue with the PLO, but paid a high price for his victory. Baker never forgave him and broke off all relations with Netanyahu. "I am not interested in having anything to do with this man," Baker told his aides. "I have no interest in him and I don't ever want to see him again." He virtually banished Israel's ambassador in Washington, Zalman Shoval, from the city. Netanyahu was surprised. He didn't understand why the Americans were so affected by this. "Baker is a professional diplomat, why does he take it so personally?" he said. "Anyone would think I cheated him in a game of golf. All I did was force him into a change of policy by applying a little diplomatic pressure. That's the name of the game and those are the rules. Aren't the Americans forever trying to pressure us into changing Shamir's policies? So what should we do, break off relations with them?"

This approach of Netanyahu's reflects Israel's constant collision course with the American administration. As far as Netanyahu was concerned, Israel and America were equal players in the international arena. He ignored Israel's total dependency on the United States. He looked into a president's eyes and treated him as an equal adversary. The problem is, however, that the Americans think otherwise. They are the superpower, not Israel; they are the ones who spread an umbrella of defense over and around this small and troublesome state in the Middle East and they expect some semblance of gratitude, not political ambushes and below-the-belt blows. We are not supposed to be able to allow ourselves things that they can allow themselves. This essential conflict can only escalate and intensify in the future, as Netanyahu continues to advance up the ladder to the very top, where the explosion will be of a different magnitude altogether.

Several years after the Gulf War, Netanyahu hinted in private conversations that the Americans—especially Baker and two senior U.S. diplomats, Dennis Ross and Daniel Kurtzer—had a hand in the breakup of the national unity government. "In private conversations, they are willing to admit it," Bibi said later. "So what? Are we supposed to feel insulted? To take revenge? To break up the coalition in the Gulf War? That's how it works in politics."

16

Allow Me to Introduce Sara

1991–1992

When Israel's national unity government broke up, Moshe Arens moved from the Foreign Ministry to the Defense Ministry. The position of foreign minister became vacant and David Levy, a long-standing enemy of Netanyahu, was appointed instead of Arens. Bibi was supposed to move with Arens to the Defense Ministry, but Levy surprised him by proposing that he stay on in Jerusalem. Someone had persuaded Levy that it was better to keep Bibi close than to turn him away. Bibi deliberated and accepted the proposal. It was a mistake on the part of both men. Netanyahu remained deputy foreign minister under Levy. It started well, began to deteriorate, and ended very badly indeed. Within a few months the minister and his deputy were totally estranged. To read classified material, deputy foreign minister Bibi would travel to the Defense Ministry, where Arens enabled him to keep up to date. And then Saddam Hussein invaded Kuwait and the first Gulf War broke out.

Israel became one of the international media coverage centers. It was obvious that as soon as America went in, Saddam Hussein would explode the coalition by dragging Israel into the fray. Hundreds of reporters, camera operators, and journalists arrived in Israel. Bibi prepared the propaganda network with his usual care and professionalism, but even he, who always thought of the tiniest detail, did not plan for what happened in reality.

Netanyahu was in a CNN studio being interviewed by Linda Scherzer, the network's Israel reporter, when they heard the siren. A barrage of Scud missiles from Iraq was landing on Israel and shaking Tel Aviv and its metropolitan area. The deputy foreign minister promptly put on his gas mask. Despite a gas mask on his face and air raid sirens wailing in the background, he did not stop the interview. Forty-seven years after the Holocaust, when the Nazis had put millions of Jews to death in gas chambers, an Israeli government deputy minister was warning his people of the dangers of poison gas that Iraqi president Saddam Hussein might fire on Israel.

Overnight, Bibi became, once again, an international media megastar. David Levy almost disintegrated with fury. Once again Netanyahu had stolen his show. It took Levy several days to issue an order forbidding Netanyahu to give interviews. Bibi was angry, but had to show restraint. He canceled an appearance on *Nightline* and rejected hundreds of additional requests for interviews from around the globe.

It was then that a revolution took place in Prime Minister Shamir's attitude to Netanyahu: suspicion was replaced by deep respect. Shamir saw Netanyahu's achievements, especially in the fields of propaganda, fund-raising, and diplomacy, and understood that this young man was valuable. After Levy tried to block him, Shamir intervened and took Netanyahu under his wing.

In the meantime, Bibi was focusing on two major objectives: establishing his own camp and building a power base in Likud, while starting a family. He planned and executed the first objective meticulously by recruiting Avigdor Lieberman and Tzachi Hanegbi from the National Union of Israeli Students in Jerusalem, as well as Danny Naveh and other youngsters from the Jerusalem student-union branch, and started to accumulate volume and legitimacy in the governing party.

The second objective was fulfilled inadvertently. Again, it was not he who initiated events. In 1980, on an El Al flight to Tel Aviv, which made a stopover at Amsterdam's Schiphol Airport, in the duty-free lounge, Bibi caught the eye of a young, blond stewardess with shy eyes. She gave him her telephone number, and he gave her his. She was Sara Ben-Artzi. Bibi, who did not make a habit of homing in on women, called her. After dating a few times, Bibi introduced her to his friends and associates at a social occasion where he was guest of honor. There was no chemistry to be seen. Quiet and introverted, Sara found it hard to integrate into the noisy inner circle that had formed around Netanyahu. The friends and activists—especially the women among them—could find no common language with her. Something was grating, not quite right. Behind his back, Bibi's friends started referring to Sara as "the problem." No one understood what he saw in her.

One day, Netanyahu announced to his friends that "the problem" was solved. He and Sara had separated. Quite a few of his people allowed themselves a sigh of relief. But several months later, he had a completely different announcement to make. He and Sara were getting married. It turned out that after their separation, Sara begged Bibi for one more date. A few weeks later, she informed Bibi that she was pregnant. Bibi was placed in a dilemma. On the one hand, he was single and wanted to have a family; he wanted a woman in his life. On the other hand, Sara unnerved him. Still, the fact that she was pregnant made it easier for him to reach a decision.

At the same time, Bibi was just beginning an affair with a singularly impressive woman named Ruth Bar, but he didn't know at that stage if it would lead anywhere. Already twice divorced, he believed that if, in addition to this, he had a child out of wedlock, his chances of being elected prime minister of Israel would plummet. Sara's pregnancy cast the dice in her favor, so Netanyahu decided to marry her. His friends were in shock, as was his mother, Cela, who asked, "Why is it necessary to get married because of a pregnancy?"

Bibi had decided, so that was that. The wedding of Bibi and Sara took place at the home of his parents, almost in secret. The intention was to maintain a low profile, so as to keep the press away and prevent them from seeing that the bride was heavily pregnant. In the end, some of the reporters got wind of the story and arrived anyway. Sara Ben-Artzi became Sara Netanyahu, the one and only. Eventually, she would demand to be called "The Lady." She brought change to Bibi's life, to his behavior, and to his personality. The change was at first impossible to discern. It happened quite slowly.

The first sign to cause concern was the way Bibi started to maintain a distance from the women in his team. Suddenly he didn't allow Yaffa Motil and Odelia Karmon, a very beautiful young woman who had been with him almost from the very beginning, to kiss him on the cheek on his birthday or any other occasion. When he introduced Sara to Motil, he made a point of adding that Yaffa was "a mother of four." Gradually, the people in Bibi's circle started to understand that something heavy and onerous was burdening him. He was becoming less free, less spontaneous, more restrained; his life and the way he conducted himself were undergoing a profound change. Something new had begun.

17

Bibi vs. Likud

1992

The next important station in Netanyahu's career was the Madrid Peace Conference of October 1991. The conference was meant to have been the follow-up accord to the first Gulf War, and Shamir's government was forced by the Americans to participate in it. During the first intifada, Netanyahu had achieved amazing results relating Israel's struggles to international media outlets. The Foreign Ministry established a seventeen-person team of cadets, fluent in foreign languages (mainly English, French, and Spanish), placing these charismatic youngsters in the most popular bars and pubs in Jerusalem where foreign reporters covering the intifada looked for interviews. It had been Eyal Arad's idea; Netanyahu made it happen. The cadets did not identify themselves as members of the Foreign Ministry, but formed close relations with the reporters. It was at those meetings at the bar, with a glass of whiskey or a pint of beer, that Israel's propaganda work was carried out, more than it was through any PR campaign. On those evenings, foreign reporters learned about the conflict from Israel's perspective. This operation did not change attitudes, but it did sometimes influence coverage.

Yitzhak Shamir headed the Israeli contingent to the Madrid conference, and included Bibi Netanyahu in his delegation. He was confident that Bibi would help Israel with the losing propaganda battle. Shamir was right. Bibi organized a huge press conference exclusively for the Arab media: he and the Arabs in the same room for the first time in history. Of course the room was filled to overflowing. Questions were asked in Arabic and translated for Bibi, who answered in Hebrew, which was then translated into Arabic. Notwithstanding the complications caused by the need for translation, Bibi gave his usual show. Almost all the Arab news channels broadcast the press conference, or referred to it. In Israel, it was broadcast on live television. Among the audience in Jerusalem was Foreign Minister David Levy, who was livid. Levy decided that was the last straw, and a few weeks later, Bibi packed up his personal effects and moved to the prime minister's office, where he was appointed deputy minister under Yitzhak Shamir.

With his new appointment, Bibi immediately set about bolstering his standing in the party. He continued to build his camp of activists and supporters, preparing for the 1992 election primaries. In the meantime, a new bill was placed before the Knesset that proposed direct elections for prime minister. No longer would there be the parliamentary democracy where a Knesset is elected, which in turn elects the prime minister. Now Israeli citizens would cast their vote in two separate ballots, one for the Knesset and one for prime minister. The candidate with the most votes would become prime minister. If he or she crossed the 40 percent threshold, that would win the first round. If not, a second round would be held between the two candidates with the highest number of votes in the first round.

Likud held intense and lengthy discussions about this proposal, and in the end they decided to oppose it. Prime Minister Shamir and Defense Minister Arens led the opposition. Netanyahu was, of course, an enthusiastic supporter. He knew that this law would provide him with the best chance of becoming prime minister of Israel, because in direct elections he could defeat any opponent. In the old voting system, he could be dependent on political combinations and parliamentary coalitions. Bibi, torn between going with his gut, or going with the party, convened his people to debate the issue. Most of them said he shouldn't go against the party. Nonetheless, Netanyahu decided to do just that, voting against his own party, Likud, in the Knesset. It was a bold decision that could have brought an end to his Likud career.

The pressure placed on Bibi was enormous. The prime minister hinted to him that it would be unfortunate if his career were to be so brief; Moshe Arens yelled at him; people were sent; and hints were made that if he dared go against the party, his political career would be over. Bibi rejected all these entreaties out of hand. Shamir summoned him a few days before the vote and offered a way out. "I'll send you to the U.S. on an urgent mission; it's a chance for you to avoid the vote," he offered. Bibi agreed to go, but only after he cast his vote. Shamir understood that Bibi was determined to go all the way on this. He called Arens to join the meeting and, together, they pressured their rebellious protégé. Bibi's close associates described the meeting like something out of *The Godfather*. Apart from placing a horse's head in his bed, they did everything. But nothing helped.

Heavy snow fell on Jerusalem the day of the Knesset vote. Bibi drove as far as Sha'ar HaGai, where he boarded an IDF-armed personnel carrier that had been sent to collect Knesset members that could not make it to Jerusalem. The vote was intense, and pressure on Bibi was exerted till the last moment. When his turn came, he announced loudly that he was in favor of the proposal. The issue passed with 56 against and 57 in favor. It was one of the most daring and auspicious gambles of Bibi's political career.

A few days later, Bibi was traveling to Tel Aviv with Sara and Eyal Arad. "Well," Sara hissed at Arad, "I hope you are satisfied, now that you've ruined Bibi's career." Arad didn't respond. It wasn't he who pushed Bibi to this vote.

When he voted, Netanyahu hadn't reckoned on the fact that Likud would lose the election that year to Yitzhak Rabin. It is reasonable to assume that if Likud had won, Shamir would have thrown Netanyahu to the dogs, leaving him, once more, out of the government, but luck was still with him, and Likud lost. Four years later the new law raised Benjamin Netanyahu to power. He won the election for prime minister but lost the Knesset election to Shimon Peres. No one remembers this episode, but Bibi's gamble had succeeded. He proved once again that when it came to personal survival, he was not afraid to make hard decisions. Twenty-three years later, he'd face a somewhat similar situation on his way to address Congress about Iran's nuclear program. Pressured against going, he delivered his speech to Congress and won the election in Israel.

In 1992, immediately after that vote, a broad Likud operation was launched to destroy Netanyahu. Avigdor Lieberman, who had become Netanyahu's right-hand man, responsible for everything concerning Bibi's presence in the field, was so alarmed he suggested leaving Likud and trying to get elected on an independent ticket. Bibi rejected the idea, establishing a well-oiled campaign headquarters. He set out to capture the field as only he knew how. But the Likud princes were convinced that this time they would succeed in destroying him at long last. They were wrong. In the elections for the party panel, Bibi came out second, only seventeen votes behind the winner, Moshe Katsav. It was an extraordinary achievement that cemented his status in the party. Not only was he not destroyed, he was able to prove that he was there to stay. Some days later, during the sevens, he repeated his previous achievement by reaching the fifth place in the first seven. The princes were horrified. Bibi smiled. His entire future lay ahead of him.

18

The Red-Hot Video

1993

In the 1992 general elections, Likud, led by Yitzhak Shamir, was defeated by Yitzhak Rabin and the Labor Party. It was the end of an era. For Bibi it came a little too early. His mentor, Moshe Arens, was due to inherit Yitzhak Shamir's leadership. However, conversations with Arens immediately after the Likud defeat led Bibi to understand that the older man did not deem himself fit to lead Likud now that it had become the opposition party. In 1996, when the next general elections were due, Arens would be seventy-one and, at sixty-seven, he believed that a younger man should now lead. Netanyahu jumped at the chance. He convened a press conference and announced his candidacy for the Likud leadership. He was only forty-three years old and had served only one term in the Knesset, but these factors were to his advantage. He was young, energetic, and something different that would shake up not only the party but the entire political system. The biggest nightmare of the Likud princes came true right in front of their horrified eyes.

There were plans to run others for the coveted leadership of Likud: David Levy and his camp, and Benny Begin, among those chosen by the princes to represent the Shamir/Arens camp. Begin was meant to bring with him his family pedigree (as Menachem Begin's son) and thus neutralize Net-anyahu's American rhetoric. It didn't put Bibi off in the least. As usual, he stormed the field. Avigdor Lieberman became his chief gofer and established Bibi's ever-expanding political camp. Tzachi Hanegbi was among his earli-est supporters, followed by Limor Livnat. The smart move was Bibi. Begin was a sentimental choice. Bibi alerted all his veteran supporters, and money continued to flow in large quantities from America. Bibi's group of busi-nessmen donors and financial supporters expanded all the time and included Gabi Taman, Sam Domb, Jack Nasser, George Meisner, Jay Meisels, and millionaire diamond dealer Morad Zamir. This group was joined by a young American Jew, Steven Schneier, who became Bibi's right-hand man in all matters concerning fund-raising and donations from abroad. He was also the main connection between Bibi and one of his oldest and closest patrons in America, the billionaire Ronald Lauder. Over twenty years have passed since then and Schneier is still there, in the same position. Lauder, however, was sent off and exiled.

Netanyahu scoured the country, visiting Likud branches from Kiryat Shmona to Beersheba at a furious rate. He established an efficient market-ing system and built a strategy that aimed at providing him, with very little effort, the victory he wanted. In David Levy he saw his main adversary. The younger Begin, as Bibi knew, did not share his father's charisma or abili-ties, whereas Levy was deeply rooted in the Likud hinterland. Bibi had a plan for penetrating Levy's strongholds in the country's periphery and con-quering them, and it was beginning to bear fruit.

But then, on January 13, 1993, the telephone rang in Benjamin and Sara Netanyahu's apartment in Jerusalem. Sara picked up the receiver. At the other end was a stranger who did not identify himself, but asked to pass on "an important message." He told a stunned Sara that her husband was having an affair, that he had been routinely meeting a woman in an apart-ment in Petah Tikva. According to the man, there was a videotape of her husband with his lover. If, by tomorrow, her husband did not withdraw his candidacy for the Likud leadership, they would release the tape, together with some very intimate details about her husband and his mistress. It's for his own good, said the stranger. If he made an official announcement about the withdrawal of his candidacy, not a word would be published, the tape would be destroyed, and it would be as if the conversation never took place.

Sara Netanyahu was in shock. Alone in the apartment with year-old Yair, she had no doubt the man was telling the truth. Too many details seemed plausible. The man had said that Bibi was meeting the woman in the afternoons, and Sara could remember too many recent occasions when she had tried to call Bibi in the afternoon and not one of his closest aides knew where he was. She was certain her husband had a mistress. She called her parents, burst into tears, and told them what happened, announcing that she was divorcing Bibi. Next, she called him. "I know you are cheating on me. I know everything," she told him. "Come home immediately." It was Bibi's turn to be flabbergasted. Just like that the roof caved in on him. Just a few weeks earlier he had begun to cool off the lengthy affair he'd been having with a married woman, after Lieberman warned him that information was being collected and a file prepared. He never imagined anything would really happen.

Bibi canceled that evening's campaign meeting and flew home. She was waiting for him, fuming, weeping, unable to listen, unable to understand, unwilling to forgive. All she wanted was for him to take his things and get out of her life, and the life of his son Yair, forever.

It was one of the hardest evenings of his life. At first he tried to deny he was having an affair, fearing a repeat of his disastrous admission of infidelity to his first wife, Micki, which had ended their marriage. He told Sara that this was "an attempt at political blackmail, an evil plot to frame" him. He promised he would get to the bottom of it, but Sara wasn't listening. She wasn't buying this version of things. "You betrayed me, you're a traitor," she said repeatedly. "I want you out of here." He understood that he didn't have any choice. Yes, he admitted. There was another woman. He even revealed her identity: Ruth Bar, his campaign public relations advisor. It was only once, a passing fling that had been over for weeks. He swore his love to Sara and their baby and asked her not to make a rash decision. But Sara did not want to listen or forgive. "I am leaving you. We are getting a divorce," she informed him. Bibi packed two suitcases, took a few ironed shirts and some suits, left the apartment, and went to stay with his parents. He felt and looked like someone in deep mourning. He swore he'd return. There was no way he'd be divorced for the third time.

In the morning Bibi called the all-powerful Lieberman to an urgent meeting. Lieberman had been pressing Netanyahu for several weeks to end the affair with Ms. Bar. His people in the field had brought back the information that the affair had been leaked. People in David Levy's camp were openly exchanging jokes at Bibi's expense, saying that he was about to become a porn king. There were signs that Bibi and Ruth Bar actually had been filmed in the act. Lieberman's agents uncovered people who rented out recording and other equipment, there were signs of bugging in Bibi's telephones and at the campaign. It seemed plausible that somewhere there was videotape. So what now?

Desperate, Bibi decided to take the initiative and attack. There was no other choice. "I'm going on TV, and making it all public. I'll pull the carpet out from under them," he said to Lieberman, who objected. "Why go to the TV?" he asked. "Go to the police chief, privately, and tell him you're being blackmailed. Let them deal with it."

Bibi wasn't convinced. He was too agitated. His wife had just thrown him out of their home. He was about to be banished from political life. But he wasn't going to fall without first putting up a fight, and he wouldn't give in to blackmail. He would show them by doing something his enemies hadn't expected: going to the TV studio and publicly admitting to adultery would spoil their plans.

Netanyahu called Eyal Arad to brief him on the blackmail attempt. Arad didn't like the idea of appearing on TV either. Netanyahu called his attorneys next, David Shimron and Dan Avi-Yitzhak. They, too, suggested he lodge a complaint with the police, and disapproved of a TV appearance and public disclosure. Throughout that day, Bibi called Sara to beg her forgiveness. Sara wouldn't budge. Then he told her of his intention to tell all on TV that evening as a preemptive strike against the blackmail. Sara was terrified at the thought of the entire nation getting a voyeuristic glance into her life. It was humiliating, but still she didn't intervene. She had already begun talks with attorney Ya'akov Ne'eman to end the marriage. She was absolutely determined. Let him go wherever he wanted, she told herself, so long as he gets out of my life.

Sara also blamed Eyal Arad for introducing Bibi to Ruth Bar. She believed he did it on purpose to get rid of her. Late at night, she called Arad at his home, after she'd thrown Bibi out, hurling insults at him. Arad responded rudely. Bibi had known Ruth Bar even before he had met Sara, but there was no point in arguing with the injured wife. As far as he and Lieberman and others in Bibi's inner circle were concerned, this business had a potentially positive side as well. If Sara were to ultimately exit his life, they believed, it might actually have been worth all the fuss and humiliation. None of Bibi's close associates liked Sara. They all agreed on this. She weighed on him, she separated him from his people, interfered in the team's work, disturbed his judgment, and was a burden on the entire campaign and on Bibi himself. Thus, if it were possible to get out of this affair without Sara, everyone would have been happy. With the exception of Bibi, of course.

In the meantime, Lieberman's people scoured the field and concluded that a "red-hot videotape" did indeed exist. The existence of the tape was backed by activists from David Levy's camp, Bibi's main rival in the race for the Likud leadership. This intel only served to reinforce Netanyahu's determination to go public. The following afternoon, Bibi called Channel A and promised an exclusive for the evening broadcast. Channel A immediately started broadcasting preliminary details of the affair. At seven o'clock in the evening Eyal Arad picked Bibi up and drove him to the TV studios. On the way, Arad consulted with some friends, all of whom advised against the appearance. "Have you seen a tape?" a leading journalist and friend of Bibi asked. Bibi said he hadn't, but had heard of its existence. "Even if you see it with your own eyes, deny it. In such circumstances, you deny everything. They are saying it's you in the tape, it's Photoshop. Who runs to the TV over something like this?" Bibi said nothing. In his heart he replied, "I do."

Bibi was charged and tense. Within a few moments everyone in Israel would know that he had been caught with his pants down. His TV interview that evening in the studio, opposite veteran crime reporter Uri Cohen-Aharonov, continues to haunt Bibi to this day. If he could turn back the clock, Netanyahu would have willingly done so. On that evening he was determined; the people around him saw a man who was terrified, in a kind of trance. Everything he had done in life, all his achievements, was about to go down the drain. His obvious panic greatly increased the intensity of the crisis. If he'd calmed himself down and analyzed the situation with a cool head, he would have seen that it could have been handled differently, more discreetly, without making a fool of himself on prime-time TV, without causing his wife so much humiliation and without inviting the entire population into his private affairs. But during those two stormy days, the voice of reason could not penetrate his troubled brain. He was in a different zone altogether as he sat there in the studio telling the nation that he had cheated on his wife and was now a victim of blackmail.

The interviewer, Cohen-Aharonov, titled the segment "Political Blackmail." Bibi liked it. "I had intimate relations with another woman," he told the nation. "That ended a few months ago. If I owe anyone an explanation, it is my wife and family. This is personal and it shall remain personal." He then hinted that the perpetrator of the attempted blackmail was David Levy.

Levy, watching at home, stared at his TV in disbelief. "I am talking about a senior Likud member," Bibi said, trying to transform Levy into a blackmailing Mafia boss.

Bibi breathed a sigh of relief after the broadcast. The terrible pressure he had been under was beginning to dissolve. Responses were good. He convinced himself that he had acted in accordance with his long-held principles that one should never give in to terror and never negotiate with terrorists. He had preempted his enemy, pulled the rug out from under their feet. Levy felt somewhat differently and convened his aides and political supporters in his Tel Aviv office. Among those present was Reuven Rivlin, who is currently serving as president of Israel. They issued a strong response to Bibi's confessions. Levy himself demanded publicly that Bibi "reveal the name of the Likud senior member." Rivlin declared that "Bibi has shot himself in the leg and destroyed himself politically." The third candidate, Benny Begin, demanded a "return to a clean and fair political campaign." The uproar was unprecedented in Israel.

The Israel Police opened an investigation into the matter. Netanyahu was questioned, Sara was questioned, Levy's people were questioned. Several months later, the investigation was closed for lack of evidence. No videotape was ever found; no evidence surfaced to support the claim that someone from the Levy camp had recorded a videotape or was guilty of blackmail. To this day, no one has testified to seeing the videotape of Bibi and Ruth Bar together, and no one has proved that such a tape ever existed. Bibi had hotfooted it to the TV studios and admitted in a live broadcast that he'd committed adultery on the strength of unfounded rumors. It was one of the more surreal episodes in the political history of the state of Israel, one that seriously impugned the judgment of Benjamin Netanyahu and his ability to withstand pressure, as well as his personal morals. Every other candidate would have caved in under such an event and, at that time, it seemed that the Netanyahu campaign was indeed sinking. For weeks after the affair, everywhere Bibi went he met with comments, calls, mocking questions, and jibes concerning the videotape that never was. The princes were convinced he was destroyed.

But Netanyahu was less convinced. It was a hiccup and he would get over it. At that time, his main objective was to make peace with his wife, to go back home, and not to be three times divorced. He called Sara dozens of times. He called her brother, Hagai Ben-Artzi, a born-again Jew with extreme right-wing opinions, who was fond of Bibi in those days (he has since gotten over it). He sent emissaries and advocates, promised to mend his ways; he declared his undying love. Sara's determination to be rid of him started to crack. At this stage, the lawyers entered the fray: David Shimron and Dan Avi-Yitzhak on Bibi's side, Attorney Ya'akov Ne'eman on Sara's side. A reconciliation agreement was drafted that exists to this day. According to urban legend, it says that Bibi is not allowed to do anything without her permission, not to go anywhere without her, not to have contact with other women without her knowledge, and so on. No one has ever seen this agreement, but Bibi returned home. Sara became a "wife" like no other, her word law. She is the ultimate CEO of everything. Bibi accepted that ruling. In retrospect, the videotape affair shook Sara badly. It caused severe emotional trauma. After Bibi and Sara reunited, relations between them changed utterly. As the years pass, the dividing line between their personalities blurs. In the meantime, Bibi achieved his first objective. All that remained was to win the primaries, become head of Likud, and leader of the opposition.

19

Rehabilitating Likud

1993–1995

Sara Netanyahu joined her husband for only a few campaign stops during the final stages of the campaign. They presented what would become permanent: holding hands, shoulder to shoulder, with Netanyahu making a point of mentioning her in every speech or greeting, always giving her credit and thanking her for her invaluable input. Before the videotape affair, she had always been behind the scenes. Now they were in this together. This arrangement would intensify with the years, until finally they fused into a single personality. "In the name of Sara, my wife; and myself, I ask you to vote for me in the primaries," Bibi called at all the campaign stops, and the audience howled. His wife became a built-in, inseparable part of his candidacy. Bibi was back on track, with renewed momentum. It was as if there had never been a whiff of scandal. The elections took place on March 24, 1993, and Netanyahu won 52 percent of the vote. David Levy trailed far behind him with only 26 percent. Begin fared even worse. Bibi had decisively won the first round. He was exhausted and exhilarated. That evening Likud held a victory parade in Tel Aviv. "Bibi, king of Israel," people sang as he arrived at the venue, his hand in Sara's. Netanyahu opened his speech with "I want to thank my wife, Sara, who has been with me all the way." Over the years to come, this opening has become standard, even un-avoidable at all such events. Netanyahu went on to promise to do everything he could to bring down the Rabin government, and called on David Levy and Benny Begin to forget their disagreements and join him in a single camp. There was euphoria in the air. Bibi was now a hairbreadth from his big dream. He was in an ideal position for taking the premiership. It had been quick and easy. All he needed to do now was wait for Rabin to stumble, and try not to stumble himself.

Before anything else, he had to rehabilitate Likud. At the historical Likud headquarters in Tel Aviv, Bibi was met with a damaged organization and debt, around 50 to 70 million shekels, a fortune, in those days. Bibi fired many staff members, appointed Avigdor Lieberman to the role of director-general, brought in more of his closest associates, and set about putting things in order. He called on his sponsors, especially those wealthy American philanthropists who had been multiplying like mushrooms after rain. Millions of dollars started streaming into the coffers of Likud. At that time, two Jewish billionaires in particular were prominently at Bibi's side, Ronald Lauder and Sheldon Adelson.

Lauder knew Bibi from his days in the UN. They had worked together in exposing the Nazi background of then Austrian president Kurt Waldheim. At that time, Lauder was the U.S. ambassador in Vienna, and Bibi was Israel's ambassador to the United Nations. The two enjoyed a strong, close, and supportive friendship, with Bibi getting the better deal since Lauder became his main patron. Lauder was a Zionist, a Jew, wealthy, and gener-ous. Bibi was the dream son of Israel. He was young, charismatic, and had the aura of a combat fighter; and then there was his brother, the hero of Entebbe. All the components that melted a Jewish heart were there, so there was an immediate connection between the two. When Fleur, Bibi's divorced wife, was looking for a job, Lauder was there. The first thing Bibi did when he landed in New York was connect with Lauder. When he wanted to estab-lish a research institute in Jerusalem with a right-wing orientation (the Shalem Center), he called Lauder. Bibi's close ties with the heir to the Es-tée Lauder cosmetics empire became well known in the city and throughout America, and Bibi used them to great advantage. When Bibi was head of the opposition, Lauder became one of the most influential people in his inner circle.

At that time, Sheldon Adelson was maintaining a relatively low profile. He hadn't yet made his billions, but still was considered a very generous donor who was always open to new proposals. Only a decade later would Adelson take off and make his way up two lists: the wealthiest people in the world and Netanyahu's biggest donors. He easily took first place in the second list, leaving Lauder in the dust. During the 1990s, Adelson was just another name in the endless lists of wealthy Jews Bibi held in his inside coat pocket. In 1991, Adelson's wedding reception was held in the elegant Chagall Hall in the Knesset building in Jerusalem. Only a carefully chosen few enjoy the privilege of holding a private family affair in the Jewish state's parliament building. Since Netanyahu was deputy foreign minister at the time, he was accused of pulling strings and using his influence to enable the Adelson wedding reception to take place in the Knesset. Bibi denied having done so, but his ties with Adelson continued to deepen. It was just the beginning of a beautiful, and valuable, friendship.

Parallel to the financial rehabilitation of Likud, Netanyahu worked at taking control of and deepening his grasp on the party. He demanded immediate loyalty from the princes and declared that anyone who isn't with him would be marked as an adversary. In every member of the Knesset he saw a potential threat, so he devoted much time to rooting out conspiracies against him, conspiracies that only he identified. It was during those early days of Bibi's Likud leadership that Bibi's infamous paranoia began to appear. He was constantly in search of the conspiracy that might threaten his rule, on the lookout for traitors, saboteurs, and schemers bent on inheriting his position. It became a routine part of Bibi's life, his daily conduct and behavior. Trusting almost no one, he is forever looking over his shoulder to catch the knife wielders and quarrel mongers before they can harm him. He became introverted, withdrawn, and gloomy. The closer he came to realizing his great dream, the more he changed. He could see nothing else, apart from the prime minister's office. It was there that he aimed every moment. He had no doubt he would make it.

20

The Oslo Surprise

1993–1995

The Oslo Accords came as a complete surprise. In the weeks preceding their unexpected reveal, Netanyahu and his people were busy planning a huge campaign that would flood the country using the slogan "Elections Now." He was doing very well in the polls, whereas support for Prime Minister Yitzhak Rabin continued to fall, having reached an impasse. Bibi's plan was to drag the country to the polls within two months, and to win. He rented billboards, hired campaign advisors and branding experts, and recruited field activists. Tapping his donors, Netanyahu had garnered a generous budget. Everything was ready. Bibi believed the time was right for a change of regime.

And then, from out of nowhere, came the Oslo Accords, a barely conceivable historic peace agreement between Israel and the Palestinians. The interim agreement between Israel and the Palestine Liberation Organization was reached after secret negotiations in the Norwegian capital. When the news of the agreement broke, Bibi was on a fund-raising tour in Europe. He dropped everything and flew home. Eyal Arad met him at the airport. Both men looked shaken and pale. Their grand strategic plan had crumbled and become irrelevant. They stopped for urgent preliminary consultations at a gas station behind the airport, and their first decision was to halt the campaign, parts of which had already hit billboards across the country. Under the new circumstances their slogan, "Elections Now," could be catastrophic. Rabin would eat Bibi for breakfast. With the momentum moved to the Labor Party they knew they'd need to go underground. They needed to lower their profile.

The news occasioned euphoria in Israel; the whole world reacting with approval. Rabin, Peres, and Yasser Arafat became heroes. Everyone was hugging everyone else, shaking hands and fantasizing about a peaceful and flourishing new Middle East. Israelis were picturing themselves eating hummus in Mecca and swimming along the Mediterranean coast to Lebanon. The stock exchange hit a new high; foreign investors began to storm Israel's economy; things looked rosy. The media decided to go with the flow. For people on the right, especially Bibi, it was hard to get a word in edgewise. Netanyahu's people fell into the political equivalent of a deep depression. "It's all over," they told him. "We won't be returning to power for decades."

Bibi said nothing. He didn't agree with this prognosis. For him, nothing was ever lost. Various scenarios passed quickly through his head, his brain fevered with the effort to identify cracks in this wall of euphoria, and within a few weeks his mood began to lighten. He collected himself and started all over again. Those days saw, again, one of the qualities that had become his trademark: to never give up. Even when everyone else thought all was lost, Bibi continued to fight. "It won't be easy," he told his people. "This agreement is not as good as it appears. We'll experience terror; there will be resistance. Now everyone is happy, but the road is long and hard and we'll have a lot to say. It is now January 1994, let's see how things look in January 1996."

In the meantime, at least he was able to convince himself. David Levy was still estranged from him after the primaries. The princes gave him the cold shoulder. Ariel Sharon kept his distance. Senior Likud members went underground, attending to their own needs, and enjoyed Bibi's distress. He found himself absolutely alone vis-à-vis the historic peace treaty, dead set against the national euphoria and global glee. He and Oslo, head to head.

Apart from Eyal Arad and Avigdor Lieberman, he also had the settlers. They were the first to fight the accords. They had no choice, because Oslo undermined the very existence of their settlements. The first protest rally organized by the Judea and Samaria council attracted thousands and brought hope to the hearts of Bibi and his people. Maybe, after all, everything was not lost. All this time, the media ecstasy continued with headline after headline. Rabin visited Morocco, Indonesia, Oman, and other Arab and Muslim states, to the sound of official orchestras playing the Israeli national anthem, *Hatikva*. Israelis were allowed to visit Qatar. Journalists fantasized about all the Arab states opening embassies in Tel Aviv "within weeks." First news of negotiations over a peace treaty with Jordan became public, and Likud seniors were convinced that they were in serious trouble. They were yesterday's news, the alarmists, the nonrelevant; whereas Rabin was presenting Israel with hope.

A distressed Netanyahu convened a political debate at Likud headquarters on King George Street in Tel Aviv. Those present consisted of his advisors, his inner circle, and his strategists. Suggestions were presented for a Likud political program that would make the party relevant again. Recognition of the Oslo Accords, with sharp reservations; agreement to territorial compromise, dividing the West Bank into Jewish areas and Arab areas; these were but a few of the ideas. Bibi was concerned. A large map covered the table and people were leaning over it, considering possible boundaries. Bibi had come with a ruler. Two years earlier, in a background talk with a journalist, Bibi had explained his position: territorial compromise, he said, was possible only from north to south; from east to west Israel would find it hard to compromise. He used his ruler to illustrate the narrowness of Israel's land in a critical region, opposite the Tel Aviv metropolitan area. It is hard to be flexible when your land is only a few dozen miles east to west, he said. On the other hand, he pointed out, in the north and in the south we have broader options for flexibility. As part of the same conversation, he hinted that he would be prepared to discuss with the Syrians a possible territorial compromise for the Golan Heights (he said this at least twice), and that if it were up to him, the peace agreement with Egypt would be an important strategic move.

During those days of Oslo euphoria, Bibi was not swayed by public opinion, and did not agree with the opinions of his advisors. When they were poring over maps and trying to figure out different territory scenarios, Netanyahu told them it was not the way he would be elected next prime minister. "It is against my concepts and my conscience," he added. He completely ruled out pathetic pleas for an alternative Likud plan in response to the Oslo Accords. He told the parable of the diver that he first heard in Sayeret Matkal. When the sea is stormy, the wisest thing to do is dive under the water. That's where it is quiet and peaceful. We'll take a dive and prepare Likud's response and present it when the moment is ripe, he said. And that moment will come, added Bibi: "I have no doubt the Oslo Accords will collapse; this peace won't last. And then, we'll resurface and show ourselves at the right moment."

In the meantime, Bibi completed his revolution in Likud. The party changed its appearance and character under its new leader. The new Likud was much less ideological than the old Likud. Brawls over key people replaced argument and ideology. It became more personal, accessible, American, superficial. Things rose or fell in accordance with the mood of the leader, who kept his cards very close to his chest. Gone were the days of stormy ideological debate and conflicting political plans. The party established by Revisionists with a burning ideology had become a one-man party. The princes did not like this. Sharon was angry, Levy growled, but Bibi led them all forward into the age of television, to personal elections, to the politics of stars, where ideology didn't matter.

And there was one more thing: anyone who did not think like the leader was deemed a "traitor." It became unacceptable to cross Netanyahu. Belonging to a different camp was tantamount to knife-in-the-back tactics. Anyone who engaged in politics in the traditional Likud style suddenly became public enemy number one. Behind closed doors, Bibi did decide to try to draft a political plan. He was keen on the "canton" plan presented to his colleague Zalman Shoval, the ambassador who returned from Washington after the fall of the Likud government. This plan granted 80 percent of Palestinians almost complete autonomy and was reminiscent of the map that was supposed to come into play after the implementation of the Oslo B accords. The difference is that as far as Netanyahu was concerned, what was to the Rabin administration and the PLO was only an interim agreement on the way to final peace, was the final stop.

Netanyahu had another issue. Apart from the settlers, Likud had no real soldiers in action. He familiarized himself with the "Judea and Samaria divisions," those devoted settlers who know how to quickly pour thousands into the field: thousands of settlers who turned up, unpaid, without expenses, with no transport or logistics. When the settlers were told to demonstrate at some road junction for a week, they simply came to the junction, set up their tents, and sat there for a week. When Likud activists were brought to the same junction, they would turn up before noon, sit on the highway for a few hours, fly a banner or two, and disappear before nightfall, but not before they were paid for doing so. Volunteers were practically nonexistent. As soon as Bibi identified this asset he acted accordingly. He moved to the right, got close to the settlers, and started to talk in their language. It was a tactical change to fulfill his political needs.

From an ideological point of view, Bibi has no real respect for the settlers. Netanyahu is not a man of action, but of words. As far as he is concerned, his speeches are much more important than the West Bank settlements. But he knew that without the powerful tool provided by the settlers, one that constantly accumulated mass and energy, he would never be able to realize his dream. So he toed the line with them, became close to them, and behaved the way they expected him to. But in private conversations he admitted that if he took over the government, they'd have to recognize the PLO as a negotiating partner. This fact could no longer be changed. When asked if he would talk to Arafat if he became prime minister, Bibi replied that he would send his foreign minister in his place. He was sure that the foreign minister in his government would be Shimon Peres. He also believed that even if he won the elections, he would form a national coalition government with the Labor Party. But all these issues were laid aside to be dealt with at a later date. There was still a lot of work to be done. At the moment he had a peace agreement to disassemble.

21

Wait for Me

1994

When the shock of Oslo began to disperse, Netanyahu gathered his wits and jumped straight into the political arena. He tightened his ties with Dore Gold, who became his closest advisor on regional and diplomatic affairs. He forged close ties with the Jordanian royal family, ties that began with an exchange of letters with King Hussein and resulted in a series of secret meetings, first in London and later in the Hashemite Kingdom of Jordan. Hussein, who possessed deep political wisdom, nurtured his relationship with the Israeli opposition leader and even shared with him information on the secret peace accords he was negotiating at the time with Prime Minister Yitzhak Rabin. On one of their visits, Netanyahu received a draft of the peace agreement evolving between Israel and Jordan and told his Jordanian counterparts, "Even I can live with this treaty."

The Syrian route was even more fascinating. Yitzhak Rabin tried to reach a peace accord with Syrian president Hafez Assad. Negotiations were secret and advanced, with Assad demanding every last inch of the Golan Heights. Rabin tried to keep the Syrians away from the shores of the Sea of Galilee. The prime minister passed on to the Americans what was coined at the time as the "deposit," or, in other words, the promise of a full Israeli withdrawal from the Golan Heights if certain conditions were fulfilled. The Americans tried to get the Syrians to agree to Rabin's conditions in order to complete the historic deal. At the height of these negotiations, Netanyahu dispatched secret messages to Damascus, according to which Assad would be better off waiting for the elections in Israel. "Let him wait for me," said Bibi, "it'll be worth his while."

It was the Americans who first got wind of this scheme. Rabin was furious. Every time the negotiations reached an impasse, the Syrians would hint to the Americans that they were in no hurry; if worse came to worst, they'd wait for the next prime minister. Bibi was prepared to conduct negotiations over the Golan Heights, and would do so in the future. That said, he believed something else entirely, that the Palestinians didn't want comprehensive peace with Israel, and that Israel was not prepared to pay the price for peace with the Palestinians (relinquishing the Golan Heights). Instead of giving back the Golan Heights, Bibi wanted to lease it. And the agreement would be based on nonbelligerence rather than peace. Assad wouldn't have to put up with an Israeli embassy in Damascus, not to mention the inconvenience of having thousands of Israeli tourists eating hummus in his markets, and the IDF would leave the Golan Heights; the Syrian army would move away from the foothills.

In the meantime, Bibi and Sara had turned their relationship around. They resumed joint public appearances, and the videotape incident seemed to have been erased from the public's memory. As anti-Rabin and anti-Oslo demonstrations increased, Netanyahu renewed his grasp on the public and started preparing for a change of government in Israel. The team included, of course, Avigdor Lieberman and Eyal Arad; the new spokesman, Shai Bazak; the political advisor Dore Gold; experts on opinion polls; and a crowd psychologist. Netanyahu believed with all his heart that his life's work was within reach, and he was determined to reach it.

In November 1994, President Bill Clinton paid a special visit to Israel as part of the White House's effort to empower the Rabin government and solidify the peace process. Netanyahu had to pull out all the stops to make his first meeting with Clinton happen, and it was brief. Bibi got his photo op with the popular American president, and told him that they would "meet again." Clinton hoped they would not. His heart belonged to Rabin, and the young opposition leader gave him a bad feeling. About a month later, the Jordanian royal family invited Bibi to a special memorial service in Karameh where, twenty-six years earlier, a painful battle had taken place between the IDF and the combined PLO and Jordanian Armed Forces. Bibi, who had taken part in the battle as a rookie in Sayeret Matkal, accepted the invitation enthusiastically. In Jordan he was received by the entire royal family, from King Hussein himself to his heir, Prince Hassan. Bibi and Prince Hassan had fought against each other in Karameh. The atmosphere was pleasant and Bibi was in high spirits. Unlike the Americans, the Jordanians showed him respect. If elected prime minister, Bibi promised King Hussein and his astonished entourage that he would strengthen the peace treaty between the two countries. Hussein wished him good health and fortune, not believing a word of it. He had followed the political map in Israel and knew Bibi was leading in the polls against Prime Minister Rabin, albeit by a small margin. Hussein held Rabin in high esteem and hoped he would win the elections, but he was also fond of Netanyahu.

22

Death to Rabin the Traitor

1995

The campaign that culminated in the assassination of Prime Minister Yitzhak Rabin in Tel Aviv's city square on November 4, 1995, began in January of the same year. Likud and the right-wing movements established a joint headquarters. Tzachi Hanegbi was Bibi's representative. The Kahane Lives and Kach movements joined in the activities, albeit uninvited. Representing Likud as man in the field was Uri Aloni, one of the movement's younger leaders. Thousands of Likud members and right-wingers started to demonstrate regularly opposite the prime minister's residence in Jerusalem and in front of his private home in Ramat Aviv. For the first time, cries of "Rabin is a traitor" and "Rabin is a murderer" were heard. They came hesitantly at first; then everyone was shouting denunciations.

A terrible terrorist attack took place on January 22 at the Beit Lid road junction. Twenty-two male and female IDF soldiers were killed and sixty-six were injured, some gravely. It was one of the worst anti-Israel terror attacks in the country's history. Two suicide bombers from the Islamic Jihad movement arrived at the junction, found the explosive devices that had been left for them, and blew themselves up among the soldiers. The second bomb detonated a few minutes after the first, targeting the soldiers who had rushed to help those injured in the first explosion. It was a horrendous sight. The attack was also a catastrophe for the peace process. In October of that year Israel retaliated, sending assassins who shot and killed, in Malta, Islamic Jihad leader Fathi Shaqaqi. It was to be one of the last orders issued by Yitzhak Rabin before he was assassinated.

In wake of the attack, Netanyahu increased his criticism of the government and announced that he would fight with all the means at his disposal this "peace process that is leading us to a Palestinian state." Public opinion polls showed a drastic drop in Rabin's popularity, while Bibi stabilized and deepened his own advantage. At the end of February, when Rabin rose to speak at a Knesset debate, the jeers and catcalls from the opposition made it impossible to hear a word he was saying. Loudest of all was Netanyahu. Rabin waited for a few moments and then shouted to Bibi, "You just shut up. When Menachem Begin made the decision to withdraw from the Sinai Peninsula, you weren't even here. You have never in your life filled any kind of position involving responsibility for security."

Bibi was stunned. Up to that moment, he and Rabin had maintained a semblance of mutual respect. Now Rabin's attack was part of a strategic decision to focus all criticism against Likud on its leader, Netanyahu. Bibi knew it was coming. He respected Rabin. It had been Rabin's decision to launch the operation in Entebbe, as well as Rabin's sensitive treatment of the Netanyahu family, after Yoni was killed, by renaming Entebbe *Operation Jonathan*. Rabin had much less respect for Bibi. To Rabin, Bibi was a potential emigrant. In a confidential conversation among close associates, Rabin asked, "Who is he anyway? I had respect for Begin and Sharon. These were men who made important decisions. Who is this Netanyahu? When did he ever have to make a decision? All he is is an American soap opera hero. He spent seventeen of his forty-seven years in the United States and now this emigrant wants to be prime minister of Israel. We should check to see if that name he gave himself, Ben Nitai, is not a sign that he intended to settle and make a life for himself there. Who's he to talk?"

Around this time, Bibi asked Shabak chief Yaakov Peri began to allow bodyguards from the nation's security unit to guard him. There was no justification for it, but Bibi had pressured Peri. After the usual pleasantries,

Bibi said, "I am surprised at you." "Why?" asked Peri. "Because there are alerts regarding my safety and, as far as I know, the Shabak, headed by you, is responsible for securing VIPs in this country." Peri responded, "I am regularly updated on warnings regarding VIP security. I have seen no such warning. Maybe it's a mistake? In any case, I'll check."

Peri turned the service upside down in his search for alerts on the safety of the leader of the opposition, Netanyahu, and found nothing. He even used keywords, which was how he found an alert regarding "Bibi." The trouble was that it referred to police superintendent Arie Bibi, commander of the Jerusalem region. It was an early alert based on recent rioting on the Temple Mount. Peri called Netanyahu. "You were right, Bibi," he said, "we've found an alert against Bibi, but it's Arie, the police superintendent." Bibi was in shock. According to Peri, it was possible to hear Bibi's heavy breathing from the other end of the line. "Yankale," said Bibi, "next time you're in the Knesset, drop in on me for a coffee?"

"Glad to," replied Peri.

And so it was. A few weeks later he sat over coffee in Bibi's office in the Knesset. "No alerts on you," Peri reiterated to Bibi. The opposition leader looked at the Shabak official straight in the eye and said, "I fear for my life." Peri later told Rabin that when he met the opposition leader's gaze, Bibi looked away. "OK," said Peri, "we'll let you have bodyguards." From then on, Netanyahu strutted around with state-supplied bodyguards. "It was a spur-of-the-moment decision," Peri said later. "I got the impression that he was afraid."

At a meeting with the prime minister later that day, Peri told Rabin, "Don't be surprised if you see Bibi surrounded by bodyguards soon." "What happened?" Rabin asked. "Have you lost your mind?" Peri smiled. "No, but Bibi was clearly anxious." Rabin sighed. "All right, I won't interfere in your decisions."

Incidentally, from the day Bibi persuaded Peri to protect him, it has been mandatory to provide security to the head of the opposition in Israel. When Peri made his decision, he wasn't thinking in terms of symbols of government. Some years later, a committee established for this purpose decided that the leader of the opposition was one of the symbols of government. What most people don't know is that Netanyahu set the precedent.

Rabin saw this incident as evidence that Bibi was a coward. Proof of Rabin's view here emerged decades later when Prime Minister Netanyahu pressured the Shabak to raise the height of the fences around his private villa in Caesarea, for fear of being hit by stray bullets from nearby Jisr az-Zarka's mosques or a still more distant sharpshooter. Has the fearless Sayeret Matkal soldier Netanyahu morphed into the cowardly politician Bibi? Possibly. But there is another possible reason for Bibi's stubborn demand for a Shabak bodyguard. He knew that Shabak bodyguards, with their suits and earbuds and their official image, would contribute appreciably to establishing his status in the popular imagination. This was important, because Bibi did not really look like a prime minister. He was young, he had never yet made a significant decision, he had appeared out of nowhere. That lack of experience was his soft underbelly, and it was at this that Rabin aimed during that confrontation in the Knesset. Bibi knew that having Shabak bodyguards would give him distinction, make him look like a prime minister. At that time, he even went so far as to add some silver to his hair, especially for his election broadcasts. For Netanyahu, physical impressions, look, and image, were more important than content. He needed to look like a prime minister. He insisted on it, and it may well be the reason he eventually achieved his objective.

Those days also gave way to a crisis between David Levy and Netanyahu. Levy had some far-reaching demands that Bibi had no intention of fulfilling. Levy put his dignity aside and announced that he was leaving Likud to establish an independent party called Gesher ("Bridge") that he hoped might threaten Bibi's chances of winning the elections. Bibi took it lightly, and rightly so. The polls indicated that any harm caused to him as a result of Levy's resignation was marginal. Netanyahu continued to lead and even increased his advantage. All this time, his strategic team was secretly planning to win the approaching elections. All options were considered, including Rabin being replaced by another candidate, like Shimon Peres, Ehud Barak, or even Haim Ramon. Bibi's people, under the direction of Arad and Lieberman, prepared a strategy for every possible eventuality.

The extreme right's campaign of incitement against Yitzhak Rabin intensified. The dozens of demonstrators outside his official residence increased to hundreds. The jeers became sharper. Screams, oaths, threats, and invectives were hurled on a daily basis. On Friday nights, the demonstrators waited for Rabin to return to his home for the Sabbath, screaming to him and his wife, Leah: "We'll do to you what they did to Mussolini." At other times, the comparison was to the Romanian tyrant Nikolae Ceauşescu, who had been executed seven years before. Waves of hate flooded Rabin as right-wing demonstrators became increasingly outrageous, breaking up every event where Rabin appeared.

The Likud team continued to lead demonstrations and anti-Rabin activity with all their might. There was a special headquarters operated by Bibi's people with the objective of turning Rabin's public life into a living hell. Activity was clandestine but its aim was obvious: to energize the right, inflame the situation in the streets, destroy every event that had anything to do with Rabin or with the peace process, and to wreak havoc. Bibi's team of helpers at that time were reminiscent of a pack of wild dogs. "That was the mentality at those meetings," said one of the participants twenty years later. "There was no red line, no ethics, no boundaries. They simply wanted to produce as much chaos as possible, and to make Rabin's life a misery."

Yaakov Peri retired from the Shabak and was replaced by Carmi Gillon. In early July 1995, Gillon arranged to meet Netanyahu, in the course of which he briefed Bibi on intelligence he had received about a plot to assassinate Prime Minister Rabin. Gillon explained that incendiary comments attacking Rabin might very well lead to an attempt on Rabin's life. Several days earlier, Bibi had led a huge demonstration against Rabin in Kfar Saba, in which he said in his speech that Rabin was "leading Israel back to the 1967 borders and preparing towns of refuge for the terrorists." At this demonstration, the call "By blood and fire, Rabin will expire" was heard for the first time. Gillon asked Netanyahu to restrain and modify the calls of the right-wing fundamentalists. "The incitement," said Gillon, "is liable to lead to a political assassination." Bibi listened but did nothing. He briefed some of his associates in the Likud leadership, including Ariel Sharon, who had announced shortly beforehand that he would not be opposing him in the primaries. "It's a Stalin-like conspiracy on the part of the government," he said.

To this day, Carmi Gillon claims that he specifically warned Bibi about the possibility of Rabin's assassination. According to Netanyahu, the warning was too general and unclear, and did not refer to Rabin specifically. Whatever the case may be, Netanyahu ignored the warning, as he had all the other writings on the wall.

Among the members of Bibi's "submarine" during those days was the psychologist Dr. Yair Amichai-Hamburger, an Oxford graduate—a credential Bibi liked. Amichai-Hamburger wore a yarmulke and held "light" right-wing opinions. After putting him through aptitude tests, Lieberman had brought him to improve headquarters. Amichai-Hamburger was a crowd psychologist who specialized in group psychology and the study of the masses. The objective was to identify and locate, with his help, the deeper streams in Israeli society, the underground trends, the fault lines, and the watersheds.

When Amichai-Hamburger understood the essence of Likud's "field activity" operated by Netanyahu and his people, he became worried. He knew what the Likud youngsters were doing, was familiar with the instructions they were given, and he was horrified. Amichai-Hamburger has never agreed to talk about this period in his life, and he is not about to begin doing so now. He wrote explicit warnings and sent letters telling Bibi and his henchmen that they were "setting free the devil." Amichai-Hamburger's doctoral thesis had focused on feuds among groups and conflicts. In his opinion, the way in which Netanyahu's people honed their differences and rivalries with Rabin's camp was dangerous. Attempts to ignite the atmosphere could be highly disastrous. The instructions to disrupt any event attended by Rabin and/or the Labor Party, to use all and every available means, and to balk at nothing in order to win by inciting, to whip up hatred, played on the most primeval instincts. Amichai-Hamburger believed this was dangerous, and he argued this view forcefully. From that moment, he was excluded from Netanyahu's inner circle. They understood that he could no longer be trusted, so simply bypassed him, continuing on their way. He watched the violence erupting and could not sleep at night. On many occasions he considered resigning and severing himself from Netanyahu's campaign, but kept postponing the decision. Later, he would deeply regret not having left in time.

Netanyahu did not rework the demonstrations or modify the rhetoric in them. On the contrary, he felt that Rabin's resilience was cracking and he understood—from Gillon, too—that the protests were achieving their objectives. The regime was wavering, fearful, its self-confidence slipping. Bibi decided to increase the pressure and ordered the Likud youth to intensify their demonstrations. His people were heard jeering at warnings and cautions. "To make Bibi win, anything is kosher," they said. It was decided to demonstrate at and disrupt any event that hosted Rabin or his senior government members. Shimon Peres, Minister of Housing Benjamin Fuad Ben-Eliezer, and many others started to experience firsthand the viciousness of the opposition. Even severe violence was experienced at some of the demonstrations, with demonstrators spitting and shoving the government ministers. Peres was banished from the Yemenite communities festival; Rabin's public rallys were disrupted; the streets were awash with waves of hostility, terror, and rage.

Yitzhak Rabin was concerned. In briefings, he warned his people against "extreme violence that might reach here." He sent a letter to the attorney general in an attempt to spur him to issue injunctions against several right-wing activists who, according to police and Shabak intelligence, had "crossed the lines of free speech." He received no response. A similar letter to the president of the supreme court met with a chilly reply. Rabin received information from the Shabak of an extreme-right conspiracy against him. He understood the situation. Nonetheless, he did not foresee himself being assassinated. No one told him that he should wear a flak jacket in public, a suggestion that would have saved his life.

But the worst was still to come: the "This Is Our Country" Zionist Camp movement, which organized many anti-Oslo activities, flooding the nation with demonstrations. The ideological cover for all this activity was supplied by extreme rabbis, mostly from the West Bank, who issued various halachic rulings that demanded the masses defend the Land of Israel. At one point, nine extremist rabbis issued a *din rodef,* which in halachic terms sentenced Yitzhak Rabin to death. The leader of the opposition in Israel's Knesset knew about this and did nothing to prevent it. Here and there he mumbled something but never came out against the violence and incitement, and did not speak out against the extremist rabbis. Nor did he discourage dozens of his supporters from standing outside the prime minister's home in Tel Aviv every Friday afternoon, chanting, "Rabin is a traitor, Rabin is a murderer, with blood and fire, Rabin shall expire!" With the vote on Oslo B approaching, he led an infamous demonstration in Jerusalem's Zion Square where huge simulated photographs of Rabin in an SS Nazi uniform were raised high. Crazed demonstrators set fire to Rabin's picture. It was reminiscent of anti-Israel demonstrations in Teheran. Bibi stood there on the balcony, at the head of the right-wing camp. The saner, more pragmatic right-wing leaders had stayed away from the event. Dan Meridor was not there; nor were Roni Milo, Benny Begin, or David Levy. Others, such as Reuven "Ruvi" Rivlin, saw where things were leading and left the balcony. Not Bibi. He stayed to the very end. He watched hundreds of children screaming "death to Rabin," and said nothing.

One month later, Rabin would be murdered in the center of Tel Aviv, by a yarmulke-wearing extreme right-winger from Herzliya, deeply influenced by extremist rabbis.

23

Arthur

1995

One evening, while a big rally of peace supporters led by Prime Minister Rabin was ending in Tel Aviv, Netanyahu's phone started ringing. Shai Bazak had called to inform him of a rumor that someone shot Rabin at the end of the peace rally in Tel Aviv. Although it was still only a rumor, Bibi summoned Bazak to him immediately, and then additional advisors. In the meantime, it was confirmed that Rabin had been shot and injured and was being operated on. Netanyahu was nervous. While Yitzhak Rabin fought for his life on an operating table, Bibi felt like a man drowning in a tidal wave. He had never even dreamed of an assassination, and he started praying for a miracle. He also tried to remember every demonstration he had participated in over the previous months. There would be no explanation for that demonstration in Zion Square, the one that several Likud leaders left as soon as they saw the pictures of Rabin in SS uniform and heard the chant "Rabin is a murderer."

In the meantime, Avigdor Lieberman rushed to Likud headquarters in Tel Aviv to personally check over the paper and computer files to make sure that the assassin, who had been identified in the course of the night, was not a Likud member, or had had any connection with Likud. Both Lieberman and Bibi knew that if Rabin had been assassinated by a Likudnik, they may as well pack up all their belongings and look for another country to live in. When it became clear that assassin Yigal Amir had no direct connection to Likud, they breathed a mutual sigh of relief. Bibi's small Jerusalem apartment was filling up with his supporters, and the telephone was flooded with calls. What were they to do now?

Bazak immediately set about composing a statement denouncing the attempted assassination. He was already passing the message on to the press when the telephone rang. Bibi picked it up, had a brief conversation in English, and hung up. Bibi was deathly pale.

"It's over. They've killed him," Bibi said.

Martin Indyk could never have imagined that one day he would face the grim task of reporting not only to Bibi but also to President Bill Clinton that his friend, the prime minister of Israel, had been assassinated. "What's going to happen now," he asked Bibi. "How does your system work? Who takes over?"

Netanyahu tried to explain to Indyk what could be expected. Don't worry, it's a stable democracy; the administration will be handed over in an orderly fashion. When the conversation was over, it was Bibi who was worried. He knew what was going to happen.

Various responses started to fill the television screen, almost all of them blaming the insane incitement against the prime minister. Almost everyone mentioned Netanyahu as the one who had led and controlled it. A cold sweat covered Bibi's forehead. "What's going to happen now; where is all this leading?" asked Sara, panic-stricken. No one paid any attention to her. Media pressure on Bibi increased; in the end he capitulated by stepping out onto his staircase and providing a response, albeit a laconic one, not allowing any time for questions and answers. One of the Netanyahu advisors (who was especially close to Sara), Rami Sadan, arrived at the apartment and said it was a lost cause, that the left would remain in power for the next fifty years. Any chance of changing the regime was gone. Bibi looked at him and didn't bother to respond. In the meantime, the head of the Shabak's bodyguard unit called to instruct Bibi to remain at home and not go out. Within seconds the entire neighborhood was flooded with police and security personnel. The Shabak placed Bibi under heavy protection. At long last he'd achieved the kind of security he believed he deserved.

Bibi was in shock; his pain at Rabin's death was genuine. He hadn't planned for him to be assassinated, nor had he dreamed that such a possibility existed. But he'd been warned. He'd seen the sights, heard the voices; too many times he'd led them. He should have taken the possibility into consideration. His political ambition had clouded all logic, all national responsibility. He tossed and turned in bed, that night realizing that the Rabin assassination could leave him with an indelible stain. But he convinced himself that he had had nothing to do with it, that he was no more than the opposition leader. He was determined to erase the stain, not to allow this disgrace to stick to him. He was terrified.

The following morning, at a meeting in Likud headquarters, Netanyahu looked like a man whose entire world had caved in on him. His long-standing secretaries noticed the tears flooding his eyes. It wasn't clear if he was weeping for Rabin, or for himself. Probably for both. He was deeply depressed.

For a few days after the assassination, Netanyahu was determined to resign from politics, sure his career was over. He was a political leper. People he encountered on the street turned their eyes away in loathing. He appeared to have lost his legitimacy. When he told some of his closest associates about his intention to resign they tried to dissuade him, but he seemed determined. Ultimately, the person who persuaded him not to resign was one of the people closest to him, but not at the time a member of his political "submarine," Yitzhak Molcho. "If you resign," Molcho told him, "you'd be marking yourself. You'd actually be admitting your guilt, and it'll hound you for the rest of your life. You must not collapse now; you must move on." Bibi listened, internalized, and understood. His personal crisis lasted a few weeks and was typical of the man who was able to return to himself many times in the course of his career after having been beaten, broken, collapsed, and sunk. These crises unsettle him, but after the initial shock, the Spirit of Bibi is always reawakened. He knows how to pull himself together, and start all over again. Bibi is the ultimate comeback kid of Israeli politics. He is the man who never, ever, breaks down.

Dr. Amichai-Hamburger resigned from the campaign team. With his resignation, he wrote Netanyahu a long, incisive, and critical letter. He wrote about the growing paranoia surrounding Bibi, about Bibi's contribution, and the part his supporters played in the savage incitement against Yitzhak Rabin. Then he left the headquarters. Dr. Amichai-Hamburger did not anticipate that things would go so far as to result in the assassination of the prime minister. To be fair, I have to add that no one in Rabin's vicinity even considered such a possibility either. But Amichai-Hamburger did identify the trend, recognized the wild forces being released into the atmosphere, and understood the dangers. He raised the alert, but no one took him seriously, so all he could do ultimately was to get out. People who worked with him in the Netanyahu headquarters were impressed by his integrity, morality, and principles, and were aware of his soul-searching during that time.

By the following morning, Netanyahu had started to recover. His first concern was that Shimon Peres would go to the polls immediately. If he did that, Bibi and Likud were finished. No one would vote for them.

Things were bad, he told Eyal Arad, but they would move forward. It's not over yet. Nothing's changed as far as the basic issues are concerned. If Peres postpones the elections, there is no reason to give up.

It was with a heavy heart that Bibi attended Rabin's funeral. The widow, Leah Rabin, refused to shake his hand. He had become an outcast. In Likud there began a quiet movement to replace him. Dan Meridor, a solid, pragmatic leader, was being mentioned as a possible replacement for Bibi and the man to rebuild the party. Bibi refused to give in. When everyone else was planning his political demise, he continued to fight. When it became clear that Peres was not calling for elections, Bibi was relieved. It was the first essential condition for his victory. Peres had missed the chance to bury Bibi politically after the assassination of Yitzhak Rabin.

Bibi's personal headquarters convened every morning in a Jerusalem café, behind a gas station. Bibi's first undertaking after the Rabin assassination was to bring back the people's confidence in him. The first polls after the assassination showed that Peres had a 30 percent lead over him. He was resolved to get out of the tough spot he occupied. "You'll see," he told his skeptical followers, "we'll get out of this, it's not over yet." He invested enormous effort in reharnessing senior Likud members to his campaign. The first to join was Ariel Sharon, after a lengthy meeting between the two. Bibi devoted much energy to Dan Meridor. As a Likud member who was also accepted by a non-right-wing public, Meridor could be the one to make all the difference. Eventually, Meridor agreed to join the publicity team. But the most significant addition to the team was a man totally unknown in Israel: Arthur Finkelstein, an American pollster and political strategist. His close friend Ronald Lauder, who had called in December 1995 and announced, "I've found him," introduced Finkelstein to Netanyahu. According to Lauder, Finkelstein would be Netanyahu's man. It was he who engineered the defeat of the legendary New York governor Mario Cuomo. He knew how to win losing battles, a genius strategist who knew no word other than *victory*. Bibi conducted a discreet check and reached the same conclusions. Finkelstein knew how to hurt an adversary, how to upset his equilibrium, how to locate weak points and compose the catchiest and most powerful of slogans. Anyone who could turn George Pataki into the governor of New York over Mario Cuomo could lead Bibi to victory.

In December 1995, he took a secret trip to New York to meet with Finkelstein. It was a short meeting. Finkelstein was prepared to join Bibi's team and named his price, $1,000 an hour. Likud's budget in those days was full of holes. Bibi had poured a fortune into his campaign and there were no reserves. When the American donors made it clear that he would "take care" of Finkelstein, the way was laid. Arthur Finkelstein was recruited and the chemistry between the two men was immediate. On the way, however, Arthur caused Bibi to lose an old friend. On the day of Bibi's secret flight to New York for the meeting with Arthur, Moshe Arens celebrated his seventieth birthday at a party in Tel Aviv. Bibi was absent and didn't give a good reason. Arens was hurt to the core. Bibi could have postponed his meeting with Arthur by twenty-four hours, but friends, feelings, and commitments are all foreign to Netanyahu when he is focused on an objective. His ability to forge genuine friendships with people, to feel commitment, to understand what the other person feels, had always been limited. Almost everyone who has worked with Bibi over the years is convinced that he suffers from a severe emotional handicap, that he possibly suffers from Asperger's syndrome, or might otherwise be on the autistic spectrum. He genuinely doesn't understand why people feel insulted by him. It is rarely his intent.

Immediately after the first meeting with Arthur, Bibi started sending him numerous and varied opinion polls, along with an accurate cross section of independent voters—whom they voted for in the past, their general political outlook, occupations, etc. Finkelstein then did his analysis, after which he told Bibi, "You're in the picture. You can win the election."

Netanyahu was determined to help this prophecy to come true. In an attempt to achieve legitimacy at all costs, he pressed former members of the security services into joining Likud. Yossi Peled, former commanding general of the IDF's Northern Command; and Gideon Ezra, deputy Shabak chief, were first. But the cherry on top was Yitzhak Mordechai, who had been commanding general of all three Commands and who was, at that time, completing his service in the IDF. Bibi seized the opportunity, promising Mordechai the post of defense minister in the government he was going to form. He also promised to appoint him chairman of campaign headquarters. He promised him the sky and Mordechai accepted. He announced his support for Netanyahu, and joined Likud. The final hurdle in the journey to the prime minister's office had been cleared.

24

Peres Will Divide Jerusalem

1995

Benjamin Netanyahu's political talents were light-years ahead of those of his rivals. When he entered the arena, Israel's politicians in everything from campaign management to the presentation of a candidate were equal to the development of a child in kindergarten. By comparison, Netanyahu was already in college. He had arrived from America equipped with the necessary knowledge and understanding of how politics work, and applied what he knew in Israel. It all started with his endless supply of money, the fruit of his connections with wealthy American donors, and he invested that money in all the right places. He imported American marketing experts with experience and expertise in products for the masses, people who on Sunday were marketing Coca-Cola and on Monday were marketing McDonald's; on Tuesday it was General Motors; and on Wednesday, Bibi Netanyahu. He felt politics was a profession, that it was possible to manipulate the masses, that it was possible to build the ideal candidate and to direct him to fit the mold of the "people's choice."

Led by Shimon Peres, Netanyahu's rivals didn't understand the power and ability of the actor before them. He had a murderer's row of experts whose titles did not reveal their talents or their relevancy to Bibi's campaign.

The mandate of these experts—among them Richard Wirthlin, a Mormon from Utah—was to make Netanyahu palatable to the Israeli voter. Since Netanyahu was already a natural actor, it was easy enough to dress him with the right ideas, masks, and poses that would make him appeal to the maximum number of voters. Bibi was prepared to say and do absolutely anything to achieve power.

The choice of Wirthlin was no coincidence, as he was considered the brain behind President Ronald Reagan's electoral success. Unlike Netanyahu, Reagan was an actor who made his living that way. His success was made possible in part because he managed to surround himself with what came to be known as Reagan's Democrats. Wirthlin and other experts devised for Netanyahu and his supporters a "laddering" tactic, the first stage of which was to conduct a series of public-opinion polls among right-wing and left-wing voters. These polls would supposedly reveal the very souls of the Israeli electorate and help Netanyahu's team amass a list of traits, quotes, and ideas that, properly deployed, would create the ultimate candidate. To create the greatest chance of winning the elections, the candidate had to be assembled, rung by rung, following a graded, ladder-like system. If a candidate could reach the top of that ladder, he or she would be able to capture the hearts of as many voters from as many political camps as possible. The candidate had to be flexible, and develop a chameleon-like ability to change, only saying the things tested in focus groups, predetermined to penetrate the average Israeli voter's innermost soul. Anyone with the intensity and tenacity to climb Wirthlin's ladder would become the "dream candidate."

Benjamin Netanyahu was the perfect client for this system. He had the financial wherewithal to pay for it. When he repeats and recites a text, he soon believes it wholeheartedly. His ability to convince himself of manufactured truths is what allows him to appear reliable. He is constantly playing a role in a movie about his political ascendancy. The machine erected around him built him up slowly, professionally, and thoroughly. He affected his own body language, facial expressions, and minimal physical gestures. He no longer had to stand in the mirror making sharp karate moves to psych himself up. He had already reached a far more advanced stage. Across the street, at Shimon Peres's headquarters, they knew nothing.

As far as they were concerned, Bibi was just another Likud hooligan trying to elbow his way to the top.

By January 1996, the gap between Bibi and Peres was beginning to shrink, now standing at 20 percent. In electoral terms, it was still a huge gap, but one-third smaller than just a month earlier. Bibi prepared an alternative campaign to use in the event that there was an agreement between Peres and the Syrians on the eve of the elections. It didn't happen. In the meantime, his people were trying to find a winning campaign slogan. All the polls showed that the strongest consensus among the Israeli public was focused on Jerusalem as capital of Israel. Even though Jerusalem had not yet been brought to the negotiating table vis-à-vis the Palestinians, it was obvious that it would happen in the future. Bibi's people needed to find a slogan that connected with Jerusalem, without exacerbating Israeli-Palestinian relations. Since the Rabin assassination, the public was sensitive, and Bibi was doing his best to avoid the matter of incitement. Someone came up with the slogan "Peres Will Give Up Jerusalem." It was marginal. Limor Livnat, the young Likud MK that served as propaganda manager in the campaign, proposed an improved version, "Peres Will Divide Jerusalem." It seemed to hit the spot. Arthur Finkelstein, on his first visit to Israel, approved the winning slogan.

The slogan was leaked to the media and met with enthusiastic responses. Bibi instructed his team to allocate unlimited resources to secure billboards countrywide for the new slogan. The entire Likud campaign shifted its focus to Jerusalem.

Netanyahu himself appeared every evening and spoke about Jerusalem; he toured Jerusalem and was photographed and interviewed there. Likud activists scoured the field. The billboards sprung up all over the country. The momentum had begun to smile on Netanyahu.

While this was happening, Hamas renewed its murderous suicide attacks on Israel. Streets ran with blood and fire. A particularly gruesome attack in front of Tel Aviv's Dizengoff Center during the Purim holiday horrified the world, and rattled Israel's population. Shabak chief Carmi Gillon resigned after the successful attack on the life of Yihye Ayash, aka the Engineer, the Hamas leader considered the brain behind the terrorist attacks. At long last,

Peres decided to schedule the elections for March 29, 1996. The race had officially started.

The wave of suicide attacks transferred the momentum to Netanyahu's camp. The traditional preelection mock elections at the Blich High School in Ramat Gan, which usually predict the winner, did not disappoint this time. Likud went in with a significant disadvantage and came out a very close second. With Peres at its head, Labor barely scraped a victory. Likud supporters at the school got a lift. The Likud billboards, and its spokespersons and activists, were at center stage. The party's legitimacy was reinstated. Coverage of Rabin's assassination was beginning to fade; replaced with the terrorist attacks, the blown-up buses, and the body parts scattered in the city streets. The game was completely up for grabs, and Netanyahu had every intention of winning.

He entered into secret negotiations with the leaders of two other rightwing parties: Rafael "Raful" Eitan, the legendary chief of staff who headed the Tzomet Party; and his bitter enemy, David Levy, who had resigned from Likud and formed the Gesher Party. The negotiations paid off within just a few weeks. Raful and Levy joined Bibi to form a large, living, and kicking right-wing bloc with Netanyahu at its core. On the other side, Peres had fallen asleep. All his energy was invested in the security issue and a desperate effort to halt the wave of suicide attacks, and the drift of public opinion in Netanyahu's direction.

And then Arthur Finkelstein appeared. The first to learn of Finkelstein's role were Eyal Arad and Moti Moral, Bibi's two campaign managers, and they were highly impressed with Finkelstein. To them, he was the epitome of professionalism. He decided that the campaign had to be based on short video clips, rather than long, heavy propaganda movies. Altogether there were three to four clips that were repeated over and over again, everywhere, brainwashing the public with short, catchy messages that would penetrate hearts and motivate fingers to do the right thing on Election Day.

Finkelstein himself remained an enigma. In the hotels he frequented in Israel, he was registered under pseudonyms. Usually, he used Eyal Arad's name. The media and most of Bibi's campaign workers, as well as the various politicians involved, were unaware of his existence. Eventually the media got wind of the mysterious American, when he came out of the shadows. Most of the time he worked from the United States, where he was sent the extensive, constantly updated polls. Occasionally he'd pay a brief visit to Israel, during which he would meet with Netanyahu. The statistics he used for tempting Bibi and his people were clear: "Looks like you're winning. It's not an easy one, but doable. We have to continue with the constant brainwashing, using all available means. Peres is going to divide Jerusalem. Period."

25

The Debate

1996

The principles Arthur Finkelstein set for the campaigns were rigid: five to six broadcasts each evening, no longer than thirty seconds long, a system Finkelstein called the hammer method. The message was repeated over and over, like Chinese torture. "Peres Will Divide Jerusalem." At the same time, Netanyahu appeared each evening on national television, filmed in a studio made to look like the prime minister's office. He was silver-haired, distinguished, a leader, dressed in a conservative suit, calmly assuring the public that he would bring a "secure peace." The objective was to put as much distance as possible between him and the demonstrations, the incitement, the shouting and ranting of the opposition, and to start presenting an image of him as prime minister. Another principle: to refrain from responding to Labor's smear tactics; to respond to nothing, and to continue along this line at all costs, all the time. Let them do what they want. We are doing our thing. And our man is Bibi.

But there was a problem with Bibi. He was starting to fall apart. The first people to notice were the ones closest to him. The stress was killing Netanyahu. His entire life was being drained into one fast-approaching date, May 29, 1996. Everything he had ever done was now being put to the test.

He knew that if he lost, all his counterparts in Likud would rise against
him as one. He had only the one chance, either to die or conquer the mountain. He was hard put to withstand the pressure. Finkelstein was updated
on Bibi's mental state and turned himself into the candidate's ever-present
personal manager. He stepped up at that critical moment and supported
Bibi. From that point every response, every message, every action, every appearance was approved by Arthur Finkelstein. "You must not dance in the
blood," he repeated over and over, instructing Netanyahu to keep a low
profile, to soften his tone, to restrain himself from visiting terror sites. And
Bibi did as he was told.

Throughout the campaign there were several attempts at mutiny, all of
which Arthur managed to quell. "Even if they raise the 'hot videotape' issue," he told his people, "we don't react." Bibi agreed with him. Their
campaign messages would be beautiful, with good music and lovely scenery, Arthur told them, but our ads will seep into the hearts of voters—our
ads will be what the public remembers on the way to voting stations. The
message: stick to our line. Nonetheless, as the campaign proceeded, Arthur did make a few exceptions: there was the clip of "Labor's disappointed
voters," and another famous one in which Peres and Arafat were seen
hand-in-hand behind an exploding wall of glass. These were winners. In
those pre–social network days the Israeli public was enraptured, almost
entirely, by election broadcasts on TV; the candidate who won the war of
advertisements would win the election. Labor's ads, as Finkelstein predicted, were indeed beautiful and well presented. Likud's broadcasts, in
contrast, were lethal. Labor's broadcasts drew sympathy. Likud's brought
victory.

The person who was troubling the people in the campaign's headquarters was Netanyahu's wife, Sara. For some reason, she was convinced that
she, too, was an electoral asset, and demanded to be filmed for a campaign
broadcast. No one had the nerve to tell her that her demands were unreal-
istic. Limor Livnat had already experienced a mouthful from her. Sara saw
in Livnat, who was young, talented, attractive, and charismatic, a potential
rival for her husband's heart. The local TV satirical program *Spitting Image*
hinted at a hypothetical, completely fictitious affair between Netanyahu

and Livnat. It was Arthur's job to reassure Sara in person that there was no truth in the story.

Now she wanted a TV ad of her own, and Arthur was called upon once again. With a glint in his eye, he ordered Bibi's staff to "do the clip." Sara glowed with pleasure. She didn't mind that the director wanted to reshoot the ad repeatedly; in fact she quite liked it. She would arrive at the set happy to be made up, dressed, and coiffed, each time anew. The production dragged on, just the way Finkelstein wanted. Time passed. Every time the ad seemed ready, someone on the team decided that it needed "touching up." And so it went, until it was too late. The elections were over and the spot was never broadcast.

In the meantime, the TV debate between Shimon Peres and Bibi Netanyahu was eagerly anticipated by Bibi's team. Labor campaigners, headed by Haim Ramon, tried to evade such a confrontation, but Netanyahu's people insisted. It was crystal clear that any evasion on the part of Peres would provide Bibi with a strong tailwind. The date for the confrontation was set for Sunday, May 26, three days before the election. For Labor it was a mistake; losing the debate at so late a date would mean that there was no chance to recover. To Bibi's people it was clear that whoever won the debate would win the election.

Arthur Finkelstein came to Israel for the debate. An improvised television studio was installed in his suite in Jerusalem's King David Hotel, where Bibi practiced for three full days and prepared for the real thing. Accurate replies were prepared for every possible question. A solid strategy was adopted to deal with every situation, including the possibility that Peres might storm Bibi, that Peres might ignore Bibi, that Peres might go for Bibi below the belt. The rehearsals were intense; nothing was left to chance. At one point they moved to the Likud studio, where a simulated confrontation was conducted with Dan Meridor playing the part of Shimon Peres. They all hoped that Peres would not be as good as Meridor. Bibi barely beat him. Preparations were completed on Sunday. Arthur was satisfied, wished them all luck, and flew back to the United States, which is what he does in every campaign. He prefers not to be there on the actual day. He left behind his assistant, Tim Roth, to oversee everything.

Bibi arrived at the debate with Shai Bazak, who tied his tie for him and accompanied him inside. The debate was recorded in the afternoon and was supposed to be broadcast in the evening. Bibi entered the studio first, took his place behind his lectern, and started to arrange his prepared comments, which were on cards. Journalists watched a live feed from a nearby room. Bibi was unaware that he was being watched by the media. He was showing signs of stress and anxiety. He asked for some water, became confused with his prompt cards, and started sweating. In their side room, the journalists were sure Peres was going to kill him. Only Shai Bazak, who was thoroughly familiar with his client, knew the truth. Bibi was always nervous right up to the moment of truth. As soon as the lights and the cameras go on, he's in his element. Eyal Arad, too, who knew Bibi better than anyone, was calm. He had no doubt how it would end. Bibi would eat Peres for breakfast.

Shimon Peres entered the debate room a few moments after Bibi. He was pale, with dark circles under his eyes; he had not slept the night before. His military secretary, General Danny Yatom, had reported that there was a real threat of terrorist attacks. Peres was troubled, tired, tense. When he began his opening speech by talking about Jerusalem, Bibi's people almost started dancing. Jerusalem? Why was he talking about Jerusalem? Jerusalem was Peres's Achilles' heel. Netanyahu squashed Peres. The debate ended with a knockout. Peres was burned out, exhausted, his messages confused and unconvincing. Bibi was sharp, accurate, and lethal. He looked like a prime minister, and he was very close to becoming prime minister.

26

Good for the Jews

March 1996

Benjamin Netanyahu is absolutely secular. In a different time and under different circumstances, he could even have been a perfect atheist. There is not in him a shred of religious belief, in the orthodox sense of the word. He does not really respect rabbis; he disdains religious trappings and rituals, which he sees as pagan mumbo jumbo. However, he has a deep respect for the Bible as the keystone of Jewish identity. His Jewish identity flows in his veins and is carved on his soul; it is the basis of the Jewish nation's right to the Land of Israel, according to Netanyahu, and it is the collective genome of the Chosen People. He does not believe in God and does not follow the commandments, does not keep the Sabbath, and does not adhere to the laws of kashruth. He derides people who kiss mezuzahs and grasp phylacteries, and has on many occasions voiced his views in front of his friends. Nonetheless, he had forged a covenant with the two branches of Orthodox Jewry, the ultra-Orthodox and the Religious Zionists, and he continues to pay the necessary lip service and graces to reinforce this covenant.

On the eve of the Simchat Torah holiday in 1984, shortly after being appointed Israeli ambassador to the United Nations, Netanyahu would invite himself to the mandatory meeting with the Lubavitcher rebbe at his court in Crown Heights, New York. In his lifetime the Lubavitcher rebbe was a kind of superpowerful magnet for hordes of Jews, including many secular Jews, who came to the famous court to be touched by the glory and receive a blessing from the revered and charismatic leader of the Chabad movement. The rebbe, who had already heard of the young Israeli diplomat, devoted a relatively long interview to him, at the end of which he placed his hand on Bibi's head and told him, "Never apologize." Over the years to come, Bibi paid many visits to the rebbe. On one of them, the rebbe told him, "You will have to struggle with 119 others in the Knesset, but surely you won't be intimidated, because G-d is on this side." This meeting took place after Netanyahu's victory in the Likud Party's primaries in 1988 and is seen to this day, in Lubavitcher mythology, as the rebbe's prophecy of Bibi's glowing future.

Ever since, Bibi maintained ties with the rebbe and his court, and even received a personal letter of congratulations on the birth of his first son, Yair. At the end of another meeting, the rebbe instructed his people to "help Netanyahu from now on and forever, unless he changes his skin." This was seen as his legacy. To the Lubavitcher rebbe, the most important thing was the integrity of the Land of Israel. Chabad ideology is very firm about this, even uncompromising. Anyone who gives back so much as an inch of the land is doomed and will be cursed. So long as Netanyahu opposed the transfer of Jewish land into Arab hands, the rebbe had ordered his followers to help him.

In the 1996 campaign, Netanyahu entrusted Ariel Sharon with the Haredi portfolio. Sharon, a veteran general, enjoyed the admiration of the Haredi rabbis and the great Hasidic scholars. They paid him respect, maintained ties with him, and welcomed him into their courts, as well as the "security briefings" he provided them with. Throughout the campaign, Sharon made his way from one court to another, as he explained to the rabbis the importance of these elections and the fact that "Bibi would defend the Land of Israel and Jerusalem." Sharon himself, one of the greatest cynics in the history of Israeli politics, was hard put to believe his own promises to his audiences, but he was interested in getting Netanyahu elected prime minister. He was eager to return to the government and worked hard to make it happen.

On Wednesday, May 15, 1996, exactly two weeks before the elections, Sharon was worried. Shimon Peres had a small but stable advantage over Bibi and Sharon. A seasoned electoral fox, he knew that they needed just one little push, a little "something more" to tip the scales. With every passing day the 5 percent advantage between the two became smaller, but Sharon feared it would not be completely erased by Election Day, and Peres might win by a hairbreadth. It was the first time in the country's history that the elections were so direct. In these elections Israelis were supposed to vote with a double ballot, one for the prime minister and the other for the Knesset. As already mentioned, the law that allowed this was passed thanks to that rebellious vote pushed through by Netanyahu. It was not necessary, therefore, to take into account coalition considerations. The person who received at least one vote more than his rival would be the one to form the government. Sharon decided to do something: he put in a telephone call to Rabbi Yitzhak Aharonov, chairman and the strongest person of Young Chabad, and asked for a meeting. Familiar with Chabad's influence in Israel, Sharon decided to try to harness the movement to Netanyahu's cause. Aharonov read Sharon's mind and agreed to a meeting with Chabad leaders but insisted on the candidate also being present. It was decided that Sharon would meet with the Chabadniks and, toward the end of their meeting, Bibi would join them. Sharon knew that not only he, but also the Chabadniks, did not believe Netanyahu. They didn't wish to make do with Sharon's promises and wanted to hear things from Netanyahu himself, to lock him into his promises.

The meeting took place on May 16, Thursday evening, thirteen days before the elections, in Kfar Chabad. One of Sharon's aides with him that night was an anonymous young man named Gilad Erdan. After Netanyahu was elected, Erdan would become personal aide to the chief executive officer, Avigdor Lieberman, and later go on to have a successful political career. At that time he was Sharon's right-hand man, who was helped by his familiarity with the ultra-Orthodox world. In his youth, Erdan had been a yeshiva student, abandoning religion later.

Throughout the meeting Sharon promised that Netanyahu would protect the Land of Israel and would ensure that no parts of it would be returned to enemy hands. The Chabadniks liked what they heard, but wanted to hear it from Bibi, too. Sharon briefed Bibi thoroughly beforehand. Chabad, Sharon told Bibi, has 210 branches in Israel; they have thousands of activists and are capable of giving us a push during the last days of the campaign; it is imperative that you come to tell them what they want to hear. Bibi understood and promised. As usual, he was late. Netanyahu's Volvo slid into Kfar Chabad at 11:00. To maintain secrecy, Netanyahu had turned up only with a driver and one bodyguard. Eventually, news of the meeting leaked out because thousands of Chabadniks showed up. With so many people pouring into the usually peaceful Kfar Chabad at such a late hour, questions were unavoidable.

Netanyahu said the things he was expected to say: how important it was to maintain the integrity of the land, how the Land of Israel belongs to the Jews. Sharon was not satisfied and wrote a note to his aides: look into the rabbis' eyes. They didn't believe him. The truth is that Sharon did not believe him either. He had virtually no respect for Netanyahu, saw him as an opportunist with very low levels of dedication and trustworthiness. A few days earlier, after leaving the court of one of the rabbis, where he'd received a promise that all the disciples of that rabbi would vote for Bibi, Sharon stopped on the stairs, turned around, and said to one of his young aides, "Listen, at this rate, our golem will be prime minister yet."

The meeting with the Chabad rabbis was a success. It led to a serious in-depth debate within the Chabad leadership in Israel. Until that day, Chabad had maintained political neutrality and did not interfere in local campaigns. It had been involved one time, within the Haredi camp, for which it later paid a heavy price. Any political involvement now would put an end to the movement's apolitical image. On the other hand, there was the Land of Israel. "If we don't help him, he might lose," said the Chabadniks. "And then we won't be able to say that we were not involved." They decided to respond to the call and step forward. A carefully thought-out slogan was chosen: "Netanyahu Is Good for the Jews." The slogan contained a whiff of racism and had been vetoed several weeks earlier by Limor Livnat and Likud headquarters. But the Chabad were not committed to a ruling party. They had no compunction about appearing racist, and were concerned about more land being handed over to the Arabs. Anyway, who would remember the slogan if they managed to bring about a victory for Netanyahu? Chabad launched its campaign three days before the elections, to leave no time for the legal system to take action, and no room for thought or protest. The idea was to go ahead with this slogan, which was to go for the jugular. By the time anyone noticed, the elections would be there and the message would have hit home. Australian millionaire and Chabad rabbi Joseph Gutnick, whose fortune from diamond mining was valued at that time at $2 billion, volunteered to finance the entire campaign. Zero hour was set for Sunday, March 26. And so three days before the election, every major road junction in Israel was flooded with Chabad supporters bearing huge banners. The streets in every large city were filled with Chabad activists carrying placards. All the banners bore the same legend: "Netanyahu Is Good for the Jews."

On Monday morning, Shimon Peres saw the Chabad people for the first time, in the course of an election tour. His car came out of Gedera, where he'd participated in a rally, and drove toward Tel Aviv. At every junction on the way he saw hordes of bearded young men with banners. Peres was exhausted and angry and suffered from an irritating infection in his eyes. The headlines that day announced Netanyahu's victory in the previous evening's TV debate. In the car, Peres was accompanied by a journalist and member of the Knesset (MK) Dalia Itzik, Peres's choice for minister of education. "What is this supposed to be?" fumed Peres when he noticed the first group of Chabadniks. "Who are these people?"

He immediately called his close acquaintance Shmuel Rabinovitz, rabbi of the Western Wall, and demanded an explanation. "They seem to be Chabadniks," said Rabbi Rabinovitz. "Bibi recruited them." Peres was shocked. All that day, as he traveled the country's roads, he encountered Chabad activists with the same banners and the same message. The country was full of them. Yesterday he had lost the television debate; today he was losing the street. Peres, a devout optimist, began to consider the possibility that he was going to lose the election.

27

Yes, Prime Minister

1996

The unbearable stress that weighed so heavily on Netanyahu during the final weeks of the campaign dissolved on the fateful day. On Election Day, Shai Bazak, Bibi's faithful spokesman, met a different Bibi, one who was relaxed and at peace with the world. After casting his own vote together with Sara at their Jerusalem voting station, Bibi asked to take a break from his official schedule and stop for a coffee. Bazak was horrified. Bibi's schedule, on one of the most important days of his life, was murderous. Where was he going to get a coffee at this time? But Netanyahu and Sara were adamant. The entourage stopped at a small café on the corner of Azza and mi-Tudela Streets in Jerusalem. Bibi and Sara sat at a sidewalk table, held hands, giggled with each other, and were photographed in the soft Jerusalem sun. Passersby gathered around them, looking on emotionally. Later, when Shai Bazak asked Bibi how he managed to be so cool on such a fateful day, he was told, "I have a rule in life: I do whatever I can, so long as what I do can change things. There is no limit to the things I am prepared to do, when there is still a change to influence. When we reach a situation where nothing can be changed, I relax. And this is the situation today. I know I've done everything. Now it is no longer in our hands."

He flew in a helicopter to the Golan Heights, where he addressed supporters in Katzrin. From there he went to Kiryat Shmona; then to Hadera,
Netanya, and other locations. He was cheered everywhere he went. The
official media were filled with reports on Prime Minister Peres's schedule
and activity and virtually ignored Bibi. With the approach of the fateful
moment, Bibi's tired body was infused with renewed energy. In the Haredi
city Bnei Brak he was to receive a special welcome. Thousands of excited
people waited for him with "Netanyahu" written on ballot notes, promising him victory. The town was plastered with posters saying "Netanyahu
Is Good for the Jews." Bibi smiled broadly as he received telephone updates
from Lieberman that the country was on fire, and that Likud supporters
were going out en masse to vote for Netanyahu; whereas the Arab sector,
which traditionally votes for Peres and the left, was asleep (as a result of
Operation Grapes of Wrath, during which errant Israeli shelling acciden-
tally killed over a hundred civilians in South Lebanon). Power smelled intoxicating to Bibi. He knew he was very close.

From Bnei Brak the entourage returned to the Hilton in Tel Aviv, where
Bibi had established his base. He usually used the Sheraton, but this time
he asked Likud to reserve the Hilton because a very large group of American friends, donors, and billionaires had arrived in Israel to be with "their"
candidate. Morad Zamir had already booked one of the suites; as did Merv
Adelson; and also Steven Schneier, Ronald Lauder's donors coordinator and
contact man. The prevalent language on the Netanyahu floor of the Hilton
Tel Aviv was English with an American accent.

Bibi asked to see the TV sample results alone with only Sara. The suite
emptied. At 10:00 p.m. two television channels announced a tie, with a slight
advantage to Peres. The commentators added that Peres's advantage was
small but definite. Peres's victory, even though not yet officially announced,
was presented as fact. The Netanyahu floor at the Hilton was confused.
On the one hand, it was a respectable tie. Who would have believed that
Netanyahu would succeed in producing a tie against Peres after the disastrous hot-video scandal, the Oslo Accords, and Rabin's assassination? On the
other hand, Bibi had lost. The atmosphere turned despondent as Netanyahu's suite quickly filled with people. Bibi kept his cool. He asked for Arthur

Finkelstein. Within minutes, Arthur was on the line. Bibi described the situation and the reports. Statistics started flowing in from various voting stations, including voter turnouts, and Bibi read them out to Arthur. Then he took a pen and started to note down what Arthur was telling him. After completing the conversation he announced: "Good, it's not over yet. There is still a chance of winning."

Outside, things looked different. Labor headquarters was abuzz with song and dance and wild yells of joy. Likud headquarters in Tel Aviv's Convention Center was dark and depressing. At around 11:00 p.m. Lieberman started pressuring Bibi to come over to headquarters. He decided to go. On the way he picked up David Levy. Bibi stepped out of the Hilton into the flashing lights of dozens of photographers waiting outside. He stopped for a moment, waved a victorious hand, and graced them with a broad smile. He was playing the part to the end, always, in essence an actor playing what history had decreed for him. From there he continued to the Exhibition Gardens, where he entered the hall in which the last of the disheartened Likud activists were waiting. With Levy at his side, he raised his arm in victory and smiled broadly. He refused to play the role of a loser and adhered to the script he had written for himself. He knew that tomorrow he'd be stabbed in the back and all his colleagues would be dancing in his blood, but here, facing the cameras and the activists, he was acting out the part of a victorious leader.

Shimon Peres spent the night in his Ramat Aviv home, surrounded by close family. He was tense and tired. The television sample results indicated a narrow victory. Peres emitted a sigh of relief, but continued to view the developments tensely. His advantage was very small. At 11:00 p.m., the telephone rang. On the other end of the line was Uzi Baram, a senior Labor member responsible for the Arab sector. Voter turnouts among the Arabs were higher than anticipated, Baram told him. Peres had been expecting this news. It should have meant that he had won. His friends dispersed. They all went to sleep with the understanding that Peres was the next prime minister of Israel.

Bibi exited the Exhibition Gardens, depleted. Eyal Arad was waiting beside his car. "Listen," Arad said, "It's not final yet. According to our data, things could still turn around." "I know," Bibi replied. "I've talked with Arthur." Arad advised him to get some rest. "You'll need all your energy and strength for tomorrow." Bibi agreed and returned to the Hilton to sleep. By the time he'd arrived in his suite, taken a shower, and organized himself, the television polls had changed and updated the results to an absolute tie. Fifty-fifty. A huge cheer shook the hotel's sixth floor. Bibi and Sara's suite filled with excited people. At a little before three in the morning, as they were still watching television, a new update came through—advantage to Netanyahu. Another, more powerful cheer roared through the hotel. The suite was now crowded with wealthy Americans, come to congratulate the soon-to-be-elected prime minister. "Listen, you could still win," Shai Bazak told Bibi. "What do you mean, could," Bibi replied. "I am the winner." And he was.

Toward four o'clock, when Netanyahu's advantage over Peres had reached 0.6 percent, Bibi went to sleep. By the time he awoke, the lead had grown to 1 percent. Fifty-one percent to Netanyahu, forty-nine percent to Peres.

With Peres, the process was different. He had gone to bed as prime minister and woken up leader of the opposition. Defeated. It was a photo-finish victory. If the elections had taken place a few days earlier, Peres would have won. Over the final weeks of the campaign, the gap between the two candidates grew smaller by the day. The advantage came at the finishing line. Had the voting law not been amended because of Netanyahu's decision several years earlier, Peres would have won the election. The Labor Party under his leadership won more seats than Likud. But the law had changed. Netanyahu's determination to vote against his party and to risk paying a political price for doing so had paid off. He got 1 percent more than Shimon Peres and won. "Good night, Mr. Prime Minister," said Sara, as her husband closed his eyes. She was saying it to them both.

28

White House in Jerusalem

1996

Benjamin Netanyahu became the youngest prime minister in Israel's history, and it showed. He did not approach the post with a sense of awe. He catapulted into it, drunk on power. An atmosphere of celebratory plunder like that of the victorious tribes of the ancient world washed over his people. Bibi and Lieberman were determined to destroy everything and create the government anew. The problem was, however, that they approached the job with only force, and no real preparation. Netanyahu had planned his conquest of the premiership and prepared that operation over the years, down to the smallest detail. What he would do when he actually got it, he didn't really know. The hard part was getting there; once there, everything would be all right. As far as he was concerned, the day after the conquest didn't matter. But the real test was still to come. Now it was time for the public to judge him. And after winning the election, his tenure began badly with an endless series of scandals, embarrassments, failures, outrageous news items, and a sense of sourness. Netanyahu the Conqueror was an unripe, childish, and perhaps even frightened prime minister. His blend of smugness—that conviction that there was no one like him—coupled with his inexperience and tendency to panic when things started to go wrong was problematic, especially when considering the rigors of the job.

It actually began nicely. Contrary to habit, Bibi lowered his guard somewhat with a victorious round of childish telephone calls to his friends. Several of his old Jerusalem friends were honored with calls in the style of "Hello, this is your prime minister. I have just finished a conversation with the Egyptian president and am awaiting a call from the U.S. president; in the meantime, I am calling you."

Always the ultimate source of Bibi's paranoia, Sara took it all to unprecedented extremes. She conducted a telephone inquisition among their friends to find out which of them had voted for Bibi and who had not. Most of Bibi's Jerusalem friends did not vote for him. Some even admitted it; after all, they had grown up in families identified with Mapai, historically the Israeli Labor party that governed the young state in the first three decades. Sara fumed. To her, the world consists of those "who are with us and those who are against us." People who didn't vote for Bibi couldn't be friends. With the passage of time, this paranoia intensified and took control of the couple. It peaked during Bibi's third term in office, when one of the couple's old friends, a distinguished medical professor who had treated Sara's father and become a family friend, received a call from Netanyahu himself. Bibi, the incumbent prime minister of Israel, asked the professor if he was friendly with a certain journalist. The professor affirmed that he was, and had even treated him for a serious illness in the past. "In that case," Bibi told him, "you can no longer be a friend of ours." The professor was speechless. He recalled that the journalist did indeed make a habit of verbally attacking Netanyahu and, especially, his wife, but he had never imagined that things would reach such a state. Several years later, however, Bibi's attitude toward the professor softened and he called him with a greeting on his eightieth birthday.

During the first intoxicating days following Bibi's victory, the office of the prime minister–elect announced that he was no longer to be referred to as "Bibi." The media would now refer to him as Prime Minister Benjamin Netanyahu. Avigdor Lieberman was now director-general of the prime minister's office. What they didn't know yet was that Eyal Arad was no longer there. The loyal and wise advisor, who'd accompanied Bibi from his first days in New York, had been thrown out, having fallen foul of Sara, who had marked him and Limor Livnat for disposal. Up to the elections, they had managed to keep it secret. Afterward, it was no longer possible to deny: Arad was banished from the prime minister–elect's office as if he'd never existed. Livnat, on the other hand, was given a ministerial position. She didn't manage to arrange a meeting with Bibi, who was terrified of it being leaked and then reaching his wife. Netanyahu knew that if he were to leave Livnat out entirely, the gates of hell would open when she told the public the reason. The drama continued until the very day he had to present his government. In the end, as usual, Sara's close confidant Ya'akov Ne'eman was summoned to break the bad news and to try to calm her down. Livnat was appointed, Sara fumed, and the matter somehow passed. For a long time all meetings between Bibi and Livnat were kept secret and recorded in code. Over the years, the issue has become much worse. In 2015, Ayelet Shaked, another mortal enemy of Sara, was appointed minister of justice, and Netanyahu never meets her in private. It is far too dangerous for him to do so.

Establishing the government became an embarrassment. Bibi and Lieberman planned to leave Dan Meridor and Ariel Sharon outside. Lieberman had marked the two as "troublemakers." To him, Meridor was a rebellious "gourmet" and something of a lefty; Sharon was dangerous, a man who could stick a knife in Netanyahu's back without warning. Sharon remained on the outside and went to fume on his farm in the Negev. Only a few weeks later, when David Levy's patience had run out and he'd announced publicly that he would resign from the government if Sharon did not join it, did Bibi give in, tailoring the Ministry of National Infrastructure for Sharon. In the end, he gave spots to all the people he had planned to shut out. Ya'akov Ne'eman brought in Limor Livnat, Begin brought Meridor, and Levy made sure Sharon was included in the government. Bibi started to learn, the hard way, lessons on the limitations of power.

Netanyahu had planned a historic revolution in government, in the civil service, and in the various corridors of power. The thesis was simple: in the time of Menachem Begin and Yitzhak Shamir after him, Likud was in government but did not really govern. Ever the gentleman, Begin left all the senior officials in their place, did not touch the regulators, did not take control of the boys in the ministry of finance, left the justice and foreign ministries to their own devices and, in fact, left all the Mapai agents in their place, and they continued to run the country. Under Lieberman's influence, Netanyahu vowed to demolish all this. "The earth shall rise on new foundations," according to "The Internationale," the standard socialist anthem from the early 1870s. Bibi and Lieberman were prepared for this, with a difference: the new world they planned to replace the old with was not socialist, but completely capitalist. It would be a world of privatization, of a free market, of removing obstacles, of weakening regulators and reducing government activity. Their plan was to control Israel, not only in theory but also, in fact, to change it. The Labor movement had built a dated and cumbersome semi-socialist welfare state. Netanyahu dreamed of a little America on the shores of the Mediterranean Sea, with a similar economy and system of government.

The plan was to establish something resembling the White House in the prime minister's bureau, to annex to the prime minister's bureau as many branches of government as possible; to replace the attorney general as soon as possible with "one of ours"; to weaken the Foreign Ministry; to take control of the treasury officials. Bibi and Lieberman dreamed of turning Israel's prime minister into a Middle Eastern version of the U.S. president. Bibi had been brought up on American political culture and wanted to instill it in the Jewish state. His plans were far-reaching and bombastic.

At the same time, Bibi began preparations for a constitutional change that would lead to a formal presidential regime. Danny Naveh, the new government secretary, spoke about this in closed forums: the objective, he said, was to create a situation in which the elected prime minister is not tied to coalition considerations and is able to appoint a government comprising experts in their fields, not career politicians. Legal experts close to Bibi began drafting a relevant bill, and preparing an opinion that detailed the authority of the prime minister–elect, in accordance with the new election law.

When all these plans reached the operational stage they failed. Within three months, it was clear that the national security council he wanted would not be formed, that a supreme economic council in the prime minister's office would not be established, and that he would not be able to annex the Civil Service Commission to his own authority. Nor would he be able to establish a powerful propaganda department that would explain the prime minister to the Israelis and the rest of the world and would bypass the Foreign Office and enable him to establish a political desk, headed by Dr. Dore Gold, that would bypass the Israeli diplomatic system.

Bibi and Lieberman set about the task with a sledgehammer. In the end, it transpired that what they had managed to smash was mostly themselves. In closed circles, Lieberman detailed his plans: to destroy Israeli agriculture, which wasn't profitable; and to revive Israel's military industry, even at the cost of closing it down. The same went for the aircraft industries. He wanted to drastically reduce the country's failing textile industry and give a push to the industries of the future, such as technology, diamonds, and computers. In retrospect, the success of these plans was limited. The budget division remained in the Finance Ministry; a supreme economic council was never established. The National Security Council was established only toward the end of his term, after Defense Minister Yitzhak Mordechai was fired. Netanyahu and Lieberman found themselves having to contend with a bureaucracy that was fighting for its life within a political system that had barricaded itself against a political newcomer, against an unconvinced public and unconquerable obstacles. Three years later, when Netanyahu was thrown out of the prime minister's office, not much had changed. There had been a few important successes and historic reforms, but the bottom line was failure.

The public had lost faith; his government and behavior were chaotic, confused, and amateurish. Ehud Barak would defeat him in the 1999 elections and sent him off to start all over again.

29

Bassiouni's Villa

1997–1998

On matters of state, Netanyahu's approach was the mirror image of his machinations in the internal political arena. He was cautious and considered, shunning adventures and striving to maintain the status quo. Left to his own devices, he would have done nothing to improve the existing situation. Before the elections he evaded questions about the Oslo Accords; after the elections he was forced to recognize them. Before the elections he claimed that he would send his foreign minister to speak with Yasser Arafat, and after the elections he did indeed dispatch David Levy on this unsavory mission. He obliged to undertake the same mission soon after Levy did.

His first meeting with President Bill Clinton took place on July 9, 1996. Clinton had already been in office for six months, Netanyahu barely one month. The joint press conference was oozing with clichés and mutual compliments. The president praised the newly elected prime minister, leader of Israel's right wing, for his recognition of the agreements reached with the Palestinians. Behind the scenes, Clinton was quoted after this meeting as saying to his people that "Netanyahu thinks he's the leader of a superpower, and we're supposed to do as he says." This quote has haunted Netanyahu to this day. He is the first Israeli prime minister to rebel against the clear hierarchy in relations between Israel and the United States. Bibi addressed the Americans as an equal among equals, completely ignoring the absolute dependence of Israel on the United States, demonstrating what has been conceived from the onset in American eyes as ingratitude. He didn't share his predecessors' respect for the benign superpower. Yitzhak Rabin treated the Americans with great respect and was a White House favorite. Shimon Peres groveled to the Americans. And even Yitzhak Shamir was forced eventually to be dragged to the 1991 Madrid conference, and refrained from intervening in the first Gulf War once the Americans had made it clear that such a move would torpedo the international coalition. Bibi behaved as if these codes no longer existed. It could be that this behavior has something to do with the many years he spent in America, years in which his personality and world view were formed. He identifies as an American in some ways, so he behaves as one of them. The trouble is, however, that while he sees himself as an American leader in exile, the Americans see him as a megalomaniac Israeli politician.

When it came to security, Netanyahu's caution was even more obvious than in the political arena, and in most cases he was not adventurous. On the contrary, he was much more circumspect about approving operations by Mossad and IDF special forces behind enemy lines than any of his predecessors. Often he would evade giving approval for such operations in order to lay the responsibility on the IDF's shoulders. On matters of security, Bibi is not quick to make difficult and risky decisions. He has a pathological fear of the possible repercussions on his political career and prefers to surrender the potential attention to be gained by such operations to avoid having to take responsibility for them. With the passing of time, his fixation on authority has intensified and, with it, his fear of losing it, which is reflected on the issue of security.

A major event clouded the beginning of his tenure. Perhaps the euphoria after Bibi's election victory loosened his inherent cautiousness, but whatever the cause, he approved the opening of the Western Wall Tunnel exit (the Hasmonean "Cave" synagogue) on September 24, 1996. The process that led to the decision to open the Cave was amateurish. Netanyahu didn't really consult with security experts, ignored a proposal to tie the opening to a deal with the Jerusalem Islamic Waqf that shares management of the site, and flew out of the country immediately after the event. Foreign Minister David Levy was also abroad when rioting broke out in the West Bank, threatening to slip into all-out war. Because the Palestinians viewed the opening of the Cave as an attempt to breach the status quo on the Temple Mount (and as efforts to dig under the mosques), the result was violence and rioting and heated confrontations between Palestinian police and the IDF. Seventeen Israeli soldiers were killed during the three days of rioting, and more than one hundred Palestinians. Netanyahu's reaction was inexplicable: He allowed himself to do a tour of three European states immediately after the opening of the Cave, a tour that mostly found a frightened, sweating Netanyahu on the phone to get updates from Jerusalem on the spread of the uprising and trying to deal with the matter from afar, talking to U.S. Secretary of State Warren Christopher and Israeli Defense Minister Yitzhak Mordechai and trying, unsuccessfully, to get Yasser Arafat on the phone.

All at once everything was turned on its head. On September 4, Netanyahu met Arafat at the Erez border crossing, a cold and insignificant meeting that took place only because Mordechai had refused to meet the Palestinian leader. For two and a half months prior to that day, Bibi had been doing everything in his power to publicly humiliate Arafat, to show him who was boss, hanging Arafat out to dry before agreeing to meet him. Now Arafat retaliated by refusing his calls. In the meantime, during a call from the German capital, Bibi received a clear and unequivocal message from his government secretary, Danny Naveh: "Things are looking bad. Come back immediately." Netanyahu canceled the rest of his trip and returned to Israel. On the plane he told journalists that he had been trying to call Arafat, but Arafat wasn't returning his calls. Some of the reporters managed to pass on this information to their editorial offices in Israel. The prime minister's bureau got wind of it and was quick to issue a denial. They did not know that Netanyahu had himself provided the information. But this was the least of Bibi's problems. The territories were in flames, an IDF force was under heavy siege near Joseph's Tomb, and Bibi found himself

having to somehow extricate himself from the burning deadlock he had
backed himself into. It took days for the riots to subside. Netanyahu's credibility was in shreds, destroyed by his will to power.

Netanyahu encountered a similar incident in September 1997. A little
earlier, in July of the same year, two Palestinian suicide bombers had exploded themselves in Jerusalem's Mahane Yehuda market, killing sixteen
Israelis. From a political point of view, Netanyahu was sensitive to suicide
attacks. He was able to win control of the government in no small measure due to the wave of suicide bombings that swept the country when his
trademark was "security at all costs." The renewal of these attacks could
have been a deathblow for him. Except that the attack in the market was
carried out by Hamas. Netanyahu knew what to do. The Hamas leadership and field operators had to be eradicated, and with them the entire terror machine. He was given two names: Khaled Mashaal and Mussa Abu
Marzuk. The trouble with Abu Marzuk was his American citizenship.
Mashaal was to be the target. The mistake was to take him out on Jordanian
soil. Jordan had signed a peace agreement with Israel three years previously.
The agreement would now be imperiled.

A botched assassination attempt on Khaled Mashaal in Amman by
Mossad ended in tragedy. Mossad agents succeeded in spraying Mashaal
with some of the substance that was supposed to cause his death, but a fight
broke out and the two agents, posing as Canadian citizens, were arrested by
police and held for questioning. Four other agents quickly sought shelter in
the Israeli embassy in Amman. Meanwhile, Mashaal was dying from the
poison gas his body had absorbed, and the Jordanian authorities began to
understand what was actually happening. A furious King Hussein threatened
to sever relations with Israel forthwith, and to impose life sentences on the
two imprisoned agents. There was an attack on the embassy to capture the
remaining four Mossad agents.

Netanyahu was facing a completely hopeless situation. He was pathetic.
He broke down and dispatched Mossad chief Danny Yatom to Jordan to face
King Hussein and tell him the whole truth. Hussein demanded the anti-
dote to the poison to save Mashaal's life. One of the Mossad agents in
Jordan was in possession of a vial containing the antidote, which had been

prepared for accidental exposure. The agent, Mishka Ben-David, received his orders from Jerusalem and handed over the vial to the Jordanians, who rushed to the hospital and administered the antidote to Mashaal, who soon began to recover.

At the same time, Netanyahu agreed to release Hamas leader Sheikh Ahmed Yassin from an Israeli jail, together with seventy additional Hamas prisoners. Only then did King Hussein's anger begin to subside. Efraim Halevy, the deputy Mossad chief and a personal friend of King Hussein, was summoned to try to repair Israel's relations with Jordan. The Israeli agents were released and returned to Israel. Khaled Mashaal became the only person in the world successfully assassinated and brought back from the dead. In time, he was to become the leader of Hamas, one of the harshest and most fanatical of Israel's enemies. Sheikh Yassin emerged from his jail cell a winner, ready to organize dozens of attacks on Israel, until the Israeli Air Force annihilated him during the second intifada. Bibi became a joke. His judgment was revealed to be sorely lacking. His decision to carry out a dangerous and highly consequential assassination on Jordanian soil, incurring serious risk to the peace treaty, was reckless. He did not consult with the authorized parties; he did not include his defense minister, Yitzhak Mordechai, in the secret operation; he had excluded everyone and was now almost alone, having to face the fallout. How paradoxical that, compared with other prime ministers of Israel, he approved very few adventurous operations behind enemy lines. He was cautious—cowardly, even. And now here he was with one of the few operations he had approved exploding in his face.

The fatal blow to his carefully created image was provided by the previous year's opening of the Western Wall Tunnel exit. Instead of the tough-guy image Netanyahu had hoped to build for himself, what came across was softness, an inability to function under pressure, and weak leadership. Israel was reluctant to use force against the gangs that opened fire against IDF units. Netanyahu's being caught up in panic and forced to demonstrate restraint was interpreted by the other side as weakness. No sooner had the flames subsided than Bibi was summoned urgently to a summit meeting with President Clinton in Washington. Bibi flew out, anxious and obedient, to the meeting, which was also attended by Arafat and King Hussein. This summit was quite different from the meeting earlier that month at the Erez Crossing. This time Netanyahu did not behave like the wealthy lord of the manor come to meet his serfs. The summit ended with a hug between Bibi and Arafat, a hug that haunted Bibi for years afterward. "I found a friend in the White House," he said about Arafat at the end of the Washington meeting. For years, Netanyahu's enemies quoted this when they felt the need to humiliate him.

Paradoxically those riots did more than just harm Netanyahu's prestige and hawkish image. They brought about renewed negotiations between the two sides and a boost to the peace process. As soon as things had calmed, Netanyahu agreed to an Israeli withdrawal from Hebron and, a year later, he was dragged to the negotiations at the Wye River conference, where Netanyahu signed over the transfer of 13 percent of the West Bank to the Palestinians as part of the second, further redeployment, which was supposed to be a part of the Oslo Accords. This period, according to the Netanyahu chronicles, symbolized his basic "operating principle" by which an easily pressured Netanyahu can be manipulated into taking pragmatic moves by means of pressure, political and security levers, and blocked escape routes. Everything Netanyahu does is an expression of the pressures to which he is subjected. The more fear and pressure that is exerted on Bibi, the easier it is to shift Bibi's position on any matter. An essential element in this principle is Bibi's conviction that such pliability will actually help keep him in office, and not the reverse. Netanyahu will never take a step that could be risky to his political survival. Bibi's real strategic objective is to remain prime minister of Israel.

This explains the formation of a secret team in late 1996 that included Americans, Israelis, Palestinians, and one Egyptian. This "villa team" worked from the luxurious villa in Herzliya Pituach occupied by Egypt's popular ambassador to Israel, Mohammed Bassiouni. The Clinton administration had developed a practical method for dealing with Netanyahu: to drag a reluctant Israeli prime minister to the negotiating table, from there to make courageous decisions (i.e., concessions), map out in advance all potential escape routes from negotiations and decision-making processes, and render them impassable. The idea actually belonged to the Israelis. Haim Ramon of the Labor Party gets the credit. Yossi Beilin, of Oslo fame, brought Ramon's thesis to the next level. One of Shimon Peres's legendary advisors known as "the blazers," Dr. Nimrod Novik, who had been the architect of the negotiations with the Palestinians, was responsible for carrying out the plan. It should be included among the most creative political guerilla operations in history. It was here that Netanyahu was unwittingly manipulated into participating in the Wye River summit. The Wye River Accords were what ultimately caused the collapse of Bibi's coalition and the early election, which Bibi lost to Ehud Barak.

First of all, it was necessary to persuade Yasser Arafat. It wasn't easy. According to the Oslo Accords, Israel was supposed to carry out three "further redeployments," in the course of which additional territory would be passed on to the Palestinians. The first stage of these had taken place immediately on implementation of the accords by the Rabin and, subsequently, Peres governments. The "Hebron agreement," which was carried out by Netanyahu, constituted the repayment of the final remaining debt from the first stage. The second phase was all Netanyahu. According to Arafat, Rabin had promised him 40 percent of the West Bank. There was no written proof of this promise, and no one on the Israeli side believed it. Netanyahu was prepared to discuss the possibility of individual percentages of the area. His infrastructure minister, Ariel Sharon, who at that time was "Mr. Security" and a crazy hawk, declared that transferring more than 9 percent of the West Bank to the Palestinians as part of the second phase would endanger Israel's security.

The job of the secret team operating out of Bassiouni's villa was to persuade Arafat to meet Netanyahu halfway and to agree to a restricted stage of something between 11 and 13 percent. The team believed that Netanyahu would, under American pressure, reach these numbers. "Your alternative is simple," the team told Arafat. "If you don't agree, nothing will happen and you'll have to wait for Bibi to lose and be replaced; or to say yes, and then you'll bring Netanyahu to a T-junction and an agreement in principle. If Bibi agrees and signs on a second phase, the meaning is that the leader of the Israeli right is adopting the Oslo Accords. If Bibi refuses, Avigdor Kahalani's Third Way Party will leave the government and the elections will be brought forward. It's a win-win situation."

On the Israeli side the villa team consisted of Haim Ramon, Yossi Beilin, and Nimrod Novik. The Palestinian side consisted of Mahmoud Abbas and Saeb Erekat; they were sometimes joined by Hassan Asfour and Mohammed Dahlan. Even Mohammed Rashid, Arafat's mysterious money man, occasionally joined the proceedings. Ambassador Bassiouni was the host and coordinator and of course in on the secret. He reported to Cairo. U.S. ambassador Martin Indyk, who lived nearby, would arrive at the villa toward the end of the meetings and receive detailed updates from Bassiouni. As incumbent ambassador, Indyk had been warned not to be caught with a hand in local politics, which is why he did not participate in the talks themselves. But he was updated and active behind the scenes, and reported to Washington, managing to be deep inside while he was ostensibly on the outside. The Israelis reported to Ehud Barak, opposition leader and potential replacement for Netanyahu. The chances of success were not huge, but it was worth a try.

Abbas and Dahlan were persuaded to accept the plan from the very first meeting at the villa. However, the problem was Arafat. The elderly Palestinian leader was stubborn. It took months to persuade him to take part in the negotiations. Abbas and Erekat invested much energy on their mission until he finally capitulated. Arafat found it hard to settle on 12 percent, but he did understand the basic principle. Arafat, trying to get orange juice from a lemon, had to be convinced that the only possibility here was lemonade. It might be sour, but it was better than nothing. Lemonade, too, said the Israelis, contains vitamin C, and the lemonade was just a reduced phase of 11 to 13 percent. Principle, they argued, was more important than the territory. What's more, when Netanyahu signs on such a phase, he is actually signing the Oslo Accords. The possibility of the right-wing Israeli leader joining the Oslo process was far more important than mere territory. It was better than waiting inactively for his fall. No one at the villa at that time could have imagined that Netanyahu would sign and then fall from power.

The team convened once a week. Arafat had a regular routine that he used to irritate everyone: he would meet with his people on their return from the villa, hear them out and be persuaded. By morning, he would have changed his mind. This continued until Haim Ramon and Yossi Beilin went to meet him in person. They extracted a reluctant "yes" from the aging Palestinian leader and returned to Herzliya. In the meantime, Nimrod Novik, the group's political brain, completed a draft of the agreement transferring 12 percent of the territory to the Palestinians. He handed this over to Danny Naveh, the government secretary and a close associate of Netanyahu. "There's a good chance that the Americans will go for this format," Novik told him. Naveh was excited. Twelve percent is a bargain for an agreement with the Palestinians and long-term political peace and quiet. He took the draft to Netanyahu. The trap was laid at the prime minister's feet.

Novik's paper was positioned accurately at the Archimedean point: it was sufficiently modest enough to avoid undermining Netanyahu's coalition, yet generous enough to leave the political process alive. The paper would have rescued Netanyahu from the deadlock that he found himself in, while his coalition partner (the Third Way Party) and the Americans were pressing him to continue the political process as the right pressed for the exact opposite. "The prime minister is prepared to give positive consideration to the paper," Naveh told Novik a few days later. "It depends. It's definitely a good basis for negotiations."

Novik's draft had already been lying in U.S. secretary of state Madeleine Albright's drawer for several weeks. She liked it. Indyk recommended going for it. She accepted the recommendation. Albright called Netanyahu and asked him if he'd be prepared to come to a summit meeting with the objective of reaching an agreement on a second phase. Netanyahu acquiesced, on one condition: so long as the extent of the phase would remain in the "low teens." Albright told him, "You got it." The summit convened at Wye and the sides agreed on a final number, 13 percent, after ten days of seclusion and dramatic negotiations. Albright gritted her teeth and completed the mission, until the successful closing of the proceedings and the signing ceremony. President Clinton presided over the debates, using all the charisma and personal charm at his disposal in bringing the two sides together. It was Minister Sharon who surprised everyone by joining in the negotiations, changing his image from a vicious hawk threatening to torpedo the whole thing to being a driving force behind the agreement. Sharon had a way of looking far into the future. He reckoned that this agreement could topple Bibi, and he wanted to be there, as close as possible, when it happened. He had already planned the battle for succession. Together with Defense Minister Yitzhak Mordechai, Sharon persuaded Bibi to sign, and he did.

As all this was happening, Bibi found himself in an embarrassing situation with Clinton, who promised him the release of the Israeli spy Jonathan Pollard in return for signing the agreement. Clinton reneged on this promise shortly afterward, when CIA chief George Tenet threatened that if Pollard were released, he and other senior CIA officers would resign. As far as the Bassiouni villa team was concerned, this made no difference. They had won the big prize and gotten Bibi right where they wanted him. They never imagined that this tactic would topple him.

30

Where's Grandfather?

1996–1999

Netanyahu's first term in office was beset with problems, systemic and governmental. Although many people had been concerned that the young Netanyahu's regime would bring with it war or a collapse of the Israeli economy, this did not happen. Bibi revealed himself to be a cautious prime minister who took few chances and maintained the status quo at all costs. The damage caused by his two earlier slipups, opening the Western Wall Tunnel exit and the assassination attempt on Khaled Mashaal, was temporary and reversible. Netanyahu paid for these two mistakes, and learned the necessary lessons. He climbed ever deeper into a comfortable, safe, and secure shell. He approved few special military operations behind enemy lines, took the fewest possible risks, and invested energy in not rocking the boat. His main problem was the way he conducted himself, the swift deterioration in the quality of government, the public reception of his administration, and the growing sense among Israelis that the person at the helm was immature, inexperienced, and not sufficiently serious. Bibi's first term in office was rife with scandal, complications, quarrels, resignations, and grave embarrassments. With the passing of time, it began to seem like

Netanyahu was not capable of running a country. He knew how to win an election, but he didn't know how to govern.

The problems began immediately. Netanyahu did not have a single moment of grace. After Eyal Arad, the obvious choice for prime minister's bureau chief, was banished and left to his own devices, Netanyahu and Lieberman launched a search for someone suitable for this sensitive post. They found Pinhas Fishler, a former IDF officer and officer in the Israel Police, who passed all the aptitude tests. Fishler managed to stay in the post for a few weeks, until he was forced out by Lieberman in a move that caused a huge scandal. Within the first few days, Fishler had come to realize that nothing could be overseen in Netanyahu's office, where chaos always reigned. An agenda was not an agenda; the prime minister was chronically tardy; the office was constantly full of friends, wheeler-dealers, and kibitzers. And there was no one who was able to take control of the pandemonium.

Netanyahu managed himself, found it hard to delegate, panicked each time something went wrong, and failed to take control of the government apparatus in order to create an organized working administration. Fishler was a straight player, and soon understood the principle of things. His replacement was no more successful. General David Agmon, a senior army officer with an excellent record, was brought in with loud fanfare, only to leave, protesting weakly, after a short time, excluded from Netanyahu's inner circle, banished and humiliated from the prime minister's bureau. What happened to the dream of a White House in Jerusalem?

Avigdor Lieberman moved around the prime minister's bureau like a bull in a china shop. On one of the first days there, he approached the bureau's legal advisor, General Ahaz Ben-Ari, an impressive and experienced legal mind, and dismissed him on the spot. "We are searching for people of a like mind," Lieberman told him, loyal to Bibi's vision that insisted on destroying everything that had been and rebuilding anew. The trouble was that Ben-Ari's replacement did not conform to civil service regulations and had to leave a few weeks later. Nothing that Bibi and Lieberman did during those first months of his term succeeded. They were unable to administer, unable to appoint, were unable to get through a week without being the subject of some public scandal or other.

Netanyahu's basic fault was his obsession with "loyal people." Loyalty, according to Netanyahu, was the main and most important—if not the only—attribute he looked for in people. And it wasn't a question of right-wing ideology, affinity to Likud, or commitment to the nationalist camp. It is entirely a case of devotion to the boss, to the Netanyahu family. Government ministers and Likud members were inevitably seen as potential rivals. As for Knesset members—no one even bothered to count them. Bibi suspected everybody without exception and tried to work around them, alone. The first to show his displeasure was Foreign Minister David Levy, who discovered that Netanyahu was conducting the country's foreign policy via Dore Gold, and neglecting to keep him informed. Next came the Foreign Ministry staff, including senior ambassadors. These were followed by senior members of the security bureau. Netanyahu had barely taken office and was already at odds with the popular chief of staff, Lieutenant General Amnon Lipkin-Shahak; the even more popular Shabak chief, Ami Ayalon; and with Mossad chief Danny Yatom. At first he kept the senior officers at arm's length from political negotiations, condescending to them one day and calling them for urgent consultations the next. In the course of Netanyahu's first term, Justice Minister Ya'akov Ne'eman, who had become a close associate, handed in his resignation following an indictment against him. Later, many other ministers also resigned. One day, with other suspects available, suspicions arose in the prime minister's office regarding female soldiers serving in the office of the military secretary. "They are not on the same page," said people in Netanyahu's circle. "Perhaps they should be exchanged for more loyal servicewomen."

The paranoia in Netanyahu's vicinity increased steadily. He trusted no one. When Dan Meridor asked one of Netanyahu's associates if Bibi could ever bring himself to trust him, he, sensing Meridor's distress, was unable to answer. However, all this was dwarfed by another, ostensibly burning issue: Mrs. Sara Netanyahu, who stole the show. From the start, stories about her had been making the rounds. Within a few months, the national legend that was Bibi's wife provided the nation with regular—almost weekly—scandals and faux pas.

In Israel, the status of the spouse of an incumbent prime minister has never been defined by any kind of law. Until the Netanyahu regime, prime ministers' wives were fairly marginal characters in the country's political setup. Some of these first ladies were more involved in their husbands' lives; some were less so. There has never been anyone as dominant as Sara Netanyahu, who has always seen herself as integral to the regime, enjoying full partnership with her husband in running the state.

A dramatic change in her behavior took place immediately after the videotape incident. Until then she had been insecure, scared, refraining from joining the inner circle. On social occasions she would stand alone, usually trying to attach herself to her husband, her eyes darting hither and yon "like a frightened little mouse," as one of the close associates put it. It all changed after that trauma and the agreement she secured in its wake. Sara was shot into the prime minister's office as from a cannon. She demanded an office of her own, including advisors and secretaries, and she became the terror of the prime minister's bureau. Her fuse was extremely short, and her demands were exaggerated and endless. Wherever Netanyahu went, she was there, a permanent shadow: state visits, events, speeches; she was always there, carefully scanning the environment, holding on tightly to the hand of her husband-partner, always receiving flattering mention of her name and importance from the prime minister's podium. Mrs. Netanyahu had a hand in every matter of state, insisting on receiving her husband's daily schedule, the right to intervene on matters regarding official posts, to interview candidates, and to veto appointments.

Netanyahu accepted it all with equanimity and total support. Since the debacle of the videotape, he'd lost his stamina vis-à-vis his resolute wife. He remembered the superhuman effort to reassure and appease Sara, and he didn't wish to fall foul of her again. Over and over again, he repeated to his associates that they were to listen to Sara, to obey her, to ensure that she was satisfied. He bought time, barely skipping from one scandal to another, resigned to his fate.

It was so, too, when endless outrages arose between the prime minister's wife and the child minders and household staff who fell in her way. The scandals were juicy and provided the public with a view of the extremely problematic personalities of their country's leaders. The sick obsession with cleanliness, the chronic stinginess, the recklessness and endless demands, all day, every day, turned the prime minister's residence into an attrition mill, spewing out casualties at a dizzying rate. It's a march that continues to this day. At one time she was known as the "problem," but no one from Netanyahu's inner circle understood the true meaning behind the woman's power. Those misguided enough to raise the problem with Bibi were subjected to an immediate reprimand and told in no uncertain terms not to interfere. Amazingly, those individuals who dared criticize matters concerning Sara discovered that Netanyahu told Sara. Many of them were forced to abandon their posts, excluded forever. Bibi had arrived on the scene with seeds of paranoia deeply rooted in his personality; Sara knew how to germinate those seeds and turn him into a fanatical paranoiac. She was protector of the allegiance, marking close associates, enemies, and the partners in accordance with their level of loyalty or perceived treachery. In time, Sara became involved in every single appointment, and it was impossible to introduce people into the prime minister's vicinity without prior approval from her. The precedent of Limor Livnat expanded over the years, with Sara opposing the appointment of Naftali Bennett to the post of minister in Netanyahu's 2013 government and the appointment of Ayelet Shaked in 2015. She would acquiesce only when there was no other choice. She studied Bibi's operating system and took control of it, an expert at pushing his buttons. The more she did this over the years, so more her covenant with Bibi would intensify, to the extent that they eventually fused into a single entity. In 2015, Sara Netanyahu was the architect of his victory in the polls, standing beside him at center stage, delivering speeches to activists, participating in meetings and discussions, making decisions.

The person who has rarely been seen in Netanyahu's vicinity since his first term in office has been his firstborn, his daughter, Noa Netanyahu. When he was first elected to head the government, Netanyahu was asked by many reporters why there were no pictures of Noa among the many family photographs behind his desk. His responses were mostly embarrassing. "The picture's being framed," his staff would say. The "framing" lasted to the end of his term. Some man, or some woman, had excluded the firstborn from the Netanyahu family idyll. Meetings between Bibi and his daughter grew ever fewer. On the rare occasions that Noa was smuggled into the prime minister's office, it was accomplished through a side entrance, to ensure that as few people as possible would witness the girl coming to visit her father. Everyone was fearful that news of the visit would reach Sara.

During the 2015 election campaign, Netanyahu's favorite newspaper *Israel Today* made no mention whatsoever in Bibi's CV of his first wife or his firstborn daughter. It is almost as if they never existed. In the meantime, Noa married, found religion, and became ultra-Orthodox. She has three children, Bibi's grandchildren. All this is barely mentioned in the media. Netanyahu is proud of being a loving husband and devoted father. He appears never to have spoken to the press of his grandchildren. Apart from a single picture from the first grandchild's circumcision ceremony, Netanyahu has almost no photographs of himself with the children; there is no quality time, no real relationship. He (and his wife, Sara) attended the circumcision of the first boy, sat with pursed lips in a corner, and left immediately after the procedure, without staying for the traditional feast afterward.

During Noa's early years, Netanyahu maintained a close and warm relationship with her. He demanded and received from her mother, Dr. Micki Weissman Haran, maximum and flexible access to the girl. In those years, Netanyahu demonstrated his love of his daughter, but then something happened. From the moment Sara entered his life, Bibi spent less time with Noa. As of today, the relationship between Bibi and his daughter and his grandchildren is practically nonexistent. When their grandfather appears on TV, Netanyahu's grandchildren are asked, "Who is that man?" They don't know. Bibi's grandchildren live a thirty-minute walk away from the prime minister's residence, but the route between the two homes is bleak. Noa and her children see Netanyahu two or three times a year, mostly at family memorial services. Even on those occasions, there is no intimacy. All those years, Noa has kept silent, as have her mother and adoptive stepfather, Doron Haran. It is a painful subject, both sensitive and explosive; but, especially, it is sad.

31

Political Rookie

1998–1999

By its second year, Netanyahu's government was a sinking ship with no captain. Bibi pursued a scorched-earth policy, leaving in its path disappointed cabinet ministers, Knesset members seeking revenge, a hostile media, and a public in conflict. In October 1997, Netanyahu was filmed whispering into the ear of Rabbi Yitzhak Kaduri, a century-old kabbalist, "The people on the left have forgotten what it is to be Jews." The sound was off, but someone read his lips. Unaware he was being filmed, Netanyahu turned into a symbol of conflict and political opportunism in Israel. He was caught in the act, the ultimate inciter. A powerful public storm broke out, joining an endless chain of media scandals both political and personal. One after the other, government ministers resigned. The first to go was Dan Meridor, followed by five others. The bottom fell out when Netanyahu fired his minister of security, Yitzhak Mordechai, toward the end of his term in office after realizing that Mordechai was considering resigning and establishing a rival party. Mordechai subsequently did establish a centrist party, together with Dan Meridor and Roni Milo (former Tel Aviv mayor and Likud member) and the former IDF chief of staff Amnon Lipkin-Shahak. Their sole objective was to topple Netanyahu. The feelings he aroused in political colleagues were all antagonistic. Almost everyone, from all parts of the political map, wanted to be rid of him. Meridor swore to do whatever it took to release Israel from the burden of Netanyahu. Milo was no less determined. Mordechai sought revenge. Lipkin-Shahak was mainly disgusted by Netanyahu.

One of the larger scandals of that term was called the Bar-On-Hebron Affair. In January 1997, a police investigation was launched to examine claims that Netanyahu and several political activists were involved in a deal to appoint Roni Bar-On to the post of attorney general, in order to get a comfortable plea bargain in a criminal proceeding that threatened Bibi's political partner, Shas leader Aryeh Deri. In return for the plea bargain, Shas would support the agreement to transfer the West Bank town of Hebron into the hands of the Palestinian Authority. Bar-On's appointment was rescinded forty-eight hours after it was announced, following heavy media response and public pressure. This made headlines for some time. Although Bar-On was not suspected of committing a crime (and later became a successful cabinet minister), the connection between Netanyahu and Deri stank to high heaven. Israel's rule of law and political appointments had been corrupted. Bibi became increasingly viewed as one whose vile transactions polluted public and state affairs.

The police investigation was lengthy and torpedoed the secret negotiations under way at the time between Netanyahu and Shimon Peres to include the Labor Party in the coalition and to appoint Peres to the post of foreign minister. Peres knew that Ehud Barak planned to remove him from the party leadership and take his place, and tried to get around the move by joining Bibi's government. The Bar-On Hebron Affair resulted in a freeze on negotiations. Netanyahu looked on, with panic, as reality closed in on him from various quarters. Frightened, he continued to fight for his political survival. After completing the investigation, the police recommended indictments against Netanyahu and others involved in the affair. His only hope lay with the decision of the attorney general, Elyakim Rubinstein, the man he'd outfoxed to get appointed as Israel's ambassador to the UN. He was sure Rubinstein would take advantage of the situation to settle the score.

Under pressure, Netanyahu locked himself in his office, severed all contact with the media, and tried to figure out how to get out of the dead-end situation. He summoned his ministers, Knesset members, associates—almost all of whom had been hurt by him, or hated him on one level or another and hoped for his political demise. He humiliated himself, groveled, begged, promised to change; said that he learned his lesson, turned over a new page. No one believed him. In the end, after a nerve-racking wait, Attorney General Rubinstein surprised him with an announcement that he was closing the case for lack of evidence. Nonetheless, he published a public report that included scathing criticism of the prime minister's conduct in the affair.

Bibi sighed in relief. He knew things would die down and he'd remain in the prime minister's office. For a while he kept a low profile, masqueraded as one who had learned his lesson and grown up, but inside, he was rejoicing. By the skin of his teeth he had survived. The case was closed; there was no indictment, time to move on. In no time at all, he was back to his old ways.

In October 1998, Netanyahu headed the government delegation to the summit conference hosted by President Bill Clinton at the Wye River Conference Center, unaware that this had been planned and cooked up at that villa of Egyptian ambassador Bassiouni. He was heading into a situation from which he could not escape. No matter what happened at Wye, he was in trouble politically. If he reached an agreement with Arafat, the right would topple him. If not, there was a good chance of the center-left ganging up on him. After ten days of heated negotiations an agreement was reached. Israel committed itself to transferring to the Palestinians 13 percent of the West Bank, the "second beat" of the Oslo Accords. Netanyahu returned to Israel, disappointed by his last-minute failure to release Jonathan Pollard, worried by the possible collapse of his coalition and criticism from the right. Still, disembarking from the plane at Ben Gurion International Airport, he declared war on the left, denied some of the commitments he'd made in the Wye River Memorandum, and tried to continue dancing at both weddings.

This time it didn't work. Netanyahu managed to implement only the first clause in the Memorandum (that included transfer of 2 percent of the territory), before his government fell. MKs from the Moledet Party, together with Likud MKs Benny Begin and Michael Kleiner, decided to give a vote of no confidence in the government. New elections were set for May 17, 1999. Netanyahu's first government was redeemed. Netanyahu was hated by large parts of the public, loathed by the media, unwanted in his own party. Things came to a head when Moshe Arens, Bibi's former patron and inspiration, decided to challenge him for the party leadership. Arens was defeated, but the message was clear: Bibi's autocracy was over. In the end, Netanyahu appointed Arens minister of defense, after firing Mordechai.

Even when he was the last man to believe, Bibi continued to fight. In those days, he was still leading the polls. His adversary, former chief of staff and Labor Party chairman Ehud Barak, did not manage to rise in the opinion polls. Even the new Centre Party formed by Mordechai, Meridor, and Lipkin-Shahak made no difference in the balance of power. In the direct election of prime minister, Netanyahu continued to lead by a small margin against Barak. Bibi knew that the Knesset elections didn't matter; the person who won the direct election would form the government. He was still seen by the public as a winner, a kind of political wizard able to juggle a lot of balls. He had no intention of giving up.

32

The Downfall

1999

As Election Day grew near, Benjamin Netanyahu's isolation grew. Advisors left, cabinet ministers resigned, associates distanced themselves. Netanyahu restricted himself to his dwindling inner circle. His paranoia worsened. He clung to Sara and she, in turn, clung to him. More than ever before, the sense that the whole world was against them united and bound them together. There remained only a handful of supporters, and Bibi and Sara together managed to convince them that they were fighting against a global left-wing conspiracy involving the Americans, the media, and others, all hell-bent on achieving his downfall. More than ever, during those harsh moments Bibi needed all his confidants, his good and trusted team that helped him reinvent himself ten years before. But Eyal Arad was now working for Yitzhak Mordechai and had sworn revenge, and even Avigdor Lieberman, the epitome of devotion, had left. Lieberman, who had been appointed general manager of the prime minister's office, had resigned in anger in December 1997, only a year and a half after the establishment of the government. It happened after Bibi and Lieberman had tried a dirty trick in Likud, whereby the 2,800-member-strong Central Committee would receive the right to elect the Knesset list. The move encountered fierce criticism from the press and Knesset members, and Bibi, as usual, got cold feet at the last moment. Lieberman was furious. This zigzagging behavior of Bibi's was, to Lieberman, the final straw. "This man is incapable of making decisions," said Lieberman to his associates. "He is a real danger to the country." He placed his keys on the table and left. But swore he'd return, next time as head of an independent political force. A few months later, he founded the independent Israel Is Our Home Party, which got its votes from ex-Soviet Jews. He no longer needed Netanyahu.

In early 1999, Netanyahu was a lonely man, with only a sparse group of followers. His campaign headquarters was nearly empty, and his slogan, "A Strong Leader for a Strong Nation," sounded pathetic. Even long-standing patron Ronald Lauder exhibited his independence by hosting former chief of staff Amnon Lipkin-Shahak at a gala dinner in New York. Lipkin-Shahak had established his centrist party with the express intention of toppling Netanyahu.

Despite past trouble with Sara Netanyahu, Limor Livnat agreed to head the campaign headquarters. Oded Leventar, an old friend of Netanyahu, was also there. Apart from them, there were a few pollsters and external advisors—Arthur Finkelstein sent his aide, George Birnbaum. Headquarters debates were carefully recorded and minutes were taken. It was a predetermined chronicle of political dissolution. Each evening they met until the small hours, wailing and complaining about Netanyahu's worsening situation and the dwindling chances of winning this election. Bibi arrived late. Usually he'd attack the refreshments and prepared food before turning, his mouth full, to the campaign broadcasts that had been prepared for the next day. Israel had only two TV channels, and every evening at a designated hour, both channels broadcast the election propaganda of all the different parties. TV viewing percentages were very high, and Netanyahu hoped to repeat the success of his 1996 campaign broadcasts. But it was a lost cause.

Each evening the prime minister would turn up at campaign headquarters; eat, drink, and edit the broadcasts; overturn predetermined policies to suit field data; and leave. "It can't go on like this," said Birnbaum. Limor Livnat laughed. "What do you expect, with the new copywriter writing all our copy and dismissing everything we do?"

But the final blow came in the TV confrontation with the third candidate, Yitzhak Mordechai. Ehud Barak, the leading candidate, refused to participate. Bibi arrived, loaded with self-confidence. Everyone expected "Mr. TV" to destroy his former defense minister, knock him out. But the strategist Eyal Arad and media advisor Avi Benayahu had thoroughly prepared Mordechai, who arrived focused and determined, and proceeded to defeat Netanyahu. Several times during the broadcast he said, "Look me in the eye, Bibi." He was referring to the negotiations Netanyahu had conducted with Syrian president Hafez Assad for a peace agreement. Bibi's emissary in these negotiations was Ronald Lauder, who flew back and forth between Jerusalem and Damascus. Netanyahu expressed his agreement in principle to discuss an Israeli withdrawal from the Golan Heights in return for peace. In the end, as always, he got cold feet. Mordechai exposed Netanyahu on this matter, dealing a harsh blow to the prime minister's reliability. The commentators declared a "clear victory to Mordechai." Bibi looked as if he'd lost it.

Limor Livnat tried to stabilize the campaign, but nothing helped. She at least did her best up to the last moment. All the others simply disappeared. In desperation, Netanyahu tried to stage a loud confrontation with the media, publicly ridiculing them for persecuting him, and coining the expression "they are a-f-r-a-i-d," which became the official war cry of his supporters. It only worked on Likud diehards. The general public was having none of this media spin. Even when popular actress Tiki Dayan called Likud supporters "rabble," Bibi was unable to do anything with it. He donned a banner, "I Am Rabble and Proud," but it was too little and too late. The country was sick of him. On one of his final campaign broadcasts, he released a hesitant and embarrassing announcement about the mistakes he'd made, and promised to change. It was supposed to make him appear human, but only exacerbated his situation. The writer Amos Oz said after the elections that the general feeling was that someone turned off a generator that had been running for over three years in the middle of the living room. Suddenly there was quiet. A collective sigh of relief was released in the country.

Almost everyone was happy about Netanyahu's departure. Almost everyone gloated. Bibi got what was coming to him.

33

Picking Up the Pieces

1999

Ehud Barak squashed Netanyahu by a large margin. The defeat came as no surprise, not even to Bibi and Sara. As soon as it was over, Netanyahu announced that he was retiring and taking a break from politics. Foreign Minister Ariel Sharon was by his side. It was a picture that had been planned long before by Sharon himself. Gradually and patiently, Sharon had spent the past year getting closer to Netanyahu. The relationship grew warmer and peaked when Bibi and Sara and Lily and Ariel Sharon had dinner together in a Tel Aviv restaurant. Sharon had never for a moment stopped mocking and disrespecting Netanyahu, but he understood that the prime minister's downfall was inevitable and wanted to be there, as close as possible, when it happened. He had maneuvered Netanyahu to the Wye River summit, knowing that it had the potential to topple Netanyahu. At the right moment, therefore, he stood at his side, the loyal minister, his close confidant, and his immediate successor. No one objected to Sharon being named "temporary chairman" of Likud to begin rehabilitating the party. It even suited Bibi. Sharon was already seventy-one, heavy of mouth and body, a politician with most of his future behind him. To Netanyahu as well as to others, he appeared the classic placeholder. None of them understood that he had a totally different agenda.

In the prime minister's official residence in Jerusalem, the Netanyahus started to pack their belongings. Bibi was in a deep depression. Sara was in a foul mood. It was hard for them to take leave of the power, of the perks of authority, of traveling in a secure convoy along the length and breadth of the country, of life at the state's expense. Throughout the "lost decade," when the Netanyahus were exiled to a political wilderness, Sara would sail away on a wave of nostalgia, remembering the convoy of cars tearing through Jerusalem, sirens wailing, oblivious to traffic lights and jams, bearing her ladyship to her chosen destination. When she was sitting in her private family home on Jerusalem's Gaza Street and hearing the sound of sirens delivering a different prime minister (Barak, Sharon, Olmert) to the official residence, her eyes would fill with tears of longing. It took her and Bibi many weeks to pack the contents of the official residence and organize themselves for the move. The Netanyahus seemed to be clinging with their last strength to the prime minister's residence, refusing to move, trying to steal one more minute.

Four months after the elections, *Yediot Ahronot* revealed what appeared to be criminal activity on the part of the Netanyahus. According to the investigation, the couple had ostensibly tried to have the state pay significant sums to cover their personal expenses. The report contained many piquant and embarrassing details. It emerged that they found it hard to pay for anything—even blatantly personal things—out of their own pockets. Mrs. Netanyahu's obsession for extreme cleanliness, her exaggerated demands for packaging methods, and many other trappings painted a disturbing picture, and even hinted at mental issues. The report led to a police investigation, which revealed that the couple had tried to conceal from the state hundreds of gifts presented to the prime minister in the course of his duty, and had tried to extract from the treasury a huge sum of money to cover the cost when they moved out of the prime minister's residence.

The Amedi affair (named after the moving company) investigation was extremely humiliating. Detectives invaded the Netanyahu household and carried out a detailed search. Nothing like it had ever happened to a former prime minister in Israel. Next came the searches of Netanyahu's office, and the storeroom in which the couple kept the many gifts from Bibi's term in office. Sara lost her cool, calling the investigators "hunters." Bibi refused to accompany her to the interrogation. He found himself sitting in an interrogation room for hours on end, facing police investigators as media cameras filmed his comings and goings like the lowliest of criminals. Sara, too, was interrogated at length, the whole while hurling insults and accusations at her interrogators. Netanyahu was mortified by the experience. Later, he would blame the police for the death of his mother, which took place shortly afterward.

Sara's responses were no less severe. When the investigation ended the police recommended an indictment against the two. No one believed Mrs. Netanyahu's claim that she was only "caring for" the hundreds of gifts her husband had received as prime minister of Israel. State Attorney Edna Arbel supported the recommendation and added harsh criticism of the couple's conduct. Attorney General Elyakim Rubinstein, the very same official who had dismissed the Bar-On-Hebron case, deliberated at length before deciding to dismiss this case. Again Bibi had gotten away by the skin of his teeth. What remained now was to pick up the pieces, gather his wits, make some money, and plan his comeback. He was only fifty, a politician just starting out, and already with a term as prime minister behind him. He had been there too early. This time he'd learn his lesson, think out a new route, study his mistakes, and reinvent himself. He knew he'd be back. He had to. He would return with renewed strength, older and wiser. He had no choice; he believed that, after Yoni's death, it was his destiny to carry out the mission. No one else could do it. Iran was already building its nuclear program and Netanyahu was building a model of the approaching catastrophe. "No one understands the danger," he thought, "better than I do." He truly believed no one but him had the historical, intellectual, and mental attributes to bring together all the sane forces in the world to stop the second Holocaust. He had inherited this view from his father and his grandfather. He was the "guardian of Israel's security," and he had no rival.

34

Back Soon

1999–2000

Benjamin Netanyahu had no intention of disappearing from the political map. He knew he'd be back, and as soon as possible. His three years as prime minister left him with a taste for more; he was addicted to the power inherent in the position. He knew that if he learned his lesson and improved his political skills, he could return.

During the final months of Netanyahu's term, Government Secretary Gideon Sa'ar became a close confidant. A young, ambitious right-winger, Sa'ar was a lawyer by profession but was working in journalism when he was called to replace Danny Naveh, who was hoping for a seat in the Knesset. Two days after the election defeat, Netanyahu summoned Sa'ar to the official residence. "We've got to start working on my comeback," he said. "If you're returning, why did you resign?" asked Sa'ar. Netanyahu was walking on his treadmill, sweaty and breathing heavily. "You should know," he told Sa'ar, "for every kilo you lose, you gain 1 percent in the polls." Sa'ar smiled and asked, "So why are you only now beginning to work out?" He understood that Netanyahu's time-out had lasted two days. He was already feeling his way back.

A few weeks later, Netanyahu decided to convene his activists and supporters for a special thank-you meeting in Tel Aviv. Despite the defeat, he wanted to keep in touch with the field. The "white tribe" had ousted him from power, but he remained popular among Likud's field activists and wanted to maintain this popularity. Sa'ar helped him draft his thank-you speech. The objective was to hint at an imminent comeback, but not to commit, to keep the people on the back burner, so they'd develop a longing for the exiled leader. It was Sa'ar who chose the exact sentence Netanyahu would say to his activists at the end of his speech: "We'll be back." The applause was deafening. *We* was a deliberately obscure term. It could mean "We Likud," or it could mean "My wife Sara and me." That he'd be back, when ready; he'd decide the time and the place. In the meantime, they could wait for him.

The battle for Netanyahu's succession in Likud was fierce. Sharon, the temporary chairman, was considered Bibi's favorite after the resignation. He was challenged by Meir Sheetrit and Jerusalem mayor Ehud Olmert. Olmert took a different approach: "The magician's era is over," he declared, hoping to make political capital with Netanyahu's enemies. He was wrong. The Likudniks didn't hate Bibi, especially not after his defeat. Sharon's support for Netanyahu helped him get elected with a broad majority and become the official Likud chairman. Netanyahu wasn't upset. He looked at the heavy-bodied, elderly Sharon, who was almost blind in one eye, almost deaf in one ear, and knew that it was temporary. Sharon would rehabilitate and reinforce Likud for Bibi. "When I decide to return," said Netanyahu to his associates, "I shall simply come and take it from Arik Sharon; like taking candy from a baby."

In the meantime, he went to work for BATM, a tech company owned by Dr. Zvi Marom. Netanyahu worked hard and Marom made him fly coach, for the first time in many years. "It's how we all fly in this company, me included," he told Bibi, who had to agree. At the same time, he began to work on rebranding himself. The "New Bibi" was supposed to divest himself of his precious image, which was hated by various sectors of Israeli society, and don a completely new persona—a conciliatory, sober-minded leader who made some mistakes, then understood and learned from them. Sara lowered her profile. No longer did she appear like a permanent shadow at his side, her hand grasped in his; she was now kept discreetly behind the scenes, giving the public a rest from her presence. Netanyahu started his reconciliation with members of the media. He met them one by one in his offices in Jerusalem where he held intimate conversations, not hesitating to admit to his mistakes and explain that he had changed. Later, Netanyahu began having the same kind of meetings with public-opinion leaders. One by one he summoned them, playing the role of the "New Bibi." He was relaxed, reconciled, and aware of his mistakes, and freely admitted to his weaknesses. He played the role perfectly. Almost everyone left his presence with a feeling different from the one they had going in. "He's worth another chance," they told themselves. Netanyahu is an excellent actor and knows how to adopt any personality with very little rehearsal time. His present character, the suffering knight, the humiliated leader who'd learned his lesson, the leader who'd reached maturity, suited him. He may not have believed a single word that came out of his mouth, but that didn't harm his credibility. He had a clear objective and he was determined to achieve it, as only he could. He knew that only if he appeared to be trustworthy, and aroused empathy and warmth, would he be able to make his way back, to dissolve the strong dissent that had accumulated against him, and to return to the public's goodwill.

The man who helped him return was his heir, Prime Minister Ehud Barak. Strange as it may seem, very little time passed before Barak had caused Israelis to yearn for Netanyahu. His government was lame, his leadership already collapsed, and his learned theories about a "quick peace process in two and a half routes" did not stand the test of reality. The Syrian route was blocked, the Palestinian route was stopped, and the coalition started to fall apart as soon as it moved. In July 2000, Barak set off to Camp David for definitive negotiations with Arafat, mediated by President Bill Clinton. Barak had been warned against embarking on this political adventure, since the situation wasn't ripe yet and no suitable preparations had been made, but he ignored all warnings. "If only I'm given a chance to spend a few days with Arafat in a closed room, I'll get a settlement," he told his associates and the Americans, who were very skeptical about the chances of success.

In Jerusalem, Netanyahu panicked. Even before, he'd been sure that Barak would sign an agreement with Syrian president Assad and call a flash election, which would be the end of Bibi, but that fear had proved unfounded. Barak lacked the mental strength to engineer a complete withdrawal from the Golan Heights down to the Sea of Galilee. He had commissioned polls that showed it would be difficult to sell to the public. Chances of peace with Syria had evaporated and another of Netanyahu's prophecies of doom remained unfulfilled. Netanyahu was equally convinced that Barak was going to attempt a quick settlement with Arafat in Camp David, followed, on the resulting waves of euphoria, by an election that would result in a win. It was a nightmare scenario for Bibi. He had convinced himself that the historic agreement between Israel and the Palestinians was on the verge of being signed. When Barak was sitting with his people in Camp David, Netanyahu was sitting in Jerusalem, mostly by himself, sweating it out. He wasn't ready yet for a political comeback. It was too early for him. He was still waiting for the state attorney's office to decide if it was going to indict him for the Amedi affair. He needed more time. Suddenly it seemed that time was running out. The stress was killing him. He started to wonder if it was all a conspiracy theory, that Barak was just trying to deny the agreement in order to accelerate Bibi's return, that Sharon was cooperating with Barak, etc.

On July 24, 2000, Netanyahu's office issued an announcement, a live, televised "personal message." News quickly reached Camp David and Ehud Barak. The assumption was that Netanyahu was going to announce his early return to politics in an attempt to prevent any agreement with the Palestinians. At 8:10 p.m., prime time on Israeli TV, all the channels broadcast Bibi's message, packaged as the message of a "concerned citizen." Netanyahu did not announce an early comeback, but offered sharp criticism of what was happening in Camp David, and of Barak's attempt to return Israel to the borders as they were in 1967, and to hand over parts of Jerusalem. "I am speaking to you as a concerned citizen," said Netanyahu.

He was in fact trying to mark out his territory and declare "I am here. Don't forget me." His goal was to maintain his position in the public's mind as the only alternative on the right. After the "concerned citizen" finished his speech, there were fewer concerned citizens in Israel. One of these was Ariel Sharon, who sighed in relief. He, too, was unprepared for a Netanyahu comeback. The second was Ehud Barak. Several days later, the Camp David summit ended in resounding failure and Netanyahu's prophecy of a "ten-kilometer-wide Israel" came to nothing. Barak returned empty-handed and Netanyahu was caught, once again, as the prophet of doom. But reality in the field blackened of its own accord. Peace negotiations were stuck. The Palestinian streets gathered like a storm, Oslo was irrelevant and struggling, a huge shadow darkened the horizon. Netanyahu was preparing, certain this prophecy of doom would come true. It had to happen sometime. And was going to be bad.

35

No Thanks

2000–2001

On October 27, 2000, Netanyahu met with a group of veteran Labor Party members in a Jerusalem restaurant. Even Yitzhak Navon was there, a former Israeli president and one of the most popular of the Labor Party's leaders. The meeting lasted two hours, during which the former prime minister lectured and answered questions. He would decide whether to compete for the premiership depending on developments. It was one of the first in a series of reconciliation meetings with his enemies in the media and with the social elite, opinion makers, businessmen, and economy experts. He had a long way to go if he was to capture their hearts. He worked hard on building the "New Bibi" brand, the leader who had matured, had lost his former tricks and shticks, no winks and mudslinging, and even without Sara. The results so far were good.

The day after the Jerusalem meeting, October 28, 2000, was the day that Likud chairman and opposition leader Ariel Sharon visited the Temple Mount. Prime Minister Barak, who was aware of the explosiveness of such a visit, had clenched his teeth and approved it. Fierce riots broke out as soon as Sharon left the Temple Mount, leaving ten Palestinians and about twenty Israeli policemen wounded. The rioting continued the next day throughout the West Bank. An additional seven Palestinians were killed. On September 30, the rioting moved to the Gaza Strip. A twelve-year-old Palestinian boy named Muhammad al-Dura got caught in crossfire with his father, Jamal, at the Netzarim junction. Video was broadcast that evening by a French TV station, bringing things to a boiling point. Palestinian protesters were joined by Israeli Arabs in the streets, confronting the Israeli Defense Forces. The video showed the boy trying to hide behind his father as the bullets flew across the junction; all the time calling for help. Ultimately, the boy was killed. Israel was quick to take responsibility for the event, although it was later reported that Dura had not been hit by Israeli fire, but was killed by Palestinian bullets. By then, it made no difference to anyone.

The Palestinian leadership lost control of the situation and the second intifada broke out, continuing until February 2005, and causing the deaths of over 1,100 Israelis and close to 4,000 Palestinians.

The violence and bloodshed accelerated the dissolution of Ehud Barak's government. The prime minister tried to calm the situation and later negotiated with Sharon to form a national unity government, but all his efforts failed. On November 29, 2000, eighteen months after taking office, Ehud Barak announced that he was ready to call an election.

The dramatic announcement caught Netanyahu in the middle of a U.S. lecture tour. Gideon Sa'ar, his confidant, gave him the news. "I'm coming right back," Netanyahu said, and gave Sa'ar the impression that he was determined to compete in the elections. Before flying home, Netanyahu made a large number of panic-stricken telephone calls, one of which was to MK Yisrael Katz, who was to embark on negotiations for enacting flash legislation that would allow Bibi to run notwithstanding the fact that he was not an MK (according to Israeli law, only a member of the Knesset can become prime minister). The second call was to Shas leader MK Eli Yishai. Shas, which had seventeen seats, was the most important faction in the Knesset. Netanyahu needed Shas if he was to pass a "Bibi law." Yishai promised to help. Bibi flew to Israel, and his associates leaked the news that "he was considering running."

The voting system in Israel distinguished between a vote for prime

minister and a vote for the Knesset. The resignation of the prime minister automatically called for an election for the premiership, whereas the
Knesset still had to complete its four-year term before another election.
Bibi was undecided. He already knew how hard it is to govern a country
and didn't believe he could do it on the basis of his party's power—only
nineteen Knesset members. He wanted the Knesset to disperse and call
for a general election that would allow him to increase Likud's power and
form a stable government. In the meantime, he left again for New York.
His people were in charge and negotiations were under way with Shas,
which had hinted to Bibi that they might support a dispersion of the Knesset, under certain circumstances. Ehud Barak resigned the premiership,
which meant that elections had to be held within sixty days. A special law
was required to disperse the Knesset. Without the support of Shas, such a
law would not pass. A poll indicated that Netanyahu would beat Barak,
but against Sharon, Barak would win. Netanyahu enjoyed a huge advantage over Sharon in Likud and if he were to decide to compete, he would
easily beat Sharon and become Likud's candidate for the premiership.
Barak had an obvious interest in having Bibi on the outside. Knowing Bibi's dilemma, Barak decided to resign. This time, too, Bibi was in the
middle of a workout in his New York hotel. This time, too, he rushed
home and convened a dramatic press conference, launching a verbal attack
on Barak and declaring that he would consider running if the Knesset
were to be dispersed. He believed that Shas would support dispersal. Some
days later, he met Shas spiritual leader Rabbi Ovadia Yosef and heard from
him: "It would be all right." The Shas promises were traditionally vague,
but Netanyahu took them seriously and interpreted Rabbi Yosef's words
as a green light.

Netanyahu acted like he had already accomplished his comeback. He told
Gideon Sa'ar that he wanted him to be his government secretary. Other
close associates, too, heard various plans and promises from him. Netanyahu had no idea that all this time, that wily old fox Sharon was operating
"special forces" in the enemy's hinterland. Sharon had ties with Shas and
close relations among Knesset members, activists and, especially, Shas's
heavy donors in America. All those levers were pulled. Sharon promised

Shas the sun and the moon if they cooperated with him, helping to lead Bibi astray, and make reality his secret dream to be prime minister of Israel.

Special effort was devoted to the Jewish billionaire Sami Shamoon, a long-standing admirer of Sharon and one of the heaviest contributors to Shas and Rabbi Yosef. Shamoon entered the fray and supplied the goods. Shas led Netanyahu to understand that it supported his demand to call for a general election. Encouraged by support from Shas, Netanyahu announced that without dispersion he wouldn't stand, which was exactly what Sharon wanted to happen. And then, at the crucial moment, Shas reneged; it wouldn't support a dispersal of the Knesset. Why should it? Shas had seventeen Knesset members. There was no reason to willingly disperse so much power.

Netanyahu understood that he'd been misled. He'd dug himself a hole and jumped in. He had to make a swift decision: should he break his promise and run anyway? Israel was in the midst of a bloody intifada; Likud had only nineteen Knesset seats. Netanyahu got cold feet. The trauma of his defeat in the past term was still with him. He hadn't planned so early a return. With a sour face, Netanyahu declared that he was passing on this election and remaining outside. Sharon's path to the premiership was thus paved. Netanyahu, who would have won easily had he decided to compete, regretted the decision for years to come. His decision not to run in 2001 caused Netanyahu serious harm: Sharon won and became one of the most popular prime ministers in the history of the state of Israel, despite the fact that his party held only nineteen seats. Only eight years later would Bibi make it back to the premiership. His "lost decade" between 1999 and 2009 was a waste of time. History had offered Netanyahu quite a shortcut, but he passed on it. Some days later Sharon had a secret meeting with Shas leader Eli Yishai in the Herzliya home of Sami Shamoon. The two politicians formed an alliance. Shas would support Sharon as prime minister and would be handsomely rewarded afterward. Netanyahu? He'd become yesterday's man.

Netanyahu never imagined he could be left on the outside. He was sure that after Barak's downfall, there would be nothing to stop him from returning to the prime minister's office. Suddenly things were happening without him. His mood was gloomy, and grew even more so when his loyal erstwhile confidant, Gideon Sa'ar, informed him that Sharon had offered him the post of government secretary. Bibi's face fell. "Offered, so what?" he said to Sa'ar. "I intend to accept," said Sa'ar quietly. "I don't understand how you can do this," Netanyahu burst out. "What do you mean?" Sa'ar asked. "I went with you for a year and a half, on a voluntary basis; now you decide not to run. The country is in a state of emergency, how can I refuse an elected prime minister?"

Netanyahu was unable to accept Sa'ar's decision. In his view, he was the only important one. The needs and interests of anyone else were completely foreign to him. Sa'ar went on: "I am doing exactly what you would have done in my place, with only one difference," he said. "What's that?" asked Netanyahu.

"At least I hesitated."

36

Self-Examination

2001–2009

Netanyahu fell into a deep depression following Sharon's election victory. He didn't believe it could happen to him. Fired from his post of defense minister after the Lebanon War in wake of the massacre in the Sabra and Shatila refugee camps, Sharon was considered unelectable. Few saw in him a serious candidate for the premiership, aside from a handful of his people. Everyone awaited Bibi's homecoming to push Sharon aside and return to his rightful place at the head of Likud, and then the premiership. But it was Sharon who taught Bibi a political lesson by taking the prime minister's office. Nothing, it seemed, would make him surrender it. The public sought a responsible adult, one who was considered security-oriented, and the public got all that in Sharon. In the meantime, Netanyahu toyed with potential appearances before the Likud Central Committee, did interviews, delivered lectures, and made other attempts at remaining relevant. In October 2001, he once again asked the Shabak to increase security in his area. In his opinion, the bodyguards provided by the Shabak were insufficient. "I am on the front line of Israeli propaganda vis-à-vis the Palestinians," he said. The VIP department refused his request. A manpower shortage was the official excuse. In private conversations, the Shabak wondered at what they deemed "Netanyahu's cowardice." They must have misunderstood the issue. It was not a case of cowardice, but of yearning for authority, for security, for the power that is inherent in the post of Israeli prime minister. Bibi found it hard to look at all this from the sidelines. A convoy of bodyguards would have made him feel better. In the meantime, all that remained for Bibi was self-examination.

He spent a lot of time thinking. Once the police investigation was completed, and after the nerve-racking wait for the outcome, Netanyahu had plenty of time to think about what had been and of what he wanted to happen. He identified his mistakes and analyzed them, one by one. He decided to build a new image for himself, one that was clean and reconciled. The objective was to cause the public to believe Bibi knew where he'd gone wrong, and that he'd made amends; to create a new Bibi. But he hadn't really changed. He only understood his political Achilles' heel and decided to protect it. This he did with his characteristic determination, making a list of reasons for his downfall and dealing with them all, one by one.

With regard to his personal conduct, he understood that he'd have to change his attitude toward his colleagues, ministers, and politicians; to pay more attention, to include them more. He was obliged to understand that he would have to keep his wife far from the public eye, for the time being, at least. The other issues were already entirely political. According to his own analysis, three elements had joined forces to bring about his downfall: the media, Bill Clinton, and the Israeli generals. Bibi knew he'd have to deal with each of these points. "When I return," he told his people at that time, "it will be with my own media. Never again will we be dependent on the left-wing media that loathes me and will do everything possible to be rid of me." At that time, too, Bibi started rehabilitating his relations with the Jewish right-wing tycoons, most of them American. The standout was Sheldon Adelson, who was still not a top member of Bibi's exclusive billionnaires' club, but was quickly making his way there. It had been a few years since Bibi had been accused of arranging for Miriam and Sheldon Adelson to have a special, actually unprecedented, permit to hold their wedding reception in the Knesset's prestigious Chagall Hall. At the time Bibi was deputy foreign minister, and the Adelsons enjoyed a close relationship with him. Neither imagined what heights the relationship would attain.

Netanyahu hoped that, when he came back, he would have at his disposal an independent media network of his own that would allow him to "pay back" Israel's so-called left-wing media. He swore they would never overthrow him again.

Nor was he prepared to go through what he'd suffered at the hands of Bill Clinton. He decided that in his next term as prime minister, he would have to weaken Israeli public opinion of the president of the United States, no matter what. It would have to be done at the very beginning. He could not ever again allow an American president to enjoy greater popularity in Israel than the prime minister.

The "generals" who had helped topple him were Defense Minister Yitzhak Mordechai, who crushed him in the televised debate, dealing that fatal blow to his image; and the hostile IDF chief of staff Amnon Lipkin-Shahak, who established a centrist party and assisted in his downfall. Netanyahu realized that he'd have to block the security establishment from Israel's political leadership. If he wanted to rule, he would have to build a firewall between politics and the IDF, Mossad, and the Shabak. In 2007, his devoted confidant MK Yuval Steinitz initiated a law that required senior officers in the security services to sit out a three-year "cooling off" period before entering politics. If you add the twelve months granted to senior officers before resigning from service, that's four years, plenty of time for whatever advantage they may have had to fade and disappear. This proposal was also signed by left-wing (Meretz) MK Avshalom Vilan, who was close to Ehud Barak. Bibi and Barak shared the goal of keeping the military separate from politics. Both feared competitors who might overtake them in the political arena. The hot name in those days was Dan Halutz, a highly decorated and respected IAF pilot and chief of staff, who was poised to storm the electoral map soon after his release from the military. He didn't make it. The law was passed, but Halutz was blocked, in the meantime, by the Second Lebanon War and the commission of inquiry that followed it. Nonetheless, if the law had always been in place, many of

Israel's best leaders would never have entered politics. The law was Benjamin Netanyahu's most important political move, and is the primary reason for his remaining alone at the top, a brilliant tactic that was something you might expect of graduates of Sayeret Matkal, as Bibi and Barak were. All attempts at rescinding the law have since been easily blocked by Netanyahu.

To ensure absolute power and zero mishaps, Bibi knew he had to take control of the country's important gatekeepers and regulators. The two police inquiries he'd undergone had been deeply traumatic for him and Sara. Twice he had waited for the country's legal authority's decisions, so now he swore it would never happen again. He was aware that his and, especially, his wife's conduct could draw additional investigations and interrogations that left only two options: to either change their conduct, or to ensure that there was always a lenient and obedient attorney general at his disposal. The first option being impossible, Netanyahu decided to focus on the second. In addition, Netanyahu marked other position holders over whom he needed control: the chief of police, the state comptroller, the civil service commissioner and, if possible, the head of police investigations. Control over all these jobs was essential to Netanyahu's future as prime minister.

Shortly after being removed from government, Netanyahu and Sara were invited to the wedding of a daughter of one of his supporters. Conversation turned to a new cable television news channel in America. According to Bibi, Israelis who traveled to New York or Los Angeles had no conception that between these two cities was the real America. This new channel was for those people, and it would be on Israel's side. It would break the CNN just-you-wait-and-see style of reporting. They wouldn't automatically take the Arab side. They knew Republican Party members and that Likud could learn a few things from them, that they could help Israel. They learned that there were evangelical Christians willing to donate funds to Israel and volunteer, too. Israel had to learn how to benefit from this phenomena.

Bibi was talking about Fox News at the wedding, and he was as excited as a child with a new toy. The conversation went on long after midnight, hours after the wedding had ended and the waiters had left the hall. Netanyahu presented a reliable and accurate analysis: Fox had indeed changed the media map in America. But he hadn't noticed the other change, one that had made less relevant the America he'd grown up in: the demographics and social processes gradually weakening the Republican Party and increasing the potential number of voters for the Democratic Party. It was a historic shift that would change America from a white continent to one that was mixed, and would increase the power of the Latino community, as well as that of blacks and other minorities, at the expense of the conservative white America that once was.

In the meantime, Netanyahu continued to formulate his comeback plan. He swore to return strong, improved, and more cunning than before. In Jerusalem, he would build a stronghold, and it would be invincible.

37

It's the Economy, Idiot

2002–2003

Ariel Sharon's growing popularity put an end to Netanyahu's comeback. He'd have to wait patiently. In November 2002, the Labor Party resigned from Sharon's coalition government. Sharon convened a consultation in Tel Aviv, in the presence of his close advisors and his two sons, Omri and Gilad. On the agenda: What shall we do? They could bring in a couple of other parties and continue to function as a right-wing government for another year, until the next elections; or disperse the Knesset and go for swift elections. Sharon did not fear a general election; he was, however, concerned about primaries against Netanyahu. His tendency was to try and bring the right-wing parties into his coalition in order to avoid elections and get rid of Bibi once again. Just then pollster Kalman Gaier entered the room and announced that among the Likud members, Sharon had an 8 percent advantage over Bibi. It was the largest margin ever. Sharon decided to dissolve the Knesset and call for elections. In addition he carried out the wise move of offering Netanyahu the post of foreign minister, in place of Shimon Peres, who had resigned together with Labor.

Netanyahu deliberated, then accepted the offer. He believed that it would be easier for him to beat the incumbent prime minister as foreign minister in the primaries. Sharon loathed and despised Netanyahu, but respected his talent for rhetoric and charisma, two traits that Sharon sorely lacked. Bibi respected Sharon as a general and a leader, but held his political ability in disdain. Netanyahu liked to say that if Sharon were less emotional in his political moves, he could have become prime minister sooner and stayed in the post longer.

The primaries took place shortly after Netanyahu joined the government. Loyal to party tradition, according to which you don't hurt an incumbent prime minister, card-carrying members went with Sharon, so he defeated Netanyahu. It was and remains Bibi's first and only defeat in primaries for Likud leadership. Despite the defeat, Bibi was given second slot on the Knesset list. In the elections that took place on January 28, 2003, Sharon led Likud to an extraordinary victory, doubling the number of seats from nineteen in 1999 to thirty-eight this time. Shortly afterward, Natan Sharansky joined Likud with his two seats. Bibi was unhappy with Sharon's rise to an uncontested leadership position. Only one hope remained for Netanyahu: a police investigation into corruption issues that continued to sully the hem of the prime minister's cloak. Israeli press was pumping many stories about Sharon and his two sons, Gilad and Omri, and their alleged ties with foreign billionaires. The Israeli Police joined and launched several investigations. Bibi followed this closely, hiding his secret hopes.

Sharon had other plans, so he dropped a bombshell: Netanyahu would be offered the Finance Ministry. The ongoing intifada in Gaza had dealt a huge economic blow to Israel's economy, which was sliding toward a recession. Sharon, a canny old fox with an understanding of politics, wanted Netanyahu in charge of that quagmire. Instead of wandering around the globe, garnering popularity as foreign minister, Sharon gave him the dirty work, where he'd be exposed to the public crossfire and criticism about Israel's recession. If he failed to turn around the economy, it was entirely his fault, and if he succeeded, the credit would go to Sharon. Bibi was aware of the trap. He eventually agreed to accept the post. He demanded and received a letter from Sharon promising full backing for any economic steps, including harsh decrees. Aware that Sharon intended to bury him in the Finance Ministry, Netanyahu decided to go for it. He would rescue the economy, he would get the country out of the recession, and he'd have the last laugh. It was the beginning of a strange and forced, but fruitful and important, partnership. On Netanyahu's part, it was a courageous and successful move.

Bibi stormed the economic crisis with everything he had. His capitalist economic approach advocating a free market, removal of barriers, and tax cuts breathed life into his new programs. He imposed on the public an unprecedented wave of harsh decrees, which were especially painful to the weaker sectors of society, the ultra-Orthodox Jews and the Arabs. The budget was cut by over 10 billion shekels, salaries in the public sector were cut, the public was forced to pay into pension plans, etc. On the other hand, Netanyahu announced sweeping tax cuts to encourage production and entrepreneurship. As expected, the plan met fierce public opposition. The labor federation threatened to strike, workers demonstrated, the streets boiled over. Prime Minister Sharon said nothing. He stood behind Netanyahu, but quietly, allowing him to suffer in the fire, with Sharon distancing himself from the turmoil.

Ultimately and after much tribulation, Netanyahu's economic program was approved by the government on March 28, 2003, and by the Knesset in May. Bibi told *Yediot Ahronot*'s Nahum Barnea, "They are saying I am doing this in order to become prime minister. They don't understand. I wanted to be prime minister in order to do this."

Fierce criticism came from all sides against the program, but Netanyahu was focused and determined. Even when David Klein, the governor of the Bank of Israel, determined that it was doomed to fail, Netanyahu forged ahead. He was convinced he'd succeed.

Netanyahu's job as finance minister in Sharon's government was the only one in his entire political career that he truly applied himself to, with no posturing and with no sideways glances. He made no attempt to appease anyone and made barely any political moves. The bottom line was that Bibi's economic program saved the Israeli economy, and opened a decade of dramatic growth and an increase in the standard of living.

Credit for this achievement goes to Ariel Sharon and Benjamin Netanyahu: Sharon for appointing Bibi and providing him with the necessary backing, and Netanyahu for carrying out the work.

Netanyahu paid a heavy price for it, though. Throughout those years he was subjected to the criticism of social organizations, and sacrificed much of his popularity among his party's supporters and in the country's periphery. The ultra-Orthodox communities were on the verge of divorcing him completely. No longer the nation's beloved son, he was branded a cruel capitalist, heartless and devoid of all social sensitivity. These sentiments wounded Netanyahu, and affected him for years to come. In the 2006 elections he crashed totally, mainly because of his policies as finance minister. Netanyahu's plan for rehabilitating the economy seriously hurt the nation's weaker social strata and damaged the welfare state by cutting government services. Netanyahu had taken all this into consideration. He had one mission and he carried it out: to rescue the Israeli economy.

In July 2003, a modest announcement was made on the margins of the economic storm: Noa Netanyahu, the twenty-five-year-old daughter of Bibi and his first wife, Dr. Micki Weissman Haran, decided to follow a religiously observant path. The announcement received relatively little media attention. Both Noa's parents were secular Jews. What pushed Noa into the arms of extreme ultra-Orthodoxy? What caused her to change her lifestyle and join the Haredi community? The question remains unanswered, though some believe there is a painful story behind it.

38

Yes and No

2004–2005

As finance minister, Netanyahu abandoned Likud's internal politics and focused on his economic program. Although he was a Revisionist, strongly opposed to all compromise and against a Palestinian state, he didn't undermine Prime Minister Sharon's peace initiatives. But then Sharon pulled out his disengagement plan and changed the rules of the game: evacuation of seventeen settlements from the Gaza Strip and a further four settlements in the northern West Bank in a unilateral move, which set off an earthquake on the right and pandemonium among the settlers. What would Netanyahu do?

Netanyahu tried to protest, but was quashed by Sharon. Bibi came under heavy pressure from the right to lead a revolt against the prime minister, but he hesitated. Bibi was not the kind of Revisionist who sanctified the territories and the settlements. He was in the middle of solving an economic crisis. When Sharon first mentioned disengagement in a 2003 speech, Netanyahu said nothing. The following February Sharon informed the Likud faction in the Knesset that he had given the order to prepare for the evacuation of twenty-one settlements. Not only did Netanyahu raise no objection, he even said that it was a done deal, that the train had already left the station. On June 6, 2004, Netanyahu voted in favor of disengagement. He'd threatened to cause a crisis but settled instead for a kind of idle compromise concocted by Minister Tzipi Livni. He realized that if he objected, Sharon would fire him. Two days earlier, two other ministers had been dismissed, and Bibi didn't wish for a similar fate. On October 26, he voted in the Knesset in favor of the plan. This time, too, Netanyahu waved the "ax of war" and threatened to arrange a field putsch for Sharon, with the participation of additional ministers. Again, it ended with a farce. Throughout the Knesset debate, Sharon sat, sunk in his chair, silent, as if disconnected from everything, while Bibi ran around the building, sweating and trying to muster support. At the last moment, when the vote began, Netanyahu rushed into the hall and voted in favor. It was a roll call, so each MK had to announce out loud whether he or she was in favor or against. Bibi's voice resonated loud and clear. Only Minister Uzi Landau voted against, and he was fired from the government the next day.

Shortly afterward, Sharon changed the composition of his coalition government by firing the ministers of the Shinui faction for objecting to the budget, and brought in the Labor Party and the United Torah Judaism Party. Netanyahu was voted in again as minister of finance and expressed confidence in the government. Again he could have voted against a government that was about to carry out the disengagement, or at least stayed out, but he supported it. In February 2005, he voted in favor of the Evacuation Compensation Law that sealed the disengagement. He adhered to his stand as finance minister and repeatedly rejected all the pleas of the settlers who made pilgrimages to him in Jerusalem, begging for his support in their struggle.

On Sunday, May 29, 2005, shortly before nine in the morning, Netanyahu made his way to the weekly government meeting. In the corridor leading to the debating room, there was the regular congregation of political correspondents and photographers waiting for news and opinions. In his hand, Netanyahu was holding a lit cigar. Bibi is more than a cigar aficionado; he is literally addicted to them, with a penchant for Cuban cigars. He receives a regular supply of chubby cigars from a long list of associates, mostly wealthy Americans and Europeans. His favorite supplier is the Israeli

American movie producer Arnon Milchan. In Israel, cigar smoking is considered hedonistic and is reserved for society's upper crust, a symbol of rampant capitalism and irresponsible behavior. The average Israeli politician would rather be seen in public hugging a Palestinian terrorist than be caught smoking an expensive cigar. But there was Netanyahu, the minister of finance who had imposed such harsh and heavy-handed decrees on the weak members of society. As Netanyahu made his way quickly toward the reporters, he remembered the burning cigar in his hand and dropped it into his inside jacket pocket. Within seconds he'd forgotten all about it, or denied it'd ever happened, and made another mistake when he stopped by the correspondents and started chatting with them. All this time, the burning cigar was getting friendly with a tissue in Bibi's pocket. Smoke started emanating from the minister's chest. Netanyahu realized what was happening. Minister Yitzhak Herzog, who was passing, helped Bibi extinguish the fire without any serious damage to anyone, except perhaps for the finance minister's good name. The correspondents laughed. Netanyahu was unmoved, explaining that he put the cigar in his pocket because "it was a no-smoking area." He then continued to explain his objection to the release of Palestinian prisoners. As far as Netanyahu was concerned, nothing had happened. He didn't understand what was wrong with the series of decisions he'd taken and why the situation was so ridiculous. To him, only the bottom line was of consequence: no one had managed to photograph him smoking a cigar in public.

Only a week before the beginning of the curfew, on August 7, 2005, did Netanyahu object, in the final government vote, to the disengagement, and resign from his post as minister of finance. Six times he had supported the move, but this had no relevance for him. He wanted to go down in history as having voted against it in the last ballot even though there was no practical worth to this objection. To Netanyahu acts are unimportant. Words, yes. Exactly as a speech in Congress is of greater importance—in his eyes—than building a new settlement.

The cause of Netanyahu's dramatic, last-minute change of position and his resignation from the government was the polls, to which he had always been addicted. He directed himself, his opinions, and his public statements in accordance with in-depth polls. It began with the "ladder" system of the 1996 elections, and continues to this day, growing ever more intense. On the eve of the disengagement, he was presented with polls indicating that Uzi Landau, the minister who had objected to the past vote and was fired, would have overtaken him among Likud voters, if they were competing in primaries for the party's leadership. This was relevant because the possibility was already floating in the air of Sharon splitting Likud after the disengagement, in order to be rid of rebel members of the Knesset. Bibi saw the polls and panicked. He was afraid of losing his right-wing base and his seniority to Landau, who had already shown his backbone and right-wing ideological loyalty by relinquishing a place in the government. Netanyahu called a press conference in Tel Aviv and declared his resignation. He was sweating heavily and felt he'd already missed the train.

A week later the IDF and the Israeli police evacuated eight thousand Jewish settlers from twenty-one settlements in the Gaza Strip and northern West Bank. Despite all the prophecies of doom, the disengagement was carried out relatively quietly. Netanyahu found himself out of the government, picking up the pieces and starting everything anew.

39

The Crash

2005–2006

Netanyahu hoped to reconquer Likud with the settlement evacuations. He was convinced that Sharon's disengagement would end in a fiasco. He challenged Sharon for the Likud leadership; he suspected that Sharon would preempt him by resigning from Likud to avoid being defeated by Netanyahu. Worried, he sought candidates from outside to reinforce him. Sharon was a much-decorated army general with many daring feats behind him, including Operation Defensive Shield, which crushed Palestinian terrorism three years earlier. Netanyahu was urgently in need of some security reinforcements. In July 2005 he had a meeting with former chief of staff Moshe (Bogie) Ya'alon, who had ended his military service when Defense Minister Shaul Mofaz informed him that his term would not be extended for a fourth year. The notice was conceived as dismissal. Mofaz was acting on behalf of Prime Minister Sharon, who wanted to appoint a family favorite, the highly respected IAF commander Dan Halutz. Frustrated and furious, Ya'alon attacked the disengagement and sought revenge. Netanyahu promised him anything if he'd declare support for him in Likud. Ya'alon was unable to join the political system immediately because of the cooling-off law, but Netanyahu was prepared to make do with external support, plus an agreement that he could join later. Throughout his career, Netanyahu had tried to surround himself with high-ranking army officers and senior members of the security services. He has an inherent respect for people in uniform, although he did not bother to remain in uniform beyond the minimum time required of an IDF officer, and was released with the rank of major. He wanted the branding "Mr. Security." It was essential for anyone aspiring to a leadership position in Israel to look tough, which is why he did his best to have as many generals around him at any given moment. One of his most important decisions during the 1996 elections was to appoint General Yitzhak Mordechai as his campaign director. Now he sought a new Mordechai to provide the necessary push.

Throughout the years, Netanyahu met with senior officers while they were still in service. He met Ya'alon after his release, but they'd been in contact before. Ya'alon did not know that some years earlier Netanyahu had met secretly with Dan Halutz, who then held the rank of major general. Halutz was Ya'alon's bitter enemy. Netanyahu and Halutz had arrived in separate cars at the Jerusalem home of Dr. Gabi Piker, a childhood friend of Netanyahu. Netanyahu held many such meetings with additional officers, either at Piker's home or at his parents' house. He wanted to meet Halutz to put a wedge between him and the Sharons, before he was appointed chief of staff. With his sharp political sense, Netanyahu realized the potential in Halutz, a highly respected pilot, charismatic, and a Sephardi Jew. He wasn't going to relinquish Halutz without a fight. Halutz agreed to the meeting in order to have a way to Netanyahu in case things went wrong with Sharon.

In the meantime, Netanyahu was getting accustomed to being the new darling of the right, and the man to challenge Sharon's leadership in Likud. His first speech on the Knesset podium was sharp and assertive: "Don't give them rifles, don't give them rockets, don't give them a port in Gaza, don't give them a giant terrorist base in Gaza; al-Qaeda and Hezbollah will establish a branch in the Strip." At long last, after almost five years, Bibi was back in his element, in his home ground: prophet of destruction, the first to issue a warning, the first to identify the dangers lurking for the nation of Israel. He was convinced that he would succeed in overpowering Sharon, with the help of the tailwind provided by Likud's right-wing core behind him. He began to smell the prime minister's office and he was hungry.

Again he was wrong. The success of the disengagement and the compliments that flowed in from the rest of the world helped Sharon conquer Likud's political center and break his own popularity record. Among the general public, he led Netanyahu by a huge majority, although among Likud members, the battle was closer. Netanyahu was counting on the settlers and the hard-core right in Likud, but his tower of expectations turned out to be a house of cards. Sharon was determined to resign from Likud and to destroy it. The prime minister was sick of his party. The "rebels" in the Knesset infuriated him, and he was sick of Netanyahu. Sharon's people encouraged him to disband Likud, which he had established thirty years before, and leave Netanyahu alone with the extremists. Sharon was in love with the idea. On November 21, 2005, Ariel Sharon announced that he was leaving the Likud Party and establishing a new party called Kadima. Fourteen MKs left to go with him. Netanyahu, who hoped until the last moment that it wouldn't happen, found himself under siege. Sharon had left him with a group of extreme rebels and a few other senior Likud members who couldn't stand him. Sharon had the important forces in Likud, leaving behind a legacy of economic decrees and the loathsome Likud Central Committee activists. Silvan Shalom had led the rebellion against Netanyahu and now assailed him: "If I considered for a moment to leave Likud, it was because of you, Bibi," he said. Shalom was the least of Bibi's troubles at that stage. There was clear evidence that the general public was sick and tired of him, too. He was rightly seen as the man who led the journey of humiliation and bullying that forced their beloved Sharon to abandon his own political home in anger. Netanyahu had become anathema. He was reminded of those bleak days after the Rabin assassination. Sharon had escaped Likud, leaving Bibi behind him among the ruins.

Silvan Shalom began a campaign of deposition against Netanyahu. He hoped to win the primaries by taking advantage of the loathing Bibi had attracted. But Netanyahu made a valiant effort and won in spite of everything. Sharon moved the general elections to March 28. His success in the primaries did not breathe the necessary new life into Bibi, and didn't help him with the general public. A few days before the elections, a putsch started to form against Netanyahu. MKs Silvan Shalom, Limor Livnat, Miki Eitan, and Danny Naveh were organizing a quick move to depose Netanyahu the day after the election. The keys to this move were in the hands of two young stars, Gideon Sa'ar and Gilad Erdan. Sa'ar hesitated. He recognized Netanyahu's desperate situation, but was not eager to depose him. On the other hand, he was reluctant to defend Bibi, only to discover the day after the elections that he was resigning from politics and leaving him to face the furious rebels. Sa'ar wanted to ensure that he was not lying on a barbed-wire fence for Netanyahu. A few days before the elections, they met for an intense conversation. "Do you intend to stay in the Likud after the elections?" Sa'ar asked. "Yes, sure," answered Bibi. "And if we only win ten seats?" Sa'ar pressed. "We're going to win at least fourteen to fifteen seats." Sa'ar wasn't letting go: "In theory we can get ten seats. Everything points to this being our bottom line. What'll you do in such a case?" he asked. "Even in such a case, I'm staying," Bibi promised.

Sa'ar decided to back Netanyahu. He convened his colleagues, Gilad Erdan and Moshe Kahlon, in a Tel Aviv café. All three were young, having served a single Knesset term, and they decided to stand behind Netanyahu. The patron of this young trio was Reuven "Ruvi" Rivlin, a Jerusalemite and one of the most experienced politicians in the Knesset. None of them was fond of Netanyahu, but Rivlin stressed that "only Bibi is able to return Likud to power in the foreseeable future." The three young men agreed. Several years later, they still can't forgive themselves for their contribution to Netanyahu's survival. The first of them to leave Likud was Kahlon, who established his own party. Sa'ar resigned after him. Erdan, whose opinion of Netanyahu didn't differ much from that of his friends, remained, with difficulty. Ruvi Rivlin was forced (figuratively) to wage a bloody battle against Netanyahu, who tried to stop his election to the presidency of Israel in 2014. Their relations have remained strained ever since. Rivlin's opinion of Netanyahu is unprintable. None of that quartet could have imagined that the artificial respiration they granted a fluttering Netanyahu in 2006 would immortalize him in power until the middle of the next decade.

Netanyahu still hoped to jump-start himself anew. His campaign was based on security warnings and economic promises: a sharp reduction in the value-added tax, huge investments in infrastructures, and a lightening of the burden on the public. Netanyahu tried to take the credit for rehabilitating the economy, but this proved to be a double-edged sword. The economic issue reminded the Likud voters and the public in the periphery of the harsh decrees that Bibi imposed on them not long before. The polls anticipated a crash landing for Bibi. He didn't understand how this could be happening to him. Six years earlier, after being banished from the prime minister's office, he was convinced he'd be back in no time. Why was it so hard? Netanyahu didn't despair.

Bibi always fights to the end, even when the chances are minimal. His brain burns with the effort to find the winning slogan, the compelling reason, the catchiest catchword to bring about the long-awaited change. He believed that the voters would come home at the last moment to raise him above the humiliating threshold of fifteen Knesset seats. He prayed for a miracle.

On December 18, 2004, Prime Minister Sharon suffered a minor stroke and was hospitalized. For a moment it appeared that the miracle Netanyahu prayed for had been granted. Although Sharon had a swift recovery, the event highlighted the health of the elderly leader, who was grossly overweight and had a plethora of additional health issues. Two weeks later, Sharon suffered a second stroke, much more powerful than the first. Against his doctors' orders, Sharon was convalescing in his home in the Negev. The journey to the hospital in Jerusalem lasted a long time. By the time he reached the operating room, the old warrior didn't have a chance. Massive internal bleeding pushed Sharon into a coma from which he never awoke. He died on January 11, 2014. Netanyahu hadn't prayed for a miracle of this sort but it's hard to believe that he did too much grieving for the old prime minister. It was the second time that a political rival of his went away under tragic circumstances (the first was the Rabin assassination). Netanyahu stepped nimbly into a new pose: stately and constrained, oozing compliments, but never forgetting to mention that he, Netanyahu, was Sharon's natural heir, the new "Mr. Security." That was the takeaway in an interview with *The*

New York Times just days after the collapse of Sharon. Netanyahu skipped elegantly over the harsh words he'd exchanged with Sharon just a few months earlier, and had only good things to say. In an interview a few days later, Yair Lapid asked Netanyahu about his first meeting with Sharon. He amazed the audience with a story of his meeting with Sharon, together with Ehud Barak on the bank of the Suez Canal, during the Yom Kippur War in 1973. Sharon was a division commander, Barak was the commander of a tank battalion, and Netanyahu was a Sayeret Matkal reserve soldier who had arrived in Israel on a special flight from Boston. An occasion such as this, in which three future prime ministers sit together in an armed personnel carrier on the front line in the course of a war, is a historic event of the first order, yet it had never been mentioned, nor even recorded in any research project or biography.

A few days later it came to light that no such event ever took place. It could be that Netanyahu stumbled across the command post of the legendary commander, Sharon, in the course of that war, but he never sat in any APC together with him and Ehud Barak, issuing orders. To this day, Benjamin Netanyahu is convinced that it did happen, but that's typical of Bibi. He tends to exaggerate, and is prone to inventions and fantasies; over the years he has become convinced of their truth and believes that they did indeed take place. All investigations show that this one never took place, but Bibi continues to insist.

Netanyahu's attempts to step into Sharon's shoes and garner his heritage failed. Bibi was defeated in the elections, bringing Likud to the greatest decline in its history. The Kadima party, headed by Ehud Olmert, raked in twenty-nine seats; Likud under Netanyahu's leadership won only twelve. On the night of their downfall, only eight MKs, out of the twelve, stood beside Netanyahu. Naveh, Shalom, Katz, and Livnat were conspicuous by their absence. The following day, Olmert was already attempting to split the Likud faction by peeling away the four rebel MKs. All four were compliant, but, for some reason, Olmert didn't want Livnat in his coalition. He exerted heavy pressure on Moshe Kahlon, who insisted on remaining in Likud. Had Olmert agreed to take Livnat, or, alternatively, had Kahlon acceded, four Likud MKs would have resigned and Netanyahu would have been left with a faction of only eight MKs, which would have made it impossible for him to be appointed head of the opposition. Under such circumstances, Bibi would surely have resigned from politics and, almost certainly, he would have descended from the stage of history, possibly forever. But that is not how it happened. Olmert's enmity for Livnat and Kahlon's devotion to Likud left Benjamin Netanyahu in the political arena. The opposition leader has constitutional status, security guards, and a nice office. It was more than Netanyahu could expect.

Silvan Shalom, who remained in Likud with his friend, didn't give up. He started collecting the signatures necessary for bringing forward the primaries for the purpose of deposing Netanyahu. He got very close to the required number of signatures, but here, too, Moshe Kahlon and Gideon Sa'ar blocked him. All this did nothing to console Netanyahu, who was lamenting his fate. The general opinion was that the Israeli public was thoroughly sick of him. He was paying the price for the cruel economic program he had imposed on the nation a few years earlier and for torturing the beloved leader Ariel Sharon until he collapsed and died. Now Bibi was a useless political wreck. He had been banished in 1999, and now, less than seven years later, he was banished again. Those were seven very bad years for him. Almost everyone believed he was finished. But Bibi didn't.

40

Renewed Hope

2006–2007

The Kadima government, headed by Ehud Olmert, was sworn in on May 4, 2006. Netanyahu remained under siege, trapped in the vice grip of senior Likudniks hoping for his downfall. "Netanyahu destroyed Likud," declared Shalom. "He disconnected the people from the party and, after such a downfall, should be going home." He was determined to banish him from the Likud leadership. Netanyahu shut himself in his home and engaged in some serious introspection. Every imaginable miracle had happened in the course of the campaign, and still he crashed. The most popular candidate of all time, Ariel Sharon, disappeared. Lackluster Ehud Olmert slipped into his shoes, although he lacked any public standing. Olmert had even presented his "convergence" plan, which was supposed to include unilateral withdrawal from broad areas in the West Bank. The plan drove away moderate right-wing votes from Kadima. Olmert's support dropped but Bibi's did not rise. His electorate spewed him out. Likud, and Lieberman's Israel Is Our Home party, were separated by only 116 votes. If 68 Likud voters were to pass over to Lieberman, Bibi would have won only 11 seats and ended in fifth place among the Israeli parties.

This humiliation had no precedent in the history of Likud. In Israel's political corridors of power, Netanyahu was a dead man walking.

On the night of the defeat, Netanyahu seriously considered retiring. He had several interesting business possibilities. He felt empty and desperate. He knew that Ehud Olmert was a gifted and experienced politician, and was sure that his management of the country would be seamless. This time, too, his pessimism went into overdrive: he knew that the brand name "Bibi Netanyahu" had zero value. Even Likud was in a bad way. The future looked grim. It was time, he told his associates: I'll care for my family, take a vacation.

Sara, as usual, was more outspoken, slamming the ingratitude of the Israeli public for failing to recognize Bibi's greatness. Bibi fell into a deep depression. It affected his lifestyle, and even his appearance. He looked unkempt, shuffling along lethargically, sometimes in a wrinkled shirt, no makeup, hair askew, a stain or two on his suit. "On such days, even Sara keeps her distance," said Odelia Karmon, who was his media advisor at the time. "She sent me to attend events with Bibi instead of going herself. There were days when no one wanted to be in his company."

According to a psychologist who worked with him for a long time, "Bibi is driven by war, constant struggle. He is a fighter, gets up every morning to a new war. He needs war, he needs enemies, and he needs a target. When the battle is decided and defeat appears final, he loses his taste for life and the will to go on. He becomes empty, at once."

Netanyahu still had his methods for getting adrenaline flowing. Once, when he returned to Israel from his post in the UN, he taught Benny Begin and Dan Meridor the karate moves. They ridiculed him. Netanyahu was addicted to it. Now, too, in the 2006 crisis, after several weeks of depression, he started to recover. "The core of Netanyahu's existence is his constant struggle for survival," says one of the closer and more loyal of his friends. "He is forever sinking and rising up. He has a phenomenal ability to recover. He is like a wild animal: the first to identify a threat, but also the first to become alarmed, to exaggerate and create empty threats. He is the loneliest man I have ever encountered. This also explains his desperate attachment to Sara, his wife, the only one who is truly loyal to him. Or so, at least, he has convinced himself. It is not love in the romantic sense. It is total and absolute mutual interdependence."

Netanyahu's life and constant struggle have strengthened his character. Once, he repeatedly recited the mantra "Don't get personal" to Uzi Arad, a former Mossad official and long-term associate. Dan Meridor once asked one of the professionals who worked with Netanyahu if he would ever be capable of trust. "Never," said the man. "If you are worth anything, you don't exist, he'll always be wary of you. If you are not worth anything, he won't count you." Netanyahu is a singular man. He has no moments of intimacy with anyone; there are no human elements in his relations with others. His point of departure has become "Sara and I against the rest of the world." Over the years several professionals have suggested that Netanyahu has Asperger's syndrome. The "chickenshit" exposé Jeffrey Goldberg published, quoting insults from members of Obama's circle, mentions the possibility that Netanyahu is autistic. Bibi seems incapable of forming human relations, has never been able to sense the needs of others; he is focused on himself and his needs. "It is not out of hard-heartedness," says one of his oldest friends, "it's just the way he is." He takes nothing personally and is capable of courting a political colleague, notwithstanding the terrible things he may have said about or done to an individual shortly before. To him, everything is relevant. "If he needs you, you are a god," says a source who worked in Netanyahu's service for years. "The moment he no longer needs you, you don't exist." According to psychologists who analyzed Netanyahu's personality, he would have made the perfect Hollywood actor: he is able to step in and out of character at any given moment and totally identify with it. When he tells a story, he believes it completely. When he creates paranoia, he is convinced with all his heart that the danger is real and immediate. In mid-2006 he had no need to create for himself an imagined reality or paranoia. His situation really was grim, and his future foggy.

On July 12, 2006, the fog was dispersed by Hezbollah fighters who invaded the north of Israel, set an ambush for an IDF reconnaissance unit, attacked it, and disappeared with two Israeli reserve soldiers: Eldad Regev and Ehud Goldwasser. Hezbollah bombed Israeli villages along the entire northern border and claimed victory. The organization had made a gigantic investment trying to hijack Israeli military personnel; after a few missed attempts, this time they succeeded. But there was one thing the Hezbollah leader did not take into account: Unlike Ariel Sharon and Ehud Barak, Prime Minister Ehud Olmert was not a general. He was a politician of a totally different kind. He didn't see the threat of war approaching, nor did he fear it. Unlike his predecessors, Olmert decided against restraint; he would not make do with artillery fire and a few IAF sorties. Israel's response was powerful and determined. The Second Lebanon War broke out, unplanned by any of the parties involved. With it, Benjamin Netanyahu's hopes to return to politics rocketed.

With the breakout of war, Olmert's popularity soared, but as the casualties mounted and the IDF floundered in Lebanon, it took a nosedive. The war ended after a month with no clear victor on either side. In Israel, the war was seen as a miserable failure, a gross humiliation against a mediocre terror organization that had challenged the mighty IDF and got away unscathed. Almost overnight Olmert was transformed from a stable and carefree prime minister to a lame duck. The exact opposite happened to Netanyahu. From a rejected and washed-out oppositionary politician, he soared to become the great white hope. The public was horrified by the condition of the IDF, which in the war was shown to be institutionally neglected, undertrained, and unable to make decisions. Israelis sought someone to fix the military. It didn't matter that as finance minister, Netanyahu had been responsible for massive cuts in the IDF's budget. Sharon was gone, Barak wasn't coming back, and the only familiar alternative was Bibi. Almost instantly he doubled his standing in the polls and became the leading candidate for the prime minister's post. Olmert's approval rating plummeted. Overnight the color returned to Netanyahu's cheeks. "This is one chance," Netanyahu told his people, "that I don't intend to miss. Get ready; we're coming back."

41

Building Up Power

2007–2008

During the war, Netanyahu tried to maintain a façade. He rebuilt his leadership with precise speeches, and with a propaganda mission in London. The rehabilitation enabled him to bring forward the primaries and catch his main rival, Silvan Shalom, unprepared. Netanyahu won and ensured, once again, his status as chairman of the Likud Party. All that remained now was to topple Ehud Olmert. Full of exhilaration, Bibi set about to accomplish this objective.

As soon as the war was over, protests broke out among the officers and reserve soldiers who returned, horrified and shaken, from Lebanon to take up positions opposite the prime minister's residence in Jerusalem. The reservists didn't know that several of Netanyahu's close associates were helping them with funding and logistics, among them tech tycoon Eli Ayalon. In 2009, Ayalon became Likud's campaign manager (personally appointed by Netanyahu). To Ayalon's credit, he served out of an ideological motive and was deeply troubled by the results of the war. He wasn't alone. Bibi was well aware of the principles of secret political warfare. The longer the reservists survived opposite the prime minister's residence, the lower the prime minister's popularity. Netanyahu therefore ensured that there would be some-one on the outside to reinforce the protest, keep it alive, help support it financially and logistically, keep the fire burning. It worked. The reserv-ists' protest wreaked chaos in the remaining support for Ehud Olmert. The prime minister was destroyed publicly. His personal charm and talents helped him hold on to the coalition, but his political immune sys-tem collapsed. Olmert was in such bad shape publicly that anything could harm him. A wave of police inquiries were opened against him, as well as an investigation by the state comptroller. Bibi knew how to handle these "gray" systems: the unmarked areas where politicians were gathering ma-terial on each other and acted under cover or by proxies to topple their foes. It included gathering as much incriminating material as possible about Olmert. The classified Olmert file was built secretly.

Netanyahu himself is more cautious, ensuring that nothing can connect him in any way to the acts themselves. Even when raising funds and talking to donors, he does so with extreme caution. According to a *Yediot Ahronot* investigation, Netanyahu's people made a habit of buying him unidentifiable cell phones, or "burners," and he would go out to the balcony at Likud head-quarters to talk to various billionaires and philanthropists. Bibi knows how to handle a dirty war and how to make it appear as clean as possible. "Once I said to him," an associate recalled, "that we need to collect material on Olmert because he's collecting stuff on us. He told me there was no prob-lem and asked me to talk with Momo."

Netanyahu established a new office for himself. Even before the Second Lebanon War, he was introduced to Ayelet Shaked, a pleasant and assertive young woman who came from the booming Israeli high-tech industry. Shaked is a rare species; hailing from Tel Aviv, she is secular, with a tech education and right-wing leanings. She closed a deal with Bibi and was due to start work in May, but didn't begin until September because of obligations to her previous employer. The Netanyahu she encountered in September was completely different from the beaten man she'd agreed to work for in May. "I'm going to be prime minister," he informed her when she ar-rived for work. "What I need now is a serious campaign manager." Shaked, who lacked any political experience, would not be able to do that job. He needed a significant personality to oversee his meteoric rise to the Likud leadership.

Ayelet Shaked brought in Naftali Bennett, who'd been highly recommended by a good friend, Erez Eshel. Bennett, an officer in Sayeret Matkal and the elite unit Maglan, had fought in the Second Lebanon War and came back deeply shaken. He had made a successful tech exit, having sold the company he founded for $140 million, and decided it was time to give back to the country. Eshel told him that Bibi was seeking a new campaign chief. Bennett was excited, so Eshel spoke to Shaked, who arranged a meeting in a Ra'anana café, near his home. Shaked wasn't actually impressed with him at first, but reported to Netanyahu, who decided to see for himself. The chemistry between them was instant. Bennett was just what Netanyahu liked, a freshly minted tech millionaire whose mother tongue was English. He wore a tiny yarmulke on his head; espoused Religious Zionism; and was talented, articulate, right-wing, and a staunch admirer of Bibi. They clicked instantly. Netanyahu understood that Bennett would march him into the Facebook era, into tech, and toward Generation Y. Ostensibly, this was a marriage made in heaven. In reality, it was the beginning of a strange relationship that would become a bitter rivalry somewhere between a Latin American telenovela and a Greek tragedy.

Bennett fell on the reservists' protest as if he'd found a vast fortune. He identified with it, too, as a graduate of the war and identified its potential as a tool for toppling Olmert. He took care of the quiet aid—the money flowing in from outside—and special operations; he helped to sharpen media messages, spinning public opinion against Olmert, and more: he presented Bibi with a plan that consisted of a long journey to bring him back into the center of Israeli society. It would be a journey to relieve pain, to soften disagreement, to capture hearts. He took Bibi out to a long series of social gatherings, including extravagant dinners at the home of well-known Ramat Gan psychologist Dr. Ilan Rabinowitz. The door to Rabinowitz's home served as Bibi's reentry into mainstream Israeli society. Several meetings took place with Tel Aviv socialites, public-opinion leaders, artists, journalists, and celebrities. Several such meetings took place with guests from the media, publishing, public relations, the business sector, and celebrity lawyers. They were not attended by Sara Netanyahu, which allowed Bibi to be more relaxed and charming, to a certain extent. By this time Bennett and Shaked had noticed the constant presence of the wife who didn't move from her husband's side, hand permanently pushed into his, and decided that it placed a heavy shadow over Bibi, and affected his behavior in the company of others. They tried to exclude Sara and minimize her involvement in Bibi's comeback campaign. Had they consulted with dozens of their predecessors, each of whom had tried in his or her way to pull a similar move, they would have known that no good would come of it and that, in the end, the bodies of Bennett and Shaked would be washed up on the beach as payment for their efforts.

In addition to dinners, Netanyahu also scoured the country from north to south, attending countless meetings in the course of what was coined "widening circles." The objective was to rehabilitate his image in economic, social, and cultural circles, as well as in the settlements and the country's periphery. Netanyahu, as usual, threw himself into the part perfectly. When there was a job to be done that required traveling from place to place, he was ready. His cadre in those days consisted of Natan Eshel, Amos Regev, Motti Giladi, Ami Doron, and sometimes Uri Elitzur. Giladi was an entertainer and Doron a journalist. Eshel worked for *Hatzofe*, Regev was an active senior editor with *Yediot Ahronot* and subsequently joined *Ma'ariv*, ignoring the ethics of his profession by attaching himself to the inner circle of an active politician. Elitzur was a respected right-wing publicist, a West Bank settler, and Netanyahu's chief of staff during his first term (1996–1999). There was also a security forum with the participation of reserve IDF officers Ya'akov Amidror and Yossi Peled; Mossad member Hagai Hadas; Shimon Shapira from Military Intelligence, who had been Bibi's military secretary during his first term, and the ever-faithful Uzi Arad.

The task facing Bennett was not an easy one. Netanyahu had a tendency to mix fantasy with fact and often got himself into trouble with embarrassing outpourings. An example is his description of his seemingly fictitious account of the meeting with Sharon and Barak on the bank of the Suez Canal, as well as his strange declaration that Italy had invited him to be minister of

finance and the even stranger story that the late minister Rehav'am Ze'evi
had been a minister in his government, which he relayed in the course of a
eulogy in the Knesset. He'd said the same thing a year earlier under the
same circumstances, but a brief examination confirmed that there was no
truth to the claim. And there were others: in an interview with *Yediot Ahronot*,
Bibi recalled seeing British soldiers in Jerusalem as a child. The trouble was
that he was born in 1948, after the British had left Jerusalem and the Mandate had ended. The paper later took responsibility for the mistake. But the
fact was that Bibi had said what he'd said and was even recorded saying it.

Netanyahu tends to believe his stories. The difference between fact and
fiction is blurred in his mind and he often builds an alternative reality for
himself, which he gradually convinces himself is true. The best example of
this is his insistence that he always objected to disengagement. Bibi denies
that he voted four times for disengagement, that he told MK Uri Ariel,
"Even in a referendum I'll vote in favor of disengagement." A lengthy
interview with Amnon Nadav on the Voice of Israel in April 2004, where
he spoke in favor of disengagement, also never happened, according to
Bibi. All this has been erased from his mind, and all that remains is his one
vote against it, one week before the disengagement took off and there was
no way to stop it. In various announcements and speeches over the years,
Netanyahu has said repeatedly that he objected to disengagement, and will
not allow the facts to confuse him. It came to a head during an intimate
birthday dinner celebrated by a group of Israeli journalists—from the
Religious Zionist stream—in 2006, shortly before the elections in which
Netanyahu's standing crashed to twelve Knesset seats. He was in a bad way
and fighting for his political life. As guest of honor he delivered a speech, in
the course of which he said he'd objected to the disengagement and voted
against it. The reporter Amit Segal tried to remind him of the facts, but
Netanyahu was adamant. Segal left the room for a moment and returned
with various reports and publications to prove Netanyahu's constant support
and vote for the disengagement. Bibi choked briefly, but went on as usual.
To this day he is certain that he voted against.

42

Salon Society

2007–2016

Together with rehabilitating his image, Netanyahu had to instill order in the complex web of Jewish millionaires he'd surrounded himself with throughout his career. For this he hired the services of media consultant Odelia Karmon, who'd worked with him on his 1996 campaign. Karmon received her fee in roundabout ways, via friends and wealthy associates of Netanyahu and by means of the nonprofit American Friends of Likud. At some stage Netanyahu became alarmed by this financial manipulation, which bordered on the criminal, and dragged Karmon to a meeting with his family lawyer, David Shimron, who recommended the immediate return of all monies paid and for Netanyahu to pay Karmon's fee from his own pocket. It was thus agreed that Karmon would receive bank transfers from Netanyahu's bank to hers.

Netanyahu prepared a detailed list of donors, consisting of names, addresses, telephone numbers, and scores. Finally he added code letters, according to which the letter *A* was correspondents, friends, and others from Israel; *B* was Olmert associates; and the letter *C* was everyone else. Wherever it said "renew connection," Netanyahu instructed the dispatch of a personal letter. The foreign billionaires were graded from one to four, according to their importance, wealth, and close association.

How did Olmert associates roll into Netanyahu's list? Wealthy Jews who support Israel are a closed reservoir, divided into two main groups, supporters of the right (like Likud) and supporters of the left (like Labor). Olmert and Netanyahu were from the same political party and sometimes shared ties with millionaires and other outstanding Diaspora Jews. Bibi marked the "Olmert associates" as a cautionary note.

At that time, Olmert was prime minister and Bibi was head of the opposition, and could not talk freely with all the Jewish benefactors. It is not customary to smear a sitting prime minister abroad.

The seeds of this donor base were planted by Netanyahu when he served in a diplomatic capacity in the United States, especially as Israel's UN ambassador. At that time he was welcomed by intellectuals, media people, high society, and in the corridors of power and money. He had a mystical talent for communicating with everyone, and leaving a strong impression on the people he met. Even civil rights leader Jesse Jackson became a friend and admirer of Netanyahu. At the time, he was running for president. In America, Bibi discovered the fervently Israel-supporting evangelical Christians, and soon became their favorite son. "There was an American look about him," recalls Eyal Arad, his media advisor. "Philadelphian English, absolute control of basic American terms, and amazing fluency. He had a natural charisma that could not be ignored." Netanyahu could adapt himself to any forum, any situation. "Once we entered a reception in honor of the wife of Andrei Sakharov," recalls Arad. "It was a home on Fifth Avenue opposite the Met, full of intellectuals and artists; a typical Woody Allen event. When Bibi entered the room, the entire room was magnetized by the tall, handsome leader. They knew him from *Nightline*; they knew his family history, including Yoni's death in Entebbe, and were drawn to him like a moth to a flame."

It was in New York that Netanyahu learned the secrets of fund-raising, and became a genius in the field. His first billionaire was Ronald Lauder, who was U.S. ambassador to Austria when Bibi led a campaign against Kurt Waldheim, former UN secretary-general and president of Austria, over his

Nazi past. Netanyahu and Lauder were diplomats appointed by their political parties (Lauder is a Republican). From the start they shared a mutual language. Lauder cooperated with Netanyahu. Lauder is a Jew, scion of the Estée Lauder cosmetic fortune, and a staunch supporter of Israel. It was obvious that this was the start of a wonderful relationship. Lauder opened the gates for Netanyahu to the world of money and Jewish power in America. Their relationship was close, intense, and good for them both: Lauder understood that the young Israeli diplomat would go far and looked upon him with admiration. In his eyes, Bibi symbolized the new Jew: courageous, self-confident, and a daring war hero. Not only did Lauder open his heart to Bibi, but also his pockets. He showered him with gifts and indulgences, making sure Netanyahu lacked for nothing.

Lauder's investment in Netanyahu was enormous, and within a decade, his young friend from the UN had become prime minister of Israel. As such, Netanyahu sent Lauder to serve as his personal diplomatic emissary to the secret negotiations he was conducting with President Hafez Assad of Syria. Lauder used his private jet to shuttle between Damascus and Jerusalem, during which he offered Assad, in Netanyahu's name, a peace treaty that included Israeli withdrawal from the Golan Heights. As usual, however, Netanyahu got cold feet at the last moment and left Lauder in a bad situation. Bibi claimed he had agreed to withdraw only as far as the Cliffs Line and didn't mean a full withdrawal. Lauder knew the truth, but forgave Bibi. He always forgave.

The belt of millionaires that accumulated around Bibi Netanyahu increased at a phenomenal rate. According to Odelia Karmon, Bibi categorized them: those with $3 million, those with $30 million, and those with $300 million. His attitude toward them depended on the wealth they had accumulated. Those who had $3 billion automatically received VIP status, not to mention any with $30 billion. Of the latter, Netanyahu had only Sheldon Adelson.

As far as Netanyahu is concerned, a man's success is measured by his wealth. In the late 1980s and early 1990s, the star of Bibi's list of rich men was Morad Zamir, a Jewish diamond merchant whose business was based in New York. Zamir was Bibi's favorite and behaved accordingly: expensive gifts to Sara, expense accounts in all the fashionable restaurants, funding office expenses and various other luxuries. When Zamir fell on hard times, he also lost his status in Netanyahu's inner circle. Odelia Karmon recalls that she had to beg Netanyahu for a promise to pay Zamir a little attention, or to have lunch with him sometime. Once Netanyahu agreed to meet Zamir for lunch at one o'clock in Jerusalem's King David Hotel. Zamir arrived on time and waited. At 4:30 p.m. Sara arrived with the children; Bibi didn't make it. It was not an isolated incident. Karmon, who couldn't bear these humiliations, challenged Netanyahu, who had no response. When Zamir's fortunes improved, so did his access to Netanyahu. But it was never the same. His star had faded.

During the past decade, since Netanyahu's rehabilitation, new bene-factors have joined the reservoir. Many billionaires flowed through Netanyahu's stock exchange, but only one comet conquered it and rules indisputably: Sheldon Adelson. Apparently, the man responsible for the official introduction between him and Netanyahu is the late Merv Adel-son. Adelson's financial ascendency placed him at the top of Netanyahu's pyramid, replacing Ronald Lauder, who was ousted and banished in shame because of another traumatic event.

In March 2011, Israel's Channel 10 broadcast an investigation by reporter Raviv Drucker into what would be coined "Bibitours": the web of million-aires who funded the journeys of the Netanyahus around the world, through-out the years. The couple demanded that Lauder, a partial owner of the media company, prevent the broadcast, and they exerted heavy pressure on him. The unfortunate Lauder didn't know how to get out of it. He knew he'd be unable to prevent such an investigation without embroiling himself in a public outcry, but on the other hand, stood to lose Mr. and Mrs. Netanyahu. As far as they were concerned, the information could not be made public. Lauder agonized, consulted, and begged, but it was futile. He compiled a list of all the positive stories broadcast by Channel 10 about Netanyahu and his family and all the negative stories published on his enemies. It was no good. Lauder was unable to prevent the broadcast. Channel 10 stood the test of journalistic democracy and ethics, but failed the test of the Netanyahu family. The police whitewashed the investigation that followed up on the broadcast, but the family never whitewashed their revenge on Lauder: when the dust settled, Lauder was the only casualty. He was banished from the court of Netanyahu as if he'd never been a part of it. With the passing of time, Bibi forgave him and was willing to renew the ties, but Sara wouldn't hear of it. All those years Lauder supported him were erased, as was any gratitude for the money or the cleaned-up mission in New York. Ronald Lauder, who had provided his every need, was no more.

That's not all. Lauder's Channel 10 was forced to issue a lengthy and humiliating apology to Adelson after airing a critical piece about him. This marked the changing of the guards at Netanyahu's side. As Adelson's status in the court of Bibi and Sara increased, so did the fallen stars and benefactors of the past find themselves instant outsiders.

In the 1990s, Lauder employed the young American Israeli Steven Schneier, who was responsible, among other things, for ties with Netanyahu. After Lauder's banishment, Schneier tried to mediate between them and return the disappointed billionaire to the prime minister's court. His efforts started to bear fruit in September 2014. Netanyahu was in New York to deliver a speech to the United Nations and agreed to meet Lauder in his hotel lobby. Lauder arrived on time and waited downstairs for two and a half hours. Netanyahu didn't turn up. In the end, a despairing Lauder left. It was said in Netanyahu's circle that when Sara learned where her husband was going, she imposed an immediate veto that Bibi was obliged to obey.

Eventually the meeting took place in January 2015, in Paris. Bibi was there to participate in the march of leaders that followed the terrorist attack on the *Charlie Hebdo* offices. This time he was alone, and agreed to see Lauder briefly in the hotel lobby. Lauder later described the scene as "strange." Relations never returned to what they'd been. Bibi's doors were closed to Lauder, as was his heart.

Sheldon Adelson is much more than Netanyahu's wealthy patron and financial backer. Over the years something resembling a father and son relationship has developed. In some sense, the elderly Adelson fills the space left by Bibi's late father; Bibi's body language when he's with Adelson is indicative of the great respect he feels for the older man. Adelson's ideology is in many ways similar to that of Bibi's father. Perhaps Bibi requires some kind of ideological lighthouse to find his way.

At the start of their relationship, Adelson was just one of many supporting billionaires. Later he advanced to first among equals. But then he rose quickly to become the be-all and end-all. The casino mogul fulfilled a dream of Bibi's and an old plan: to effectively have his own media entity. *Israel Today*, a daily newspaper distributed free all over the country, has become the nation's best-"selling" tabloid, pushing aside all others, including *Yediot Ahronot*, owned by Bibi's bitter enemy Arnon "Noni" Mozes. Adelson invested many millions in *Israel Today*, which regularly serves as the Netanyahu family's mouthpiece. When it comes to Bibi, it's hard to find a single critical word in it. Over the years, Adelson's investment in the paper had increased, in what appeared to be an an effort to destroy the Israeli media market and bring down the *Yediot Ahronot* media empire.

When Adelson is in Israel, Netanyahu visits him in his Tel Aviv apartment for face-to-face meetings. In Israel the custom is to come to the prime minster and not vice versa. They have a telephone hotline, and it was Adelson who encouraged Netanyahu to join the unsuccessful campaign to overthrow Obama in 2012. In the United States, Adelson is central to a large support system for Netanyahu. Israel's ambassador in Washington, Ron Dermer, is often referred to as the ambassador to Las Vegas. Dermer has attended the auditions where Adelson examines Republican candidates before deciding whom to invest millions of dollars in to rid the White House of Democrats.

Second on the list is American billionaire Spencer Partrich from Detroit. The "Bibitours" investigation exposed documents of Netanyahu in which Partrich is referred to as "a wealthy friend, Netanyahu's flying taxi in the U.S." Partrich used to fly Netanyahu in his private jet throughout the United States and host him in various locations. He, too, has a hotline to Bibi.

For many years Arnon Milchan has been included in Netanyahu's inner circle, but he is worth a separate reference. Milchan is a Hollywood producer, a proud Israeli who continues to hold Israeli citizenship but conducts his business in Los Angeles. For many years, he has been in and out of the courts of all the Israeli prime ministers and most of the country's senior politicians. Milchan likes to be involved; he gives advice, carries out missions, passes on messages, softens quarrels, and is there to counsel when needed. He is close to Shimon Peres, Yair Lapid (who once worked for him), Avigdor Lieberman, Silvan Shalom, Ehud Olmert, and others. Almost everyone has been his "son." It was Milchan who mediated between Netanyahu and Livni after the 2009 elections, and between Netanyahu and Yitzhak Herzog in 2015. He is politically well versed; partner to Shimon Peres's endless programs, to Tony Blair's creativity, and to most of the political intrigues in Israel. Milchan has his finger in every pie, and he loves every minute of it. He is unable to say no. Shimon Peres likes to say that "when he sees a wall, he is sure it is a door." This is probably the secret to his success in Hollywood, and what turned him into a major force behind the scenes in Israeli politics.

Somewhere in 2014, Milchan introduced the Australian billionaire James Packer to the Netanyahus. It was an immediate love affair. Later, it became a police investigation against Netanyahu, who was suspected of having received many expensive gifts from both Milchan and Packer.

43

Matters of the Psyche

It is not just Sara Netanyahu's behavior over the years that has given rise to rumors of mental issues in the prime minister's household. Many of the people who have worked with Benjamin Netanyahu over the years, including a considerable number of his close associates, are convinced that neither is devoid of symptoms that could indicate one mental problem or another, including psychopathy. "They have similar disturbances," says a person who was very closely to Netanyahu for many years. "Bibi is a psychopath, and his behavior touches on that of Sara's. They speak the same language. She is the controller, and he is the controlled. She is the handler, and he is the handled. The family connection here creates a melting pot, they are intertwined with each other, which is what leads to their bizarre lifestyle and behavioral disturbances."

A person who knows the couple from close up, and has been included in their inner circle for many years, describes them in more professional terms. He lists the familiar symptoms of psychopathy:

1. Parasitic lifestyle
2. Impulsivity

3. Glib and superficial charm
4. Grandiose self-worth
5. Pathological lying
6. Conning and manipulativeness
7. Skilled at operating people
8. Lack of remorse or guilt
9. Callousness and lack of empathy
10. Failure to accept responsibility for own actions
11. Vindictiveness against anyone who tries to destroy the inflated self-image

"The most famous villains in history were like this," the man continued. "When international leaders say that it's impossible to believe a word Netanyahu says, they are referring to this, too."

"Narcissists expect everyone else to recognize their superiority," says one of Netanyahu's veteran aides. "They are forever demanding confirmation, are afraid that others envy them; they have absolutely no ability to empathize and have a strong sense of entitledness. The fact that Netanyahu has lived most of his life at the expense of others, or the expense of the state, and doesn't understand what's not right about that, proves the thesis." He explains, "Even when he was living in an apartment that an Australian millionaire placed at his disposal, he was forever complaining: why was there no hot water and why was the maintenance unsuitable, and it never even occurred to him that someone was doing him a favor. These are classic symptoms of narcissistic personality disorder."

A childhood friend of Netanyahu provides a supplementary theory: "One of the reasons for narcissism is oversensitivity from a young age. Bibi was a very sensitive child. He was soft, with artistic tendencies; wanted to be an architect or an artist. He suffered deeply from the exaggerated criticism of the adults around him, the remote father and the stormy mother, the over-achievement, a chronic lack of attention and love. His problems were not simple ones. That's the reason he surrounds himself with grasshoppers who won't endanger his greatness. His was what is known as a 'severe emotionally abusive childhood.' Incidentally, Yoni also had issues, which were reflected in his loss of leadership in Sayeret Matkal and the intention to dismiss him as its commander. It wasn't easy to grow up in the Netanyahu household."

A typical incident illustrating the intensity of Netanyahu's narcissism is described in Odelia Karmon's book *The Confidant*. In the President Katsav sexual-assault affair, Karmon was revealed as "A" from the transport ministry. For many years her identity had been kept secret until the day *Ma'ariv* published an interview with her on its front page. The attached picture was blurred. Bibi, who was leader of the opposition at the time, recognized Karmon, his former press advisor, and called her. She was sure he was about to ask her how she was feeling, how she was getting through the difficult days. That's not what happened. If he'd managed to recognize her from the picture, then almost anyone could have done so, too. That was the reason for the call. It certainly wasn't pleasant. Karmon was disappointed that Netanyahu was concerned only for himself. "Now they're trying to destroy me," he informed her, and claimed that if it emerged that his personal assistant was one of Katsav's accusers, Bibi would be blamed for trying to destroy Katsav politically, in order to prevent Katsav's return to the political map, just as he was nearing the end of his term as president. "Bibi," Karmon begged him, "it's not about you; it's about me." He wasn't listening. He was in a panic. Again, he was making a mountain out of a molehill. "I suggest you do a lie detector test," he told her. "Not one, but two. Two separate polygraph institutes, so they won't say we've stitched this up in advance. Get them to ask you if I sent you to testify against Katsav. Say I didn't, and you'll be telling the truth." Karmon couldn't believe her ears. The tale Bibi had woven in his imagination was groundless. She wasn't the one who broke open the Katsav affair, and her testimony wasn't relevant because it came under the statute of limitations. Yet Bibi was placing himself center stage in this insane movie, about a personal tragedy that could get him into trouble, neither understanding nor caring that his former close personal assistant was in the throes of an emotional upheaval and undergoing a powerful personal trauma.

According to a top-level official who worked with Netanyahu and is well versed in intelligence issues, there is no doubt that the CIA prepared a psychological profile on Netanyahu, which members of the administration, headed by President Obama, studied closely. "If you look at the famous 'chickenshit' article," says the source, "[you'll have seen] the term *Asperger's*. *Chickenshit* is a slang term, which reflects the president's opinion of the prime minister; that he's a coward, both on the security level and on the diplomatic level—a weakling, who is unwilling to take risks. But *Asperger's* is a term from the field of psychology. It seems the Americans know a few things about Bibi's problems, which is why this word found its way into the report and was mentioned to Jeff Goldberg. It wasn't accidental."

The source also recalls many conversations over the years with Americans who have admitted that the psychological file constructed by the CIA around Bibi's problems includes some very complex issues. "It is common practice among the Americans," says the source. "Almost every foreign leader of any importance has a psychological profile compiled by experts, who are fed by many years of media reportage and professional observation." The source stresses the fact that when President Obama first walked into the prime minister's residence in Jerusalem, he made a point of praising Sara's beauty. "He didn't do so by chance. It was the result of personality analyses and psychiatric findings; indeed, everyone in her vicinity knows that if you want to captivate Sara, you have to say that she's beautiful and then she's all yours. And, so is Bibi. I know it sounds insane," says the source, "and it really is insane, but that is the reality and everyone is fully aware of it."

In private conversations, a significant number of Americans express doubt as to Netanyahu's mental competency. The term *mentally ill* is heard often in these conversations. Moreover, history teaches us that many world leaders have suffered to some extent from narcissistic personality disorder. It is hard, without some measure of narcissism, to achieve a position of leadership and survive the exhausting political path.

A highly experienced, top-ranking American diplomat, who served in Tel Aviv during Netanyahu's tenure as prime minister of Israel, best summed up the situation. His final telegram to Washington at the end of his mission included a very telling recommendation to the State Department: "You'd better make sure that whoever you send to replace me is a psychiatrist."

44

The Intoxicating Scent of Power

2007–2009

On September 6, 2007, a secret nuclear reactor near Dayr al-Zawr in Syria was bombed by unidentified aircraft, and completely destroyed. News emerged that this was the work of the Israeli Air Force. President George W. Bush claims in his memoirs that Israel had discovered the Syrian nuclear installation. The information was provided by an Israeli Mossad agent who'd hacked a computer belonging to a Syrian nuclear scientist staying in Vienna. The information was passed on to the Americans, who were then kept updated as events were unfolding.

Israel never took responsibility on the attack on the Syrian reactor. It is customary in Israel for the prime minister to keep the opposition leader updated on sensitive security issues in face-to-face conversations. Around that time, Netanyahu was trying to join Olmert's government. Netanyahu knew that such an event would bolster Olmert and stabilize his administration. The fear, once again, was that his life's dream of returning to the prime minister's office could fade into the distance. Netanyahu informed Olmert that he would join his government if national security issues became sufficiently complex. Ya'akov Ne'eman, Netanyahu's veteran consigliore, had already drafted a handwritten agreement for his inclusion in the coalition. It was never typed, so it could not be leaked. The jobs and portfolios destined for Likud remained open, although there was mention of Netanyahu receiving the security portfolio; in addition, Silvan Shalom, Yuval Steinitz, and Gideon Sa'ar would join the government. Netanyahu virtually forced himself into the tent. He was afraid of the train setting out without him, and with it his comeback plans.

The destruction of the Syrian reactor that was attributed to Israel by the foreign press happened with zero aftermath. Assad was restrained. No war broke out. Netanyahu, on the contrary, was accused of a lack of restraint. He tried to claim, falsely, that he took part in major decisions that were made. Olmert was incandescent with anger. He wanted to pick up the phone and reprimand him, but refrained. Those were sensitive days and such a conversation could easily leak. In his vicinity, people were saying, "Bibi is sick and dangerous. A man devoid of all discretion."

The destruction of the Syrian reactor that was attributed to Israel stabilized Olmert's status in the polls, but a wave of police investigations that followed media reports brought the prime minister to the end of his rope and he resigned on September 21, 2008. President Peres called on Tzipi Livni to form an alternative government. Netanyahu's time had come; he had waited for this day for almost a decade. He wasn't going to miss this chance. To return to government, he had to prevent Livni from forming a government, and force her to call an election. For Netanyahu, it was now or never.

Netanyahu formed a small, intimate team whose task was to prevent the establishment of a new government. The four-man team, headed by Netanyahu, convened every day in Tel Aviv, where the fragrant scent of Netanyahu's cigar became the smell of power.

The polls showed an unprecedented seventy Knesset seats for Livni's center-left bloc, ten of which belonged to Arab MKs. The right and ultra-Orthodox stood at fifty MKs. Gideon Sa'ar understood that the key lay in the Arabs' hands. If Livni entrenched them and got them to promise to abstain at the swearing-in of the government, her success was promised. Sa'ar

had a close relationship with Arab MK Ahmad Tibi, one of the more brilliant parliamentarians in the Knesset, and checked in with him every day.
When Sa'ar asked Tibi if the Arab MKs' concerns had been addressed and
he said they hadn't, Sa'ar was puzzled by the apathy of Livni and her people.
Tibi made it clear that the Arab MKs would be prepared to abstain in return for economic concessions and minimal cooperation, but no one had
approached them. Livni exhausted herself, and wasted some of the time allocated to her for forming a government, on negotiations with her most
natural and easiest-to-achieve allies, Ehud Barak's Labor Party. It took her
three valuable weeks to seal a deal with Barak, who belonged to the center-
left camp, instead of dealing with far more essential sectors. She didn't know
that Barak was working for Netanyahu and was intentionally trying to exhaust her, so that Bibi had time to block all other options. Barak preferred elections to a government led by Bibi. He knew he'd be defense
minister after the elections, whatever happened. He'd sealed that deal with
Netanyahu.

In the meantime, Netanyahu dealt with two big prizes: the Senior Citizens' Party, headed by Rafael "Rafi" Eitan, who had seven Knesset seats;
and Eli Yishai's Shas party, which was a member of the coalition. First came
the Senior Citizens. They were a one-term party and didn't want elections;
Bibi just needed to come to an agreement with them. But Livni spent unnecessary time negotiating with Barak, so Bibi pounced on the pensioners
with all his force. He bombarded Rafi Eitan with declarations of love and
signed a written agreement with him according to which he'd be a minister
in the next government even if the pensioners did not make it through the
elections. He also stormed all seven pensioners in Eitan's party, with high-
falutin' promises that by most indications he had no way, and no desire, to
fulfill. He didn't care; they were old, didn't understand politics, and already
had one foot outside the Knesset.

Despite all his agreements with Rafi Eitan and his MKs, Bibi was still
not appeased. He asked for a fictional agreement to be drafted between the
seniors and Likud and turned up at 7:30 one morning at Eitan's home with
the first draft. "Relax, Bibi," said Eitan, "I have no intention of entering any

narrow government under Livni." Netanyahu smiled and said, "I still want us to run together." At that moment he would have happily married the eighty-three-year-old. Even Sara would have agreed to it, so long as he didn't sign with Livni.

At the same time, Bibi expended an enormous effort in putting a wedge in the heart of Livni's Kadima party, which included a group, at least four strong, of MKs who supported Livni's bitter rival for the party leadership, Shaul Mofaz, who held center-right views. The first of these four, Ze'ev Elkin, agreed to join Likud before the elections with the support of Netanyahu. The remaining three were dealt with more cunningly. A friendly journalist was encouraged to call each of them separately and ask a single question: Would they be willing to serve in a government established on the Arab vote? They all replied in the negative. Immediately, an announcement was made that four Kadima members opposed a government based on the Arab vote. There was no going back. The way to a narrow government that would achieve a majority vote on the back of abstention of the Arab MKs was thoroughly blocked. Livni was furious and was certain that Mofaz was behind the conspiracy, not knowing that Gideon Sa'ar and his friend Silvan Shalom had planned and executed the whole thing.

What remained was to rope in Shas. During his terms in the Knesset, Netanyahu had worked at length with Eli Yishai and Rabbi Yosef as well as with Yaakov Litzman and the United Torah Judaism Party. It was obvious that Rabbi Yosef preferred Bibi to Tzipi, but he was still traumatized by the years his party had been in the opposition and didn't want to find himself on the outside once again. As soon as he understood that the Kadima option no longer existed, he knew it would not happen. Bibi swore not to repeat past mistakes vis-à-vis Shas as he had in 2001, when he allowed Sharon to make a fool of him. Itzik Sudri, Shas's legendary spokesman, joined Netanyahu's negotiating team. While Livni was toiling against Eli Yishai, refusing to announce that there would be no negotiations over the future of Jerusalem, and hesitating whether to agree to the party's economic demands, Netanyahu had finalized all the details with Yishai and the rabbi. He promised them everything they wanted, and Livni was blocked.

Netanyahu behaved during those weeks like a wild animal. Taking no prisoners, working around the clock, mortgaging the country's future on baseless promises, negotiating with everyone possible and focusing on his never-changing life objective. With the help of his efficient team, he divided the political components from each other, and led them to the elections. The first part of his mission was crowned with success.

45

Back Home

2009

The comeback plan was nearly complete. Netanyahu tried to create the illusion of a new Likud by bringing in reserve IDF generals Yossi Peled and Uzi Dayan; as well as the former chief of police, Assaf Hefetz, who was promised the Internal Security portfolio in Netanyahu's government. Dan Meridor and Benny Begin returned and fresh new forces joined, too, such as Miri Regev and Tzipi Hotovely. Netanyahu was everyone's patron. Each one carried in his or her pocket a personal promise of one sort or another. The new Likud membership card was "smooth." Until recently, it listed the party's principles. Not anymore; there were no principles, no discord; everybody was welcome to climb aboard for a ride. Even Yuval Rabin, son of the assassinated prime minister, murmured something to Bibi's credit, at a strange press conference they'd convened together. It happened on the eve of elections, when Tzipi Livni's Kadima soared at the expense of Barak's Labor. Bibi was worried that Livni could still beat him in a photo finish. Kadima's negative campaign against him was gaining ground. The decisions he made as finance minister to rescue the economy took center stage. Yuval Rabin declared in their joint press conference that he was voting Labor, which was what Bibi wanted, to strengthen Barak at

Tzipi's expense. Rabin added that he hoped for national unity with Netanyahu leading the way.

The Likud campaign was unfocused. Netanyahu was worried. He had entered the fray full of self-confidence, but that was gradually slipping away from him. Could he miss yet again? Behind the scenes, Sara dominated, while in the campaign headquarters, much effort was made to keep her out of sight. They tried to modify his appearances, sending him on diplomatic errands with foreign leaders and foreign media that were within his comfort zone. Lieberman's campaign slogan: "Lieberman, I believe you" was a body blow to Bibi. There was less belief in Bibi, and Likud reached the finishing line winded and full of well-justified fears. Livni received twenty-eight seats, Bibi finished with only twenty-seven; and Barak's Labor won thirteen seats, as did Lieberman. A tie. The keys were in the hands of President Peres, who had to entrust one of the MKs with the task of forming a new government. This time, too, Netanyahu expressed a reason to panic. "Peres will entrust Tzipi," said a terrified Bibi to his entourage. "He doesn't want me in government." One of his advisors took preventive measures: a journalist was dispatched to former president Yitzhak Navon to ask him what he would have done in such a situation. Navon, an honest man and Labor veteran, said that he would entrust the task of forming the government with the person who has the best chance of doing it right. In other words, Bibi was the right choice. The story was never published, but someone made sure President Peres heard Navon's view of the matter.

In the meantime, Lieberman took advantage of the situation to have some fun. He remained silent when asked who he was recommending to form the government. If Lieberman had recommended Livni, it would have given her a significant advantage. He passed around identical questions on state and religion to both Livni and Netanyahu and left for vacation in Moldova, leaving what remained of Bibi's nerves to fray. As usual, Bibi started writing the worst-case scenario's script: Lieberman will recommend Livni. The hints Lieberman passed on to Bibi failed to reassure him. Lieberman had said essentially it would be all right. In the end, it was.

Lieberman returned to the president and recommended that Netanyahu form the government. He would pay whatever it took to whomever it took.

He'd arrived. He was back. Sara was returning to the official residence. They did it together. They stuck with each other, were dependent on each other all the way. No one was going to stop them now. The ten long years in the desert were over, at long last.

Long live the king, and the queen, too.

46

A Very Broad Coalition

2009–2013

At the beginning, Netanyahu toyed with the idea of forming a government with Tzipi Livni's Kadima. His natural coalition partner, Avigdor Lieberman, vetoed any idea of including Ehud Barak in the government, so Bibi was in trouble. Apart from anything else, if he was to carry out his plan to build the "Netanyahu Stronghold" in Jerusalem, he would need time and a period of stability. He knew exactly how he would take control of all branches of government, conquer all the positions of power, and replace all the gatekeepers with his own people. A broad coalition would have allowed him to achieve all this in comfort.

Negotiations between Likud and Kadima were conducted between Gideon Sa'ar and Tzachi Hanegbi, with the objective of establishing a unity government on the basis of parity and rotation, with Tzipi Livni receiving the final third of the term, a little over a year, as prime minister. Livni demanded a full rotation, half the term as prime minister. Alternatively, she agreed to a third, if the coalition were narrower and would be dissolved in the event of Kadima's exit. Netanyahu deliberated. He had no intention of giving Livni half a term. If she agreed to a third, he could dissolve the government before the time came for the rotation between them. "We have a government without you, why should we give you half a term?" Sa'ar asked Livni in a telephone conversation. In the meantime, efforts were made to bring Netanyahu closer to Livni to decrease suspicion and, especially, Sara's hostility toward her.

The two couples, Benjamin and Sara Netanyahu and Tzipi Livni and Naftali Spitzer, shared a single unsuccessful evening together. They met one Saturday evening at Livni's Tel Aviv home. Livni cooked and didn't particularly excel at it. It was supposed to be a casual meeting, an attempt at appeasement, but it didn't really work. Bibi and Sara were accustomed to elegant reception rooms, quality refreshments, top-shelf alcohol, and expensive cigars, none of which were available in the Livni household. The chemistry between the couples was minimal. The ice didn't break. All Livni remembers from the event was the sight of Sara Netanyahu perched on the sofa in her living room and rising to demonstrate, with her hands, how the planes would take off from a northern air force base on their way to bomb Iran. The Iranian nuclear bomb must be prevented at all costs, she said, and her husband echoed her words. Netanyahu, too, was in shock from that evening, having come to understand that as far as Livni was concerned the Palestinians constituted a more important and urgent issue than Iran's nuclear program. "She's completely unhinged," he told Sara, who agreed.

Meanwhile, Avigdor Lieberman lifted the ban he'd placed on including Ehud Barak in the government. All at once, there was no more flirting with Livni, and the rotation was shelved. Netanyahu formed his second government with the ultra-Orthodox, Lieberman, Labor, and the Jewish House Party. The government was sworn in a little before midnight on March 31, 2009, to make it before April 1 and not be recognized as an "April Fool's government." As he descended from the podium, Netanyahu encountered Gideon Sa'ar and Yuval Steinitz. "You did a good job," he told Sa'ar. "And you'll do a good job, too," he said to Steinitz, who was surprised to be appointed finance minister.

The new government consisted of thirty cabinet ministers and eight deputy ministers, the largest-ever government in Israel. Lieberman was appointed foreign minister. Ehud Barak remained minister of defense. A strategic alliance was forged between Barak and Netanyahu, based on common interests: Netanyahu's need for a "responsible adult" who could sell the new government to the world and be its "store window," and Barak's need for a political patron to clinch his control of the Defense Ministry despite his unimpressive results in the election. For Netanyahu it was orgasmic: his revered Sayeret Matkal commander working for him. Barak, who dismissed him in 1999, was now at his mercy and serving in his government. That said, Barak was indifferent. He knew Netanyahu too well, and had no respect for him. As far as Barak was concerned, Bibi was Yoni's less successful younger brother. Sitting with Alon Pinkas in a New York restaurant, Barak was asked to explain who this man is?" "He speaks in Republican English, talks about his father, talks about history, Churchill. What's he about?"

Pinkas was a casualty of Netanyahu. Before the elections, Bibi had courted him passionately. Pinkas, a Labor Party member, close to Barak and Shlomo Ben-Ami, an articulate expert on America, was a big prize for Bibi, and he was promised the ambassadorship in Washington. On the eve of the elections, Pinkas endorsed Netanyahu. Right after the elections, all the promises disappeared, as did Netanyahu. Barak smiled. "He's not like us," he said. "He's not from here." What do you mean? Pinkas asked. "Ignore his biography, the fact that he was born in Jerusalem and served in Sayeret. In the end, he's just a scared Diaspora kid." Barak once told Uzi Baram, "No matter where Bibi was, he'd always be number two." Netanyahu's father had the same opinion of his son; he said in an interview that Bibi would make an excellent number-two man.

But now Bibi was number one and laughing at everybody, including Barak. To his close associates he said, "Barak is great, when he's small," and proceeded to keep him that way. Somehow the Bibi/Barak partnership managed to hold on for the entire four-year term of the second Netanyahu government. For the first time, nearly all the political tricks, the diplomatic intrigues, and the maneuvers carried out by Netanyahu during this term were drilled in Barak's brain and implemented harmoniously by the two.

Benjamin Netanyahu's second government was formed to make everyone happy. Thirty ministers, eight deputies, generously distributed titles and honors; superfluous ministries were established, four ministers without portfolio were appointed, and new positions were invented that were not needed. No one remembered Rafi Eitan, who'd received a written promise of a ministerial position even if he didn't make it to the Knesset. Like the other pensioners, he was left by the roadside. Bibi no longer needed them. He kept his promises only to those who had the potential to harm him.

Netanyahu's most important move in this term may have been made even before he'd established the government. Indications are that he carefully crafted his choice for minister of justice, Ya'aKov Ne'eman, and Attorney General Yehuda Weinstein, to best protect his interests. Ne'eman had been Netanyahu's loyal consigliore for decades and was responsible for the reconciliation agreement between Netanyahu and his wife after the video crisis. Weinstein had also represented the couple during the police investigation into the bill presented by the moving company Amedi and the official gifts Sara wanted for herself. Their loyalty to Netanyahu was unquestionable. Ne'eman received his position by personal appointment by Netanyahu. Once appointed he would have significant responsibility for determining who would serve as attorney general and it can be assumed was charged by Netanyahu with assuring that the post went to Weinstein, no simple matter. The goal was clear. The incumbent attorney general, Menachem "Meni" Mazuz, was scheduled to end his appointment in February 2010, in less than one year. If Weinstein replaced Mazus, Netanyahu could feel confident that Weinstein's six years in office could provide him and his wife with six years of peace and quiet. According to sources, Netanyahu met Ne'eman and Weinstein prior to the 2009 elections and before he formed his government on March 31. Ne'eman was appointed minister of justice and a few months later Weinstein was the AG. Mission accomplished. Weinstein's six years in office were calm and quiet for Netanyahu. No investigations opened, no unnecessary questions asked.

Netanyahu was on his way, right foot forward.

47

The Country Is Me

2009–2016

As soon as he returned to power, Netanyahu tackled a mission that was of foremost importance to him, i.e., buttressing his regime. The objective was to brand himself as the nation's father, a leader who was irreplaceable; to instill in the masses the same belief that drove the Netanyahus, that no one was more suitable to lead, and without him, Israel was lost. At the same time, he set about taking control of every station of power, the gatekeepers of democracy. Netanyahu's thesis was simple: When you are strong, you set the agenda; and when you are perceived to be irreplaceable, you are safe. No snowballing police investigations could ever harm a powerful prime minister, who provides the daily picture of national security and the weekly spin. The new Netanyahu was Mr. Consensus, Protector of the Nation, symbol of Israeli sovereignty, the one and only man for the job. At the same time he flushed out the political system, leaving a leadership vacuum. If Netanyahu got his way there would be a chronic dearth of serious rivals, no leaders; any serious competitors would be jettisoned from the political arena after their legitimacy had been undermined. The objective was to leave Netanyahu at the top in splendid isolation, surrounded by political dwarves. He wanted to create a "Gulliver" effect.

To make this plan happen wasn't easy. For instance, a law was created solely to bring about the political destruction of popular former chief of staff Gabi Ashkenazi, who had political aspirations once he'd attained his release from the IDF. It also involved close attention to small, ostensibly marginal matters that had cracked Netanyahu's image in the past and would now have to be overcome. For example, Netanyahu suffers from hyperhidrosis (excess sweating), which is exacerbated by stress. Other leaders ridiculed him for it, suggesting that this was a sign of weakness or panic. For years he was haunted by pictures of himself sweating heavily when he needed to give the impressions of being cool and composed. Overcome by this embarrassment, he had every room in his offices air-conditioned to near subzero conditions.

Each event attended by Netanyahu is a carefully planned state occasion. Political and economic declarations, press conferences, and announcements all fit the same format: There is the podium, the flags, and other symbols of power. Bibi takes his trademarked scenery wherever he goes. The idea is to engrave in the public's awareness the idea that Bibi and the state are one and the same. He is the state.

It is hard to find an official picture of Bibi without a flag in the background. His tie will usually be blue, his shirt white. Everything is blue and white. Only on days when he is pushing for combat or nationalism will his tie be red; meetings with Obama, for example, often got a red tie. Netanyahu, who learned how to face the camera decades ago in New York, was not ashamed to learn again. Aware of the fact that he was conceived as a cold and emotionless person, he learned to laugh, his head thrown back to show what it looks like when the prime minister is laughing out loud. The stage instructions are carefully thought out. He must never be photographed from below, to avoid the appearance of a double chin. He must not be photographed from above, because that would make him look short. He must be photographed only from the side, usually from his good side, the one that does not show the scar on his upper lip. The camera has to be at eye level. On occasions where dozens of cameras are present, Netanyahu knows with extraordinary precision which camera is photographing him at any given moment. He is a media animal, a dream presenter. His people will always be in control of the camera's angle, of the staging. As far as Netanyahu is concerned, it does not matter what's happening, what is broadcast, and what is reported. It's the picture that counts.

So long as Netanyahu's regime has lasted, his paranoia increases. His second government succeeded to survive a full term, 2009–2013; a rare thing and due mainly to its exaggerated size, which provided a stable coalition. In 2013, Netanyahu won the elections due to a last-minute union with Avigdor Lieberman; but the resulting coalition was unbalanced, or so he believed. Yair Lapid managed to get in, suffering every minute of the hated Naftali Bennett and Ayelet Shaked. Separated from Lieberman, Lapid feared the revenge of the ultra-Orthodox parties, which were excluded because of him. In 2015, Netanyahu won the election against all odds. The public seemed thoroughly sick of him and his unprecedented last-minute fear-mongering, but his opponent, Yitzhak Herzog, failed utterly on the national security front, an essential for anyone who wants to win an election. This time Netanyahu formed a minimal coalition of only sixty-one MKs, and without his old ally Avigdor Lieberman, who decided to stay outside the government, largely because he thinks that Netanyahu got a police investigation started against him on the eve of elections. Lieberman planned to take over the premiership with Yair Lapid and Moshe Kahlon.

During these years, Netanyahu burned bridges and important connections with many senior Likud members and fellow travelers. The popular Moshe Kahlon was forced to resign, establishing an independent party. Gideon Sa'ar, the most sophisticated and popular politician in Likud, could no longer stand Netanyahu and his wife, and resigned. President Reuven Rivlin, a veteran Likud icon, became an enemy when Netanyahu tried to sabotage his presidential election in every way possible. Dan Meridor was thrown out of Likud and Benny Begin was left out of the government. Netanyahu lost all faith in the outside world, retreating into his inner circle and intimate family. It was just Bibi, the wife, and the heir apparent, Yair Netanyahu. The second circle of trust is two men: the family lawyers, David Shimron, who deals with all internal matters; and Yitzhak Molcho, who takes care of all external affairs. These constitute *la famiglia*. An intimate governing unit, fortified, loyal, and impenetrable. The third circle is logistical and consists of his patron Sheldon Adelson alone. Next to him is another lawyer, Yossi Cohen, who is responsible for the "gray area," together with Natan Eshel, Mrs. Netanyahu's personal assistant, and Shlomo "Momo" Filber, a veteran confidant and special operations expert. This is the staff through which Netanyahu has control of the country and the lives of its some eight million citizens.

Apart from fortifying and perpetuating the survival of his regime, Benjamin Netanyahu set himself three additional missions when he took up office in 2009: to block the Iran nuclear program at any cost; to kill the peace process with the Palestinians without having to pay a price for it; and to survive unharmed the Obama administration, doing his utmost to ensure that it lasted only one term. Netanyahu seemed to ignore the way that these three missions were dependent and intertwined with each other.

48

Finale

Early 2016

In summer 2011, a group of young people set up an improvised tent camp on Tel Aviv's Rothschild Boulevard, in protest over the cost of housing in Israel. Within days the camp had become an unprecedented grassroots protest that led to a series of additional mass rallies in other towns in Israel. On one night at the height of the protest, a million Israelis demonstrated in various towns and cities countrywide. The "Summer Protest," as it was coined, or the "Social Protest," shook Netanyahu's regime to its foundations. The public demanded social justice, and the message was clear: Israelis were sick of the existing order, the ever-growing social discrepancies, the rampant capitalism, and the high cost of living. Netanyahu responded in his usual way, with panic. He saw the protest as a left-wing conspiracy to overthrow him. He dispatched Eyal Gabbai, the general manager of the PM's office, to wander around, in disguise, among the protesters on Rothschild Boulevard to try to understand what if anything was behind the protests; who was pulling their strings. At the same time Netanyahu established a public committee to meet the protesters and discuss their demands, some of which he subsequently gave in to. By the end of summer, 2011, Bibi looked weak, a hedonist detached from the people. His popularity sank.

Shortly after the end of the protest, Netanyahu negotiated the release of captured Israeli soldier Gilad Shalit, after he'd spent five years in Hamas captivity in Gaza. His predecessor, Ehud Olmert, had refused to negotiate a deal with Hamas, because he knew it would harm Israel's ability to defend itself. The Shabak warned that the release of a large number of convicted terrorists with blood on their hands could cause a new wave of terror against Israeli citizens.

Considered a much more extreme hard-liner than Olmert, Netanyahu had a plan during the first two years of his regime: He was adamant in his refusal to release Palestinian murderers in exchange for a captured Israeli soldier. But the summer protests changed his thinking. Additionally, he needed to change public opinion. In the name of political expediency, he opted for a deal with a terror organization. Israel released more than a thousand Palestinian prisoners, many of them cold-blooded murderers. It was classic Bibi. After having "educated" the world not to surrender to terror and never negotiate with terrorists, after writing books and convening congresses and delivering hundreds of speeches and berating all the prisoner-exchange deals made by Israel over the years under other prime ministers, he was the one to cave in to terror, carrying out one of the most shameful incidents in Israel's history.

With the return of Gilad Shalit, Bibi's popularity hit new heights. It was an act of political genius. Demands for Shalit's release came mostly from Israel's political center-left, a sector that does not traditionally support Netanyahu, and it was there that he became the hero of the day. He had set aside historic principles, all his beliefs and doctrines, for political profit. Here, again, was proof that Netanyahu had no real ideology except for his commitment to staying in power. His philosophy is flexible, changeable, because its real objective is power, not serving the country. Everything flows from Bibi's firm conviction that what's good for him is good for everyone.

Taken from any historical point of view, Bibi's results are not impressive. Obama got his second term in office. On the Iran issue, Bibi failed dismally. He promised hundreds of times that if Israel had no choice, it would be obliged to deal with Iran's nuclear threat itself. He established an expensive military option against Iran, threatened and planned and prepared to use it, but at the moment of truth, choked. And Israel remained at the mercy of the superpowers. At the same time, his behavior severely damaged the strategic relationship between the White House and Jerusalem. His stubborn insistence on fighting the Iran agreement right up to the last minute and on speaking to both houses of Congress, in blatant defiance of President Obama, hindered Israel's ability to receive any significant security upgrade through American aid. The final military aid deal, about $3.8 billion a year, was a lot less than what the administration would grant Israel if Bibi had not rejected Obama's hand a year earlier. It was not only about money. There was a golden opportunity to reach strategic cooperation and unprecedented understandings between the two states on the Iranian issue and other important topics. In his book *Doomed to Succeed* Ambassador Dennis Ross hints that president Obama considered placing Massive Ordnance Penetrator bombs in Israel, if Netanyahu would halt his war against the Iran deal on time. That never happened. Israel paid dearly for Netanyahu's failed gambles.

As for a Palestinian state, Netanyahu drew a tiny victory. He did manage to bury the Palestinian issue, persuading most Israelis that there was no partner for peace, thus succeeding in extracting himself from Obama's plans. The problem is that on the way to achieving this, he lost Israel's international credibility, exposing it to various diplomatic threats, which has culminated in the current wave of Palestinian terror, which began in October 2015. There is no solution on the horizon. If there is a victory somewhere in all this, it is definitely a pyrrhic one.

Even with his famous flagship issue, the war against terror, Netanyahu's record was and remains feeble: during Operation Protective Edge, which began July 8, 2014, Hamas fired rockets on Tel Aviv for fifty-one days, while Netanyahu hesitated and instructed the IDF not to get involved in a war inside Gaza. His promise to topple the Hamas regime remained unfulfilled. Israel achieved a pathetic draw in a war against a small, besieged terror organization. The Gilad Shalit prisoner-exchange deal put the lid on the failure of Netanyahu's antiterror policies, and the outbreak of the new wave of terror in late 2015 was yet another nail in the coffin of Bibi's image as a great fighter against terror.

Benjamin Netanyahu is the devoted student of his father, Professor Ben-zion Netanyahu. In 2003, the professor published his book *The Founding Fathers of Zionism*, in which he reviews the activity of five of the movement's outstanding leaders. The book illustrates the professor's great fondness for Benjamin Ze'ev Herzl, founder of Zionism and visionary of the Jewish state. In his book, Prof. Netanyahu analyzes rationality vis-à-vis Mapai-ism. In other words, people of vision versus people of action. It was Herzl who dreamed of a state, believed in his dream, defined it, and instilled it in the hearts of the Jews of Europe. On a practical level, Herzl did not shine. Mapai—the forerunner of today's Israeli Labor Party—established the state of Israel (under its powerful leader, David Ben-Gurion) and was the epitome of action. Saying less, doing more. Establishing facts on the ground.

Netanyahu, father and son, belong unequivocally to the people of vision. They don't know how to translate ideas into action. They place no importance on action, as such. It is marginal.

As far as Herzl was concerned, it was vital to obtain the required charter for the establishment of a Jewish state for the Jewish people in the Land of Israel. He spoke to congresses and conventions, wrote books, and strove for international recognition. Thus, too, was Netanyahu Sr. and his father; thus, too, the grandson, Benjamin Netanyahu. For these men, appearance is more important than action. Anyone who ever worked for Netanyahu knows that preparations for a photo op before a meeting are more important than the meeting itself. Netanyahu is more concerned with what is reported than with what happens. Micro-tactics are not for him. He exists for the big strategy, an important speech in Congress or the UN, an important document—recognition and illusion. To him, the written word is the supreme value, the height of achievement. When attempts were made to persuade him that there was no need to produce a book about his dead brother, Yoni, his response was, "You don't understand the power of the written word. It changes history."

"If you understand Netanyahu," says one of his closest associates, who worked with him for many years, "he has already actually attacked Iran. To him, every assertive speech he gave in the UN or Congress, or anywhere else, against Iran is more important than any physical attack. Netanyahu's natural battleground is on the floor of Congress, not some nuclear enrichment site in Natanz. He inherited this tendency from his father, who got it from his own father, and Herzl, who coined the phrase 'If you wish it, it is no myth.' For Netanyahu, this phrase changed history. The actual labor was carried out by others."

Practical Zionism is completely alien to Netanyahu. He scorns it. Netanyahu is the exact opposite of Ariel Sharon, who established settlements and scattered them over every hill and valley in the West Bank. Sharon loathed words and speeches, and was attracted to acts. Which is why Sharon was the one who destroyed first the Sinai Peninsula's Yamit settlement following the peace treaty with Egypt, and then the twenty-one flourishing Israeli settlements in the course of the disengagement from Gaza. Netanyahu will neither build nor destroy. He prefers to talk, to try to change history by way of the word, not with the sword and the plow.

As one who recoils from action, Netanyahu is not eager to open unnecessary fronts, keeps his distance from dangerous confrontations, and tries to stay away from sweaty reality. An exception is his unprecedented struggle with President Obama which, except for a few idyllic and unconvincing sparks, persisted throughout their mutual two terms in office. Both of them, suspicious alpha males, skipped the "sniffing out" stage, and clashed powerfully almost from the first moment. In the course of his overlap with Netanyahu, Ehud Olmert said, "Even with Obama I can get along." Netanyahu replied, with hooded eyes, "Give me George Bush anytime, and see how far I'll get with him." But no one gave Bush to Netanyahu. He got Clinton for his first term, and Obama for his second. To Netanyahu, Obama was a total loss, almost from the word go. Guests at the Netanyahu home often hear the family's opinion on the American president. "He's a Muslim," Bibi and Sara's older, more dominant son, Yair, makes a habit of saying, to his parents' pleasure. *Muslim lover*, *anti-Semite*, *Hussein* are Obama synonyms in the Netanyahu household. But, in fairness, the other side uses derogatory names and expressions to describe Bibi. Obama was surrounded by aides and advisors who loathed Netanyahu, and had hated him since his first term. They considered him a liar, manipulator, and political charlatan. "When I write my memoirs," Bibi likes to tell his associates, "Obama will have to go underground. I'm going to write some things that will cause him considerable embarrassment."

In the final analysis, Benjamin Netanyahu is a saga of missed opportunities. On November 21, 2016, he succeeded in beating David Ben Gurion's record in the length of a continuous term in power. He was soaked in an endless line of scandals and political fights; still, his reign seemed stable without a dominant threat. The credit he has built among the Israeli public over the past seven consecutive years of his regime has allowed him to do practically anything he wants. He could have marked a target and aimed for it, burst through any political dead end, changed the paradigm, been a leader. But Netanyahu is not cut out for real leadership. He is here to protect the existing situation, to identify the dangers to him politically, and to do so at the cost of any opportunities. He is the ultimate presenter of the catastrophes of the wandering Jewish nation. He is a leader blessed with talents and abilities, intelligence, deep understandings. He is quick on the uptake and has substantial analytical skills. How unfortunate it is that all this is wasted on personal survival, adherence to the status quo, and fearmongering. Had Netanyahu had the courage to hope, he could have really influenced history. As of March 2016, he had succeeded in bringing Israel back to the same spot left by Prime Minister Yitzhak Shamir in 1992, a country devoid of vision and hope, stuck, isolated. A people that dwells alone. Donald Trump's shocking victory in the American election sowed new hope in Netanyahu's heart. Trump seemed to be too good to be true but Bibi was realistic enough to acknowledge that Trump's real interest is Trump. At least he avoided Hillary Clinton.

PART TWO

✡

DANGEROUS RELATIONS

48

Israel and the Palestinians

2007–2008

If you compare Obama's CV with Bibi's," a close Netanyahu associate said in early 2015, "you'll understand it all. There's absolutely no comparison." The dawn of Obama's second term was breaking as Bibi was beginning his fourth with no end in sight. This is an analysis in retrospect, but it indicates the warped foundations on which the shaky relationship between the two leaders was established. When the foundation is bad, the building collapses.

"Before entering the White House Obama hadn't achieved anything of significance," continued the close associate, who was involved for a long time with the relationship between Washington and Jerusalem. "He didn't hold any significant job before the Senate, he was a less than mediocre student, and no one knows how he got accepted to Harvard. When Obama was smoking grass like some flower child in Chicago, Bibi was an officer of excellence in Sayeret Matkal, the IDF elite commando force. Bibi was accepted by all the most prestigious universities in the United States, Yale, Harvard, and MIT; he completed a BA at MIT with honors and an MA at Harvard in record time. He was number two in the Washington embassy; Israeli ambassador to the UN; deputy foreign minister and foreign minister; minister of finance, who rescued his country from a severe economic crisis. He is one of the best speakers in the world and since the age of forty-seven has served as prime minister of one of the hardest countries on earth to govern. He is an impressive man, and still a handsome man even at age sixty-seven. He was raised and spent many years in the United States, his English is perfect, his French is good, he is an experienced and seasoned politician, and his geostrategic outlook is amazing. The only sphere in which Obama can give Bibi a fight is in delivering a speech. So what wonder is it that in 2009, when Obama finds himself facing Bibi, he is simply afraid?"

This is a condensed analysis of what happened and, especially, what didn't happen between Bibi and Obama during their almost eight mutually bad years. It is based on facts, but tends to favor Netanyahu. It lacks two central facts: Barack Obama became president of the United States at about the same age as Benjamin Netanyahu was when he became prime minister of Israel. And Obama overcame the Clinton family's mighty campaign machine and was elected the first black president in history. Anyone who sneers at a man with such a record is making a big mistake. Moreover, in 2009, Obama was one of the most revered leaders in the world, while Netanyahu was numbered among the world's most objectionable leaders. But Bibi's people wouldn't let these facts spoil their thesis. "Bibi lives with a profound sense of mission," says the close associate. "He was born for something, he was destined for something, he has a mission. Obama found himself, against his better interests, in the wrong place at the wrong time. He is the antihero who has come to spoil the party."

In addition to all these issues, Obama and Netanyahu possess diametrically opposing character traits and world views. Obama is a liberal, an eternal optimist. As a leader he is averse to the use of force, believes in soft power, recoils from tricks of leadership and façade; he is pragmatic and direct. He would always prefer dialogue to threats, diplomacy over war. He is an appeaser who was voted into office exactly for this reason: to extract America from the two quagmires it had sunk itself into in Afghanistan and Iraq; to make peace with the Muslim world; to soften its image as the brutal, conquering, and bombing empire; to rest a little. Netanyahu is

"Mr. Suspicion," with a grim view of the world, who ignores opportunity when it might upset the status quo. Netanyahu only sees danger and hostility. He is addicted to his projections of forcefulness; he is an expert at leadership tricks and power poses, even if there is nothing real behind them. He is an alarmist who knows how to warn and arouse, and not only is familiar with the language of force, but knows how to use it. Notwithstanding these differences, the two leaders share several similarities. Both are great orators, great speakers, dripping with charisma. They both have cold, noninflammatory personalities that find it hard to create human warmth and closeness. One of them strives to open his country to the world; the other prefers to close it. And, by an accident of history, they have found themselves having to face each other.

They first met at the airport in Washington in spring 2007. Bibi was Israel's opposition leader and Obama a senator in the run-up period before the actual campaign. They were both there to speak at the American Israel Public Affairs Committee conference. Yes, Obama once liked AIPAC. The young Democratic senator asked to meet the veteran Republican Israeli politician. Due to timetable issues, the meeting took place at the airport. They were given a room and Netanyahu arrived first with former senior Mossad official, close associate, and advisor Professor Uzi Arad, who would become, two years later, Bibi's national security advisor. With them was Dr. Dore Gold, also a veteran political advisor and former Israeli ambassador to the UN. Obama arrived with only one advisor and a notebook in which he wrote his impressions. "We didn't know a lot about him," Arad recalled. "His walk was panther-like. Reminiscent of James Coburn." Netanyahu sat in a deep armchair; Obama took a chair beside him. It looked more like an interview, with Obama in the role of assiduous student, interrogating the silver-haired leader, trying to draw as much as possible from his knowledge and wisdom. Arad wasn't really following the conversation. He didn't believe that this young African American was destined for greatness. Netanyahu was attentive, and gave the impression that he was enjoying the pose adopted by Obama opposite him. They took their leave with the usual civilities and, when Obama and his assistant walked out, Netanyahu turned toward his people, saying, "He's got it." Arad and Gold didn't quite understand. "The young man who was just here is a sophisticated political animal. He can beat Hillary," Bibi added, and deep in his heart, he hoped it would happen.

As far as Bibi was concerned, Obama could be a dream come true. In all America, it was impossible to find a family he loathed more than the Clintons. Bill Clinton cost Bibi the election in 1999. Enjoying enormous popularity in Israel, Clinton imposed on Netanyahu a series of humiliating lessons. Netanyahu knew that Obama was running against Hillary Clinton for the Democratic nomination, but didn't hold any special hopes for him. After the meeting at the airport, Bibi changed his view. He saw that Obama would be a serious rival, and crossed his fingers for him. Regardless, Netanyahu hoped for a Republican president, but if he had to choose between Hillary Clinton and Barack Obama, he preferred the latter. He knew it would be easier for him to push Obama on the Israeli public. A black president, mysterious, with no record of support for Israel and a middle name like Hussein would be an easy rival. Ideologically, Netanyahu knew that Clinton was closer to Israel than Obama, but Obama would be much more comfortable politically.

The second meeting took place fourteen months later, in July 2008. Netanyahu's prophecy had come true, and Obama was already an official presidential candidate. The presidential candidate came to Jerusalem at the head of a distinguished delegation, while Bibi headed the opposition in the Knesset. Both faced general elections. The meeting took place at Jerusalem's King David Hotel, where Obama was staying. Martin Indyk, Susan Rice, and Dan Shapiro accompanied him. Netanyahu brought Uzi Arad, Yitzhak Molcho, and Ron Dermer. The Americans recall that even then, months before the election, Netanyahu's people referred to him as "prime minister," an unprecedented tribute in Israel. For them, he had already won. The meeting was scheduled in advance, and planned down to the last detail. Both sides were tense and both had something to lose. Obama feared that any hitch could damage his fund-raising campaign. Bibi might say something that could be misinterpreted at home. Netanyahu shared the same fears: that Obama might say something that could be interpreted as support for Tzipi Livni.

The fears proved groundless. Arad coordinated all the issues in advance with a contact in Obama's entourage and all the messages were formulated together, down to the most sensitive resolutions. Nothing was left to chance. Bibi and his people were surprised to see the dramatic change in Obama since their past meeting. He'd matured and come of age. Netanyahu opened by saying, "Barack, I have the feeling that at our next meeting we'll both be in an official position." Obama laughed. Yes, he hoped to reach that official position, but he prayed not to find Bibi opposite him. Netanyahu felt the same. He, too, hoped to win the election, and prayed not to have to work with Obama. In other words, Obama hoped for a victory for Tzipi Livni and Bibi hoped John McCain would win. Still, the meeting was excellent. Obama determined the pace. Bibi arrived with organized notes; Obama arrived without notes but knew everything by heart. He said everything Bibi wanted to hear, stressed the importance of halting Iran's nuclear program, not only because of Israel, but because it would lead to a nuclear arms race in the region. He praised the special relations, the strategic alliance, everything that an American presidential candidate tells an Israeli leader on the eve of an election. After the meeting, comments issued by the two entourages were optimistic and positive. It was the last time this would happen.

49

Not Even One Brick

The second Netanyahu government was sworn in on March 31, 2009, at night, to avoid the awkward date of April 1. Netanyahu preferred to postpone the first meeting as leaders with President Obama for as long as possible. He was apprehensive about this meeting and wished to study the new president beforehand, to consult with his people, and to come to the meeting fully prepared. Ultimately, the meeting was set for May 19, 2009, almost two months after Netanyahu took office. In the meantime, his team had been trying to carry out an assessment of overall Israeli policy. They studied the various negotiations Olmert held with Syria, coordinated by Turkey (eight rounds of negotiations in Istanbul), they studied the conversations between Dov Weissglass and President Bush on the matter of settlements and expanding the West Bank settlements, they looked at the negotiating route in Annapolis with the Palestinians, and other strategic issues.

Netanyahu's people were convinced they had made a thorough and extensive study of all these issues, but they were the only ones who thought so. Olmert's people thought otherwise. They were surprised by the amateurishness of their successors. Netanyahu's people were not interested in meeting them for a thorough and organized briefing. They were quick to settle in at their new offices. Shalom Turgeman, Olmert's veteran political advisor, who also served Sharon and Barak, was overlooked. His overlap meeting with Prof. Uzi Arad lasted half an hour. Turgeman, a human database of all the sensitive negotiations, special relations, and interregional meetings held by Israel's prime ministers since the days of Ehud Barak, went home without passing on any of this information to anyone, as did other senior officials. Some of the future glitches between Washington and Jerusalem can be attributed to this lame beginning.

Netanyahu always looked askance at Obama. The same thing can be said for Obama. Neither of them had any great expectations of the other. Obama was surrounded by people like Rahm Emanuel, who had squabbled with Netanyahu back in the Clinton days, as well as other Jewish officials who were not famous for their fondness of Netanyahu. Bibi, on the other hand, was awash with prejudice and saw Obama as a genuine strategic threat: left-wing, liberal, devoid of any real affinity for Israel or any noteworthy record with AIPAC. Netanyahu was certain that Obama would try to dissolve the discrete strategic understandings between Israel and the United States. It was the most sensitive issue on his agenda, a historical matter that went back to the days of Golda Meir and President Nixon and consisted of American backing for Israel's policy of ambiguity vis-à-vis the nuclear issue, and the political umbrella that the United States provided Israel with over the decades. Knowing one of Obama's main goals was nuclear disarmament, Netanyahu suspected that on this existential field he could expect a nightmare. A small Israeli delegation preceded the Washington visit to prepare the various issues. It included Bibi's national security advisor, Uzi Arad; his political advisor, Ron Dermer; and Yitzhak Molcho, his personal emissary. Arad was entrusted with two key issues: strategy and Iran. During that year, U.S.-Iran relations had started to thaw, so Israel was concerned. Molcho was given the Palestinian portfolio. Here, too, Netanyahu knew, it wasn't going to be an easy ride with Obama. Netanyahu expected Obama to demand a decrease in construction in the West Bank, but believed he could get the Americans to agree to continue building in the settlement blocs.

In Washington, they met Obama's national security advisor, Jim Jones;

Gary Samore, who was responsible for nuclear issues in the National Security Council (and headed the Middle East desk); and other officials. The atmosphere was good. Arad remembered his contacts from the Clinton administration. The ice was soon broken and everyone acted like old friends, managing the preparations with ease. From the beginning, General Jones agreed to Israel's request for a joint U.S.-Israel coordination mechanism on the Iran nuclear issue. Both sides agreed to the approach being multifaceted; that coordination would be ongoing, extensive, and accurate; and pressure on Iran would increase continually. The Americans asked for secrecy; outwardly, their relations with Iran had been thawing. The Israelis agreed willingly. Uzi Arad was surprised, and favorably impressed. The approach established at that meeting lasted until 2013, when Tom Donilon, General Jones's successor, would leave the White House, and Ya'akov Amidror, Arad's successor, left the prime minister's office.

As for strategy, the teams' success came as even more of a surprise. Gary Samore agreed immediately to ratify all past understandings. In return he asked for Israel's commitment with the United States on all issues requiring a consensual decision. Samore set about drafting the letter of ratification and Arad flew to Israel to hand Netanyahu the draft. Bibi read it, pretended to be displeased, but approved it. The fact that the Americans were prepared to ratify and even upgrade the understanding with Israel on so sensitive an issue ruined his thesis. He didn't believe it possible. His suspicions wouldn't dissipate; possibly even the opposite was true. "They are up to something," thought Netanyahu. "It's too good to be true."

The Palestinian issue was much less successful. Molcho was subjected to some harsh criticism from the American side and, although he returned to Israel concerned, he was not depressed. Bibi had already been through the Clinton administration and survived such situations. It was going to be all right. There was already a way to cut a few corners. After all, the tidings brought home from Washington by Netanyahu's vanguard were not bad at all.

As the visit approached, Netanyahu's military secretary, General Meir Califi, began to feel uneasy. From his time with Olmert, he was used to orderly staff work, an efficient agenda, with all the necessary discussions determined and preparations made, and meticulous study of all relevant material. He found it hard to deal with the new reality in which there was no boss in the office, where the agenda was merely suggestion, chaos reigned, anonymous emissaries came and went, and there were no regular reports, no staff meetings, no organized thought and no management of any kind. Califi reached out to the man closest to Netanyahu, Yitzhak Molcho. "Let's start by agreeing that this meeting never took place," he told Molcho. "Now tell me, what is the objective of the meeting to Washington? Have you written out an objective? Do you know what you wish to achieve?"

Molcho stuttered something. "What are you suggesting," he asked. "When we arrive, Obama's door will be open to us." General Califi replied, "The objective is that even when we leave, the door will remain open to us. Now all we need is to think how we can achieve this. Did you study the political process in Annapolis? Everyone is talking about the Annapolis process. Think of a way to continue with it. Even by using your methods. If you don't, take along a substitute. The Americans are going to ask about it."

Califi was concerned. He knew that no one was going to sit down with Turgeman, and realized there hadn't been an organized overlap period, and that all the understandings and processes left over from the Olmert administration had not been studied and internalized. He was used to order. Under Olmert, the chief of staff, Dr. Yoram Turbowitz, used to summon the senior staff every day at exactly 7:00 a.m., to summarize the previous day and define the current day. Olmert arrived at exactly 7:45 a.m. and they would both go into his office to start the day. When Califi asked whom Netanyahu's chief of staff was, he was introduced to a good-natured guy with a yarmulke, who looked as if he'd just dropped in from a typical nineteenth-century eastern European Jewish shtetl. "Pleased to meet you," said Natan Eshel, a man lacking political and/or diplomatic experience, or even any significant managerial talents, a kind of minor bookkeeper who had been general manager of a tiny newspaper before rising to the position of deputy general manager of Adelson's *Israel Today*. Eshel was a favorite confidant of Mrs. Netanyahu, with orders to report directly to her. Eshel had perhaps the most important role since he bore responsibility for the household needs of the prime minister's wife, a job that would later embroil the Netanyahus in a police investigation. Califi was shocked. He asked Eshel why no regular staff meetings were held, why no teamwork was recorded. Eshel waved a hand in disdain. "I am not here for that," he replied. "I have other jobs to do." Califi set about writing an extensive memorandum to the prime minister, in which he stressed the importance of organized teamwork, of a professional staff, of task delegation, and of defining authorities. They all read his paper, including Netanyahu, but did nothing. The prime minister's office continued to operate like a grocer's shop in a remote village. The chief of staff reported to the prime minister's wife, the political emissary was actually a private lawyer and the owner of a flourishing law office; spokespersons got changed with the frequency of dirty socks; and chaos reigned. On one occasion Califi told Bibi that there may well be some excellent people in the office, but there was no team. Bibi nodded his head and moved on.

In Netanyahu's eyes, one of President Obama's more worrying appointments was that of George Mitchell as the U.S. special envoy for Middle East peace (2009–2011). In Netanyahu's world, Mitchell is seen as a hostile element. The Mitchell Report, prepared by a team headed by him and dealing with the circumstances that brought about the second intifada, constituted the basis for President Bush's "Road Map." This report included a recommendation to freeze Israeli development in the settlements, a recommendation that was especially explosive to a right-wing government headed by Benjamin Netanyahu. Mitchell was appointed immediately upon Obama's taking office, three months before Bibi became prime minister of Israel. He visited Israel and met Netanyahu when the latter was still opposition leader. Bibi felt uneasy after this meeting. He sensed that there'd be problems with the guy, but still couldn't gauge what they might be.

In the plane on the way to Washington, Netanyahu was worried. The Israeli daily *Yediot Ahronot* ran a special headline in honor of his journey: "Bushar in Return for Yitzhar," The Obama administration was willing to meet him halfway on the Iran issue, on the condition that he meet them halfway on the Palestine issue. But Bibi didn't know what they were cooking up for him, expressing his suspicions in conversation with the reporters on the plane. Sweating, and cracking his fingers, he asked repeatedly what Obama expected from him. He suspected that Obama wanted him removed from power, and even said so out loud.

His reception in the United States capital was good. The Americans behaved according to protocol and it was clear they were trying to present a relaxed atmosphere. The media were briefed accordingly, and the meeting with the president commenced. In accordance with protocol, each leader brought his staff for a discussion of the issues on the agenda. At a predetermined time, everyone was then asked to leave; this, too, according to protocol. The time had come for the traditional closed-door meeting between the two leaders. In relations between allies, it is customary for leaders to move to the edge of the official meeting space for a more private coming together. There is no note-taking, and no other witnesses. It is possible during this part of the meeting to speak freely, and say things that are not permitted by protocol. Obama and Netanyahu's tête-à-tête was supposed to last one hour; it lasted almost twice as long. No one could recall so long a closed-door meeting in the White House between the president and an Israeli prime minister. Staff members and advisors don't like closed-door meetings. First of all, it leaves them outside the loop. Also, such a meeting is liable to cause problems. The staffers waited outside, impatiently. Uzi Arad looked at Defense Secretary Gates, who looked back at him. Both of them looked at their watches. The Americans were more concerned than the Israelis. They suspected that the veteran Netanyahu, with his greater experience, might be giving the inexperienced, Johnny-come-lately President Obama the runaround. Fifteen minutes before the end of the meeting, the two national security advisors, Robert Gates and Uzi Arad, were summoned inside to record in duplicate the minutes of the closed-door meeting that had just concluded. Obama did the talking, speaking for Netanyahu: We agreed on this, we spoke of that, we decided to carry out this, you stressed this, and I emphasized that. Arad found nothing special in the summaries. At the end Obama asked Netanyahu if he had anything to add.

Bibi didn't, but for some reason his face was ashen. The advisors left the room, and a few minutes later so did Obama and Bibi. The meeting was over.

It was one of the hardest meetings Netanyahu had ever endured: stuck in a closed room with no witnesses or documentation, and the leader of the free world world had given him a fierce slap across the face. "I demand," said Obama, "that you stop building in the West Bank." Netanyahu cleared his throat, tried to bargain, asking: What about the settlement blocs, the agreements? But Obama cut him short. He wasn't interested in blocs or agreements; he demanded a total cessation of building—immediately, in all the areas, everywhere, including Jerusalem. Bibi tried to raise the issue of natural population growth, the needs of the local population, but Obama continue to block him. No growth. Total halt. Later, the expression "not even one brick" would come into common use and became a symbol of the collapsing relatonship between the two leaders. The expression is credited to Secretary of State Hillary Clinton, but the Americans swear she never uttered it. "It was never said," says a senior White House official. The phrase could have been an attempt on the Israelis' part to undermine the Obama administration. With or without a single brick, the significance of Obama's demands was the same. Israel must cease all building in the West Bank, period. Netanyahu paled. "Even if I agree," he told the president, "my coalition won't allow me to do it." Obama was unimpressed, and continued to insist that Israel had to stop all building in the "territories." Here Netanyahu began to bargain, suggesting that Obama arrange a gesture from the Arab world. "Such as what?" President Obama asked. "A handshake from the king of Saudi Arabia, for example," Netanyahu replied, and Obama promised to try. But it didn't encourage Netanyahu. He didn't understand the sudden hostility, or what the president wanted to accomplish. The suspicions he had exaggerated about while talking to the press on the flight over were realized in full. Obama was out to get him, and wanted to topple him.

Benjamin Netanyahu was in shock. His people noticed his agitation as soon as he walked out of the meeting. Still, he decided to keep the matter to himself until they were back home. He didn't want details leaked too early.

He wanted the upshot from this first visit to continue to appear rosy and upbeat; perhaps he was still hoping that it was a passing nightmare. On Obama's side, there was a certain smugness. Obama had kept private the discussion of the freeze on settlements to avoid having the issue discussed publicly. "When the president sits opposite you and says things directly to you, it has an effect," recalls a senior White House official. "Anyway," he added, "at that time, the Israelis were leaking almost every conversation we had with them. We preferred to keep this secret until the president said it face-to-face to Netanyahu."

After the meeting, Obama was asked how it had gone and he described Bibi's shock in great detail. Later that day, Obama sent Vice President Biden to Blair House, the official diplomatic guest residence, to meet Netanyahu, reassure him, and evaluate the damage done. In Blair House, Biden met a prime minister in emotional turmoil. Looking at the floor, Bibi asked repeatedly, "What do you want from me?"

Following the meeting with Obama, Netanyahu continued on his regular round of meetings on Capitol Hill. There, too, he heard things that concerned him, mainly from Democratic senators and congressmen. When had the America he'd known disappeared? None of the people he spoke to knew about Obama's demand to freeze building in the settlements, but their tone with him was somehow similar. Netanyahu's meetings on the Hill that were supposed to reassure him only exacerbated his concern.

Only after his return to Israel did Bibi summon his team for an update. Now it was their turn to be shocked. More than anyone else, Arad took it all to heart. "We've failed," he shouted at his staff. They hadn't fully prepared the prime minister for this ultimatum, had fallen asleep on duty. Arad's remorse did not change the situation. Netanyahu found himself in a deep pit. The goods Obama demanded of him were impossible to deliver. To halt building in the territories, with their 350,000-strong Jewish population and robust population growth, was tantamount to killing Jewish settlement, or at least causing it irreparable damage. Obama wanted to push for quick negotiations, and as things stood, he wasn't going to relent until Netanyahu was brought to his knees. In early June, two weeks after the

Washington meeting, Netanyahu received another message from Obama: *The New York Times* reported that if Israel refused to freeze settlement activity in the territories, the United States would consider canceling its automatic support for Israel in the UN Security Council. Bibi knew it was a serious threat. With the demand for a freeze public, Mahmoud Abbas couldn't move forward unless Israel stopped building. Obama had caused Abbas to climb up the tree, and Netanyahu realized there was nothing he could do.

50

The Immediate Suspect

2009

Netanyahu was not the only one to fear Obama. Even before Obama had overcome Hillary Clinton in the Democratic Party primaries, *Ma'ariv* published this headline: "Fear in Jerusalem: Obama Is Moving Toward the White House." At that time, Ehud Olmert was still prime minister, and for Israelis from all parts of the political map, Obama was worrisome. In talks between Obama's staff and AIPAC, all the right boxes had been checked. That was the routine. Candidates had to "prove" to the pro-Israel lobby his or her commitment to Israel, to its security, to its prosperity, and to the need to maintain a qualitative edge over its enemies. There is an Excel sheet with boxes for every position and statement required of a candidate. Obama's team worked quickly to make sure their candidate said all the right things. The Obama campaign circled back to make the necessary clarifications verbally. The trouble with Obama was that he had absolutely no record of anything concerning Israel, for or against. He had never stood a real test. Although he surrounded himself with Jewish advisors, these were the kind of Jews whose left-wing views are synonymous with Peace Now, the Israeli equivalent of J Street.

One of the senior Israeli embassy officials in Washington had a talk with

Sallai Meridor, Israel's U.S. ambassador. "I have read everything there is to read on this Obama," said the official. "Nowhere does it indicate that he is pro-Israel. In my opinion he is nonaligned at best; at worst he is pro-Arab." Meridor replied, "You are an alarmist. I spoke to Dennis Ross and a long list of Jews in the administration who know Obama and are willing to vouch for him." The ambassador's words were not convincing, and he himself was undecided. There was an extensive debate about Obama. To this end a separate venue was arranged, and senior embassy members were invited. The special "seminar" was dedicated to the Obama question. They discussed what would happen if Obama wanted to open diplomatic relations with Iran, and there were extensive conversations about building in the settlements. All these eventualities, which were conceived at the time as extreme, eventually materialized.

Netanyahu had done his best to prepare for his first meeting as leader with Obama. He turned to people who were supposed to know the president or his people well. One of these was Shimon Sheves, ex-Rabin chief of staff, who was close to Rahm Emanuel. Netanyahu met Sheves by chance, and asked him for help in preparing the visit. Sheves agreed in principle and Netanyahu said he'd call to arrange a meeting, but didn't. Alon Pinkas, former Israeli consul general in New York, someone associated with the Democratic Party, was also recruited. "I need your help," Netanyahu told Pinkas, who said he'd be happy to comply. They met in the lobby of Jerusalem's King David Hotel. "We don't come from the same place," Pinkas told Bibi, who agreed and added, "I really appreciate your help. I am afraid of Obama. I don't understand what he wants; Hillary will be secretary of state, she's been haunting me since her husband's administration, Rahm Emanuel is going to be chief of staff and he hates me." Pinkas raised an eyebrow. "Bibi," he said, "do you really believe that this is what they think of you?"

"Do you think they don't think those things about me?" Netanyahu replied.

"They are not in their jobs in order to hound you," Pinkas explained. "That's not how it works in America. As far as they are concerned, you are quite marginal."

Netanyahu asked if there was anything to be done, if their attitude toward him could change. "Yes," Pinkas replied, "it all depends on your first trip there. And the rapport you succeed or don't succeed in creating with the president." During those days, Netanyahu toyed with the idea of appointing Pinkas Israel's ambassador in Washington in hope of building trust between him and the Obama administration. Netanyahu and his people only spoke Republican English, and what he needed was someone to translate him into Democratic English. But the idea soon dissolved. Although Pinkas publicly supported Netanyahu on the eve of the 2009 elections, he changed his mind after Bibi formed his government. It was Bibi's inherent mistrust of Pinkas, who had been close to prime ministers and foreign ministers from Israel's left (Peres, Barak, Ben-Ami), that did the trick.

Another person Netanyahu tried to get help from in building a relationship with Obama was Alan Solow, an American lawyer from Chicago, chairman of the Conference of Presidents of Major American Jewish Organizations (2009–2011) and one of Obama's main supporters, someone who has enjoyed a lengthy and trusting relationship with the president. Netanyahu met Solow on the eve of the elections, in the course of Operation Cast Lead, when Solow was in Israel as the head of a group of Jewish leaders. Ehud Olmert was still prime minister at the time, but Bibi was poised to replace him. Obama was already president, and Netanyahu was starting to make preparations. Ron Dermer was also present at the meeting with Solow. After taking office and before his first meeting with Obama, Netanyahu summoned Solow urgently back to Israel. When the prime minister of Israel beckons, you come. Solow arrived in Israel on a one-day flash visit, but the meeting with Netanyahu was, as usual, delayed because of Netanyahu's habitual lateness. He has been known to keep people waiting for as long as one or two hours, totally unaware that others might have things to do. It happens with cabinet meetings and meetings with foreign leaders. A schedule, as far as Netanyahu is concerned, is less than a suggestion. Solow sat in the prime minister's office. It was evening and he had to catch a flight back to the United States at midnight. "Tell the prime minister that we'll meet in Washington," he told Netanyahu's secretary and made to leave, but just then Bibi arrived. The prime minister appeared helpless. "What does Obama want?" he asked Solow. "Why does he insist on a two-state solution? He knows it's not easy for us. I have political constraints." Solow replied with a question: "What do you want, Prime Minister? What is your policy on the Palestinian issue? How is it to be resolved?" Netanyahu started to detail his policy, spoke about demilitarizing Palestinian territories, about the Israeli presence in the Jordan Valley, and the fact that refugees would not be able to return to their land. The question was whether Netanyahu would mention the 1967 lines and/or Jerusalem—the most explosive issues he had with Obama. "I don't know what you should say, Bibi. I am not a politician," Solow said in the end. "You're a political leader and you've just shown me the way you want to see a solution to the Palestinian problem. From what I am hearing the president saying, I don't think there are such big discrepancies between the two of you. You talk of demilitarization of the future Palestinian state, on Israeli presence in the Jordan Valley; it seems to me the president is saying the same thing. Maybe your approaches don't exactly overlap, but the spirit is the same. Obama is smart enough to know that it's impossible to return refugees to Israel. You both agree that the territory will be split and that there will be some kind of Palestinian state, it doesn't matter at the moment how it'll be defined. [Let me tell you,] Bibi, the president is very sensitive to the security of Israel. It's absolutely genuine with him. In your place, I wouldn't worry too much about the language or the terminology. I would ask the president what his plans are. How does he see things at the end? You are both intelligent people; you both reached your positions at almost the same young age; don't patronize, take care when you speak, I am sure that if this is the spirit, you'll find a common language. You, too, have to detail your own vision and how it's going to end, as you see it."

Netanyahu listened carefully to Solow. Then he pulled out a sheet of paper and wrote on it with theatrical flourish: "Do not patronize." Solow laughed. So did Bibi. The problem was that Bibi didn't act on Solow's advice. In retrospect, Solow would say: "To this day, Bibi hasn't shared with Obama his vision and hasn't detailed how he sees the solution. He mostly evades and bargains; thus Obama's frustration. He believes that Bibi is no more than a manipulator, who never for a moment intended to do anything."

The first official meeting with Obama was bad, but it was nothing compared to what would come to pass further down the road. Two weeks later, Defense Minister Ehud Barak was sent to Washington for a "retrieval visit." Barak was the only card Bibi had to play. He was a Labor man, leader of Israel's dying "peace camp," and had good connections in Washington, especially among the Democrats. He tried to find a way to sweeten the bitter pill Obama had prescribed to Netanyahu. "Conduct has to be fair," Barak told reporters. "We can't expect that illogical things will happen." The media took this bait, but not President Obama. He was adamant, "like a Rottweiler with its jaws locked on something," according to a close associate of Netanyahu. "He refused to listen to any alternative." The American media leaked that the United States was reconsidering its veto policy in the UN Security Council, and that President Obama would not honor letters from President Bush to former Israeli prime minister Ariel Sharon, which at least gave the impression of U.S. recognition of Israeli settlement blocs in the West Bank.

Barak's visit turned into a fiasco. While there, he was also tasked with rooting out information about President Obama's historic speech in Cairo, which was planned for June 4. The prospect of this speech frightened Jerusalem at least as much as the demand for a freeze on building. Netanyahu's worst nightmares came true before his eyes. Barack Hussein Obama favored the Arab world over Israel. He was openly humiliating Netanyahu, avoiding an official visit to Israel, flying to Egypt and making a stopover in Saudi Arabia instead. It was as if Israel didn't exist. "He's declaring war on us," Netanyahu told his aides. "They are going to change their policies. They want to topple me. We're in for a hard time." The White House did not provide Netanyahu's office with an advance draft of the speech in Cairo, as had been customary for decades. All attempts to clarify and understand what Obama had planned had failed. Netanyahu was a nervous wreck. But in just a few months his revenge would be served cold when he delivered his famous Bar-Ilan University speech, in which he recognized the principle of a two-state solution. No draft of the speech was sent in advance to Washington. This time it was the Americans' turn to bite their nails and try to extract details from the media. Bibi's problem was that he was trying to play against Obama as an equal. He allowed himself to take risks, and acted like Israel was America's patron and not the other way around. It was exactly like Bibi's first conversation with Clinton, after which the president said to his aides, "He thinks he is the superpower and we are here to do whatever he requires."

51

The Bastards Changed the Rules

2009

As the time approached for President Bush to cede power to President Obama, Israeli prime minister Ehud Olmert's political advisor, Shalom Turgeman, instructed Sallai Meridor, Israel's ambassador in Washington, to create a memo detailing every agreement and understanding in place between the United States and Israel for when the baton passed from the Republicans to the Democrats. Meridor's report was the result of some extensive and thorough work. He compared the relations between Israel and the United States to couples figure skating. "Both sides know where the ice is thick and where it's thin, where they have to take care and where they can skate freely." Both sides also know that all around them, the entire Arab world is looking on. There must be no stumbling. In preparing his report, Turgeman was helped by Elliott Abrams, a Bush advisor and a leading supporter of Israel. Ambassador Meridor knew that the coming period would be critical and that nothing must be left to chance—issues such as nuclear opacity, settlement blocs, international backing when attempts were made to isolate Israel over the nuclear issue, the veto in the Security Council, and many other matters. Then Meridor left and Netanyahu dispatched Michael Oren to Washington.

The choice to appoint Oren could have been conceived in Washington as a positive gesture on Netanyahu's part. According to Elliott Abrams, "Bibi could have sent a political ambassador, but chose not to, and instead picked an academic, a historian with no political profile, a moderate man, who supported Sharon's withdrawal from Gaza. And what did Netanyahu get from the Americans in return? Only trouble. Netanyahu's conclusion was that for his next term in office, he would send his own man, Ron Dermer."

Ambassador Oren's reports from Washington to Jerusalem were worrying. In a press conference with Israeli foreign minister Avigdor Lieberman, Hillary Clinton was asked about the natural population growth in the settlements and rejected it out of hand. There was no natural population growth. The United States demanded an absolute freeze on building. Again, this act was conceived as a repudiation of the Bush letters. Oren called Rahm Emanuel, and asked for clarification. "You can't repudiate former understandings," said Oren. "You are erasing the differences between Gilo, which is a part of united Jerusalem and Itamar, an isolated and secluded settlement which is outside the concensus in Israel. It'll cause long-term damage." Emanuel responded emphatically, "Supposing there were such understandings, if we think they are not effective, it's our right to say so, isn't it? We can't be committed to everything that the previous administration thought." Oren understood the extent of the problem. Incidentally, this was the first and the last telephone call Emanuel received from Oren.

In the embassy this is accredited to the fact that the office had not yet received the appropriate instructions, but ever since that telephone call Oren almost never managed to reach the White House chief of staff or the NSA. The intimacy and hotline between the Israeli embassy and the White House chief of staff were things of the past. The man entrusted with relations with Oren was Dan Shapiro, head of the Middle East desk. That was Oren's glass ceiling. Condoleezza Rice, in contrast, had made a habit of meeting every Israeli government minister who arrived in Washington. She even hosted Shaul Mofaz in her private residence. Hillary Clinton put an end to this custom. Michael Oren barely met her. When Israel's energy minister arrived in Washington, he met only the assistant secretary of state for energy resources. In the embassy this apprenticeship was coined "the taming of the shrew." According to a senior embassy official, "It was obvious to us that they were changing the rules of the game. They want to get away from the Bush legacy with maximum speed. There was no longer what we called 'effective intimacy.' There are no more updates, no open discourse. We felt a freezing cold gust of wind. Israeli presence in the White House had almost disappeared. Michael Oren would call Emanuel, Jim Jones, and Stephen Hadley, but almost always the person who called him back was Dan Shapiro. We were treated like one more third-world country, and that's it."

In the White House, no one understood the Israeli complaints. The feeling there was the exact opposite. "All day long we were on the phone with the Israelis," says a senior American official. "Truly, on a daily basis, with Dermer or Uzi Arad, we responded to all their requests; and Jim Jones was also accessible, and every fortnight Barak would turn up here and Mitchell in Jerusalem. Our feeling was that the intimacy was at a maximum. It's no longer possible to conduct a more intense discourse as before. On all issues."

This disparity reflects the dissonance between the sides in mid-2009. Ambassador Oren felt isolated. In conversations at the time, he reported alienation, distance, and a sense that "the special relationship" with America was over. According to him, this was characteristic of the Obama administration, which suffered from an inability to maintain special relations with anyone. "He would even have clashed with a Meretz [left-wing] government," Oren said in private conversations.

One of the senior officials in Olmert's government said: "When Bush replaced Clinton, the principle was ABC: Anything But Clinton. Now, in the changeover between Bush and Obama, it was ABB, anything but Bush. We tend to forget that during the first year of the Bush administration, the president was hostile to and furious with the Ariel Sharon government after the prime minister delivered his famous Czechoslovakia speech, in which he compared U.S. coalition-building in the Arab world to British appeasement of the Nazis in the 1930s. Then, too, there was a feeling that Israel was being thrown to the wolves, except that then several things happened that strategically changed the situation. The first was the 9/11 terrorist attacks, followed by proof that Palestinian leader Yasser Arafat had been lying. In the Obama administration, such things didn't take place."

In the meantime, in Jerusalem, Netanyahu heard, and nourished his fears and anxieties. It was clear that Obama had taken out a contract on him. The term "throwing Israel under the bus" was born. The administration rode roughshod on the traditional principles of bilateral relations between the countries: "no surprises" and "no daylight." The Americans surprised Netanyahu with the demand to freeze settlements, and the disclosure of all their differences with Israel, contrary to their policy of not washing dirty laundry in public. It seemed occasionally that the administration enjoyed exaggerating its struggle with Netanyahu, that there was a clear intention of informing the world that the rules had changed. That Israel's automatic immunity was no longer in place, that there was a new boss in town. Netanyahu knew that the Arabs would be the first to notice these cracks. His fears increased and he continued to scrutinize Obama tirelessly over the Iran issue, and his concern grew. Likewise, Obama continued to scrutinize Bibi over the Palestinian issue, and his concern grew. The crisis was a foregone conclusion. The administration approached the various components of its relationship with Israel separately. On the Iran issue, which came under the auspices of strategist Uzi Arad, Israel was respected, but its opinion carried no real weight. On the Palestinian issue, which was dealt with by Molcho, Netanyahu was bullied. The security issue was the only area where the administration decided to continue business as usual, actually increasing aid and intelligence cooperation. Such was the essential policy formulated by Rahm Emanuel for Obama before he moved into the White House. The United States would remain committed to Israel's security, but not to its policies. The United States would continue to supply all Israel's security needs, but on all other issues, Israel would have to toe the line with administration demands if it wanted to maintain its status. The winking policy concerning the settlements was a thing of the past. Israel needed to understand that there would be repercussions to continued settler activity.

For his first visit to the Middle East as president of the United States, Obama chose Saudi Arabia and Egypt. On June 3, 2009, Obama arrived in Riyadh, bowed down to the Saudi king, and asked him for help with Netanyahu. Obama presented a plan where Israel would freeze building in order to resume negotiations and the Saudi king would agree to meet

Netanyahu and shake his hand. The Saudi king waved Obama away as one would a pesky fly. It was a stinging public humiliation for Obama, news of which reached Jerusalem via intelligence reports. The following day Obama was already delivering his speech in Cairo. Both Egypt and Saudi Arabia border on Israel from the south, but the president had decided to skip a visit to Israel. "He's here and not stopping over; we're out of the loop," Bibi told his people and prophesized, "Obama intends to isolate us and get close to the Arab world." In Jerusalem they watched the Cairo speech with burning eyes. "This is the behavior of a powerful president?" Netanyahu asked. "Look at him groveling to the Saudi king. At this rate, in a few weeks' time no one in this region will even be counting him."

In Jerusalem, the speech was received like an ice-cold shower and the media, encouraged by Netanyahu, focused on one message: "Israel was no longer America's spoiled little baby." A public-opinion poll in Israel showed that most of the population was in support of surrendering to Obama's demands for a freeze on settlement activity, but a worrying number of Israelis (53 percent) believed Obama's policies were bad for Israel. This poll happened before Netanyahu's aggressive brainwashing campaign against Obama, which destroyed the American president's image in Israel. A warning light flickered in Washington, but no one noticed it. Obama's people could smell Netanyahu's blood in the water, and they rejoiced. They believed they could bring him to his knees easily and everything would be all right. Later they would understand the extent of their strategic mistake. "The Israelis are going to hate Obama in the years to come," wrote the Israeli daily *Maariv* a day after the Cairo speech. George Mitchell, by contrast, was quoted in Israel saying, "The culture of winking is over. All these years the Israelis have been lying to us."

The Cairo speech also revealed the extent to which discrepancies between Israel and the United States are based mainly on commentary and misunderstanding. "Here, too, the Israelis missed a great opportunity," says an Obama associate. "Instead of seeing the advantages and the big things the president said, they are inventing all kinds of phobias. Here the most powerful man in the world, the president of America, arrives in the capital city of the Arab world. He informs them that America's historical alliance

with Israel is eternal, but if they want to drive a wedge, they can forget it.
He talks about anti-Semitism; he talks about the Holocaust, about Holocaust denial. He is actually telling them that Israel isn't going anywhere and
they better get used to it. Instead of this, they take things out of context,
claiming the president was saying that Israel was established only because
of the Holocaust." Obama's people were furious. They quote the speech to
back up their reaction. "Is only Bibi allowed to mention the Holocaust twelve
times in every speech? Is it a crime for the president to do it?" This business of mentioning the Holocaust as one of the causes for the establishment
of the state of Israel had significant segments of the Jewish community up in
arms against Obama. In the White House, commotion broke out. "I
spoke to all of Obama's Jewish advisors," recalled one of the president's associates. "No one understood the president's speech in the way it was interpreted by those with an agenda. But no one was listening to us. Later, Yossi
Kuperwasser (former chief of the Research Department in IDF Military Intelligence) said at an official event for American Jews that Obama didn't
understand that the Jewish people see Israel as their homeland, and are not
there because of the Holocaust. That nonsense was bandied around, instead
of looking at the main issue, that the president of the United States had
turned to the Arab world and said to forget about destroying Israel, that
Israel and America are together forever, period. What bothers the Israelis
is that he didn't talk more about them, and that he didn't stop for a visit in
Jerusalem. Two weeks before that he sat down with Bibi, didn't he?"

In January 2016, PBS aired a movie on relations between Obama and
Netanyahu on the program *Frontline*. Several of Obama's close associates
admitted there, for the first time, the fact that the decision not to visit
Israel after the Cairo speech was a big mistake. Not everyone agreed. A senior American official said that same month, "It wasn't necessary to go to
Jerusalem after Cairo. The president had met with Netanyahu shortly before. The real mistake was that President Obama didn't come in August 2010,
after they announced a freeze on building in the West Bank, in order to
launch negotiations and get the two sides into the room. This was a missed
opportunity."

The Cairo speech highlighted the fact that Washington and Jerusalem are essentially different, with totally contradictory world views. Their respective leaders, too, have opposing personalities. They were deaf to each other.

After the Cairo speech, people in Netanyahu's office started making more use of Obama's middle name, Hussein. In the Israeli media, quotes from Netanyahu associates started to appear describing Obama's Jewish advisors as self-hating. The reference was mainly to Rahm Emanuel and David Axelrod. These quotes infuriated Washington, and damaged the atmosphere even further. At that time, Alan Solow and Rahm Emanuel were organizing a meeting between the president and a group of Jewish leaders, in an attempt to lower the flames and kick-start the relationship. The meeting took place on June 13, 2009, and was attended by sixteen key Jewish leaders. Although lengthy and charged, the meeting was sincere and beneficial. The Jews claimed that violation of the "no daylight" principle was harmful. According to Malcolm Hoenlein, "The Arabs see these conflicts and understand that they need to continue applying pressure." Others felt the dirty laundry should be left at home. Obama replied that during the eight years of the Bush administration, there may not have been daylight, but there was also no progress. On the contrary, Israel's situation had deteriorated; there was a war in Lebanon, rockets fired from Gaza; it was more dangerous than ever. The Arabs needed to know that when it comes to Israel's security, there was no daylight and the United States is firm in our support. On the political side, there might be disagreements; sometimes there could be differences of opinion. It will increase the United States' validity as mediator and improve the chances for genuine dialogue. The president stressed there was no reason to panic about disagreements with Israel. Things needed to be talked out. America's commitment to Israel is deep, unconditional, and nothing would be gained by hiding disagreements.

That meeting ended on a friendly note, and the president succeeded in persuading the Jewish leaders of the authenticity of his commitment to Israel's security. However, someone told the media the exact opposite, and the headlines the next day focused on the president's desire to distance himself from Netanyahu and sharpen the discord between Israel and the

United States to continue with his journey of rapprochement with the Arab world. Moreover, the president was described as encouraging the "daylight" of dissent. It was not his intention. His words were taken out of context, something that would happen throughout the years to come. This event was typical of dozens of similar clashes throughout that year: a tragedy of errors and misunderstandings, some deliberate and planned, spiced with a large pinch of prejudice. In Netanyahu's world there was no hesitation about calling Obama a Muslim, black, lover of Arabs, and hater of Israel. In Obama's circle, it was the flip side of the same sentiment: Netanyahu is a liar, a charlatan, unwilling to take risks and unable to make decisions. He understands only force.

52

I'm Going to Speak, Too

2009

On June 5, Hillary Clinton fanned the flames. At a joint press conference with the Turkish foreign minister, she announced that there was no knowledge in the administration about a memorandum of understanding achieved with Israel over building in the West Bank settlements, and that she did not recognize informal or oral agreements. She said the administration was not prepared to accept any further building in the settlements. She was sharp-tongued, critical, and piercing. According to her, there are documents that prove the opposite; these documents state that no other document can contradict the commitment that Israel undertook in the Road Map. Netanyahu was furious. In the Washington embassy, things were going haywire. AIPAC was receiving operational commands, and the Hill was burning. Obama's friend Alan Solow was stressed out about it and called the White House. "The Israelis are saying that you tore up the Bush letters and threw them out of the window. Have you checked with Bush, Condi, or Hadley? Maybe there's a case?" The response Solow received was clear: Everything checked out. The administration was on firm ground. Years later, e-mail was leaked that had been sent by Hillary Clinton to Condoleezza Rice about the letters. Rice led Clinton to understand that everything was fine, that there was no American commitment of the kind the Israelis were claiming. All this did not console Netanyahu, who felt the administration closing in on him from all sides. There was no way out. At a government meeting the next day, he announced that he would soon deliver a speech in which he'd detailed his government's principles for achieving peace.

Three days later, the White House distributed a picture of Obama having a telephone conversation with Netanyahu. The president is sitting back in his chair, one foot on the desk. In one hand he is holding the telephone receiver, with the other he is signaling with his thumb and forefinger that this is exactly how he wants Netanyahu to act and this is exactly what he wants him to do and that he's waiting for the speech in hope that the Israeli prime minister does exactly what is expected of him. The picture drove Netanyahu crazy. He was busy drafting the speech, together with his advisors. One of them, a well-connected American, was surprised to see Netanyahu suddenly pull out the picture and show it to him. "It was taken like that on purpose," Netanyahu said. "It's meant to humiliate me, it's an attempt to hurt me, they are off the rails and will do anything to get me down on my knees and they need the whole world to know it. You tell me, why are they doing it? After all, they know I am preparing a speech, that I am about to recognize the two-state principle. So why are they doing this to me?"

Later, a senior White House official analyzed the picture and said that it wasn't meant to humiliate Bibi. The media team saw the picture and decided it was good. It was relaxed. Had it been shown to the White House staff, they might have said it wasn't a good idea because in the Middle East a foot on the desk could be viewed as an insult. But that didn't happen, and it was still completely innocent and utterly misconstrued. What the Israelis did with this picture was simply insane. In Jerusalem, they didn't want to hear. Netanyahu was already locked into victim complex. The picture was to the already failing relationship between Netanyahu and Obama like gasoline on a fire.

Netanyahu conducted a further round of talks with American Jewish community leaders, in an attempt to understand what Obama wanted; he was convinced that the president wanted him overthrown. According to an American official very close to Netanyahu, Obama was surrounded by people who couldn't stand Bibi, including those who had known him during the Clinton administration. They had told him that there was no chance of him succeeding in the Middle East, so long as Bibi was prime minister of Israel. They prayed for Tzipi Livni to win the elections and were disappointed on learning that she had won one more Knesset seat, but that Netanyahu had formed the government. They were sure that if they were to weaken Bibi a little more, he would fall and there would be a change of regime in Israel. They were sadly mistaken. They had not read the map, and had no understanding of what had happened to Israeli public opinion after the withdrawal from Gaza, when it became clear that any withdrawal from a territory turns it into a base for terror and rockets. They continued to whisper in Obama's ear that he should undermine Bibi just a little more, until he collapsed. They should have done the opposite. To calm his fears, to reinforce his self-confidence, to let him understand that America was not going to abandon him, but rather wanted to push forward his agenda. Instead, they pushed him a little more. It was a missed opportunity of historic proportions. Their hatred for Bibi drove them out of their minds.

At that time Bibi was told by a well-known American Jewish community leader who was close to the Obama administration as well as to Netanyahu, "Obama is African American. You mustn't forget that. African Americans have an automatic solidarity with oppressed minority populations. There is a tendency to see the Palestinians as some kind of deprived black people. The fact that the Palestinians are the underdog turns them into the favorite. It isn't about hatred for Israel, or personal loathing toward you. It's something much deeper. It's a way of thinking. A world view. They connect it to Israeli interests. They believe that peace between Israel and the Palestinians will provide Israel with a security asset that will reinforce Israel. Don't try to find inciters to turn Obama against Israel. It's the president who believes in pushing for a solution; he's not doing it because he has anything against Israel. On the contrary, he believes it's for Israel's good. The trouble is that if no one is listening on the Israeli side, that's when the distancing begins. And this is when we get to the settlements, which he

conceives as the major obstacle to the entire story. There are ways to deal
with this. If the president can be convinced of your good intentions, Bibi,
that's when there's a chance of you becoming friends. Talk to him, get him
to understand what it is you really want."

Netanyahu didn't buy this thesis, and preferred the conspiracy option
sold to him by his own people. In the meantime, he commissioned several
secret in-depth public-opinion polls and discovered that the public in Israel
supported him and not Obama. He was reassured. It meant that Obama
could not influence the Israeli voting public. After the bitter herbs fed him
by Clinton during his first term in office, Netanyahu was suffering from a
scary sense of déjà vu, so he was determined to prevent a second bout of it.
No American president was going to knock him to the ground. He would
do everything in his power to turn the president into a lame duck in the
eyes of the Israeli public. He would belittle him before anyone understood
what was happening, and rob him of his validity. If Bibi got his way, Obama
would be seen as a person who hated Israel. The sooner the Israelis understood this, the better and safer would things be for Bibi. And the plan
succeeded, especially because Obama himself helped it along. He played
perfectly into Netanyahu's hands. So, on the home front at least, Bibi was
less nervous. All that was left was to try to calm the rest of the world. This
he hoped to achieve with his Bar-Ilan speech.

On June 14, 2009, Netanyahu delivered the speech, which was warmly
received in Israel and the rest of the world. His small victory over Obama
was that an advance copy of the speech was not passed on to Washington
in advance. A few hours before the speech, Bibi spoke with Vice President
Biden, but told him only the most general of issues. In his speech, Netanyahu recognized for the first time the principle of a two-state solution
and agreed to the establishment of a demilitarized Palestinian state, under
certain circumstances. In return, the prime minister demanded Palestinian recognition that Israel is the nation-state of the Jewish people.
Netanyahu spent many long days composing the speech. He worked with
Ron Dermer, his minister for strategic affairs; Moshe Ya'alon; and a long
list of advisors. In Netanyahu's view, the speech symbolized an important,
historic waiver.

Bibi is a man of speeches. Speeches go down in history; they change it, form it. He sits with people, collects ideas, then sketches a general outline, receives a rough draft, and starts to work on it for hours, days, sometimes even weeks. He agonizes over every word, every comma, every exclamation mark and question mark. Had he not opted for a career in politics, Bibi could have been an excellent literary editor or even a brilliant journalist. He'll introduce changes, delete, add, and reedit until the last moment. The final changes are all done by hand, on the last printed draft. It's as if he believes every letter has the power to change the world. From Netanyahu's point of view, the Bar-Ilan speech was on the same level as a dangerous commando operation, with the mission of rescuing himself from the danger zone. It was the first time that a right-wing leader from Israel's nationalist camp had recognized the two-state solution. It came with reservations, with a stutter, with conditions, but Bibi managed to extract from his own mouth the term "Palestinian state." The speech, so he believed, would give him breathing room. He knew that his terms would not be met and the circumstances would eventually allow for a Palestinian state to become a reality in the near future. So long as things remained on paper, he could continue to sit in the prime minister's residence in peace.

International responses to the speech were positive, but not overwhelming. The White House was restrained and described the speech as "a step in the right direction." Netanyahu's people expected much more. They tried to get something more dramatic out of the Americans, but no one called it a historic speech or a definitive speech or speech of the decade. There was polite restraint. Because they hadn't received a draft of the speech in advance, they had no time to prepare. Someone in the White House had to work quickly, which meant less was more. Netanyahu, who had sweated over this speech for weeks, was disappointed.

53

Freeze and Stagnation

2009

Ten days after the speech, Netanyahu set out on a tour of Europe, in an attempt to capitalize on his new status as peacemaker. At a meeting with French president Nicolas Sarkozy, Netanyahu raised the novel idea of constructing high-rise buildings in the settlements, in the style of San Gimignano, a small-walled medieval hill town in the province of Siena, Tuscany, in north-central Italy, which was famous for the towers that rise above all the other houses. In this way, Netanyahu explained, there would be no need to expand the settlements, while providing solutions to the natural population growth of Jewish settlers. Completely in tune with Obama, Sarkozy was unimpressed: He told a disappointed Bibi that the demand was a total freeze on building in the settlements. This did not help reduce the enmity that continued to flow in from Washington. In private conversations, Vice President Biden said, "Netanyahu had better wake up and stop preaching to the U.S. that the settlements are essential to security." Similar sentiments were voiced by Clinton, Mitchell, Admiral Michael Mullen, and Rahm Emanuel. The message was that the rules had changed. Washington had changed. It's money time, and Bibi had better stop stalling—time for action, not words.

Bibi had delivered a speech, offered proposals, was prepared to make concessions, but Obama was immovable. "I don't want to drag it out and deceive anyone, but the merchandise the Americans want is not possible," Netanyahu said in a closed-door meeting with reporters in Paris. "Does anyone know what the Americans really want? Do they have a genuine objective, or do they just want to clash with me? Does anyone have an idea? Do they want an agreement? If they do, they should let us reach it in a logical manner." Netanyahu's body language expressed genuine distress, something new for him. His usual wheeling and dealing was no longer relevant. He'd been taken to the edge of the cliff and asked to jump off, and he hates to jump.

And the bad winds continued to blow. As a result of Israel's intention to build homes in the compound of the Shepherd Hotel in East Jerusalem, Ambassador Michael Oren was summoned to a meeting with Jim Steinberg in the State Department. Ostensibly, the meeting was supposed to deal with routine political issues, but as they were wrapping up, Steinberg and his people surprised Oren with an ultimatum. Israel was not to build in the hotel compound. The American warning was leaked by the prime minister's office to the Israeli press, and made headlines. Now it was America's turn to fume. Ambassador Oren tried to sweet-talk Washington, as did other senior Israeli officials. They tried in vain to convince the Americans of the importance of a presidential visit to Israel, and the response was always the same: There would be a visit when there was something to report, when significant progress had been made. They didn't understand what the Israelis—including experienced Foreign Office personnel—were trying to explain to them: that Israelis need first to be convinced that America hadn't abandoned Israel. It was critical to any progress. The *Jerusalem Post* published an opinion poll that showed only 4 percent of the Israeli public supported President Obama.

It took almost a year for the Obama administration to wise up. There had been no progress. On September 22, 2009, during the UN General Assembly, President Obama summoned Netanyahu and Mahmoud Abbas to a highly publicized, futile summit meeting. Apart from a few handshakes for the cameras nothing was achieved.

In late October, Secretary of State Clinton arrived in Jerusalem and, for the first time, she praised Netanyahu's proposals to "restrain building" in the settlements. She also called on Abbas to accept his proposals in order to open direct negotiation with Israel; the key change here was "restrain," not a "complete freeze." But there was a new problem. Abbas was no longer able to climb down from his high horse, stuck on the "not even one brick" sentiment. The fiasco spread from Jerusalem to Ramallah and Washington. Instead of a freeze, Washington got political stagnation.

But bad blood had already spread throughout the region. In November, Netanyahu set out to speak before the Jewish Federations of North America's General Assembly. His people begged for a meeting with the president in the White House, but were given no firm answer until the last moment. On the flight to the United States, Netanyahu still didn't know if he'd be meeting the president. It's the Americans' preferred method to squeeze out further concessions and more moderate declarations to tempt Abbas back to the negotiating table. Eventually, the meeting took place late in the evening, with no reporters, photographers, or statements after the fact. The atmosphere was sour. The Israeli embassy was an isolated stronghold in a hostile zone, with the staff investing enormous effort to crack the administration's walls. On a whiteboard in one of the embassy rooms, a list had been compiled of all new appointments made by the administration, their connections, and possible channels to their cooperation. If they were Jews, their synagogue was there; who sat next to them; who could influence them. The atmosphere was heavy.

On November 20, the Jerusalem municipality announced the building of nine hundred new homes in the Gilo neighborhood. The neighborhood is located in East Jerusalem. Immediately, the White House issued a sharp reprimand. Netanyahu wasn't bluffing; it was a blatantly bureaucratic move that required no political approval, but nonetheless the American response was harsh. "I feel sorry for Bibi," said one of his cabinet ministers that week. "Since taking up office, there's been hardly any building. Former prime ministers Sharon and Barak did much more building and the Americans didn't give them so much grief."

On November 25, Bibi gave in, announcing a ten-month freeze on build-ing in the West Bank, excluding Jerusalem. "It is not an easy step," he said, "but we are making it from national considerations and in the hope that we can work determinedly with our American partners to achieve peace." The freeze did not include public buildings such as schools, kindergartens, and synagogues. At the same time, U.S. emissary George Mitchell convened a press conference at his end in which he, too, announced the freeze. "The decision to freeze building will help to proceed toward a solution for the conflict," he said.

Mitchell was wrong. Obama was wrong. The Americans were wrong. In retrospect, not only did the freeze not move things forward, it actually held them back. A precious year was lost. The most important year, the first year of both leaders' respective terms in office. The sides arrived at an impasse, exhausted, loathing each other. The freeze killed relations be-tween Israel and the United States, and did nothing to improve relations between Israel and the Palestinians.

Even Obama's people have since admitted, in hindsight, that the freeze had been a fatal mistake. In Israel, an argument persists as to whom it was who initiated the freeze. Who gets credit for this piece of genius? Who was the one who harnessed all the energy of the Obama administration in order to halt building in parts of the West Bank for ten months, and in the pro-cess kill the chances of a real peace process? The answers are varied. One explanation is that it was George Mitchell, the presidential emissary, who headed the international committee that analyzed the circumstances behind the outbreak of the second intifada. The report sharply criticized Israeli policy in the West Bank; this resulted in the Road Map, which included a freeze on building. "Mitchell was obsessed with this issue," said a senior gov-ernment official in Olmert's administration. "He was the one who first used the term *freeze* and the position that a freeze would be needed regardless of including natural population growth. That there was to be no building to accommodate even natural expansion was a provocation. This happened in 2001, and many jokes were told about the idea in the Sharon administra-tion. Arik [Sharon] would ask what would happen to a child born in Ma'ale

Edumin, during the freeze. Does he get sent to live with his grandmother in Haifa? It was Mitchell who talked about a full freeze with Obama, including natural population growth."

The Americans had been warned about the freeze. Obama's first two and a half months in office had overlapped with the Olmert administration. Olmert had met Hillary Clinton, and passed on messages to Obama. Israel's message had been unequivocal: Don't try to reinvent the wheel. There is already a process in place and has to be continued. The Annapolis route is a good platform. Don't try to force things on Bibi that he can't do, don't appoint a special emissary. Opt to continue negotiations from the point at which they stopped. The Palestinians themselves didn't raise the matter of a freeze, and were persuaded in Annapolis that it would only cause harm.

But the Americans did try to reinvent the wheel. For a start, they decided to tame Netanyahu and put him through a harsh education, the result of which was that they tamed themselves, too. The freeze came when both sides were completely disconnected. George Mitchell set up togetherness talks, which only placed greater distance still between Netanyahu and Abbas. "It was an unforgivable strategic mistake," said a veteran Israeli official. "If they had invested all that energy in renewing the Annapolis process, the result could have been completely different. Annapolis was an orderly process, not only with Olmert and Abbas, but also with Tzipi Livni and Abu Alaa. A kind of continuity could have happened, but they wanted to start over, because they didn't want to move on with anything from the previous administration. They allowed Abbas to build exaggerated expectations, and nothing was achieved. The beginning of the end was when Obama went down on his knee before the king of Saudi Arabia. President Bush's first speech on the Middle East ended with a quote from the Bible, whereas Obama's first speech in Cairo ended with a quote from the Koran. It took Bush a year and a half before he paid serious attention to the Middle East. First, he had to study it and give it thought. Obama took office and immediately pulled out all the stops. He wasted an opportunity when Netanyahu was still weak. Defense Minister Barak was willing to approve generous gestures in the field, and Bibi, seeking American recognition, was prepared to take risks. They demanded of him the one thing that was difficult for him to give, and wasted all their energy on it."

This is not Netanyahu's people talking, but a senior official in Olmert's government who was deeply involved in the peace process and is no fan of Netanyahu. He felt that it wasn't accurate to say the Obama administration deviated from the commitments of the Bush administration vis-à-vis Israel. That includes the Bush letters, which were accepted by a large majority both in the House and the Senate. Obama did much to advance the mutual cooperation and security between the two countries, and equipped Israel with things it had never been given before. He renewed and upgraded the Memorandum of Understanding on U.S. Military Assistance. He backed Israel in every war against terror. The Obama administration's silence during Operations Pillar of Defense and Protective Edge was more noticeable than the backing given by the Bush administration for Operation Cast Lead, since at that time the relations were intimate and the Americans were involved. This time it couldn't be taken for granted, but still it was there. It happened as John Kerry was exerting all his energies and strength in the Middle East and Israel was pulling him around by the nose, exhausting him for no reason. It happened because the first stage on the Road Map required an end to terror attacks, which happened, and the second stage was the establishment of a Palestinian state within temporary borders. Israel was recruiting the whole world against a Palestinian state within temporary borders, and the United States vetoed it. Why?

An Israeli official well versed in the peace process and intergovernmental relations said, "At the beginning of his mission, Mitchell checked with Netanyahu to see if he was prepared to continue with the Annapolis process. Netanyahu's response was negative. Let's not forget that in the meantime, Operation Cast Lead had begun and it was impossible to simply return to Annapolis. So Mitchell went and looked at the Road Map and repeated the call for a freeze. It was the default. The mistake," said the official, "was that he accepted Bibi's refusal and hadn't tried to appeal it. You are America. Be creative. Break down Annapolis to its various components. Start with borders and security, for example. If they'd gone full force for Annapolis, they would have broken through, and the difference is that then they would have been in the midst of negotiations, and not with mutual alienation and hostility, as was the case after the announcement of a freeze." The official added, "Whatever doesn't happen during the first year, won't happen. By the time they came to the freeze, a year had already passed, and they were approaching the midterm elections. Congress sent Nancy Pelosi to the president to make it clear that if he wants health-care reform, he needed to get off Bibi's back about extending the freeze, and that's how it all died peacefully."

The Israeli side was also wrong. "Bibi is sure he's Captain America," said an Israeli expert on Obama/Netanyahu relations. "But the problem is, Bibi's America is fighting a rearguard offensive. Ron Dermer is his contractor for American affairs, and it's more of the same." Dermer is a second-rate political activist from Miami Beach who travels between Miami, New York, and Los Angeles. He knows the Hispanics? He knows the twenty states where whites are becoming a minority? He knows the minorities' coalition? From the beginning Bibi and his people didn't read Obama correctly. Bill and Hillary Clinton were all they knew about Democrats. Maybe John Kerry, too. But Obama is nothing like them. They had no idea who they were facing. They didn't understand the sources of Obama's strengths: the new America, colorful, sparkling; the America in which an average donation to an election campaign is $100, via the Internet. They didn't understand that Obama was taking off the cowboy hat, that destructive power was being replaced by soft power. That whatever it cost, he would get America out of Afghanistan and Iraq and would try to gradually disconnect from the Middle East, in favor of stronger relations with Asia and the Pacific. That he will try to establish an international coalition against global threats. Obama wanted to contain China while simultaneously coping with it. He wanted to achieve energy independence, and declared war on proliferation of weapons of mass destruction. Obama's primary objective was to have a clean break from the Bush legacy, and then to reshape and rebalance the United States, its priorities and its status in the world. The notion of rebalancing is crucial to understanding Obama.

Netanyahu should have been prepared for all this. Obama had a strategy. But Bibi had given this no thought at all. He was used to the Clintons with their clever politics, conducting themselves politically and going with the flow with no specific strategic outlook. As the first black president, Obama saw himself as a man who had to get things done. He didn't set out on any grand war, but did not hesitate to kill terrorists, and turned the use of drones in targeted killings into something commonplace and routine. In Obama's America, Israel also had to change. No longer was it a small country surrounded by enemies, having to hold on to territories in order to defend itself. It was a regional superpower whose existence and strength left no room for doubt. Obama saw Israel as more of a Goliath than a David. He feared a Jewish force that abused its power. He was not pro-Israel. "Netanyahu walked into Obama's administration without knowing that it was a trap," says the official.

Others are convinced that Rahm Emanuel is responsible. "As a former Israeli," says a former senior official in Netanyahu's office, "Emanuel was responsible for understanding how best to deal with Netanyahu, and it was he who dripped poison in Obama's ear. One of the things Emanuel repeated was that it would be impossible to make progress until Israel completed building in the settlements. Emanuel was thoroughly familiar with Israel's 'blind eye' culture. Netanyahu had already fooled him once during the Clinton administration, when he signed the Wye agreement and immediately pulled out of it. Since then, Emanuel has brought a lot of bad blood. Incidentally, during the first term, too, Netanyahu tried to bypass Clinton via Congress and failed."

"Netanyahu and Obama," says an Israeli military official of the highest level, "had one thing in common. Each man had a special advisor who supposedly understood the other side. Bibi's advisor for American affairs was a former American named Ron Dermer. Obama's advisor on Israeli affairs was Rahm Emanuel. What Dermer did here, Emanuel did there. Each one incited his boss against the other's boss. Obama developed a problematic view of the Palestinians as victim. It was difficult from the onset, and advisors make a difference. The only one who tried to redress the situation was Dan Shapiro, but it was too little. Dennis Ross, too, had the ability to cool down and release tensions. Ross has an amazing ability to organize the president's thoughts, to explain to him what Netanyahu means when he speaks of painful concessions. But the tone, at least at first, was set by Dermer and Emanuel. During the first meeting between the president and the prime minister, in a broad forum, Dermer interrupted Obama in midspeech, saying, 'Mr. President, I beg to differ.' This kind of thing is not done in the Oval Office. But Dermer was not there to soften blows or round corners; he had come with an agenda. He and Emanuel should have ignored the entrenchments and insults, ignored the misunderstandings and arm wrestling, and tried to explain to each other the constraints and fears of each side. It didn't happen, and that's a pity."

While Mitchell and Emanuel are the immediate suspects, their role was probably only marginal. "There was an argument inside the administration about the freeze," recalls one of the key players in the Obama administration during those years. "Although Mitchell had already written about the freeze back in 2001, it wasn't his idea. We sought something that would serve as a lever for negotiations and make it clear that the rules had changed. At some point we understood that it had to be connected to the settlements." The idea had come from the president; Mitchell agreed, Rahm Emanuel was excited, and so was Hillary Clinton. It was decided that Obama would inform Netanyahu personally of this demand at a private meeting, so it wouldn't fizzle out among clerks, allowing Netanyahu to wriggle out. It's different when the president is sitting opposite him, looking him in the eye, and working the demand. The freeze was Barack Obama's idea. The decision was made in the Oval Office. The aides and advisors simply carried out his policy. Circumstantial proof of this can be seen: during the pre-freeze period, when an Israeli delegation headed by Minister Dan Meridor, together with Molcho and Uzi Arad, set out for talks with the Mitchell and his team in London. Those were troubled times, and American pressure was heavy with regard to the building freeze. Meridor had been sent by Netanyahu in an attempt to reach a compromise. The meeting took place at the residence of the American ambassador in London. Meridor brought with him several proposals for compromise, including a suggestion to exclude Jerusalem and to allow for natural population growth equal to the rest of Israel, rather than the higher growth rate among the settler population in the West Bank. He proposed excluding the consensual settlement blocs together with the Jewish neighborhoods in Jerusalem. Every time Meridor and his team raised one of these proposals, Mitchell and the American team asked for a break and went up to the second floor to call Washington. In Israel the thinking was that the calls were to the president himself, or to one of his senior advisors. Every compromise offered by Israel was rejected by Washington. "No good," Mitchell came back after each telephone call, letting the Israelis understand that orders came from above, from the Oval Office. It was Obama, and no one else, who was unbending.

At a certain point the Americans agreed to accept a freeze on building on the other side of the security fence, except that this proposal contained an obvious flaw. The freeze did not have a time limit; it'll have to be a permanent policy of yours, said the Americans. And Israel refused to agree to this. It would be better to freeze everything for a predetermined period of time.

54

A Knife in the Back of Ambiguity

2009–2010

Only one subject troubled Netanyahu more than a freeze on building in the territories, and that was the issue of nuclear strategy. America's backing for Israel's nuclear ambiguity, which was based on a series of understandings, most of them verbal, was achieved over time between the two sides, and without which Israel could have found itself under heavy international pressure, isolation, and possibly even sanctions. From the first moment, Netanyahu feared that Obama, who had a clear agenda of universal disarmament of weapons of mass destruction, would betray Israel on this critical issue, too. The positive messages brought by Arad from his preliminary visit to Washington did not reassure Netanyahu.

In the course of that visit, in May 2009, Obama dropped a suspiciously hot potato on Netanyahu's table, when, with no prior warning, he invited Israel to a special conference led by him to discuss nuclear security. "We have invited only forty countries, including Israel," the American contingent told the concerned Israelis. "The president sees this as one of his flagship issues. This is an extremely important summit meeting." The Israelis were hard put to say anything good about this flagship issue. As far as Israel is concerned, a nuclear summit is a recipe for disaster. "Don't worry," they were reassured, "the agenda is neutral, nothing you need to worry about: how to prevent terror organizations from taking control of nuclear weapons, how to secure nuclear substances, etc. It's about security, that's all. Israel has a lot to contribute, based on its broad knowledge on the subject. The president has great faith in controlling WMDs."

For Netanyahu, this was far from reassuring. He feared Obama's hidden intentions. Uzi Arad tried to assure him. "It's a very comfortable agenda for us," he told Bibi. "They are guaranteeing that there won't be anything problematic." Arad persuaded Netanyahu to participate, so the prime minister informed Obama that he would attend in person at the head of the Israel delegation to the conference, which was scheduled for March 2010. Shortly thereafter, Israel appointed—as did the other participating countries—a special ambassador to the conference, and preparations commenced. But that was when problems began. Word reached Netanyahu that a large Arab country was also invited to the conference, a country that could make trouble. Again, Netanyahu feared an ambush. Arad was less concerned and called Gary Samore. "You've got nothing to worry about," the Americans reassured him once again. "The gavel's in Obama's hands, it's his conference; he's controlling the timetable and the agenda and the speakers and everything else. Nothing's going to happen that we don't want to happen." Netanyahu relaxed, ostensibly. But then, only a few days before the conference, the new military secretary, General Yohanan Locker, arrived with fresh intelligence that the Arab delegate planned to use the conference to protest the fact that Israel had not signed the Non-Proliferation Treaty. They were going to demand that Israel sign. Bibi was alarmed. Arad was annoyed. The intelligence provided by the military secretary was—in his opinion—insignificant. After all, the Americans had promised unequivocally that there would be no trouble. Arad felt that the newly appointed military secretary was trying to impress Netanyahu, and tried in vain to diminish the damage. Netanyahu's phobias had been just below the surface, but now, at the very last moment, he had uncovered a conspiracy. "The president is preparing an ambush," said Bibi, and canceled his trip. Arad fumed. He'd spent enough years with Netanyahu to know how easy it was to scare him. Arad was one of those who scared him, too, occasionally.

But in this case, it wasn't necessary. The Americans had received a personal promise from Netanyahu and would be furious. At the last moment, Netanyahu was persuaded to send Dan Meridor, who was responsible for intelligence matters. Meridor headed the Israeli delegation, which also included Brigadier General Shaul Chorev, director-general of the Israel Atomic Energy Commission; and Professor Uzi Arad.

There was another reason for Netanyahu's absence from Obama's conference. The conference was scheduled to take place only a few weeks after the visit of Vice President Biden in Jerusalem and the ensuing fiasco. Netanyahu was not popular in Washington at the time, and he feared that his appearance at the nuclear conference would make him a sitting duck. But he needn't have worried. There was no ambush; Obama ruled the conference with an iron fist and allowed no one to cross the line. Israel got through it OK with one exception: Netanyahu was enraged by Meridor's moderate speech. He summoned Uzi Arad to the sterile room at the Israeli embassy in Washington and gave him a strong reprimand over the phone. Netanyahu had expected a far more assertive Israeli message and was in a fighting mood, for no real reason. He assumed that the man responsible for Meridor's appeasing speech was Brigadier General Chorev, whose job had been to brief him in advance. In that same telephone conversation, Netanyahu asked Arad if there was a way to fire Chorev and to replace him with Gideon Frank, his predecessor. Arad, appalled, asked Netanyahu to calm down.

But the Americans were the ones who were unable to calm down. Netanyahu's unexplained absence from a conference so important to the president infuriated them. Furthermore, Netanyahu had missed a golden opportunity to meet the presidents of China and Russia, the German chancellor, the president of France, the British prime minister, and many others. Forty of the most important world leaders had come together at that conference, and only the prime minister of Israel remained at home, trembling with fear. According to Arad, it had been a unique opportunity to meet and engage in party talks with everyone, on a single platform. Netanyahu had been eager to meet some of them as early as possible. He had virtually begged for a meeting with the Chinese president, but the Chinese gave him the runaround until finally accepting him in 2014.

The same could have been achieved four years earlier if he hadn't succumbed to his fears.

But the nuclear problems weren't solved with President Obama's conference. They had only just begun. Two months later, the Non-Proliferation Treaty Review conference was scheduled to convene in New York. The conference convenes every five years and Israel takes no official part in it. Every time, the Arab states, especially Egypt, attempt to pass anti-Israel rulings, and every time the United States and Israel are able to defeat these rulings by means of various alliances, coalitions, and complex deals. This time, too, there was advance intelligence that Egypt was planning to push through a resolution to rid the Middle East of nuclear arms by 2012. The United States explicitly promised Israel that such a proposal would not be supported. The promise was in writing, and Israel was relatively calm. Except Netanyahu wasn't, until that is, Arad read a statement on the nuclear issue which called for demilitarizing the world, including the United States. Netanyahu's expression was grim. "I told you so," he told Arad. "Prime Minister," replied Arad, "what I just read was indeed said by a president, but it was President Bush Sr. and he said it in '91." Bibi was not reassured.

This time, however, Netanyahu's fears were realized in full. The Arab states proposed appointing a special emissary to promote the establishment of a zone devoid of nuclear armaments in the Middle East, and wanted to convene a special conference to this end. The Americans were supposed to block this initiative, but a series of failures, including the intervention of that year's conference chairperson (who was from Ireland), created a situation in which the conference actually voted to approve the appointment of an intermediary and a committee for disarming the Middle East. Netanyahu was shocked to the core, and interpreted what had happened as a move on Obama's part against Israel. "As far as he was concerned," recalls an Israeli security official of the highest rank, "Obama had hurt Israel's most important life-insurance policy. Israel had an express promise from America, a promise that wasn't fulfilled at the conference. Bibi was absolutely stunned."

Later the Americans admitted that there had been a mistake and promised to provide Israel with a replacement life-insurance policy, with "plenty of safety latches." Again, Uzi Arad was entrusted with the task and shuttled between the White House and Jerusalem, producing an additional series of letters containing express American commitments to support Israel's nuclear ambiguity, not to agree to Israel being singled out on the nuclear issue, to demand that Pakistan be included in the proposed "demilitarization conference," and to demand that all decisions have to be made by consensus, as well as other commitments that constitute a historic upgrade of strategic understandings between the two countries.

The bottom line is that failure in the 2010 Non-Proliferation Treaty conference did Israel more good than harm. The resolutions that passed at that conference dissolved over the years; nothing came of them. Understandings between Israel and the United States were upgraded, and additional letters and documents were written that anchored everything that had been achieved and even added to it. The pinnacle was an official letter published by national security advisor Jim Jones on the White House Web site. The letter was supposed to have been handed to Netanyahu in person during a visit which, although scheduled to take place in Washington, was postponed at the last moment because of the Turkish-flotilla *Mavi Marmara* affair. Netanyahu was unable to contain himself and briefed Israeli reporters that a historic breakthrough had been achieved in strategic negotiations between Israel and the United States. The postponed visit took place shortly afterward on July 6, 2010, the letter was released, and the crisis passed. What didn't pass was the accumulated bad blood between the two bureaus and, especially, between the two leaders. In this incarnation, Benjamin Netanyahu and Barack Obama were most unlikely to become fond of, or have any faith in, each another.

55

Bibi Didn't Know

2010

Vice President Joe Biden and Benjamin Netanyahu are old friends. In March 2010, frustrated by the lack of progress on the political front, President Obama decided to activate Biden, ostensibly his secret weapon vis-à-vis Netanyahu. The Palestinians had no faith in Israel. Building continued apace in East Jerusalem, and the Palestinians refused to renew negotiations. Biden's job was to give Netanyahu an additional prod to provide the necessary gesture (halt building in Jerusalem, or recognize the 1967 armistice lines as a starting point for negotiations). That would be enough to renew the talks. Biden's visit was also meant to be compensation for Obama's having skipped Israel the previous year. The vice president was coming to visit. It was time to turn the page, and get back to the negotiating table.

Instead of a new page, there was war. In the middle of Biden's visit to the Holocaust memorial museum, Yad Vashem, an announcement was issued by the Interior Ministry's District Committee for Planning and Construction, confirming that plans had been submitted for the building of 1,600 homes in the East Jerusalem Jewish neighborhood of Ramat Shlomo. The freeze did not include Jerusalem, but this announcement, at the height of

Biden's visit, was tantamount to a ringing slap in the face. It was a targeted killing of all efforts to renew negotiations, and a painful humiliation for the vice president of the United States. The Americans believed that it was planned and commissioned in a calculated way.

The Americans could not believe this was happening to them. One-third of the freeze period was already over, and now things were at an impasse. Netanyahu had thumbed his nose at them and humiliated them in public. From Yad Vashem, Biden was scheduled to continue to a state dinner in his honor at Prime Minister Netanyahu's residence. He returned to the hotel to "freshen up," but the following day he told Palestinian Authority leader Mahmoud Abbas that he'd been deliberately late for the dinner. Biden sat in his hotel suite and talked to Obama and several other senior staff members. One of the possibilities he considered was to leave Jerusalem and return to the United States immediately, or to leave for Ramallah and skip the dinner at Netanyahu's. The Americans were incandescent. If Israel's Military Intelligence had intercepted those telephone conversations, it is doubtful if anyone there would have believed they were talking about Israel. It sounded more like a discussion on North Korea.

In the end, Biden turned up at the dinner an ostentatious hour and a half late. Despite the genuine effort made by the vice president to complete the visit in Jerusalem in a civilized manner, America's fury was palpable, and censorious. Ambassador Michael Oren tried to save the situation by creating a kind of optimism: Oren asked Netanyahu to go to the airport to see off the vice president with a handshake, but Bibi didn't arrive. Netanyahu's name was mentioned repeatedly in the White House that day, each time accompanied by a different curse word. The crisis caught President Obama in the White House, with Tom Donilon and several of his closest staff members. Hillary Clinton was out of town. Dan Shapiro and Dennis Ross were with Biden in Jerusalem. Everybody who'd been exposed to the events of that day recalls that Barack Obama, usually a cool and calculated man, had never been so furious. Even in the harshest moments of his campaign, the president's people had never seen him like this. Senior administration officials competed with each other over who could hurl more verbal filth at Netanyahu, his infidelity, his arrogance, and his sheer chutzpah.

In the meantime, in Jerusalem, Dennis Ross, Dan Shapiro, and Ambassador Oren joined forces in an attempt to cool things down. Ross and Shapiro didn't accompany Biden to Ramallah, instead spending the day in Jerusalem together with Ron Dermer and Michael Oren to arrive at a solution. The Americans were divided over whether Netanyahu knew about the announcement on the building in Ramat Shlomo. Had there been a deliberate intention to humiliate Joe Biden? Dan Shapiro was in the minority among the Americans in his belief that Netanyahu had been unaware of the announcement. Shapiro was familiar with the chaos that reigns in Israeli government and understood that it was entirely possible they had fallen upon a comedy of errors. But he was unable to convince his colleagues in the White House, or any of Biden's people. In the meantime, however, he and Ross had come up with a solution of kinds, according to which Israel would refrain from building in Ramat Shlomo for two years and avoid promoting the project they had announced; as well as several other promises. For his part, Biden was supposed to say a few words on the subject at a speech he was scheduled to deliver at Tel Aviv University the following morning. It was all agreed in advance. Ross, Shapiro, Oren, and Dermer were sure the crisis was behind them. The dispute was settled. They accompanied the vice president to the airport, watched him board Air Force One, and sighed in relief at another bridge crossed. But they were so wrong.

The thinking was entirely different in Washington. There, the president and his people were angry. That night, Ross, Shapiro, and Oren took off for the United States on a commercial flight (Biden had flown to a different destination). While the three were still in the air, the White House's revenge was planned, to be carried out by Hillary Clinton. There was no need to convince her. She had known Netanyahu long before they did.

Secretary of State Clinton called Netanyahu to berate him about settlement building. Apparently, there had never been such a conversation between so senior a representative of the U.S. administration and an Israeli prime minister. The State Department took the trouble of leaking the contents of the conversation, which lasted over half an hour, with Clinton doing most of the talking. Clinton said that the Israeli announcement about the building in Jerusalem is "sabotging the bilateral relations with the US in the deepest manner possible." She stated that the administration is convinced the Israeli act was done and planned on purpose. "It is a shame," she said, "and it was a public slap in the face of VP Biden." Then, she dictated to the PM a detailed list of demands for immediate answer "within 24 hours." This came from the highest level in the White House, said the secretary. The list was long and most of the American demands were humiliating and impossible to implement, "I will wait for your answer," said Clinton. "If you will not be able to comply, it might have unprecedented consequences on the bilateral relations of the kind never seen before." Again, Netanyahu was in shock. He tried to explain to Clinton that the District Committee was not under his jurisdiction, that he was surprised by the announcement, that there had been no intention to embarrass the vice president. Netanyahu was telling the truth, but Clinton was in no state to listen, so it made no difference. "What do you mean by 'unprecedented repercussions'?" Netanyahu tried to ask, but Clinton only repeated, "I am telling you again, Bibi, these instructions come from the highest level. . . ."

Ross and Shapiro knew nothing of the conversation and only after landing in Washington did they become aware of the commotion. They realized that it had all been cooked up in the White House, between the president and Clinton. The conversation became a definitive watershed in the relationship between Jerusalem and Washington. But in the end, the fury subsided and there remained only a murky puddle of frustration and some more bad blood.

But something more remained on the Israeli side. "Bibi managed to manipulate Obama," said a senior administration official. "He entered the lion's den and came out in one piece. He began to understand that Obama's bark is much worse than his bite, that there is no reason to fear him, and that it's easy to beat him by stalling and using political tactics. Bibi began to understand that he could get himself out of any trap Obama laid for him, and he stopped fearing him." Another American senior administration official adds, "We have to admit that Bibi taught Obama a lesson. At first he was in shock, but he quickly recovered, studied the material, learned his weak points by heart, and exhausted him. On the building freeze, too, and the reprimand, Bibi triumphed. The freeze we got in the end wasn't the freeze we'd demanded, it was full of holes, the Palestinians were aware of this and therefore didn't go with us, and in the end it all died. And the worst thing is that Bibi's conclusion from all this was that he could beat Obama in the long run, by wasting time and exhausting everyone until Obama gave up, and that's exactly what happened."

Yet a senior Israeli government official, with many years' experience in handling relations with the U.S. administration, pointed out: "Obama failed to extract a fee from Netanyahu and that was his biggest mistake. With Bibi, you need to come with a big stick and cause him to believe that you'll use it. The moment Obama choked over the freeze, and after the reprimand from Clinton, Bibi knew it would be all right. It's been so ever since."

Netanyahu's victory in the Palestinian arena was a pyrrhic victory, says a senior member of the Obama administration, "because Obama, too, learned a few things, that it's impossible to work with Netanyahu in a real and close way, and that there will never be any trust between them. He decided that if Bibi didn't meet him halfway on issues that were important to him, he would distance himself from issues that are important to Bibi, such as the Iran nuclear program."

In the meantime, Israel's Washington embassy continued to broadcast distress signals. The Obama administration had no intention of returning to the intimate relations with the Israeli embassy of yesteryear. On the contrary, the luckless Israeli ambassador, Michael Oren, who landed in Washington at five in the morning immediately after the reprimand, was promptly summoned that afternoon to the State Department for an official demarche. Oren was in a fighting mood. "I don't intend to keep quiet," he told his people. "I'll give as good as I get." He arrived for the meeting with his chief of staff, Lior Weintraub. Clinton's deputy, Jim Steinberg, made Oren stand while he reread the text of the reprimand to him word for word. "Write it down," he told Weintraub, who didn't manage to write it all and asked for the printed document but was refused. "I'm the first ambassador," Oren responded, "that the Obama administration has summoned for a reprimand, right? I need to understand, as soon as Ahmadinejad visited Damascus and announced that he'd throw Israel into the sea, you summoned the Syrian ambassador for a reprimand? No. You decided to send your ambassador back to Damascus. You are making a mountain out of a molehill. There is no one in Jerusalem who doesn't believe that this crisis is a fabrication. Do you really believe that Netanyahu knew about the Dictrict Committee's announcement? Every time anyone builds anything in America, is Obama informed? You are upgrading this crisis on purpose, you use every mistake we make in order to exert pressure on us, to wring us dry, in order to extend the freeze and impose it on Jerusalem, too."

In Washington the next day, the situation began to improve. The Americans, too, were beginning to understand that they'd exaggerated. Administration officials promised Ambassador Oren they would lower the volume on the Sunday political programs. Oren promised Jerusalem that tranquility was on the way. Then it was Sunday, and with it came David Axelrod, senior advisor to the president, who once again launched a frontal attack on the Israeli government. In Jerusalem, Netanyahu asked what happened to the promised calm. On the phone to Washington, he asked Oren the same question. Oren managed to connect to Rahm Emanuel and accused him of planning the whole thing to increase pressure on Israel. The whole system was alarmed. And indeed, the Israeli embassy looked more like a place in wartime. The Jewish community saw the incident as a multivictim terror attack. In the end, that's what it was.

For the president, the Jerusalem visit was an important event. Obama's loss of faith in Netanyahu had been a process that included several highs. The Biden visit was one of the more important highs in this process. In Obama's view, Netanyahu could not be taken seriously, nothing could be achieved with him, and he was incapable of conducting himself with integrity, or keeping promises. The situation was not yet irreversible, although the direction was clear. The responsibility for trying to exploit the Biden crisis as an additional lever for placing pressure on Israel lay on the shoulders of Obama's chief of staff, Rahm Emanuel, whose approach was that every opportunity should be used to place pressure on Netanyahu. However, the Americans missed this opportunity. According to an Israeli official, they didn't know how to take things to their conclusion, and before long Jerusalem understood that their threats were idle.

Still, the suffering continued in the Washington embassy. Time after time the "no surprises" principle was violated by the Americans in what seemed like revenge for Israel's surprise building announcement. When it was decided to return the American ambassador to Damascus, Dan Shapiro called Michael Oren less than an hour before the decision was made public. When rumors spread that the administration was conducting indirect contact with Hamas via conflict resolution specialist Rob Malley, no one bothered to reassure the Israeli embassy. It actually appeared that the Americans were enjoying the situation. Israel knew that Malley was updating White House officials on his talks with Hamas, but there was no one to complain to. The same thing happened when Israel learned of Bill Barnes's talks with the Muslim Brotherhood in Egypt. When asked directly, Barnes replied disingenuously, "If someone was with the Muslim Brotherhood and left, does that mean that we are in contact with them?" Such was Israel's strategic dialogue with the United States at that time. Efforts to upgrade communication to the respective foreign ministers, Avigdor Lieberman and Hillary Clinton, were rejected by the Americans. The most they would agree to was Deputy Foreign Minister Danny Ayalon opposite Bill Barnes. The talks were superficial and sterile. A cold wind blew between Washington and Jerusalem, but the real storm was still to come.

56

Human Bridge

2009–2012

Barack Obama received over 70 percent of America's Jewish vote, which is traditionally given to the Democrats. But the more enlightened leaders of the larger Jewish organizations in the United States knew that Obama's arrival in the White House was not going to be smooth vis-à-vis strategic U.S.-Israel relations. They knew Obama represented a new America, one that wasn't fully recognized in Israel. They knew that Jews of the liberal persuasion surrounded him, whereas the right governed in Israel. They anticipated a clash and tried to soften the blow. And there was another, more sensitive issue. Obama was the first black president of the United States. According to a veteran American Jewish leader and Obama supporter, "Obama is African American and, as such, his personality automatically gravitates toward solidarity with the Palestinians, who, too, are seen as people of color. It's inherent in Obama, whether he admits it or not. We knew this and tried to build a bridge. By the way, this is not unique to Obama. We saw it with Colin Powell and Condoleezza Rice; we saw it with Susan Rice and of course we see it with Obama. It's not a case of anti-Israel. Not at all. But it's a natural pull toward the weak and the disenfranchised. When the president mentions that little boy in Ramallah, he talks from the heart. He feels genuine empathy. It isn't merely liberal bullshit as Bibi's people thought."

Abraham Foxman identified the urgent need to create trust between both leaders. The veteran ADL president, possibly the most accepted and well-connected Jewish leader between both leaderships in both capital cities for decades, decided to take the initiative. He approached Elie Wiesel, Nobel Peace Prize laureate and the world's most famous Holocaust survivor, and asked him to try to form a close personal relationship with the president and help connect him informally to Netanyahu. He knew that Wiesel was close to Netanyahu, and believed that both Obama and Netanyahu might enjoy this route. Wiesel's reply was positive, in principle. When he learned that Obama was scheduled to make a tour of the extermination camps in Poland, Foxman called Dan Shapiro to suggest he take Wiesel on the trip. "He was in Bergen-Belsen, why shouldn't you take him with the president?" Shapiro was less enthusiastic: "We invited him and he said he couldn't make it." "Can't be," Foxman replied, adding that he was having lunch with Wiesel that afternoon and he'd look into it. Wiesel insisted no one had invited him, so Foxman arranged everything with Shapiro. Presidential bureaucracy was sidetracked and Elie Wiesel joined the much-publicized journey to the death camps. The connection was made and a relationship began to flourish between the two. With Foxman's encouragement, a routine was started where every few months the president and Elie Wiesel met for breakfast or brunch, usually on a Sunday. They discussed various topics, with a focus on the Iranian danger, with Wiesel keeping Foxman updated. During one of these meetings, Wiesel suggested writing a book with the president.

The idea didn't materialize, but it is testimony to the two men's once close relations.

This idyll was broken as the 2012 elections approached. Wiesel told Foxman that he thought it was over. Foxman asked why. "He asked me to announce my support for him, and I refused, because I have never done something like that," Wiesel replied, adding that the president's people asked him to at least accompany him on a tour of Florida and talk about their special relationship. Wiesel refused this, too. "I don't identify politically," he said, "and they led me to understand that it was over." Foxman tried to re-habilitate the lost relationship around the time of Obama's 2013 visit to Israel, but to no avail. At Netanyahu's controversial congressional address in March 2015, Wiesel, at the time over eighty-five years old and rarely appearing in public, sat close to Sheldon Adelson and his wife, Miriam.

There were other attempts to bring Obama and Netanyahu together. Abra-ham Foxman, who took to heart the alienation between the two leaders, tried to solve the issue at an earlier stage of the first term and discussed it with Netanyahu's emissary, Yitzhak Molcho. They both agreed that it was imperative to find someone with access to the president, someone who didn't have to go through Rahm Emanuel. They hit on Joe Biden, a veteran friend of Israel, who enjoyed a firm and independent relationship with the presi-dent. He'd been friendly with Bibi for years and appeared ideal for the job. Earlier Netanyahu had tried to persuade Foxman himself to undertake the task, but Foxman demurred. With Netanyahu's blessing, Foxman took the idea to the White House and the vice president, who liked it. It was later dropped because too many people disliked it. Emanuel, Tom Donilon, and Denis McDonough disapproved, but the greatest opposition came from Hillary Clinton. Turning Biden into a special emissary between Obama and Netanyahu would bypass her authority and power, and turn her into a lame duck. And she wasn't having that.

57

Between the Snub and the Lecture

2010–2011

On March 23, 2010, Netanyahu left for the United States. This time, he took along his defense minister Ehud Barak for reinforcement. The prime minister was going to give a speech to AIPAC and his staff had begged for a meeting with the president, which was eventually scheduled. Beforehand, Netanyahu had a difficult meeting with Hillary Clinton. The meeting with Obama was unpleasant and should go down in the history of Obama/Netanyahu meetings as "The Snub." Instead of a debate, the conversation was about the freeze and the need to extend it to the areas of East Jerusalem, in order to bring the Palestinians to the negotiating table. Netanyahu tried, as usual, to exhaust the president, but with no success. Obama presented him with thirteen demands that were tantamount to ultimatums and required immediate responses. When Netanyahu tried to buy time, Obama did what no other U.S. president had ever done before to a previous Israeli prime minister: He stood up and left the room, leaving Netanyahu alone with his entourage. The official explanation was that Obama had taken time out. The rumor was he had gone to put his daughters to bed. The joke, passed around by the Israeli delegation, was that Obama preferred putting his kids to bed over allowing Netanyahu to put him to sleep. But there was nothing funny about the situation. Tension ran high. Obama had actually turned the tables on Netanyahu. He walked out and left the prime minister to continue the debate with the American team. Let us know when you have something to report, was actually the president's message.

Nothing like this had ever happened between Israel and the United States. Netanyahu, who didn't know what to do, sought a safe place for urgent consultations. Bibi didn't trust security in Blair House, believing that the place was under constant surveillance. In good weather, he would gather his people in a corner of the garden behind the presidential guesthouse and discuss sensitive issues there, but this time, Netanyahu was not given the right to stay at Blair House. He didn't wish to talk in the hotel, so the delegation was driven to the Israeli embassy to use a sterile room with a secure telephone line. The room was opened. Netanyahu, who was in a foul mood and had a terrible migraine, crowded in along with all his entourage. He asked for a bag of ice, for his head. "It's not as cold as our reception at the White House," someone whispered. In the meantime, Ehud Barak was wandering around outside asking where he could get a cup of "cold tea." He was referring, of course, to a shot of whiskey. Later, Barak had the pleasure of dismembering the combination lock to the sterile room. It was another great day in the history of Obama/Netanyahu relations, a day that began in near secret, at an irrelevant hour, and with no media coverage, and ended in farce. The message was clear to Netanyahu: Israel is not a welcome guest in the White House. No wonder Bibi had a migraine.

The American version sounded predictably different. Michelle and the girls weren't even at home at the time. Obama's health-care reform bill was signed that day, for him a historic moment. Netanyahu had invited himself to Washington and forced a meeting on Obama. Despite everything going on, Obama met him. True, it may have been a mistake to call it a "private visit," but the meeting lasted ninety minutes. There were still some unsettled issues and disagreements, but there was a real desire to reach an understanding. The president suggested that the Israeli team stay on, and continue to work on consolidating proposals. He told them that he would come back if necessary. At the same time, his friends and staff arrived to celebrate the health-care bill. The Israelis said they needed more time and the president suggested they stay at the White House and work there in the Roosevelt Room. His own team would remain with them and he would return if necessary. So he says. He was friendly, he was to the point, he meant what he said. And, indeed, the Israeli team stayed with their American counterparts until midnight. The following morning the media reported the Israeli claim that they'd been led out of the back door past the garbage carts, that there were no cameras, only humiliation.

An associate of Obama recalls that the meeting with Netanyahu had been lengthy. The debate was supposed to continue among the two teams and the president was available if he was needed. But according to an Obama official, the Israelis were making a big deal out of it all, using it to get at the president, never keeping promises, and humiliating him vis-à-vis the Palestinians and the Arab world.

The farce sums up the entire story. The Obama/Netanyahu relationship is riddled with incidents that began with a misunderstanding, escalated with tendentious leaks to the media, and a great deal of bad blood. In many instances, such as the one described here, there was more smoke than fire. But that's what emerges when relations are built upon a shaky foundation, where there is no personal chemistry, and endless mutual loathing.

At that time, stories were rife about the president's so-called animosity toward Israel. "None of these stories are true," Obama's people insisted. One claim was that the Americans were dithering over the issuance of visas to Israeli scientists. Malcolm Hoenlein even called Obama associate Alan Solow, who called the White House and discovered that there was no truth to the story. Obama's people were sure it was planned and deliberate, that Bibi wanted to sabotage Obama's legitimacy and to present him as a Jew-hater and enemy of Israel. He wished to invalidate Obama as potential trouble for the Israeli electorate, and succeeded in doing so. The problem was, however, that on his way to achieving this, Netanyahu balked at nothing, and he really did succeed in ruining any chance of a working relationship with the president, in the process seriously undermining the alliance between the two countries.

On July 6, 2010, Obama and Netanyahu met once again for what was described as a meeting of reconciliation. This time, the media were permitted to cover the meeting, and the atmosphere was much improved. Ambassador Oren joked that "there'll be more photographers than at the Academy Awards." Martin Indyk had the impression that Obama and Netanyahu were finally learning to work together. Obama had recently approved a budget increase of more than $200 million for Israel's Iron Dome project. The Americans realized that the stick method had failed and decided to try the carrot instead. The settlement freeze was in its final third stage, with no progress made. Obama provided some impetus, giving an interview to Israel's Channel 2, in which he stated his belief that Netanyahu could bring peace. "The fact that he is not perceived as a dove could only be an asset to him. I get the impression that the prime minister is not here just to 'heat the seat,' but to be a statesman who leads change." It is not clear what caused Obama's surprise optimism, but it could have been a response to progress in secret talks between Israel and the Palestinians in London, which were mediated by the Americans. Netanyahu, too, appeared pleased. In contrast to the earlier, humiliating visit, this time he stayed in Blair House and wandered around Washington a welcome guest. It didn't look quite like the beginning of a wonderful relationship, but perhaps like the end of an unpleasant rivalry; if not necessarily a peace pact between Israel and the Palestinians, then maybe peace between Obama and Netanyahu.

At that time Netanyahu was negotiating with the leaders of the largest Knesset faction, the Kadima, over the possibility of it joining the coalition. Tzipi Livni would be appointed foreign minister responsible for political negotiations. In his talks with Kadima, as well as with President Shimon Peres, Netanyahu hinted that he was ready to make a surprising political move. The various emissaries who conducted the negotiations on his behalf produced a steady stream of whispers and rumors. "Just you wait," they said. "He'll surprise us all. You wouldn't believe how far he's willing to go. He wants to make history." Over his years in politics, he made much use of the sentence "I'm going to surprise you all." But somehow it always ended in disappointment.

In summer 2010, some of this optimism managed to seep into the hearts of Obama, Clinton, Shimon Peres, Tony Blair, and several others who were trying to restart the political process. On August 20, Hillary Clinton announced that Netanyahu and Mahmoud Abbas would be coming to Washington together on September 1, and that the White House intended to have a peace agreement "within a year." President Obama made a similar announcement a week later. Netanyahu adopted the mode of a "historic leader" who was going to bring change. It happens to him from time to time. He'd just spent a few days in a seminar with Shimon Peres. The old fox understood that the most successful tool for persuading Bibi was his wife, Sara, and invited the couple for a series of cozy dinners at his official residence. There, he dragged them through extensive ideological discussions on the wonders of peace. Peres came out of the experience with the feeling that it was possible. "Bibi is no fool; he understands the situation," he said. All that remained was for him to act on it.

The meeting between Netanyahu and Abbas took place in early September. There were bombastic declarations; there was even a handshake. No progress was made. The Palestinians demanded an extension of the settlement freeze; Netanyahu refused. A further summit meeting took place in mid-September in Sharm-al-Sheikh, and the following day Abbas came for an additional meeting at the prime minister's official residence in Jerusalem. Then, too, no progress was made. The freeze ended at the end of the month, and Israel returned to building in the settlements. President Obama wrote to Netanyahu offering a series of incentives if Israel would extend the freeze on settlement building. Obama even agreed to recognize a long-term military presence in the Jordan Valley if an arrangement were reached. A similar letter was sent to Abbas, with improved incentives for the Palestinians if they would only return to negotiations. Behind the scenes, Defense Minister Ehud Barak tried to manipulate Netanyahu and the Americans into a package deal for extending the freeze; he failed. George Mitchell met Obama and Abbas, and the Europeans exerted pressure from their side, but Netanyahu continued to ponder, and claimed that the freeze would topple the coalition. Israeli foreign minister Avigdor Lieberman declared in the UN General Assembly, "A peace treaty between Israel and the Palestinians is not practical." Lieberman has a habit of saying out loud what Netanyahu is thinking.

Attempts at resuscitating the peace process continued for months. On

November 7, Netanyahu left for the United States again for a series of meetings with senior administration officials, but without the president, who was on a visit to East Asia. Before the trip, the prime minister's people spread rumors about a "political upheaval," that Prime Minister Netanyahu was ready to make difficult decisions. Right after the zig came the zag in the form of new Israeli building initiatives in Har Homa and Gilo, two Jerusalem neighborhoods that lay beyond the 1967 lines. Obama was quick to condemn the plan from Jakarta, the capital of Indonesia. Netanyahu countered that "Jerusalem is not a settlement, it is the capital of Israel." Negotiations continued about extending the settlement freeze. Ehud Barak worked on a package that would give Israel an additional squadron of stealth bombers, and an improved aid package in return for an additional three-month freeze on settlement building. Barak conducted an endless series of lengthy talks in Washington. Netanyahu continued to spin tales and work on public opinion while preparing the coalition for the possibility of a three-month extension. On his way home to Washington, Obama voiced his appreciation. But then it became clear that contrary to hints Barak had made about the stealth bombers coming free of charge, Israel would have to pay for them out of their military aid budget. The "Jewish settlement freeze" bombers were nicknamed the JSF planes. A scandal broke out in Israel and caused mayhem in Netanyahu's coalition. The headlines had mentioned a gift and now it appeared that it had to be paid for. Ehud Barak was blamed for being deliberately vague. Barak likes being vague, but it was Netanyahu who gave him leverage. As usual, the truth is somewhere in the middle. In Barak's negotiations with the Americans the question of payment for the squadron remained vague. Actually, it was ignored. The Israeli side thought it would be a gift. The Americans knew it wouldn't. When Tom Donilon learned there was an issue, he declared that payment would come out of Israel's military aid allowance.

On November 11, at the height of the saga, Netanyahu and his people had a tense meeting with Hillary Clinton in New York. Instead of lasting one hour as scheduled, the meeting lasted several. In the middle, Netanyahu left for a birthday meal with his wife, Sara, and returned later to resume the debate. He was in his element and "sucked the Americans dry."

Netanyahu, and especially Molcho, deliberated on every word, every comma, and every period, driving the Americans crazy. At the end of that marathon meeting, Clinton hoped she'd never have to see Netanyahu again in her life and "wished they'd leave us alone." Incidentally, it should be said that Barak's stitching together of the military deal was coarse; many details were not concluded, disagreements were left unsettled, misunderstandings remained misunderstood. Aides came and went from that meeting. George Mitchell tried to organize a last-minute deal sweetener for Netanyahu and went out to see if he could arrange permission from Saudi Arabia and other Arab states for El Al planes to fly in their airspace. Mitchell failed. And then Natan Eshel stepped out to check if the Ramot neighborhood was outside the Green Line, or just parts of it. Endless debates continued over kindergartens, synagogues, infrastructures, what could be built, and what could not. Dan Shapiro's resonant voice could be heard asking the participants, "How long are you going to continue with these stupid quarrels?"

One of the American proposals was for Israel to carry out a "silent" freeze, with no official announcements. Netanyahu tended to agree with this approach and it was agreed that he'd return to Israel, to convene the cabinet and pass the proposal. But then the ultra-Orthodox Shas faction demanded that the government also announce new building projects not included in the freeze. Shas wanted to have something to show its right-wing electorate. Molcho called Washington and described the latest events. "Know what?" said the Americans. "We give up. There's no deal." At the end of the marathon, what should have been clear from the beginning became clear: There was no deal and no extended freeze. The Americans were exhausted, angry, and unwilling to continue negotiation with Netanyahu. In Congress and in the media, fierce criticism was voiced against the administration for having been prepared to pay billions of dollars in return for a further three-month settlement freeze. Obama and his people were sick and tired. But there was an amusing angle to it all: For a long time the Israelis continued to blame the Obama administration for changing their minds at the last moment over the "quiet" extension, while the administration continued to blame Israel for being unable to confirm the deal without making additional building announcements. The Americans didn't know that Bibi had had an alternative. Before leaving for the meeting with Hillary Clinton, Bibi met in Jerusalem with opposition leader Tzipi Livni, who told him, "If you need to freeze settlement building again in order to finalize negotiations, count me in." Under such circumstances, she would agree to join the government, or provide an external safety net. But at the moment of truth, Bibi preferred Shas and its right-wing base to the political left. It was Bibi's choice. In Washington the sense of revulsion was so deep that the Americans had even stopped being angry. They'd had enough of this war of attrition.

President Obama turned to his plan B, which came in the form of a speech about the future of the Middle East. The president decided that it was time to define the vision of the future of the Middle East.

On May 2, 2011, the most wanted man on earth, Osama bin Laden, was killed in Pakistan by U.S. Navy SEALs in the course of Operation Neptune Spear. Obama had played his cards well; the timing was perfect not only to demonstrate leadership on the Middle East, but to teach Netanyahu a thing or two. At the same time, Netanyahu had been invited to deliver a speech in May, before both houses of Congress. Both talented and charismatic speakers, the two men were like two gunfighters.

Tensions arose in Israel's Washington embassy as the time approached for the president's speech. Michael Oren and his staff tried in vain to get an advance snippet. At a meeting between Oren and former deputy national security advisor Antony Blinken, the latter described the bin Laden killing. Oren wanted to know if the president's speech was going to focus on the Middle East. Blinken was evasive, said that the president might mention Europe first, that things happen, and that any mention of Israel would be marginal. A few days later it turned out that there had indeed been a speech: Obama's vision for the post–Arab Spring in the Middle East. In Washington everyone who could be was briefed on the speech, including research institutes, foreign media, and ambassadors; everyone except the Israelis. Oren was beside himself, and in Jerusalem the anxiety level soared. Netanyahu lost his fear of Obama. His close advisor, Ron Dermer, told him that Obama would be a one-term president.

On May 16, 2011, three days before the president's speech, Netanyahu addressed the Knesset in Jerusalem with a speech that outlined what he conceived of as an appropriate permanent agreement with the Palestinians. It was a relatively moderate speech that included the phrase "for the sake of peace, I am willing to relinquish parts of our homeland." The speech included reasonable parameters for peace. Netanyahu said he would demand an Israeli military presence on the banks of the Jordan River, sentiments that were construed as ultra–left wing and revolutionary for him. For the first time, the prime minister did not talk of Israeli sovereignty over the Jordan Valley, only of a military presence on the waterline, without specifying for how long. The man most encouraged by this speech was minister Dan Meridor, who invested many hours of his time in attempts to persuade Netanyahu of the necessity of the peace process. Meridor managed to spend considerable time with Netanyahu behind the back of his regular "babysitter," Yitzhak Molcho, while maintaining close contact with the Americans and encouraging them to support Netanyahu. "It is possible to work with Bibi," Meridor often said to the Americans in those days, "you just need to know how." Meridor knew Netanyahu would express similar sentiments before the American Congress. Later, Meridor would say in private conversations that the Americans missed the point of Bibi. Instead of hugging him, they pressured him. President Shimon Peres considered himself the godfather to Netanyahu's pragmatic speech. He felt that at long last something was beginning to move. The flash seminar he'd given Bibi and Sara at the president's residence was bearing fruit. There was renewed hope in the president's heart, and in Bibi's heart, too. Prime Minister Netanyahu believed he was prepared for the trip to Washington.

On the eve of Netanyahu's flight to Washington, a headline in *Yediot Ahronot* informed him that President Obama was about to place new parameters for solving the Israeli/Palestinian issue. Frightened telephone calls flowed in accompanied by the anticipated logic: "This is how you treat an ally?"

So it seems, and it was only the beginning. The five days between May 19 and 24 were planned and orchestrated with deadly accuracy and resolution. The president's speech was scheduled for Thursday, May 19, 2011, close to the time Netanyahu was due to take off for Washington. The prime minister, having heard things before boarding his plane for an eleven-hour flight where he had no way of contacting the outside world, could only sit and stew. The Americans hoped the lag time would make it impossible for Bibi to brief the well-oiled Jewish/Israeli machine in Washington. Netanyahu's meeting with Obama was scheduled for Friday afternoon, shortly after he landed. The tight schedule would make it hard for Netanyahu to respond off the cuff, and do what he does best: to inflame the Hill and, especially, the Republicans. On Sunday, Obama was supposed to speak before AIPAC, followed by Netanyahu, and on Tuesday there would be a finale: Netanyahu's address to the two houses of Congress. The biggest duel of words in history, between two of the best orators of their generation. Obama opens; Bibi closes. In between, they are colliding in AIPAC, and Bibi the guest has a one-speech advantage (before Congress). The best show in town.

One day before Obama's speech, information reached Jerusalem that the president was going to refer to the 1967 border as a basis for negotiations between Israel and the Palestinians. Netanyahu made an angry phone call to Hillary Clinton and tried to persuade her to press the president into refraining from doing so. Clinton wasn't interested, and Netanyahu realized he was in trouble. A few days earlier it appeared that, contrary to procedure, the Americans were unwilling to receive Netanyahu's special envoy, Yitzhak Molcho, for a round of meetings to coordinate and prepare for the Obama/Netanyahu meeting. They said it was all coordinated. From their point of view it was probably true.

A few hours later, President Obama took the podium and fired the opening shot for the five stormy days to come. His visionary speech included several allusions to the need for new leadership, and criticism of leaders who allowed themselves to remain hostages to yesterday's restraints while renouncing the opportunities of tomorrow. But the real blow came with the president's statement that "Israel and Palestine should be based on the 1967 lines with mutually agreed swaps, so that secure and recognized borders are established for both states. The Palestinian people must have the right to govern themselves, and reach their potential, in a sovereign and contiguous state." The speech contained several things that were unpleasant to Palestinian ears, but no one in Netanyahu's vicinity heard them. As Netanyahu saw it, Obama had breached a taboo and set a dangerous precedent. According to the witnesses, Netanyahu looked like an angry bull being taunted by a matador. From the plane in Tel Aviv, Bibi's entourage leaked, "As soon as the plane lands in Washington the prime minister expects to receive some clarifications with regard to his statements." This quote infuriated the Americans but, as Netanyahu was already in the air, they decided to talk to Ambassador Oren, letting him know that Israel was not in a position to dictate terms with the White House. The Israelis responded that there must have been some problem in translating the prime minister's words as he boarded the plane. The Americans weren't buying it and asked what kind of problem. Are you Pakistanis? Don't you know English? And so on, until Netanyahu landed in the American capital, which this time was prepared for his arrival as it had never been before.

On the political front, Bibi was pleased with the Republican Party's strong reaction to Obama's speech. Former governor Mitt Romney, subsequently the Republicans' presidential candidate, declared that the president had thrown Israel under the bus. His colleague Newt Gingrich said it was the "most dangerous speech given by an American president in terms of Israel's survival." Such was the atmosphere surrounding Netanyahu when he arrived at about 6:00 p.m. for the meeting at the Oval Office. Upon Netanyahu's arrival, the Quartet (the United Nations, the United States, the European Union, and Russia) published an announcement, giving its wholehearted support for the president's speech. This, too, was preplanned. Netanyahu was surrounded. Facing him was the omnipotent American president; all around was the rest of the world: Europeans; Russians; the Quartet; and, of course, the Palestinians. The Americans had ambushed Bibi and were sure he'd blink. They were wrong.

The meeting between the president and the prime minister, which should have lasted fifty minutes, went on for twice that time. After it, the media were invited in for a photo op that turned into one of the most publicized and controversial battles between an American president and an Israeli prime minister. This time it was Netanyahu's turn to strike. After Obama's reasonable introduction, Netanyahu straightened his tie, looked the president squarely in the eye, and embarked on what later became known as the lecture. In a lengthy tirade, the prime minister delivered an educated lecture full of historical facts to illustrate to the president why Israel could never return to its 1967 borders, and laid down a set of nonnegotiable conditions for peace talks. Obama's look was frozen as Netanyahu explained to him how the Middle East worked. Not a muscle moved in the president's face; his stoic cool was admirable. And it all happened on his home turf, in the Oval Office, in front of the American media. In a live television broadcast, the head of a tiny Middle Eastern sponsored state, a dependent, was trying to give him a lesson in history, statesmanship, and responsibility. In the Israeli embassy, someone was counting the seconds: it went on, according to an Israeli official, around six minutes that seemed more like an eternity. Afterward, Obama and Netanyahu shook hands for the cameras—a particularly forced handshake—and took their leave of each other. They still had to face a working dinner, but things would no longer appear the same. Something had happened that evening in the Oval Office.

In the middle of the visit, Dr. Dore Gold, a member of Netanyahu's entourage and a fellow guest in Blair House, had an article published in *The Wall Street Journal* that infuriated the Americans. The Israelis tried to explain that the article had been submitted long before and that there had been no intention for it to coincide with the visit, but the Americans pointed to the inclusion of quotes from the president's speech, which loudly overturned the Israeli defense. There were voices in the White House calling for an immediate dismissal of the Israeli delegation from Blair House. It didn't happen, but everything else did. The atmosphere between the sides was tense and hostile. The Israelis were accused of humiliating the president. Relations between Obama and Netanyahu, which had never been good, were at an all-time low. Netanyahu's people tried to cool things down. Bibi was interviewed in the American media praising the president and the administration to the skies, and even visiting the Liberty Bell. The Israelis hoped for a miracle that would enable a return to the White House under reasonable circumstances. The Americans promised no such thing.

This catastrophic meeting between Obama and Netanyahu was their seventh. The only thing left for both sides, in light of the obvious hostility and mutual suffering, was to emphasize the number of meetings between the two men. *Ha'aretz* editor Aluf Benn wrote that the latest meeting had pitted the "revolutionary" against the "conservative." This was an accurate definition. Ultimately, the technical differences between them are not big. However, there exists a huge conceptual, ideological, and moral discrepancy, which perhaps can best be understood through the eyes of a pair of close friends, one Obama's, the other of Netanyahu.

Accord to Obama's man, the president could have been clearer in his speech. He could have better explained the matter of the 1967 borders. But he also talked about a territorial swap, which puts him in the same place as Bush, who recognized "demographic changes in the field." It's easy enough to understand that there is not much difference between them. But the Israelis saw only what they wanted to see. The moment there's a territorial swap it's not really about 1967 borders. So instead of the prime minister praising the president for recognizing the blocs, because a swap of territories is a de facto recognition of the settlement blocs, and instead of thanking him for his support of a Jewish state, and instead of thanking him for a demilitarized Palestinian state and strict security arrangements and the fact that there would be no right of return or long-term presence in the Jordan Valley, and instead of thanking him for his firm stand beside Israel and the unprecedented security aid, instead of all these, Bibi gave the president a public lecture and humiliated him in his own home. According to the official, it was as if Bibi had deliberately distorted Obama's words; he had forced Obama to explain his vision in his speech to AIPAC. And in spite of all this, Obama didn't renege on any promise he'd made to Netanyahu, did not compromise Israel's security, and did not seek revenge, which proves that Obama was and remains cool, even though during that week Netanyahu had dealt him a few very bad blows. He offended him and humiliated him and distorted his words, but Obama did not consider for a moment to respond irresponsibly, even though Netanyahu infuriated him as few had done beforehand. The resulting situation between them is hard to conceive and asymmetrical. Actually, it appears that only Bibi can attack Obama on the issue of Iran, to criticize his policy and preach to him at every opportunity, and the president is obliged to accept and understand.

But when Obama addresses the Palestinian issue and offers advice that is no different from decades-long official U.S. policies, Netanyahu explodes. He obviously knows that no matter how revolting his behavior, the president is committed to Israel's security and will do nothing to harm it. Above all, it is a sad state of affairs. Netanyahu said what he said in the Oval Office even though, beforehand, during the meeting, he had received from Obama an exact and detailed explanation of what he meant in his speech, and knew that he had no reason to worry. He simply prepared an ambush for Obama, in cold blood, inside the White House.

And Netanyahu's friend, a member of his inner circle, who was with Bibi during this visit, said the Israelis didn't believe that the president was at all upset by Netanyahu's speech in the Oval Office. The following day, they sat together in Blair House, where Bibi showed a picture of himself marching toward the car together with the president, and Obama appears relaxed and friendly, and there's a Marine standing there and they are all smiling and everything appears all right. The picture was taken after the so-called lecture. Obama said nothing to Bibi, and did not behave in an unusual way when they parted later. So the simple conclusion is that only after Netanyahu left, and Obama stayed behind with his advisors, did they start to make the case that the prime minister had humiliated him in public. It wasn't Obama's real feeling, it was an idea that all the Netanyahu-haters around Obama later planted in the president's head and heart. Netanyahu spoke from the bottom of his heart there in the Oval Office; he felt he was representing the Jewish people throughout the ages, a nation that has been persecuted and suffered and was almost annihilated; it was his job to stand up and represent them in the struggle. He had no intention of humiliating the president. Even if he exaggerated a little, there was no need to make such fuss. The thing is that they were lying in wait for him, they wanted trouble, they loathe him in such a way that almost anything he does or says will turn into a confrontation. Let's not forget that almost every time Bibi visits Washington, there is a harsh surprise waiting for him. Once it was an interview with Jeffrey Goldberg, once a humiliation, and once a speech. This business goes both ways, and it was usually Obama's people who initiated these quarrels.

The tragedy is that both those "spokespersons" are correct. The president really wasn't moved by the lecture. Obama is even-tempered and not easily flustered. He really did accompany Netanyahu calmly and parted from him with warmth, as Bibi described. The president's people saw things differently, especially Chief of Staff Bill Daley and deputy national security advisor Denis McDonough. When the president reentered the office, he was told that he'd been humiliated. That interpretation was shared by reporters present at the event, and it emerged in the coverage that pointed out the humiliation. Obama had not taken it seriously, but soon aligned himself with the majority view. From the start there had been no chance of a connection between Obama and Netanyahu, who are forever like oil and water, cat and mouse, Republican and Democrat. To work successfully together there needed to be a lot of goodwill, close associates to mollify each leader when necessary, constant bridge-building and mutual encouragement. None of this has ever been present. When Netanyahu came face-to-face with Obama in the Oval Office he was representing centuries of catastrophe-filled Jews; it was like David facing Goliath. Obama saw it the other way around: In his eyes Netanyahu was no David, but more of a Goliath, reminiscent of leaders of South African apartheid in its twilight years, the grim alarmism and fossilized conservatism being tossed by the new age into the junkyard of history. Obama, for his part, represented hope, opportunity, and the informed world view that identified a new possibility at every turn, whereas Netanyahu saw a real and mortal danger.

58

"A One-Term President"

2011–2012

During 2012 Netanyahu was concerned with two main issues: praying silently for Barack Obama's fall at the end of the year; while trying, simultaneously, to get the president to attack the nuclear installations in Iran. In between, Netanyahu continued to work on developing and upgrading Israel's military option in preparation for the eventuality that Israel would have to carry out an attack on Iran alone. Netanyahu believed that he was able, with Ehud Barak at his side, to issue such an order to the IDF if there were no other choice. He was determined not to allow Iran entry into its famous "zone of immunity"; it was his historic duty to prevent it.

In all these objectives, Netanyahu failed. Ron Dermer's oft-repeated promise that Obama was a "one-term president" was wrong. There was no attack on Iran. Netanyahu choked, and Obama won the election.

In Israel, toward the end of 2011, depression began to set in. The summer protests that brought hundreds of thousands of Israelis into the streets faded away, mainly because of the release by Hamas of the Israeli soldier held hostage, Gilad Shalit. The main concern that awaited Israel without a political breakthrough was what Ehud Barak coined a "political tsunami." On November 9, 2011, the well-known Israeli historian Benny Morris published an article in *Newsweek* titled "Is Israel Over?" It caused significant waves. In it Morris describes Israel's ever-increasing ills, its weakening liberal and democratic character, the social cracks, the external threats, and the general feeling of dissolution. Morris anticipated a wave of Palestinian violence washing over the country in the near future. His prophecy was realized in October 2015, when an onslaught of terror broke out and continues as this book is being written. But in September 2011 and in early 2012, Netanyahu was still able to rest on his laurels. Around the same time as Morris's article, *The New York Times* published an op-ed piercingly critical of Netanyahu, in which it determined that the prime minister was isolating Israel; but Bibi didn't flinch. Himself a practiced alarmist, he was used to threats and dark prophecies. At that time he was concerned with two things, toppling Obama and Iran's nuclear race.

The G20 summit in Cannes, France, provided Netanyahu with an excruciating dose of embarrassment when French president Nicolas Sarkozy, described the Israeli prime minister as a "liar" in a private exchange with Barack Obama that was inadvertently broadcast to journalists.

"I cannot stand him, he's a liar," Sarkozy told Obama. Obama responded with: "You're fed up with him? I have to deal with him every day."

Neither leader apparently realized that microphones that had been attached for a press conference had already been switched on, allowing journalists to hear the conversation.

It was a rare opportunity to hear, clearly, what world leaders think of Netanyahu. But there was more to it: As the conversation continued, and despite what they had said about Bibi, the U.S. president urged Sarkozy for help in persuading the Palestinians not to bring their request for recognition of a Palestinian state to the UN. This conversation is a perfect example of America's duplicity: on the one hand, disgust and complete lack of faith in Netanyahu; while, on the other, continuing to back Israel in the stormy international arena. Obama never made real use of the stick he held. Even when playing the carrot-and-stick game with Netanyahu, the carrots were given generously, but the sticks were held at both ends, rendering the game ineffective, which caused Netanyahu to lose his fear of Obama at an early stage in their relationship.

Netanyahu's feeling of political siege worked wonders for him. He was used to such a situation. To him, the Jews were under constant siege, even when it appeared they were not. On January 19, 2012, *Jerusalem Post* editor in chief Steve Linde revealed that at a meeting some weeks earlier, Netanyahu had told him, "We have two enemies, *The New York Times* and *Ha'aretz*. It is they who are determining the agenda for the anti-Israel campaign all over the world." When Linde and several other reporters present at the meeting asked Netanyahu if he believed that the media really does have so significant an effect in forming the world view of Israel, Netanyahu replied, "Yes, absolutely." As someone who bases his policies on speeches and words but keeps his distance from actual accomplishment, he has a mystical belief in the power of media and its task in defining victory or failure. He still blames his 1999 failure in the polls on the media, especially on the left-wing media, and he sees in them a real threat to Israel and Zionism.

In early March 2012, Netanyahu flew once again to the United States, for another meeting with President Obama and to deliver another speech to AIPAC; a reconstruction of the previous year's catastrophes, except this was an election year in the United States. Obama was fighting for his second term and aspiring to remove the nuisance called Netanyahu from the agenda. Bibi's aspirations were completely different. He was hoping that Obama would lose the election, Netanyahu still believing with all his heart that Obama was a danger to Israel. Netanyahu lived and breathed this feeling twenty-four hours a day, and it continued to intensify. He still had his secret weapon in the form of Sheldon Adelson, the generous gambling mogul, who was willing to invest as much as it took to replace Obama with a president who was friendlier to Israel, and more hostile to the Iranian nuclear program.

In his 2012 AIPAC speech, Obama went out of his way to prove how committed he was to Israel's security, and announced that he would never allow Iran to become a nuclear power. Once again, he stressed that all options were on the table and praised himself for generous security aid he'd delivered to Israel. Obama was in the middle of a fund-raising campaign and wanted calm on the American Jewish front. This was not a good time for dissent with AIPAC or other Jewish organizations, especially because of the relatively significant weight the Jewish vote had in states such as Florida.

Obama went on to hone the message on the Iran issue. Secretary of Defense Leon Panetta, who also spoke before AIPAC, insisted that if there was no choice, the president would use force. Obama stressed once again that he had no intention of allowing a nuclear Iran. These messages were all intended to keep Netanyahu in check, to modify his rhetoric, to allow him to climb down from his high horse and make it possible for the president to get through 2012 safely.

In the meeting between the two men, however, the messages were completely different. Obama made it clear to Netanyahu that an Israeli attack on Iran before the U.S. elections would be a grave mistake. The United States would not back such an attack, Obama said, and made sure that Netanyahu understood that logistic aid or air- and sealifts of ammunition and equipment the day after were very much in doubt. Netanyahu said nothing; his answer to the president in his AIPAC speech.

The next day, Netanyahu delivered his famous "duck" speech: if it looks like a duck, walks like a duck, and sounds like a duck, it's a duck, only this duck is a nuclear duck. Netanyahu said that it was time for the world to start calling this duck by its real name. He also pulled out the response of the 1944 U.S. administration to the World Jewish Congress request regarding the Jews of Europe, a response that was, of course, negative. But he quickly pointed out that the Obama administration was different. Netanyahu was placing Obama in the historical defendant's seat, as someone who could, once again, abandon the Jews to their fate. He neglected to mention that then, in 1944, his own father, Prof. Benzion Netanyahu, did exactly as he was doing that day: attempting to set the Republicans against a Democratic president, on behalf of the Jews. The only difference was that in 1944, Netanyahu Sr. had extenuating circumstances and valid justification; the Holocaust of the Jews of Europe was at its peak. Netanyahu related to this, too. The Jewish nation had changed. Today, we have our own nation-state, and the objective of the Jewish state is to defend Jewish lives and to ensure the future of the Jews. He added that Israel has waited for diplomacy to work; we waited for the sanctions to work, and could not allow ourselves to wait much longer.

This time, too, Netanyahu's speech at the AIPAC conference infuriated the White House. He had placed valuable ammunition in the hands of the Republicans just before the definitive months of the election campaign. It gave the impression that Israel was, once again, being thrown under the bus. He had raised the volume, instead of lowering it. Obama noted these things, and repressed himself. He had an election to win.

In mid-May, *Time* magazine published a cover story with the headline "King Bibi." "At a moment when incumbents around the world are being shunted aside, he is triumphant." On July 29, the Republican presidential candidate Mitt Romney arrived in Israel. A few days earlier, as a preemptive strike, Barack Obama had signed an agreement for tightening security cooperation with Israel, including an additional $70 million budget to continue funding the development of the Iron Dome system. The White House hoped that these presidential steps would cancel out the effects of Romney's Jerusalem visit, which was aimed specifically at the many Jewish voters in the wavering states of Florida and Pennsylvania. It was a mistake. Romney was on a state visit to Jerusalem; he had come straight from London, where he'd received a cool welcome, and Jerusalem was a huge compensation for his trouble getting there, a visit closely planned in full coordination with the prime minister's office. The objective was to present Romney as the incumbent president, to help the American voters see how things would be if Romney were elected.

Romney's visit was treated as a state affair, with top-level meetings and intimate dinners with the prime minister and his wife, full media coverage, and plenty of photographs. The prime minister's office did everything possible to stage a warm hug between the two men. There was no comparing Romney's 2012 visit with that of presidential candidate Barack Obama in 2008. The White House had harsh words for Israel's interference in U.S. politics. The elections were in two months, and if Barack Obama was reelected president, Netanyahu would pay for his behavior.

Two months later, a video campaign emerged in the United States featuring Netanyahu warning (in his own voice) against an imminent Iranian nuclear bomb. Threatening music accompanied the words "The world needs American power, not apologies." The ad was claimed by an unknown organization called Secure America. Here, too, all signs led to Netanyahu and his followers. In September, shortly before the scheduled UN General Assembly in New York, Obama's people refused Netanyahu's request for a meeting. Enough is enough, said the Americans. According to a senior White House official, it was hard to set a date for a meeting with the prime minister because the prime minister's schedule was hard to decipher. "We can never tell when he's acting as Israel's prime minister, and when he's working as Mitt Romney's campaign director," said an American official. In the White House they feared that a meeting with Obama might constitute an excuse for a parallel meeting with Romney on U.S. soil. They wanted to avoid a situation in which Jewish voters might see the warmth and closeness of a Romney meeting juxtaposed with the hostility and coldness typical of a meeting with Obama. In the meantime, a list was published of Romney donors revealing that 19 percent of Romney's contributors were Netanyahu associates, and also regular contributors to Bibi. As if anyone in the White House needed this smoking gun.

Throughout those months, Netanyahu continued to lash out against the Iran nuclear program and complain repeatedly about the foot-dragging of the United States and the West. In the White House there was no doubt in anyone's mind that Netanyahu was trying to brand the president as weak and ineffectual, and sully his leadership. Bibi was wandering around the presidential election as if he were dealing with primaries in Likud. In the White House they finally understood that Netanyahu, the object of their disdain and revulsion from day one, was going for the jugular. What did he know that they didn't?

Not much, it turned out. Until the last moment, Netanyahu believed that the president he hated so much was on his way out of the White House. Ron Dermer swore to it. He ignored the polls, the commentators, and reality. He had an educated paradigm, backed by a personal thesis, according to which, at the last moment, all the wavering states would fall in Romney's direction. He was absolutely certain, and he convinced Netanyahu, too. A senior Likud member recalls Netanyahu's certainty that Romney would win, even though the polls showed the opposite. "Don't pay attention to the polls," he said. "I know America. Romney is the next president."

On Election Day, Dermer opened an improvised operations room in the prime minister's office in Jerusalem. All day he sat there facing a computer with TV screens and other connections, telling anyone willing to listen that Romney was winning. Even when the polls and television channels announced Obama's victory, Dermer continued to insist. "It's not over yet." When he was told that Romney needed a miracle, Dermer was sure the miracle was happening. He grasped his beloved paradigm with all his might, even when it began to crumble. With it, Netanyahu crumbled, too. The day after the elections, people saw a broken man. He had built an entire empire of plans and expectations on a President Mitt Romney. Now he'd have to continue with Obama. Benjamin "Mr. America" Netanyahu had disregarded for four years what everyone said, that Obama was a two-term president.

59

Chapter B

On January 15, 2013, a week before the elections in Israel and two days before the start of his second term, Obama gave Netanyahu a personal gift, a kind of cold vengeance served for his interference in the American elections. It came in the form of a series of interviews with Jeffrey Goldberg, the journalist and political commentator closest to the president. Goldberg wrote a special article for Bloomberg, with quotes straight from the president's mouth. "Israel doesn't know what its own best interests are," Obama said, "and each new announcement by Prime Minister Benjamin Netanyahu of settlement expansions is leading Israel down the path of near-total isolation. Netanyahu is a coward, on the road to self-destruction." When the president learned of the plans to build Jewish housing in the area outside of Jerusalem known as E-1, he didn't even bother getting angry. He told several people that this sort of behavior on Netanyahu's part is what he has come to expect, and that he had become inured to the self-defeating policies of his Israeli counterpart.

What Obama still didn't understand was that such statements actually helped Netanyahu. Over the past four years, Netanyahu had completed what had appeared to be an impossible mission, to portray Obama as an enemy of the Israeli people. In the past, had an American president said such things about the Israeli prime minister, it would have caused a political earthquake. But in 2013, the Israelis were indifferent to Obama, just as he was indifferent to Netanyahu.

In Israel, meanwhile, Netanyahu was leading in the polls. No real genuine rival had stood up to challenge him. A few weeks earlier he had joined forces with Lieberman's Israel Is Our Home party, a move that promised him the election. However, instead of the forty-five seats Netanyahu and Lieberman had expected, they received thirty-one. Yair Lapid was surprised by coming in second place with nineteen seats. In any case, two months after Barack Obama, Netanyahu, too, won an election, his third term coinciding with the start of Obama's second. They were not rid of the other. The difference was that Obama had an expiration date (January 2017) and Netanyahu doesn't. He will stay there as long as the Israeli public wants him. He will see Obama leaving the White House as a prime minister, although his political horizon is not so clear anymore. A heavy cloud named Yair Lapid is out there, accompanied with a series of heavy police inquiries about personal misconduct.

In the White House, there was an assumption that Netanyahu would try to amend his previous behavior and change direction. They believed that Bibi learned his lesson. He had Obama for four more years, in political terms an eternity. It was time to make peace, to mend what needed mending and move on. The White House was mistaken. Something amazing had happened to Netanyahu. He completed whatever inner evolution that had been crawling within him over the years and completely lost his fear. He still needed Obama for the Iran business and would play the game outwardly, but inside he was finished with Obama. Bibi had always been a cautious, if not anxious, leader. He had gone to great lengths to avoid rocking the boat, but suddenly he found courage. There were reasons: He had been in the lion's den and he got out safely, which gave him confidence. He also had the billionaire Sheldon Adelson, with all his force, and the Republican Party as well. Most important, he had caused Obama to be hated by the Israeli public, turning him into a strategic political asset. Each time Netanyahu clashed with Obama, Israelis cheered from the sidelines. Using his inherent political wiliness, Netanyahu managed to turn a burden into an asset. Obama helped him by making every possible mistake on his way to the dubious distinction of being the most hated American president of all time in Israel.

At the beginning of Chapter B, it appeared that Obama actually internalized his past mistakes. His second term opened with an announcement of a state visit to Israel on March 20. This time, both sides swore, it had to be a success. And it was. The credit for this goes to the tireless American ambassador to Israel, Dan Shapiro, and to Ron Dermer, Netanyahu's pick to replace Michael Oren in Washington. For Dermer, the visit was a kind of audition. The Americans were not thrilled with the potential appointment, and voices in the White House were hinting that Dermer, friend of Adelson and the Republican Party, would not be welcomed warmly. Obama's people remembered his activity in Mitt Romney's election campaign. Dermer had an organized plan for overcoming the administration's opposition. The president's visit was the first part in this plan. It went well and was easy. Both leaders wanted it to succeed. Bibi knew that after missing his chance to act in Iran, his life's mission was dependent entirely on the American president. The president, for his part, had not yet given up on the vision of an Israel/Palestine arrangement. John Kerry, his new secretary of state, planned to make the mission his top priority. Obama wanted to give relations with Netanyahu another chance.

It was an excellent visit. On the Israeli side the man in command was Ya'akov Amidror. Dermer helped him and did his best to let the Americans know of his efforts. On the American side it was Ambassador Shapiro who saw the visit as a definitive event that was meant to end the bad period and turn over a new page. There were moments during the visit when Obama and Netanyahu appeared relaxed, smiling, almost enjoying each other's company. For the first time in the history of their relations, all the advisors and aides made a real effort to bring them closer together, and not the other way around. It began with the landing of Air Force One at Israel's Ben Gurion International Airport. Apart from the state reception, in the presence of President Shimon Peres, Prime Minister Netanyahu, and other dignitaries, the president was scheduled to receive a demonstration of Iron

Dome, Israel's mobile all-weather air defense system, a battery of which was standing in wait on the edge of the runway. The event was planned with military accuracy; while still on board the plane, Obama was fitted with a microphone. Netanyahu was fitted with one, too, and the two were connected to the media feed that was controlled in the operations room and broadcast live to all the international TV and radio networks. The two men were getting closer while being broadcast, and spoke to each other with warmth and friendliness throughout the ceremony.

President Obama inspected the guard of honor with Israel's aging President Peres at his side. After the speeches, the highly secured convoy moved a few hundred yards to the edge of the runway, where the U.S.-funded and Israeli-developed Iron Dome defense system waited. Also at the ceremony was Amir Peretz, minister for the environment from Tzipi Livni's party. Not many people knew that Peretz's presence at the ceremony was agreed upon in the course of recent coalition negotiations, and that Peretz had been the defense minister who decided to develop Iron Dome against the military establishment's protests. He wasn't impressed with the relatively junior post offered him in the recent negotiations, so was awarded as compensation the privilege of meeting Obama at the airport. Peretz was moving up in the world, and he liked it.

With the tour over, the American and Israeli delegations were scheduled to return to the secured convoy, which would take them to a Jerusalem-bound helicopter. Obama, however, who had just landed after an exhausting transatlantic flight, suggested doing the hundred-yard distance to the helicopter on foot. The president wanted some air. Gil Shefer, Netanyahu's chief of staff, who immediately understood the potential here, pounced on the idea. He was looking for a winning picture. Obama and Netanyahu started to walk along the runway when the president, who was feeling the Israeli heat, suddenly decided to take off his jacket. Shefer, walking to their right, signaled to Netanyahu to do likewise. Netanyahu hesitated for a second before whipping off his own jacket. Barack Obama, in a white shirt and a blue tie, held his jacket nonchalantly over his shoulder. Bibi Netanyahu, in a white shirt and a blue tie, did the same. To Obama it came naturally. He is the coolest president in American history and he sauntered casually over the runway, his tie blowing in the wind. Netanyahu was more uptight, tightening the belt under his belly, not quite knowing how to hold the jacket on his shoulder; beside the athletic president, he appeared clumsy, but he went with the flow, and in so doing, proved his acting talent and adaptability to unexpected situations. Within ten seconds, here was the winning picture. The two leaders, one older, one younger, similarly dressed, walking side by side, making small talk. It was almost romantic. Later, Netanyahu complained that he'd been embarrassed; he knew he looked far less elegant than the president. Only later, when the picture was printed on the covers of three hundred magazines and was featured on important Web sites worldwide, did he understand. It was the closest he and Obama had ever been. It wasn't to happen again.

The idyll continued throughout the visit. When Obama entered the prime minister's official residence on Balfour Street in Jerusalem he was welcomed warmly by the entire Netanyahu family, and stood for a few minutes with Sara and Yair, the older son. Obama had done his homework thoroughly in preparation for this visit and made a point of flattering Netanyahu and his handsome sons, who "look like their mother." Sara Netanyahu was delighted. The special file compiled on the Netanyahu family by experts, including the CIA, psychiatrists, and intelligence personnel, also contained the fact that Mrs. Netanyahu has an obsessive addiction to flattery, especially regarding her good looks. It is common knowledge among all the couple's friends and associates, who make a point of fawning over her, verbally and in writing. Now it was the president's turn. On other occasions during the visit, Obama was charming and pleasant toward Mrs. Netanyahu. He helped her with her chair, listened assiduously to her, and generally singled her out for special attention. "It's obvious that she is completely charmed by him," said an associate of the prime minister. "Obama has done an impressive job on her." It was no coincidence. President Peres, too, when wanting to persuade Bibi to embark on political negotiations, knew that the key was in Sara's hands, and devoted considerable energy in getting her on his side.

Obama left nothing to chance during this visit. He knew by heart the names of everyone involved; he brought special gifts for each and every staff member (sweets, pictures of the White House, cuff links with the presidential seal, etc.). He was the ultimate charmer, and the atmosphere was homely and friendly. Ambassador Shapiro brought his three children to a farewell dinner. Everything looked rosy, pink, and sickly sweet. So much so that in summing up the visit after the president's departure, Netanyahu was worried. He'd spent four years vilifying Obama with much success, and he was concerned that this visit would improve the status of his nemesis. "Don't worry, it's not going to happen," he was assured.

Several political achievements were noted during the visit. Netanyahu agreed to a "quiet freeze" on building outside of the settlement blocs, and promised Israel would stop halting Palestinian tax revenues. The pinnacle came in the form of a telephone call from Netanyahu, with Obama's mediation, to Turkish prime minister Recep Tayyip Erdogan, in which he apologized for the *Marmara* incident. The Americans had invested considerable energy in these efforts, which were aimed at placing Israeli-Turkish relations back on track. Netanyahu hesitated. But it was Ron Dermer who persuaded him to agree to the president's plea. "Let's do it," Dermer had told Netanyahu, adding, "It's important to the president." Netanyahu agreed. The conversation should have taken place from a communications caravan brought especially to the airport in time for the president's departure to Jordan. Obama and Netanyahu sat there with their senior advisors; time was running out, but it was impossible to get hold of Erdogan, although it had all been coordinated down to the smallest detail. Every word of the conversation had been rehearsed. Netanyahu was supposed to say certain things that had been formulated and written, Erdogan was supposed to respond in kind. Suddenly, Obama noticed that Bibi was going over the text in his copy of the conversation and correcting something. The prime minister was trying to slip something in about the Israeli soldiers. Obama understood the potential catastrophe. The Americans knew that Erdogan would receive a simultaneous translation of Netanyahu's words and if he noticed even the tiniest deviation from the original text, there would be an almighty scandal. "Leave it, Bibi," Obama said quietly and suggested he read the text as it was approved by them, without changes. "Don't worry. It'll be OK." Netanyahu then looked at the president and saw he was serious. In the meantime, Erdogan was located and his voice could be heard on the other end of the line. Obama and Netanyahu spoke with him; Bibi apologized for the *Marmara* event and they agreed to maintain contact with a view to reconciliation. Even Erdogan, a well-known party pooper, was unable to spoil this moment. It seemed that, though forced, perhaps the marriage between Obama and Netanyahu could become a happy one. It was time for the honeymoon. Neither of them believed it would last, but at least they enjoyed the moment.

60

At Home in America

2013–2016

Ron Dermer was born in the United States and moved to Israel in 1997. His personality is split between America and Israel. He is a devout Zionist, but America still defines him in some ways. Dermer had a dream, to be Israel's ambassador to the United States. To go home to his second motherland, as the representative of his historical, first motherland. Between Dermer and the realization of this dream was the Obama administration. The White House rightly marked Dermer as a devout neoconservative, his heart and soul joined to the Republican Party, closely associated with the Bush family (especially Jeb) and the man behind Mitt Romney's state visit to Jerusalem on the eve of the presidential elections. The information that flowed into the White House about Ron Dermer during the first four years was nothing short of incriminating. He was closely associated with Dan Senor, senior foreign policy advisor to Mitt Romney, and had ties to Sheldon Adelson and Rabbi Shmuley Boteach. Dermer never hesitated to challenge the White House on every possible occasion. Americans remember his comment during one of the first Obama/Netanyahu meetings: "Mr. President, I beg to differ." It was Dermer who told Israeli reporters, "This idea of two states for two peoples is a stupid and childish solution to a very complex problem." He took every opportunity to say that Mahmoud Abbas was not a partner for peace. The Americans wanted Dermer in Washington almost as much as they wanted Netanyahu in the prime minister's office in Jerusalem, so there was a real possibility of them not approving his ambassador's credentials.

Netanyahu hesitated. Notwithstanding his respect and close association with Dermer, he could not embark on a campaign to validate the appointment. He began to come to terms with the fact that he would need to find another ambassador. Dermer was affronted. At one stage, he left for a long family vacation in the United States. He severed relations with Netanyahu, and started to renovate his home in Israel, but still hoped to persuade Bibi to change his mind. It was the first conflict between the two. In the meantime, Netanyahu decided to appoint Gilad Erdan ambassador to Washington. Erdan, an ambitious rising star in Likud, needed some time out from the political swamp in Israel and believed that the Washington appointment would accelerate his way to the party's leadership.

But Dermer didn't give in; he had a different program. He made it clear to Netanyahu that he would only accept the Washington appointment. His first step toward quelling American opposition to his appointment was the successful presidential visit to Israel. Dermer continued to attack on several fronts by attaching himself to Jewish American Democratic leaders; he participated in the prestigious Saban Forum, which enjoys close ties with the Democratic leadership, and invested all his energy in lobbying influential Democrats like Joe Lieberman, Secretary of the Treasury Jack Lew, Congresswoman Debbie Wasserman Schultz, and possibly even Valerie Jarrett. But Dermer placed most of his chips on Secretary of State John Kerry, notably by hosting, with Rhoda Dermer, a private family dinner for Theresa Heinz and John Kerry in Washington. Dermer sold himself anew to the Americans, with great panache. He would be a loyal ambassador, he would connect Netanyahu with Obama in the best possible way; he wouldn't trip landmines and was familiar with all the boundaries. All this, with the addition of the convincing leverage of Jewish activists who were willing to vouch for his new pragmatism, influenced the White House, but opposition to Dermer was still very strong in the Obama camp.

Kerry, thinking that Dermer was too close to Netanyahu in Jerusalem, pushing him further to the right, actually wanted him brought to Washington, where Dermer's damaging influence would be reduced, he'd fall in with the Obama administration, and would help to maneuver Netanyahu. Still, Obama wasn't having it.

In the meantime, national security advisor Tom Donilon was about to complete his term in office. One of the jobs Obama wanted him to do before leaving was to inform his Israeli counterpart, Ya'akov Amidror, that Dermer was not wanted in Washington. Nearing retirement and working on a very tight schedule, Donilon forgot to pass on the message. It was a big error, one that caused considerable damage. Meanwhile, in the prime minister's office, Netanyahu was worried about the Dermer appointment and asked Gary Ginsberg, an intimate associate who was close to the Obama administration, to check the climate regarding Dermer.

For many years Ginsberg and Dermer were close personal friends. Ginsberg admired Dermer's wisdom, knowledge, and talents. He went back to Netanyahu and told him it was going to be fine. To this day no one knows the basis of Ginsberg's assessment, how he checked things out and whom he spoke to, or if he actually did anything. It's possible that he simply felt that the Americans would be forced to approve the appointment. He wanted to help Dermer out and took the risk. Whichever way, Ginsberg gave Netanyahu the green light to go ahead, and everything was all right. He may have done it on his own initiative, and he might have been given a hint or a wink from someone in the White House against the president's wishes. The bottom line is that Ginsberg's move had a touch of genius. He was right. He'd said that nothing would happen if Dermer was appointed and indeed, nothing has happened. The administration, sluggish as usual vis-à-vis Netanyahu's caprices, contained the insult, and approved the appointment. President Obama fumed. When reports reached Jerusalem of Obama's reaction, Netanyahu called to apologize. Only then did Netanyahu understand how strong the opposition to Dermer had been, and that Ginsberg's green light had been fake. Non-approval of Dermer's credentials would have caused pandemonium, and the Americans chose to pass. "It wasn't supposed to happen," Bibi admitted to Obama. "I should have asked you directly." Surprised by Bibi's frank regret, Obama decided to move on and judge Dermer by his behavior and not by his past deeds. Dermer became Israel's ambassador to the United States and fulfilled his dream, which for the White House would turn into a nightmare.

A silent partner to Dermer's work in the United States was sure that Obama's people were exaggerating, that Dermer wasn't the brain behind Romney's visit and didn't help with his presidential bid. According to this Dermer associate, it was Dan Senor, Romney's senior aide, who did it to create the impression that he and Netanyahu were close, for his own political gain. They later begged Dermer not to deny what happened. Even the fund-raising dinner was no exception; American candidates make a habit of holding such dinners in Jerusalem, and Dermer wasn't there. They tried instinctively to sully him in the administration's eyes, if only because of his reasoned opinions. They found it hard to cope with his claims, so turned him into an enemy of the people.

The honeymoon between Dermer and the Obama administration didn't last long. During 2014 and 2015, Dermer was considered one of the main reasons relations between Washington and Jerusalem began to deteriorate. In late 2014, Dermer participated in a public "audition" held by Sheldon Adelson for potential Republican candidates for the 2016 presidential campaign. That same month, the Voice of Israel reported that national security advisor Susan Rice refused to meet with Dermer. Lists of visitors to the White House published in *Ha'aretz* in April 2015 revealed that Dermer had only one working meeting in the White House, with Philip Gordon in 2014. Dermer had become persona non grata in Washington. Susan Rice agreed to meet with his counterpart, Israel's national security advisor Yossi Cohen, on the condition that he arrive without the ambassador. Still, Netanyahu let him keep the job. A partial break with the White House was preferable to surrender. Netanyahu seems to enjoy seeing the president squirm. Dermer's access to Adelson was more important than relations with the administration.

Ron Dermer oversaw the struggle in the United States over the negotiations with Iran. Netanyahu continued with his hysterical warning speeches, reaching new heights with his September 27, 2012, "Looney Tunes" speech in the UN General Assembly, when he drew a red line on a cartoon bomb to show the Iranians' uranium. Iran made a point of cross-ing that line, shifting the focus to the development of a broad ability that would enable them a quicker route to nuclear power once they decide to do so.

Netanyahu was furious about the interim agreement signed with Iran in Geneva on November 24, 2013, which didn't prevent him later from prais-ing the fact that the Iran nuclear program was not only frozen but had suffered a setback. At a certain stage, those overseeing the process, in-cluding the United States, lost all interest in listening to Netanyahu. He had no influence among the world leaders involved in the negotiations, or close to zero. Netanyahu's policies now focused on the American arena.

After the final agreement was signed in Vienna on July 14, 2015, Netan-yahu turned to his alternative plan. Ron Dermer believed that the president could be beaten in Congress. The underlying logic resembled his as-sumption that Obama was a one-term president. For the president to lose in Congress with a two-thirds majority, Dermer, Netanyahu, and Adelson would have needed a long series of miracles and wonders. Anyone with eyes in his head knew that there was no chance the president would lose such a vote in an election year. But Netanyahu decided to fight to the end, despite everything. It was his own personal decision, taken against the advice of many of the senior officials in the Israeli security establishment who felt Israel should enter negotiations with Obama for a strategic compensation package. Netanyahu rejected this proposal out of hand. He refused to go down in history as the one who had participated in the surrender agreement with Iran. Once again Netanyahu's decision hinged on his imagined place in the history books and not on pragmatic reality.

Netanyahu's speech before both houses of Congress on March 3, 2015, just prior to the elections in Israel, marked the lowest point ever recorded in relations between Washington and Jerusalem. Again, the man who made it happen was Ron Dermer, in coordination with John Boehner, then speaker of the U.S. House of Representatives. Communications were kept secret. In the White House, no one knew a thing, so the announcement that Net-anyahu would arrive in Washington to speak out against President Obama's Iran nuclear agreement sent shock waves throughout the administration.

Even in their worst nightmares, no one could have imagined a guerrilla operation like this whose sole purpose was political humiliation, meddling in internal political affairs, and exploiting the Republican Party with the aim of harming a sitting president.

The invitation to Netanyahu had been extended without the president's knowledge. On the day it was made public, the American ambassador, Dan Shapiro, was in Washington, a broken man. "It's unbelievable," he said in a private conversation. "The Israelis didn't even give us a right to hear about it. Not even a telephone call to let the president know that Netanyahu was arriving." The day before Netanyahu's surprise visit, John Kerry spent several hours with Ron Dermer making lengthy telephone calls on behalf of Israel, to help on an unrelated issue. It was an outrage that Dermer had left Kerry in the dark. Israel received help from the United States on an almost daily basis and, in return, they were insulted in the most unforgivable way.

American ambassador Shapiro felt betrayed. He had spent years trying to stop the dam from bursting and to keep relations above water, trying to build something new, or at least to preserve the existing order, and then something like this happened. "I feel as if they've cut my legs off," Shapiro said in a private conversation. Even during the worst days between the two countries, he had remained a hardworking ambassador, accessible, efficient, and never giving up. He had earned the trust of the Israelis and had done his best to maintain a reasonable level of communications between Washington and Jerusalem. He was devastated. It was a personal affront that took Ambassador Shapiro a long time to recover from. He found it hard to understand the ingratitude. "We are investing all our energies here, funding the Iron Dome project, defending Israel in every international forum, veto when requested, do our best, upgrade security relations, and this is what we get in the end. Every day we get requests for help from Israel and we do the best we can. How could they have done something like this?"

This event became a fault line in the relations between Obama and Netanyahu. The White House staff repented; they should have broken the Netanyahu, Adelson, and Boehner axis. They should have learned their lesson after the 2012 elections and defused the threat, but they did nothing. Israel's move tore apart the Democratic lawmakers and forced them to choose between their president and Israel, divided the American Jewish community, and even managed to arouse anger within AIPAC, the all-powerful Israel lobby in Washington. Heavy pressure was exerted on Netanyahu to cancel his journey, but he was adamant. And he had good reason. It wasn't Iran that concerned him at that moment, but the Israeli voters. For the first time he was lagging behind in the polls, and this was the real reason for his trip to Congress. He knew that the speech would reinforce his image at home. When he stood on the podium in AIPAC, or the UN, or Congress, or any other important international forum, he was at his best, and the Israelis would forgive him for everything. This was also the reason that the original date for the speech, several weeks before the elections, was amended and the new date was set for two weeks before Israel's Election Day.

The commotion that exploded in America's political establishment in the wake of Netanyahu's appearance in Congress was colossal and drew into itself everything that was in its way: AIPAC, Jewish Democratic lawmakers, Jewish organizations, and leading media reporters.

American-Israeli billionaire Haim Saban, who is closely associated with the Democratic Party, was immediately assailed by Democratic lawmakers. Saban, who has been active for years in maintaining U.S.-Israeli strategic relations, was beside himself. In private conversations he said that the speech was more harmful than helpful to the ultimate goal, to stop the deal. He didn't understand how Bibi, who knows America, was not aware of it. He lost the White House, but he had Congress. Now he'll lose nearly half of Congress. Saban said that hundreds of Democrats talk to him; they are desperate, and Netanyahu forced them to choose between their president and their sympathy for Israel. It's insane and deliberate sabotage to the traditional bipartisan support for Israel in Congress. The prime minister sacrificed deep, long-lasting cooperation for a narrow political gain back home. Saban tried to exert his influence on Jerusalem and on Netanyahu, but failed. Two staunch Israel supporters, Senators Dianne Feinstein and Richard Durbin, sent Netanyahu an urgent letter, asking him to reconsider his decision to address Congress. "This unprecedented move threatens to undermine the important bipartisan approach towards Israel—which as long-standing supporters of Israel troubles us deeply." As an alternative, they invited him to address Democratic senators in a closed-door meeting. Netanyahu rejected the invitation. AIPAC, too, did not know how to handle this unprecedented event. No one had consulted AIPAC before embarking on it. Although the lobby continued ostensibly to back Netanyahu, behind closed doors senior organization officials understood that the speech would cause strategic damage.

The pressures increased. In the Israeli military establishment, too, they didn't approve of the prime minister landing behind enemy lines and embarrassing President Obama. Associates of the prime minister offered various bridging tactics. It was suggested to postpone the appearance until April, after the election, to avoid the appearance of making the speech for political reasons of his own. Netanyahu rejected this, too. The White House signaled that as far as the president was concerned, it would be a declaration of war, but Netanyahu did not flinch. "He didn't see anyone in front of him," said another associate, describing Bibi's mood during those days. "He decided to do it, and that was that." It was a new stage in the struggle between Obama and Netanyahu. The new Bibi moved from defense to offense and caught the president by surprise, in his own backyard. He would land in Washington without the president's permission, no matter what he said. By Netanyahu's side in this journey, like a firm rock, stood Sheldon Adelson and Ron Dermer. "Don't be afraid," they told him. And he wasn't.

Netanyahu's speech was magnetic, eloquent, and convincing as usual. He won his applause and numerous standing ovations. His media surrogates in Israel pumped out the speech around the clock, and the TV channels broadcast large chunks of it. Netanyahu was tense, but gave his usual show. The speech, this time, was written with the help of his secret ghostwriter, Gary Ginsberg, who was employed in the White House during the Clinton administration and is associated with the Democratic Party. Ginsberg, has, over recent years, held a number of key positions in large media organizations, including News Corporation. He is currently with Time Warner. For many years, Ginsberg has been closely associated with Hollywood producer Arnon Milchan, who introduced him to Netanyahu. Notwithstanding the differences in world view, they clicked. Ginsberg is extremely well versed in all the mores of modern America, and is a genius with words and imagery. He is always present at Netanyahu's important visits to the United States and, when called, comes to Israel to help Netanyahu write his key speeches. Ginsberg has never spoken to the media about his relationship with Netanyahu and maintains complete discretion. He is responsible for Netanyahu's definitive speeches, including the "duck" and the "Looney Tunes" bomb speeches. He is also said to have participated in drafting the dramatic address to Congress.

Since Netanyahu sees his speeches as unambiguous and is actually governing through these addresses, his office attaches historical importance to them. Before each speech, the office distributes pictures of the writing process and rehearsals. The pictures are high quality, with the necessary lighting and scenery and, of course, the impeccable makeup and hair one would expect from a leader of this caliber. His speeches in English are considered far better than those in Hebrew. No matter what achievements he chooses to flaunt when he leaves public life, as far as he is concerned, the real show will be the display of artistic, beautifully designed and executed pictures of his speech-writing processes. Real actions have never been Netanyahu's forte.

As the date approached for the speech, the pressure on Netanyahu increased, and the media/political struggle surrounding the event intensified. Caught between the White House and the prime minister's office and AIPAC, the Jewish lawmakers were torn to pieces. Netanyahu's back was protected by his patron, Sheldon Adelson, who made hundreds of telephone calls during those days to members of Congress. Adelson also ensured the presence of Jewish leaders in Congress to show support for Netanyahu. Abe Foxman, for example, was plied several times by Adelson. More than anyone else, Foxman symbolized the Jewish/American dilemma of those days. Politically, he is centrist, very close to Israeli prime ministers (including Netanyahu, and always very well received in the White House). Abraham Foxman is a warmhearted Jew as well as a devoted and loyal American. He supported the prime minister on the Iran issue, but he thought the congressional speech was unnecessary. Needless to say, he received a call from Adelson, who said he didn't wish to shout at him, but where does his chutzpah come from to tell the prime minister to stay at home. Foxman wasn't shocked. He has had a long and fruitful relationship with Adelson and is familiar with his style. He repeated to the gambling mogul what he'd said to the media: that he supports the prime minister and his stance on the nuclear issue, but he believes that it would have been wise to choose a different time and place in which to speak. Adelson could live with that, and asked if Foxman would be coming. Foxman had no ticket, but Adelson promised to arrange one for him. Foxman arrived at the event, armed with a ticket, which, fortunately, had arrived at his office from the Democrats' direction, so he wasn't obliged to sit in the same frame as Mr. and Mrs. Adelson, Rabbi Shmuley Boteach, and Elie Wiesel. Like many American Jews, Foxman came away from the event torn. Netanyahu had placed the friends of Israel and America's Jews in an impossible situation and sabotaged the traditional concept of bipartisan support for Israel.

Unwilling to be outdone by Netanyahu, President Obama spoke before and after Netanyahu's speech and did not hesitate to criticize Israeli interference in the private affairs of America. A well-known Jewish leader found himself in the White House shortly after Netanyahu's congressional speech. On the television screen the president was in the middle of a press conference, in which he criticized the speech. "Aren't you overreacting a little?" the Jewish leader asked a White House senior official he was meeting with. The man stood, closed the office door and asked his guest to sit. "This is something really big," he said grimly. "You don't understand how big it is. We get to hear what Bibi says in private conversations, and the wedge he is pushing into American society." The Jewish guest tried to argue, "It's stupid, what does it matter what he's saying, ignore him, let him fuck off." The senior White House official insisted, "You are wrong. It's a huge story and can't be ignored. It's the prime minister of a foreign country and he comes here to the floor of the U.S. Congress, takes advantage of the fact that the Republicans barely recognize the president, to rake in a political fortune. He comes to Washington to stand up in Congress and cast doubts on the president's intelligence and judgment. It's not done. We can't just ignore it. We are taking it all very seriously."

Netanyahu, too, was taking the situation very seriously, and continued with all his strength in struggling against the agreement. Obama fought back. It was an unprecedented battle between a sitting president and a prime minister of Israel, over a vote in Congress. On May 21, an interview by Jeffrey Goldberg was published in *The Atlantic*, included scathing criticism of Netanyahu's Election Day warning that "the Arabs are flowing in their masses toward the voting stations," as if "Arab Israeli citizens were somehow portrayed as an invading force that might vote, and that this should be guarded against." He also pointed out Netanyahu's assertion that "a Palestinian state would not happen during [his] watch," and that making such sentiments "has foreign policy consequences."

The following days, Obama addressed the Adas Israel synagogue in Washington. Here he was more reconciled, described his conflicts with Bibi as momentary disagreements, and praised the strategic ties between the United States and Israel, and his absolute commitment to Israel's security. Obama wore a yarmulke, blessed the Conservative Jewish congregation with "Shabbat shalom," and talked about the necessity of a peace process and a two-state solution. Ron Dermer was conspicuous by his absence. In addition to the *Atlantic* interview and the synagogue appearance, there was another intimate meeting between Obama and Jewish leaders in the White House. During these intimate meetings, Obama spoke of his unrequited love for Israel. He went out of his way to prove his love for the Jews, and his admiration for Jewish history and the story of the establishment of Israel, as well as his sensitivity to all forms of anti-Semitism. It's easy to learn, from what he says, that he is frustrated by the fact that his love for Israel is not returned. Someone in the congregation thanked the president for his unwavering sensitivity and apologized for the hurt he described. The president replied that he didn't think *hurt* was the right word to describe his feelings, and his interlocutor agreed, adding that it was important for the president to understand that there is no doubt regarding his motivations, only his judgment. The problem with many members of the congregation in the room was that the president had actually defined himself as a Jewish American liberal, or a Conservative Jew. "It's not right to look on Israel from that vantage point," said another of the Jewish leaders in the room, "because Jewish American liberals or Conservatives don't live in Israel and it's impossible to know from here what's better for Israelis who live there. The right way is to look at Israel from the point of view of an American."

In the aftermath of this meeting, a feeling of disquiet spread through some of its participants, about the president's talk of being an unrequited lover; as if his love for Israel was only one-way, because unrequited lovers have a tendency to become bitter and hateful and perhaps even vengeful. It's an explosive situation.

Netanyahu was going for broke. Now, too, Ron Dermer was there to blow wind into his sails. "We can win in Congress," Dermer believed, and infected Bibi with his belief. On the other side, the Obama administration decided to extend the hand with the carrot. Senior administration officials passed on messages to Netanyahu according to which the administration would be willing to sit down with Israel to discuss an especially generous compensation package. But now Netanyahu wasn't interested in handouts. First he wanted to win the election. President Obama spoke with Netanyahu in early April, after the interim agreement, and immediately after the final agreement was achieved in July. During all these conversations, Obama suggested they end the conflict and set out on a new path. Every time, Netanyahu rejected the proposal. Obama told Netanyahu that he was prepared to start working with him on security, on the compensation package immediately. Netanyahu suggested they do that after the agreement was passed. In other words, he rejected any of the president's attempts at appeasement.

Even after addressing Congress and raking in all that political credit, Netanyahu wouldn't let go. Even then, Netanyahu continued to fight, deciding not to enter into negotiations with the administration. Ambassador Shapiro was unable to understand how Israel was capable of rejecting their offer. "They don't want to talk to us," he wailed in a private conversation. "Bibi simply doesn't want to enter into a dialogue even though he knows that at this stage it's possible to receive a lot more." The Americans offered to improve what they were willing to give Israel on the condition that he lay down his arms and stop fighting the agreement just before it was being brought to a vote in Congress. Netanyahu refused. He was adamant. He was sure that Israel would get everything it would have been given earlier, because the Americans had no choice. Netanyahu was thinking of history. He believed with all his heart the Iran agreement was a modern incarnation of the Munich Pact and he wanted no part of it. He wanted to isolate himself historically from anything to do with this obscenity. Again, as usual, Bibi was much more interested in the historical outlook than the present. In the two months during which Netanyahu conducted his losing battle against Obama in Congress, Israel lost whatever vestiges of the respect it had enjoyed in the White House. Netanyahu's battle against Obama ended in a knockout. When asked by a close friend if he regrets having urged Netanyahu to speak in Congress, Ron Dermer insists he had no regrets whatsoever. When asked if it could have been done differently, Dermer insists it could not; Israel held on to its principles to the end.

The fight intensified as September approached and, with it, the fateful congressional vote on the Iran deal. Netanyahu, who had already won the elections in Israel, believed he could win in Congress, too. Proof of this belief is the call he put through to billionaire James Tisch, asking him urgently to come to Jerusalem. Netanyahu knew that Tisch was a close associate of New York senator Chuck Schumer, a Democrat, a Jew, and an avid supporter of Israel. The assumption was that many fellow Democrats would be waiting for Schumer's decision on whether to vote in favor of or against the Iran agreement. Netanyahu felt that an announcement from Schumer that he opposed the agreement would bring him closer to victory. In July, a large rally of right-wing Jewish organizations took place in Times Square against the Iran agreement, with a focus on placing pressure on Schumer. Tisch boarded his private plane, flew to Israel, and had a ninety-minute meeting with Bibi, who gave him the full presentation: You have to make it clear to Schumer that you will take a very dim view of the possibility of him not opposing this dangerous agreement, and that he would have to shoulder the historic consequences. Tisch, who felt uncomfortable with the situation, promised Netanyahu something vague. Shortly after, Schumer announced his opposition to the agreement.

By this stage, even the most fervent Republicans did not believe there was a real chance of achieving the two-thirds majority vote required to overcome a presidential veto in Congress. But Netanyahu continued to fight with all his strength. He continued to disregard all the hints and emissaries flowing in with messages from Washington. He was in a trance. He did not want to repeat his mistake over the disengagement agreement with the Palestinians, which he supported all the way, before repenting at the last minute. He ignored the constraints of the day and the hour. He was dealing with history here, specifically with his own place in it.

This historical messianism was added to Netanyahu's ever-increasing self-confidence and power-drunkenness, which followed six consecutive years as prime minister of Israel and led to an unprecedented act. According to a senior American Jewish leader, Netanyahu told him in 2014 that he had effectively erased the Obama administration. As far as Netanyahu was concerned, it no longer existed. He didn't recognize this administration. When asked by the Jewish leader: By what right does something like this happen—after all, relations with an administration do not belong only to him—Netanyahu replied that he pins his hopes on the American people, and his relationship with Congress. He had no expectations from Obama. The leader recalled how he thought, at the time, that this was insane.

This was not simple bragging. Netanyahu boycotted Obama's final two years in office. He had lost all fear, and it sometimes seemed that he was actually seeking public confrontation. He knew why. Each time Netanyahu hammered Obama in public, his stock among his traditional voters grew several fold. The process of turning Obama into Netanyahu's electoral asset was complete. Not for nothing did Bibi reject all efforts to create a road back to civility between himself and the president. If he'd even so much as considered a conciliatory move, such as dispatching the liberal, center-left Alon Pinkas (former Israeli consul general in New York) to Washington to allow him access to the president, now he was distancing himself from the White House deliberately. But Netanyahu's motive was not purely political. He genuinely believed that Obama was a historic mishap, a strategic catastrophe that befell the Western world in general and the Jewish nation in particular. Netanyahu felt a blend of disdain, disgust, and disappointment regarding Obama. If during Obama's first term Netanyahu had still tried to hide it, by the second half of the second term, he no longer bothered.

Netanyahu's feelings and behavior were reciprocated to a certain extent by the other side. Despite his cool demeanor and the pointed behavior, Obama was not unaware for a second of Netanyahu's attitude and understood, almost from the beginning, that he was being patronized. In a conversation with one of the women closest to President Obama, a highly respected senior Jewish American leader poured out his heart and said he was extremely worried about what was happening, because the president was deeply and emotionally hurt by Israel's attitude toward him. Because it is unrequited love, there is a fear that it might make him dangerous. Imagine, she replied, that you are president of the United States, the strongest superpower in the world, and there's one little country that depends entirely on you in almost every sphere, a country you are fond of and support, and you wake up on Sunday, go to church, come home, and find that on every television channel the leader of that little country is lecturing to you on how to handle your foreign policy, your intelligence, your political efficiency, and your street wisdom, and gives you public advice and scolds you. And the following day, it happens again. Same thing. And the week after, too. The American Jew became defensive: That's an exaggeration; he doesn't do it every week. To which the lady replied that in a roundabout way that he did. In fact this guy has said practically every word possible about the president except the word *nigger*. When the man said that's not fair, the response was: But that's the feeling we get.

After it was all over and the president had passed the nuclear agreement and defeated Netanyahu in Congress unconditionally, the question was: What next? This time, too, there was no lack of mediators to go back and forth to the prime minister's official residence. This time, too, neither of the leaders was overly enthusiastic. "What more can be done?" asked one of those emissaries of Susan Rice. "Is there another way to repair the situation?"

Rice thought there might be. As far as the president was concerned, the peace process was extremely important and goodwill in this sphere could be useful. Obviously, a peace treaty couldn't be achieved in the remaining time of Obama's last term in office, but the situation could be improved. Again, the hot potato dropped in the lap of Netanyahu, who immediately rolled it into the garbage. His November 2015 visit to Washington did not reap the expected results. Netanyahu deliberated and decided, in the end, not to offer the Palestinians the benefits he had agreed on with the Americans. His right-wing government did not allow room for maneuvers, and he preferred his narrow sixty-one-member minority right-wing coalition to cooperation with Obama and the international community. A large number of American Jewish community leaders were heavy-hearted. One of them recalls having called the prime minister to suggest he call the president, show him his good intentions, talk to him man to man, explain why he'd fought until now over the Iran nuclear deal, and tell him it was still possible to move on. Obama made his move: He was interviewed in the *Forward*, spoke to the Jewish Federation online, had another conversation with Jewish leaders. He was holding out his hand to Netanyahu and he couldn't allow himself to leave it hanging in the air.

During those dreadful days of the collapse of relations between the White House and Netanyahu, the American-Israeli billionaire Haim Saban tried to help. A close associate of the Clintons, Saban is in direct contact with President Obama and makes frequent visits to Israel. Although he is not among Netanyahu's natural admirers, they have a fair relationship. Saban is no Likudnik, but he has a basic respect for a sitting Israeli prime minister and a love for the country he grew up in. He cares deeply about the relationship between Israel and the United States, and in recent years he has been working hard to improve it. Netanyahu's deference for billionaires is automatic, so he respects Saban and is aware of his close ties with the White House. Saban was actually a back channel in which Netanyahu could keep contact with the curent mood in the White House even in the hardest times. Obama used Saban as an unofficial route to get messages from Netanyahu. Saban hoped it was still possible to save the relationship between Bibi and Obama. "We must overcome and heal whatever it is that's going on between you," Saban told Netanyahu in a conversation in Jerusalem after the 2015 election victory. Bibi agreed, but provided no workable suggestions. "I know that in the next two years I'll be eating a lot of margarine from the

White House," he told Saban, meaning that the automatic support from the White House is at risk. Saban replied that there wasn't even any margarine left. "You know," he added, "there will be attempts to drag Israelis to the International Court of Justice in the Hague, from the simplest soldier to the highest-ranking officer. The Americans are currently protecting you, but it won't go on forever." Netanyahu agreed. "It could include me, too, and when it happens, Obama would be pleased," he said. "How much longer do you think you can poke them in the eye? They've had it up to here," Saban asked.

Sheldon Adelson is Haim Saban's exact antithesis. Both men share an undying love for Israel, but Adelson is Netanyahu's patron, pulling strings and interfering on his behalf. Saban is merely an acquaintance, in comparison. During the collapse of relations with the Obama administration, Adelson's influence was dramatic. Most of Netanyahu's close associates believe it was Adelson's unwavering support that gave Netanyahu the self-confidence to engage in an open struggle against the Obama administration, Adelson being an extreme-right-winger and sharp critic of the two-state solution or any other compromise. It is not always clear who in the Netanyahu-Adelson relationship controls whom. Is it Bibi who is deeply rooted in the right, with Adelson protecting him; or is it Adelson who actually drags Netanyahu to the extreme right, forcibly making him adhere to the Republican Party and preventing him from conducting himself in a reasonable way with the administration? In any case, it was Adelson's approach that achieved a clear victory and, after the 2015 elections, the peaceful solution was removed from the government's agenda. For the first time in many years, Netanyahu was prepared to pay the price for his break to the right, but at that stage, there was no one to pick up the tab.

From that moment until the end of Obama's presidency, there was no private channel of communication between the Israeli prime minister and the U.S. president, an unprecedented dangerous situation that seemed to bother no one. Netanyahu fullfilled his mission: He outmaneuvered Obama without paying a real personal price. On the contrary: He used the American president as an asset. This is exactly what he wanted to happen. In his view, between 2008 and 2016, there was no America. That

thing called Barack Obama was a strange enigma, an embarrassing historical mistake. Netanyahu yearns to find the America he once knew, the
conservative, pro-Israel, Republican America. He prayed for a suitable
Republican candidate who could beat Hillary Clinton and be grateful for
Adelson's millions. His prayers were partially fullfilled. Donald Trump
did beat Clinton against all odds, but Trump is grateful to no one and has
never been a real Republican. In the meantime, Netanyahu concentrated
on the main immediate benefit from Trump's victory: He managed to
avoid Clinton, who could yet cause him to yearn for Obama. The family
DNA burned into her does not bring good tidings to Israel's prime minister. Although she is much less liberal and left-wing than Obama, when it
comes to Netanyahu, the Clintons have had more than their share of grief.
During Bill Clinton's first term in office in 1997, Netanyahu was on a visit
to the West Coast when the president was also there. The prime minister's office requested a meeting, and the White House demurred because
of a full schedule. The president was sitting in the house of a friend in Los
Angeles. The friend, a wealthy, well-connected Jew, asked him: Since you
are here already and you're not really busy, why won't you meet with Bibi?
Clinton responded with a sudden burst of anger: "It's not going to happen," he said. "That man has insulted me and the presidency, he makes
promises he doesn't keep, he caused me to promise things in his name to
other leaders, and disappeared." In 1999, after Netanyahu was toppled
from power and Ehud Barak replaced him, the Clintons were happy. "We
are so relieved," said Hillary to an associate. "You have no idea how long
we've been waiting for this." Since then, and to the present day, things
have only deteriorated. Clinton's experience with Netanyahu in her term
as secretary of state was torture. The attrition that Netanyahu imposed
on the first term of the Obama administration was a difficult experience.
The endless debates, the delays, the unfulfilled promises, the stubborn
persistence on small details, all these very nearly drove the secretary of
state out of her mind. During one of her endless telephone conversations
with Netanyahu—according to one of her assistants—Clinton took the
handset and banged it on her head several times. She looked as if a steam-
roller had driven over her after a marathon meeting in New York, in which

she tried to reach an agreement with Netanyahu over an extension of the building freeze in the territories.

Bill Clinton was the guest of honor in the rally and memorial events on the twentieth anniversary of Itzhak Rabin's assasination, held in late October 2015 in Tel Aviv. One of the memorials took place in the Rabin Center. During the cocktail reception, a small group of guests in the VIP lounge stood and gossiped: Dov Weissglass, former chief of staff of Prime Minister Ariel Sharon, Alon Pinkas, former Israeli consul general to New York, American-Israeli billionaire Haim Saban, and Rita, a famous Israeli singer. Tamir Pardo, head of Mossad, joined the group. Weissglass introduced him to Saban. The conversation focused on "the full list of Bibi's lies." Weissglass was the prime speaker, when President Clinton joined the forum. He listened carefully to the whole list, slightly amused. "That's all you have?" he asked Weissglass, and everyone burst out laughing.

To Hillary Clinton, Netanyahu is simply insufferable. Bibi considers Clinton a much more dangerous enemy because it would be harder to incite the Israeli public against her. The two of them, Clinton and Bibi, have spent the better part of 2016 praying for a miracle so they don't have to work with each other. Unfortunately for Clinton, the miracle did happen. For Bibi, it happened more than once: He has extracted all he can from Barack Obama. Obama beat John McCain and Mitt Romney, but lost to the Republican Benjamin Netanyahu. Israeli blogger Tal Schneider popularized a new term for Bibi: *Republikudnik*.

Once, when Bibi was being interviewed on an American Sunday talk show, the subtitle on the screen described him mistakenly as "Benjamin Netanyahu (R)." For just a moment, there he was: a conservative Republican senator, maybe from one of the southern states. It suited him. Israelis love him best when he is being impertinent, argumentative, and fighting for Israeli interests against the strongest country in the world. Netanyahu understands this gives him leverage. At his famous "lecture," he did not speak to Obama. He looked at the president, but spoke to the Israeli public, to the congressmen and -women, the evangelicals, and America's conservative Jews. From Netanyahu's viewpoint, he wasn't representing Israel, but the Jewish nation. He has adopted the traditional sense of victimhood and turned it into a way of life. He pumps the Holocaust and Jewish suffering and, based on this, his starting point is that of entitlement and persecution. It is, at once, a victimhood collective and personal. One of his election campaign advertisements describes the pogrom that almost resulted in the death of his grandfather in Europe. It was there that the victimhood of the Netanyahu family began and continued throughout the generations. Netanyahu lacks the ability to understand someone else's narrative; he is unable to see the other side or to feel solidarity with it. He is completely oblivious to anything that is not traditional Jewish victimhood. And against this background he is unable to recognize things that are done for him. Senior American officials have often mentioned that they have never heard him utter the words *thank you*, even though America has done great and important things for Israel during his tenure. An Israeli official once thanked Ambassador Samantha Power for something, and she responded sadly that this was the first time she had ever heard these words from an Israeli. Netanyahu has a habit of taking for granted everything that is done for him. He tends to focus on whatever is not done. He is a persecuted Jew. That's all there is to it.

How will history judge Netanyahu the leader? It is an open question. Netanyahu is still here, alive and kicking. Actually, it is one of Shimon Peres's people, an intelligent, veteran Israeli, well versed in the rules of negotiations over the generations, broadly connected in Jerusalem, Washington, and almost all the Middle Eastern capitals, who provides this explanation: Netanyahu is the one Israeli prime minister who least feared the U.S. president. Netanyahu trembled at the thought of Bill Clinton throughout his first premiership; his second, beginning 2009, was the same way, but as time went by, he managed to relax. He entered a planned conflict with Obama, attacked him face on, sidestepped him, and manipulated him. He is an ideologist who succeeds in fooling everyone at the same time. It is fascinating to see the way he's developed opposite the U.S. presidency since the beginning of his premiership, when he overcame his fear, to the end of the Obama era, with Netanyahu and Dermer convinced they'd made a clown of Obama.

According to this man, Netanyahu has grown into the position. In Netanyahu's own eyes, he has become the Jewish version of Winston

Churchill. He has adopted a trait he never had before: composure. He is no longer quickly alarmed. He works through enormous risks, conducts himself calmly when everything is up in the air, and is convinced that he can beat Obama on his own playing field, manipulate him, scatter mines, mislead. After all, the Americans are forever being replaced; whereas with us, it's always the same faces. The same Mahmoud Abbas and the same Saeb Erekat, the same Netanyahu and Lieberman and Barak and Tzipi Livni and all that jazz. The only thing that's needed is to keep toppling each incoming president. Obama actually allowed Bibi to manipulate him. His choice of Mitchell as emissary to the Middle East was a bad one, according to the same source. Where everyone is a snake you have to be a bigger snake, too. Mitchell couldn't distinguish between true and false, so was led astray. The only appointment worse than Mitchell's was that of John Kerry, a good man, but naïve, full of good intentions and devoid of the animal instincts necessary for survival in the Middle East. Bibi saw that right away as well. He knew how to sort out these weaknesses and exploit them. Admittedly he's a Republican, but he was raised in America and understands the codes. Together with Dermer, also an "American," and the gigantic economic umbrella provided by Adelson, the third American, they built an invincible axis whose objective was to survive Obama safely. Did they succeed? It depends on your viewpoint. As for the nuclear issue, they were defeated. And the Palestinian issue? They succeeded. They survived Obama, but without peace.

PART THREE

✡

IRAN, IRAN, IRAN

61

Iran

1992–2009

Benjamin Netanyahu prides himself for having been the first to pinpoint the Iranian danger. He is partially correct; Netanyahu made a major contribution when he raised the issue not only on Israel's agenda, but also to that of the rest of the world. Back in 1992, Netanyahu was claiming in the Knesset that Iran was striving for a nuclear bomb and would achieve its goal within three to five years. This extravagant evaluation was not realized, but may have contributed to the seriousness with which his prophecies were taken in the future. At that time, Yitzhak Rabin was prime minister of Israel, and he warned at every opportunity against the Iranian threat. Rabin coined the term "Khomeinism without Khomeini," repeating it in many of his speeches and meetings with world leaders, although Iran's nuclear program was in its embryonic stage and unrevealed as yet to the West. When Netanyahu was elected prime minister for the first time in 1996, the Iran issue received preferred status. Bibi was exposed to intelligence courtesy of the head of the research division in IDF's Military Intelligence ("Aman"), Brigadier General Amos Gilad, known as Israel's "Mr. Intelligence." This was all it took to put in motion all of Netanyahu's inherent apocalyptic instincts. His genetic penchant for identifying pending catastrophes pushed him to announce during his 1996 address to the U.S. Congress that Iran was galloping toward the acquisition of nuclear arms. America was not really blown over by the news, but Netanyahu was. The Iranian nuclear prospect fired his imagination, and he homed in on it like a moth to a flame. Netanyahu became obsessed with Iran. He had a firm factual basis; he identified a genuine danger. Iran was indeed advancing toward a nuclear bomb and later increased its pace. Iran's supreme leadership was resolved to turn Iran into a nuclear superpower. As far as Netanyahu was concerned, a nuclear military Iran was tantamount to the end of Zionism, and threatened a second Holocaust for the Jewish people. This was a gross exaggeration on his part, and turning the Iran issue into a messianic obsession was harmful. Unlike other Israeli prime ministers such as Rabin, Sharon, and Olmert, who made sure to keep Israel behind the scenes in the anti-Iran political campaign, Netanyahu placed himself center stage. He turned Israel into the world's barking and snarling guard dog, goading the rest of the world into action and threatening to attack by itself. At the same time, he warned against a second Holocaust, as if he were politicking in the Warsaw Ghetto. The prime minister equated the Iran threat to the gas chambers, identified Iran with Nazi Germany, and claimed that the treaties between the West and Iran were no different from the Munich Pact.

He was asked by several people to refrain from these comparisons. One of these people was Shaul Chorev, head of the Israel Atomic Energy Commission, the secret body responsible for all of the country's nuclear issues. According to foreign sources, Israel has an active nuclear reactor in Dimona, a nuclear research reactor at Nahal Sorek, and a nuclear arsenal consisting of between eighty to two hundred nuclear warheads, some installed in Jericho ballistic rockets. According to this information, and in accordance with reliable evaluations provided by various intelligence services, Israel is a nuclear superpower. Chorev implored Netanyahu to stop comparing the Iran agreements to Munich. Surveys showed that Netanyahu's campaign of fear had succeeded in causing anxiety among Israel's population.

According to an Israeli civil servant, "Instead of frightening the Iranians, Bibi has frightened the Israelis." Notwithstanding Chorev's pleas, and those of other security officials including Military Intelligence chief Amos Yadlin, and other politicians, Netanyahu charged full steam ahead with this kind of propaganda: A nuclear Iran was a danger to Israel's existence, a new Holocaust was likely to happen, Israel couldn't allow this to happen, and if the world did not deny Iran the nuclear power it strives for, Israel would have to, even if by force. The more of these fear speeches Netanyahu delivered, the more convinced he became by his own prophecies of doom. Iran turned into his life's mission, the one thing that interested him and the main engine for his own political growth. Who else was there to defend Israel from a nuclear Iran?

During Netanyahu's first term in office, much effort was made to persuade the United States that the Iran threat was indeed tangible. To this end, Netanyahu dispatched his best people. In 1998, General Amos Gilad, from IDF's Military Intelligence, together with Ron Prosor, the congressional delegate at the Israeli embassy in Washington, attended a meeting with Vice President Al Gore at the White House. Also present was national security advisor Leon Fuerth. Gilad and Prosor presented their hosts with intelligence to prove that Iran had a military nuclear program. Years later, Prosor recalls, "They thought we were insane, and didn't take us seriously."

Netanyahu's minister of defense during that first term, Yitzhak Mordechai, was the messenger. He was a moderate, which gave him more credibility with the Clinton administration. On his third official visit to Washington, Mordechai met with his counterpart William Cohen. Together with General Shlomo Yanai, head of the IDF Planning Department, Mordechai introduced the U.S. defense secretary to fresh intelligence on Iran's nuclear intentions. Before this meeting, Mordechai had received the latest updates from Yoram Hessel, former chief of global operations, intelligence, and the foreign relations division of Mossad. Even in the Pentagon, Israel wasn't having an easy time selling the threat. In all the confrontations until then, the Americans didn't know how to swallow the Israeli obsession with Iran's nuclear ambition. Iran's Islamic revolution was young, fewer than twenty years old; Khomeini had died only nine years before, and Iran's military nuclear program sounded like science fiction. To this day, the meeting with William Cohen is seen as the moment America began to consider the threat a valid concern. After examining the material provided by Mordechai, Cohen said, "Mr. Minister, I am happy to inform you that on this issue, we are on the same page."

Netanyahu lost the 1999 elections and left the prime minister's office without getting anywhere on the Iran nuclear program, which continued to move forward. Throughout his "lost decade" (1999–2009), Netanyahu had no leadership status and was unable to make any relevant decisions. For a brief period, he served as foreign minister under Ariel Sharon, then as minister of finance, but the government's focus during those years was on putting an end to the second intifada and dealing with the country's calamitous economic crisis. The Iran threat had been pushed aside, though in reality it marched forward. In 2002, the Iranian uranium enrichment facility in Natanz was exposed together with news of Iran's nuclear race. In an interview with *Ha'aretz*, Professor Uzi Arad, Netanyahu's national security advisor from 2009 to 2011, said that during that year there was no one to explain to the Americans the wisdom of "going for Iran, instead of invading Iraq." Arad must have forgotten that there had been someone who had explained to the Americans that it was preferable to invade Iraq. This "advisor," in this case, was Benjamin Netanyahu. In September 2002, even before his return to Israeli politics, Netanyahu delivered a speech to Congress in which he said, "There is no question whatsoever that Saddam is seeking, is working, is advancing towards the development of nuclear weapons. . . . If you take out Saddam, Saddam's regime, I guarantee you that it will have enormous positive reverberations on the region." The Americans listened to Netanyahu, toppled Saddam's regime, but found no signs of any nuclear technology or any kind of nuclear material in Iraq. In the meantime, they got al-Qaeda in Afghanistan and Daesh (ISIS) in Iraq, and the existing order in the Middle East has crumbled. Netanyahu built himself a reputation for being an alarmist who makes mountains out of molehills. It could have been his undoing later, when the mountains he saw turned out to be real, but at this time no one believed him.

Netanyahu resigned from the Sharon government in 2005 and, after the 2006 elections, became leader of the opposition. During those years, Netanyahu occupied an office in Tel Aviv's Europe House, which had been placed at his disposal by the building's owner, businessman Moti Zisser, who was at the time one of the richest men in Israel. It was a small, rather Spartan space that contained a large dry-erase board on which three words were written most of the time, "Iran, Iran, Iran." Visitors to this office heard countless lectures on the subject, accompanied by his habitual drawings and demos on the whiteboard.

Netanyahu returned to power in 2009, and brought Iran back with him. He prayed for a Republican president and received not only a Democrat, but a liberal African American whose world view was all about appeasement, whose life's work was devoted to ending unnecessary wars, to achieve peace in the Arab and Islamic world, and to be a soothing presence. Netanyahu was wary of Obama from the first moment. And the feeling was mutual. Netanyahu's problem was an unwillingness to compromise, but he needed to be flexible on the Palestinian issue in order to get his foot in the door vis-à-vis the Iranian issue. At first he seemed to go with the flow, delivering his Bar-Ilan speech, but as soon as he realized that the Obama administration was not as firm as the Bush administration, and that this president could be easily manipulated, he decided to put everything on the line. He was not about to pay the price of the peace process without first receiving guarantees that, ultimately, he would be getting the real deal. He didn't want to relinquish anything in return for promises. He suspected Obama from the word go, and possibly even earlier. Above all else, it was imperative to him that he remain in power. He was absolutely convinced that his political survival was crucial to the security and future of the state and the nation. "The state is me," he believed, and believes to this day; first and foremost, he had to remain in power. "After that, we'll see what happens." To remain in power, he wouldn't compromise on the Palestinian issue. It is for that reason that he missed the Iran issue.

62

We Have the (Military) Option!

2009

Following his election victory in 2009, when Netanyahu began negotiating his coalition government, IDF spokesman General Avi Benayahu wrote a special memo to chief of staff Lieutenant General Gabi Ashkenazi. The title was "Work with the 'Incomer.' " Most of the security establishment's big brass were unfamiliar with Bibi. To the chief of staff, the generals, and heads of the various departments and intelligence organizations, the newly elected prime minister was a complete enigma. Benayahu, who served as media advisor to Defense Minister Yitzhak Mordechai during Netanyahu's first term in office, worked closely with the prime minister and knew him well. "Last time," Benayahu told Ashkenazi, "the security establishment made a serious mistake by pushing Netanyahu into a corner. To his last day in the PM's office, they never saw him as one of theirs, treated him as an outsider. He didn't get on with chief of staff Amnon Lipkin-Shahak, with Minister Mordechai, Shabak chief Ami Ayalon, and Mossad chief Danny Yatom. They had marked him out almost from the beginning. What actually happened is that they missed out on him." Ashkenazi asked his spokesman why he thought it was a loss. "Because Bibi is a man you can work with," Benayahu said, surprising Ashkenazi. "He's not as extreme as people think. True, he made a mistake with the Western Wall Tunnel and the attempted assassination of Khaled Mashal, but in the end, Peres didn't have the nerve to give back Hebron. Then Bibi came along, had a cup of coffee, smoked a cigar, and gave it back. Then he went to Wye Plantation and signed the Oslo Accords. He wanted to get out of Lebanon, but the IDF didn't let him. You need to know how to work with him. The problem is that he wasn't allowed into the club. In the end, he nearly withdrew from the Golan Heights during the negotiations with Assad that Lauder brokered."

Ashkenazi asked Benayahu for his advice. "Invite him here, before he takes up office. Informally. Just the two of you. When he arrives, put your feet up on the table and put an ashtray down, so he'll feel comfortable enough to smoke a cigar. Give him the feeling he's one of the guys. That he's wanted. After that, everything will flow. I suggest you give him a little seminar right here, especially on the Iran issue. That's the one that's closest to his heart."

Ashkenazi, who respected his shrewd spokesman's political insights, bought the idea. A few days later, in early March 2009, Netanyahu, prime minister–elect, arrived at military headquarters for a meeting with the chief of staff. As planned, the meeting was informal. Netanyahu was due to take up his new position in less than a month. Ashkenazi laid out before him the situation vis-à-vis the country's security, as well as the challenges and the dangers Israel was facing. When he reached the Iran issue, he called in the extended team responsible for Iran, under the leadership of its special project manager, deputy IDF commander in chief General Dan Harel. Together the two military leaders briefed Netanyahu on Iran's advances. Then they reached the chapter on "Israel's preparedness." Now Netanyahu's eyes began to sparkle. He was unaware that the IDF was so deeply embroiled in preparation for a real military option for attacking Iran's nuclear infrastructure. As the briefing progressed the prime minister–elect grew ever more excited. He asked to hear more and more, asked in-depth questions, and arranged a further meeting. At one point Netanyahu asked Ashkenazi if he could use the telephone. Ashkenazi led him to his office and pointed to the phone. "I'll leave you alone," he said. "You can stay," Netanyahu said, smiling, then called his wife, Sara. As it happened, the two were planning a romantic evening out to celebrate their wedding anniversary. "You'll never believe what I'm seeing here," he reported to her emotionally. "I'm going to be late this evening, I can't help it, I'll tell you when we meet, you won't believe what you hear." Nothing in the world could have supplied Netanyahu a more justified alibi for missing an anniversary dinner with Sara than the Iran issue. It was an obsession that beat in both their hearts, equally. By then their personalities had already fused into a single entity, and she understood.

Over the years, Netanyahu's sense of mission on the Iran issue had turned into something genuinely messianic. He and Sara often repeated to anyone willing to listen that Bibi had to return to power in order to save the nation of Israel.

He inflated the Iranian threat to biblical proportions. Bibi has always believed with all his heart that the threat is real. He has a talent for grandiose exaggerations that somehow seep through into his subconscious and turn into an alternate reality. When he saw that the IDF had not been entirely inactive, and that a genuine military option existed for an attack on Iran, he was gripped by a kind of mini-euphoria. Ashkenazi and his officers were subjected to a flood of compliments. "I am so surprised," he told them. "The stuff you have prepared here will provide space for decision making; it is very impressive." They agreed that Netanyahu would return the following day for the rest of the briefing and so it was. In the end, this improvised seminar lasted three consecutive days, during which Netanyahu was exposed to Israel's most closely guarded secrets. On the one hand, he was deeply concerned by the Iranians' meteoric nuclear advances, details of which he had just been shown. On the other hand, he almost fell off his chair when saw what the IDF was preparing. The plans were creative, but they were still in the early stages. Netanyahu was still impressed, and believed he had seen the seeds of Israel finally having an option for genuine action. It was for this that he had been elected, he believed.

63

The Iranian Brotherhood

2009–2012

The day after the first meeting, Netanyahu updated Minister of Security Ehud Barak on what Ashkenazi had shown him. Barak noted the excitement. Bibi sounded like someone on steroids. In Sayeret Matkal, Barak had been Bibi's esteemed commander. Barak knew him inside out and almost immediately noted the potential. Those were the days of coalition negotiations between Netanyahu and the various relevant political parties. Barak's Labor Party had suffered a painful loss, winning only thirteen Knesset seats, an unprecedented low. Realizing that the voting public was not interested in him, Barak sought a new political engine that would return him to the arena. Netanyahu's obsession with Iran would provide Barak's new lever. From that day, in early March 2009, Barak became a completely different person; it was as if he was reborn. He became the main supporter of the hawkish approach that pushed for an Israeli attack on Iran's nuclear infrastructure. He supervised all the staff work, personally managing the debates, overseeing the progress of building the military option, and pressured the various security branches and politicians in order to garner support. A wily and sophisticated politician, Barak understood that the Iran issue could be his life insurance policy with Bibi. He knew that there was no support in the security establishment for an attack on Iran. He also knew that Netanyahu needed a significant security crutch to lean on. In the past Barak had been prime minister, defense minister, and IDF chief of staff. He was Israel's number-one soldier, the ultimate proponent of national security. It was upon him that the existence of a military option depended. The power and influence granted him by Netanyahu as a result of this situation were far greater than that of an electoral lever. Barak was intent on transforming himself from Netanyahu's highly respected commanding officer during his time in Sayeret Matkal into the supreme security authority from which Netanyahu could draw legitimacy for the greatest campaign of his life. This was the plan, and Barak executed it with a touch of genius. Barak and Netanyahu's Iranian fraternity was born during those three days in early March 2009. But Barak, being a seasoned and cynical strategist, knew there was also a third party to this fraternity, the American side. He knew that the Americans were chary about the possibility of an Israeli attack and realized immediately that he was holding in his hands a life insurance policy: Bibi could not attack Iran without him. In Washington, likewise, he was the only one capable of preventing such an attack. Thus the Israeli defense minister became the fulcrum between two supremely powerful forces. He made the most of the situation throughout the next three years.

Unlike Barak, Netanyahu's intention regarding Iran was authentic. In the dozens of speeches he made on the subject during those years, he was telling the truth. When he promised that if diplomacy failed, Israel would act on its own, he believed wholeheartedly in every word he said. He lived the pose, was enamored of the mission, and persuaded himself that he was capable of carrying it out. Had he undergone a polygraph test on the question of whether he would dare attack Iran if there was no other way to stop its nuclear program, he would have said yes, and he would have been found to be telling the truth. Over three long years, Netanyahu and Barak drove the entire world crazy with the Iran issue, and scared the Americans to death, as well as the Europeans and some of the top echelons of Israel's security establishment. They sunk many more billions of dollars into the military option, expanding, intensifying, and improving on it. They embarked on exercises, training, and real practice runs in preparation for the day of reckoning. They encountered an unprecedented crisis of confidence with the United States, which included a cold war between the two countries' intelligence services, when both sides attempted to confuse, to conceal, and to deceive one another. Ultimately it all petered out, as it should have from the onset. Israel did not attack Iran in 2011 and 2012 for two reasons: Barak didn't want to, and Netanyahu didn't dare. It was the chronicle of a failure foretold.

64

Dangerous Relations

2012–2015

Mossad chief Meir Dagan was the man who held the Iran file. Following a lengthy slump in operations, Dagan, an IDF derring-do operations man, returned Mossad to its former glory. Under Sharon and Olmert, Dagan had focused on international terror, the Iranian nuclear program and, according to foreign sources, the Syrian nuclear program as well. With Netanyahu's arrival, the Iran issue took over Mossad's agenda, its three most important issues: Iran, Iran, and Iran. All of Israel's energy and resources were pledged to this end, even at the expense of other crucial fronts. Dagan's successes were impressive and his tenure was extended several times. He was in office for almost nine years. During his final year, his relations with Netanyahu ran aground. In Israel, the prime minister is the direct commander of Mossad and the Shabak. Dagan had been appointed by his old friend Ariel Sharon, and the two were perfectly suited. Both men were introverted, tough men of action who loathed chitchat, avoided pathos, and disdained clichés. Netanyahu is the complete opposite, so relations between them deteriorated steadily to the point that during Dagan's final year in office, it was impossible for both to be in the same room.

The tense atmosphere and the mutual scorn allowed only minimal co-operation between them.

Dagan was especially infuriated by the fact that Netanyahu tried to dodge responsibility for dangerous operations. Dagan saw no similarity between the image Netanyahu tried to project and the situation inside the room. Unlike previous prime ministers, Netanyahu was averse to approving operations presented to him by Mossad, and continued to drag after him the trauma of the failed assassination attempt on Khaled Mashal. He didn't like to take personal risks; as far as he was concerned, such a risk would be worse than endangering the country, because no one could replace him on his Iran mission. Netanyahu's system was simple: In meetings with the Mossad chief, he simply did not respond when Dagan asked him for approval of planned operations. Since these meetings are recorded, Netanyahu did not wish to be heard approving an operation, preferring to keep silent, or nodding his head, or simply telling Dagan to "move on" to the next clause. But Dagan refused to move on. "Mr. Prime Minister, do you approve, or do you not approve?" Dagan would insist on a reply and Netanyahu would continue to hold his tongue. On several occasions Netanyahu could be heard saying, "I leave it to your discretion." Dagan insisted, "My discretion does not matter; you are prime minister." Seeing that it was impossible to argue with him, Netanyahu preferred to hint to Dagan that certain operations had not been brought to him for approval. He chose not to know. "Just keep the military secretary updated after it is carried out," he would say to Dagan, who refused. "According to law, you have to approve an operation." When reminded of the meaning of the term *law*, Netanyahu panicked. His fear of the law was burned in his awareness from past run-ins with it. In private conversations, Dagan did not hesitate to call Netanyahu a coward. To Dagan cowardice was anathema. "He'd always try to distance himself from anything that could become dangerous, he never accepted prior responsibility for actions that might go into a tailspin; only in retrospect, if the operation succeeded, would he be quite ready to take credit for it." Dagan believes that Netanyahu is not only a coward, but also a liar. He does not buy into the theory that Netanyahu believes his own lies and is therefore not really a liar.

"No," says Dagan, "in some of his lies, he knows that he is lying. Sometimes he believes his own lies, sometimes he doesn't. He is a qualified liar." When these relations between the two men became public, Netanyahu's people tried to claim that Dagan was taking revenge on the prime minister for not extending his tenure for a tenth year, but it is not true. Dagan was ready to retire.

In the 2015 elections, Dagan mustered all his strength, which had dwindled in the wake of a complicated kidney transplant and a fierce struggle with a cancer that had spread throughout his body, and arrived in television studios and rallies to say loud and clear that Netanyahu was a danger to Israel's security. "This is the first time," he said in a private conversation, "that I am terrified for the country's survival. Netanyahu is a real danger to the existence of the Jewish state." Netanyahu has never been popular among Israel's security heads, both active and retired, but the disdain and resentment displayed by Dagan toward him was unprecedented. The prime minister refused to approve Mossad's plans to carry out a unique and daring operation, even though several opportunities arose in the course of his time in office to do so. Dagan knew that Netanyahu feared the repercussions of such an event, and continued to look out for his own political skin. He misses Olmert, who, he knows, would have approved this daring operation out of strategic considerations and without a thought for his own political fate. Dagan's plan to get rid of one of the sworn enemies and perpetrators of terror against Israel was rejected by Netanyahu. Dagan presented an operational plan that was as original as it was brilliant, with a high chance of success. But Netanyahu refused. He didn't want to take the risk. Those were the only two large operations that Netanyahu refused to approve. On all the other cases, Dagan developed a system for getting approval: He would bring with him several other Mossad senior officials to the meeting with the prime minister, sometimes even the team commanders destined to carry out the operations. Dagan knew that in the presence of others, Netanyahu would wish to appear courageous and he'd have no choice but to approve the operation. Moreover, Dagan knew how jealously Netanyahu guarded the "commitment to security" image he had built for himself over the years, and that he feared that his hesitation in the presence of large forums would be leaked to the press. On occasion, too, following a meeting in which approval had been granted, Netanyahu would be quick to summon Dagan back to his office to reconsider the decision. Dagan was able to pre-guess those cases in which Netanyahu might change his mind.

Dagan was very fond of falafel, a famous national oriental dish, and after meetings with Netanyahu, he made a habit of getting some. When it seemed to him that he'd be called back, he would go to the nearby Mahane Yehuda market for his falafel. When he believed this wouldn't happen, he would drive the distance to Abu Ghosh. When he wasn't sure, he would choose to eat at the Turk's in Mevaseret Zion, just outside Jerusalem. Dagan's rate of accuracy in those gambles was high, and he ate a lot of falafel in those years.

A definitive crisis in the relations between Netanyahu and Dagan took place in the course of a private meeting at the prime minister's residence on Jerusalem's Balfour Street. Usually such meetings take place in the office; for some reason, this time Dagan was summoned to the official residence. The two were sitting in the prime minister's secure study when the door opened and in walked Netanyahu's wife, Sara. The Mossad chief fell silent. "You can continue, Meir," said Bibi. "Sir, I would prefer to continue when we are alone," Dagan replied. "It's all right," said Netanyahu, "Sara is up to speed. She knows everything, she is partner to the secret." Dagan refused. "I need to receive approval from Yuval," he said. "As far as I know she has no community clearance." The Yuval he was referring to was Yuval Diskin, head of the Shabak at the time, who was responsible for all matters concerning Israel's security clearances. The matters under discussion at that meeting between Dagan and Netanyahu came under the definition of Israel's highest level of secrecy and, in order to be exposed to them, maximum security clearance, known as intelligence community (nicknamed "community") was required. Mrs. Netanyahu had no security clearance of any kind. When she understood that the Mossad chief was firm in his refusal to continue, Sara stood up and stomped out of the room, slamming the door behind her. Meir Dagan was never again summoned to the prime minister's residence.

Even before this incident, there had been several lengthy discussions between the Mossad chief and the prime minister in which the essential differences in the two men's world views were revealed. On one such occasion, after a tricky professional argument, Netanyahu asked Dagan, "Tell me, why don't you try to indulge me?" Dagan replied, "I don't think it's my job to indulge you." Bibi pointed out, "You are subordinated to me." To which Dagan replied, "Yes, and if you are dissatisfied with me, you can release me from my position. My loyalty is to the country."

Another time, Netanyahu told Dagan proudly about a speech he had delivered to the AIPAC lobby. Dagan said that he didn't believe in speeches. "I don't recall a single speech of yours," he added. There was an argument. "Speeches make history," Netanyahu replied, and listed some of his important speeches, including the Bar-Ilan speech, the speeches he'd delivered to Congress, AIPAC, and in the UN General Assembly, adding that he remembered all of Churchill's speeches. "Yes," replied Dagan, "but Churchill didn't make do just with speeches. He also took action." It was a direct hit, and Netanyahu fumed.

65

A Secret War

2009

The job of preventing Iran at all costs from achieving nuclear military power was entrusted to Mossad and Meir Dagan. At first it appeared that Iran's nuclear race could be stopped by means of a covert war waged, according to foreign publications, by Israel and the United States against Iran at that time. That war had a code name, "Olympic Games," and according to foreign sources, it included the use of fighters and opposition forces inside the country, and cyber warfare as well as assassinations. However, as time passed it became clear that while it was possible to delay Iran, it would be impossible to prevent it from achieving nuclear power by these covert means. The only choice was the use of real military force. Netanyahu reached the conclusion that only an open and powerful military attack would succeed in stopping the Iranians; in other words, a war between Israel and Iran. Before Netanyahu returned to power in 2009, Dagan had committed himself to preventing the Iranians' march to nuclear power until 2015. And he fulfilled this commitment. As far as he was concerned, the fact that Iran had not obtained nuclear power, in spite of all its efforts, constituted a huge Israeli achievement. According to Dagan, "Every year there are 150,000 new students of mathematics and physics in Iran. The nuclear bomb is a weapon system that was first used in 1945. All the drafts and formulations can be found on the Internet. A nation such as Iran, with valuable stores of human and infrastructural resources, with determination and power, should have achieved nuclear power long ago."

During those years it appeared that foreign intelligence elements had managed to penetrate the Iranian system, causing vast damage. Iranian nuclear scientists were murdered or disappeared, strange explosions took place, computer worms had penetrated operating systems, and a long and creative series of sabotage attacks within and outside Iran caused serious damage to the country's nuclear program. This covert war was reportedly conducted in cooperation between the Israeli Mossad and the CIA, and it extracted a high price from Iran. In private conversations, Meir Dagan made no mention of Israeli involvement, but pointed out that "Iran's defense is intelligence and their evaluation of the situation is no worse than ours. They understood that they were exposed, [and] they decided to slow down and they knew why. Add to this the escalating regime of sanctions and the result was a decision not to push forward with the nuclear program, but to keep advancing slowly and carefully, to maintain a safe distance, until a suitable opportunity presents itself."

In May 2009, less than a month after Netanyahu's swearing in, Western news media reported that the Israeli Air Force had practiced an attack on Iran. According to reports, more than a hundred F-15 and even F-16 fighter jets had been deployed in the exercise, which included aerial refueling. The jets flew westward over the Mediterranean Sea, exceeding the distance equal to an eastward flight toward Iran's nuclear sites and back. According to a senior Pentagon official, this was the first indication of the Netanyahu government's intentions. The first stage in Netanyahu and Barak's joint plan was to set off all the warning sirens in the West. At the same time, the IDF was ordered to escalate the completion of the military option, the budget for which was virtually unlimited. In the IDF, the top echelons identified a change in strategy. "Bibi is serious," said Ashkenazi to his headquarters officers. Meir Dagan in Mossad, together with Yuval Diskin in the Shabak and Amos Yadlin from the Military Intelligence branch, understood that

Israel was embarking on a new era. At the same time, Israel's media came to life as an ever-increasing number of scenarios and speculations began to appear. Netanyahu and Barak did nothing to stop the stories. Netanyahu formed special teams to work on the Iran issue and established the Forum of Seven, an intimate ministerial group destined to become the secret forum dealing with the Iran issue. In addition to Netanyahu and Barak, the forum consisted of ministers Moshe "Bogie" Ya'alon, Dan Meridor, Benny Begin, Avigdor Lieberman, and Shas leader Eli Yishai. Later the forum added an eighth, Yuval Steinitz. When Lieberman resigned from the government after being served with an indictment, former Shabak chief minister Avi Dichter replaced him.

The main objective of this forum was an in-depth study of the Iran issue. It consisted of an unprecedented seminar spread over dozens of meetings, each lasting many hours. Eight Israeli government ministers were exposed to all the intelligence material; discussed all aspects of a possible attack on Iran, all the potential repercussions, all the scenarios, and all the assessments. Netanyahu's plan was for this forum to formulate the necessary operational outline, which he would then present to the cabinet for approval. The forum's meetings were classified top secret; the ministers were required to leave their cell phones outside, to sign confidentiality agreements, and to become partners in the state of Israel's closest secret. There was no stone that this clandestine security seminar did not turn in checking out Israel's military option in Iran. All the theories were examined. Never in the history of Israel had there been so complex and extensive a theoretical security journey as this, on so fateful a subject. The debates were prepared according to an orderly progress graph compiled by Netanyahu's military secretary, General Meir Califi. They probed the subtlest resolutions; dealt with all conceivable eventualities and scenarios, all potential repercussions, all the results and all the risks. The problem was, however, that the forum had no legal validity. To decide on going to war (an attack on Iran was tantamount to war), Netanyahu would have had to achieve a majority vote in his political-security cabinet, which is a statutory body. The forum was a body established for debate and study purposes only; it had no authority. But Netanyahu and Barak gradually forgot this detail. They considered a majority vote in the forum for an attack on Iran to be something of great importance.

In 2009, Western media channels started publishing reports and exclusives relating to Iran's advances in its nuclear race. Anonymous sources leaked stories to the media, flooding it with material that almost always proved accurate. Most of the material was credited to Iranian opposition sources. Iran was forced to expose its secret nuclear facility near Qom after news broke that Western intelligence agencies had discovered it earlier. In late September 2009, a London newspaper reported a meeting between MI6 and Meir Dagan, where the MI6 chief related Saudi Arabia's objection to Israeli fighter jets flying over Saudi airspace on the way to attack Iran. He also reported at that meeting that Iran was secretly developing detonators for a nuclear bomb. Israel did not respond. Iran responded with a successful dispatch of a Shahab 3 rocket capable of reaching targets within Israel. Iranian president Mahmoud Ahmadinejad announced that "Israel would never dare attack Iran." As in a Hollywood action movie, the tension built.

66

Crazies: Get Down off the Roof

2009

Netanyahu and Barak's plans encountered the first problems when it became clear that all the security heads in Israel were united in their objection to the Iranian adventure under their current conditions and timing. Chief of Staff Gabi Ashkenazi was excited during the first year by the flow of cash and improved abilities, but there was a vast distance between this and the actual operation. Mossad chief Meir Dagan led the opposition to the plan and was joined by Military Intelligence chief Amos Yadlin; Shabak chief Yuval Diskin; General Amos Gilad from Ministry of Defense; and even the air force commander Ido Nehushtan, followed by his successor Amir Eshel. In the forum the situation was not a great deal better. Aside from Avigdor Lieberman, none of the other ministers actually sided with Bibi and Barak. Dan Meridor, Benny Begin and Moshe "Bogie" Ya'alon, who was the minister for strategic threats, all registered their objections. The Shas party leader, Eli Yishai, wavered. And he tipped the scale.

Bibi and Barak tried to persuade the security heads by every possible means. The elegant dinner Meir Dagan was invited to at Barak's luxury apartment in Tel Aviv was almost romantic. Dagan was later invited to Netanyahu's Caesarea residence. Ashkenazi and Yadlin were similarly feted.

But it changed nothing. The security heads were opposed in principle to a military attack on Iran, believing that Israel should go for such an attack only as a "last resort." They believed that it was impossible to carry out such an attack without strategic coordination with the United States, that a "renegade" Israeli attack could, in their opinion, do much more harm than good.

Under such circumstances, Barak and Netanyahu found it hard to obtain a majority vote among the ministers. Here, too, they tried everything: intimate meetings, beseeching, and even manipulation, the most sophisticated of these attempts were exercised on Shas leader Eli Yishai. Shas is an ultra-Orthodox Haredi party, disconnected from matters of security and worldliness. Yishai was an Orthodox politician with little knowledge of military issues. At one point, Yishai was shown a presentation that led him to believe that the generals were actually in favor of attacking Iran. Yishai was horrified to learn at one of the crucial debates that the situation was the complete opposite. At that time, the Shas party had a single supreme leader, Rabbi Ovadia Yosef, an octogenarian Torah scholar and genius whose world was the Torah law. He was the only arbiter, the first and the last. Here, too, Bibi and Barak tried all the manipulative tricks at their disposal. For weeks on end they played a sophisticated game of chess with their counterparts, all trying to overcome each other. Occasionally plans came unstuck, manipulations collapsed, and opposing results were achieved. The best example was a meeting between Moshe "Bogie" Ya'alon and Rabbi Yosef. Netanyahu and Barak hoped that Ya'alon would succeed in explaining to Yosef the dangers of a nuclear Iran and promote his support for an Israeli military attack at a time decided upon by the cabinet. But Ya'alon, who did not object in principle to an attack, but believed Israel was still far from a situation that would force it to attack, achieved a contradictory result. He did describe the gravity of the situation but went on to explain to the rabbi the dangers of an Israeli attack without American support. The meeting between Ya'alon and Yosef, which was supposed to bring Shas into the supporter's camp, backfired.

Rabbi Yosef's opposition intensified and his representative in the forum, Eli Yishai, joined the opposition camp. It was then that Bibi and Barak realized that Ya'alon was not with them. He was a former chief of staff, well versed in all the relevant material, but he hated unnecessary adventures. Despite also having lost Yishai, they continued to try. One day Ya'alon ran into Chief of Staff Ashkenazi coming out of a meeting with Netanyahu. "So they're trying to get a decision out of you, too?" he asked.

Netanyahu also held lengthy conversations with Dan Meridor, as well as launching into arguments in the forum. Meridor, formerly a promising Likud prince and proud Revisionist, had, in those years, become a voice for the party's moderate, pragmatic, and sane members of Netanyahu's government. He was a security buff, but also a realist. "Your concept is mistaken," he told Bibi and Barak. "You can't drag the Americans into this. We can't force them to attack. That's not how it works." When Netanyahu insisted, Meridor told him, "You know America, and you're quite a good American player, but the America you are familiar with is Republican. America is not only the president. There's Congress, there is public opinion, there's the media. The main problem is that there is no support in America for another war. After Afghanistan and Iraq, even the Republicans aren't in a hurry to get involved again. That's why the campaign of intimidations is superfluous."

Meridor and Benny Begin, son of the first Likud prime minister, Menachem Begin, were the heart of the axis that opposed an attack on Iran without the United States. The objections put forward by Begin, son of the "father of the theory" who had attacked Iraq's nuclear reactor thirty years prior, were significant. Both men believed in the impossibility of preventing a nuclear Iran by military means. There was a limit to power. Iran was not Gaza or Lebanon. In the end, it could harm Israel's deterrence. Meridor even refused to meet Rabbi Yosef on the matter. "I'm prepared to study a page of the Talmud with him, but not to discuss these issues," he said.

67

"Don't Surprise Us"

2009–2010

In Washington, the warning lights started to flicker shortly after Netanyahu again entered the prime minister's office. The United States operates a substantial number of intelligence collecting systems in Israel, according to *The Wall Street Journal*, and efforts at garnering intelligence have escalated significantly since the tension began with Iran. Israel's security activity was leaked almost immediately, as were the establishment of the Forum of Seven and the issues it addressed. United States ambassador to Israel Dan Shapiro worked overtime, using all his connections in Israel's top echelons to extract details on what was happening in the country. He met and interrogated numerous Israelis with access to Netanyahu and Barak in an attempt to understand what the two were planning, and how serious they were. During those years, Shapiro was the most worried man on the American side. As the first forward observation officer, he was supposed to supply the warning. All this responsibility rested on his shoulders, and he was confused. His sources told him that Bibi was serious, and that Barak was out of his mind. Others said that Barak was serious, and that Bibi was out of his mind. Some said that it was an Israeli fraud, and others still believed it was genuine. Shapiro tried to establish relations with the Israeli security system, especially with former generals, in an attempt to understand what was happening. The number of versions he heard equaled the number of people he talked with.

Meanwhile, in Washington, the stress level was constantly on the rise. It wasn't clear, and it needed to be. They first focused on Israel's security minister, Ehud Barak, who also operated as a kind of foreign minister for American affairs in Avigdor Lieberman's place. During this time period, Barak visited Washington more than any other security minister. He maintained a bland façade but gave the Americans the impression that Netanyahu was serious. At some point the Americans began to see that Barak was playing a game, but that they were hard put to identify what it was. They opened additional channels, as many as possible. Meir Dagan received a good number of concerned telephone calls from Secretaries of Defense Robert Gates and, later, Leon Panetta. It turned into a weekly ritual. "I hope you are not serious about those things you are saying," Gates would say to his friend, the Israeli Mossad chief. "I would like to stress that an attack on Iran is contrary to American interests. We are deployed in the Middle East, we have forces in Iraq, in Afghanistan, we have divisions in the Gulf, you'll drag us into a war we are not prepared for and don't want." In every meeting by a senior American security agent in Israel—and these visits grew in number—the Iran issue always led the agenda.

Things were similar with Gabi Ashkenazi. To this day, Ashkenazi is not convinced that Bibi and Barak's Iranian operation was anything more than a sophisticated game of fraud. Had he believed that it was real, he would have gladly cooperated. "If you want to wave an ax of war, there's no problem," he used to tell the prime minister and defense minister. Ashkenazi stood at the most sensitive fulcrum between the American and Israeli security systems, and knew the Americans were unimpressed by the speeches and threats issued by Netanyahu and Barak. They would only be concerned by evidence of genuine preparations, training, exercises, and acquisitions. In long conversations with Admiral Michael Mullen, Ashkenazi would say, "Admiral, you don't know how serious this is. I'm telling you, our politicians are extremely serious. You should take it seriously." Mullen passed on the message. Concern in Washington increased when these words were joined by acts, such as the big May 2009 airborne maneuver, which was followed by other military activity. Ashkenazi had an interesting experience after the big maneuver. Even before all the Israeli aircrafts landed in the bases, an American Marine from the U.S. embassy appeared at the IDF Kirya base in Tel Aviv, bearing a secure telephone. Admiral Mullen was on the line, wanting to talk to Ashkenazi. "Gabi," said the admiral to the general, "I hope you are not going to surprise me." Ashkenazi was unreadable: "If you don't want us to surprise you," answered Ashkenazi, "you know exactly what has to be done." This relationship between Ashkenazi and Mullen was strategic to maintaining the intimate axis between the armed forces of America and Israel, as well as for mutual reassurance. Mullen would vent his grievances: "Gabi, my friend, you know we have too much on our plate right now." Ashkenazi replied, "So at least prepare some plans, make yourselves look as if you intend to do something." Over the years, Ashkenazi often heard this question and his reply was always the same. Throughout those years, it was understood that the situation was under control. Israel never promised it wouldn't surprise the United States. Somehow a fraternity developed between the people in uniform on both sides, and the personal relations between Ashkenazi, Dagan, and Yadlin and their American counterparts remained a kind of anchor of mutual respect, fair play, and sanity.

Ashkenazi's dilemma, as well as that of Dagan and their colleagues, was not simple. On the one hand, the senior Israelis wished to placate the Americans, to explain to them that they themselves did not support an attack that was not coordinated with the United States, and hinted that the politicians would not carry out such a move without support from the military. On the other hand, they were committed to the policies at a political level. It was unclear who was on the political level. The military was subject to the government. Netanyahu and Barak did not have a majority in the forum, and it was not clear whether they had a majority in the cabinet. Nonetheless, Mossad answers directly to the prime minister. The senior Israeli officers involved found themselves in a no-man's land. Most of the time they participated in a pantomime of "hold me back." Feelings were mixed. The posturing may have helped accelerate sanctions, placing more pressure on Iran, but they were not convinced that Netanyahu and Barak would settle for the deception. They feared their behavior would ultimately lead to a war. For long periods of time, Ashkenazi believed that Netanyahu and Barak's intentions were real. Dagan, too, feared this possibility, and said that even if their plan was to withdraw at the last moment, it could well be too late to block the escalation. Only Military Intelligence chief General Amos Yadlin was almost completely convinced that these were idle threats. He wasn't as fearful as the others. According to Yadlin, Netanyahu wanted to attack, both believed and dreamed of carrying out such a move, but he was unable to achieve it on his own. The second man, Barak, was putting on a show. He didn't really believe in the process and when the moment of truth came, he would bolt. Years later, Yadlin would reenact those days in closed forums: Barak, for his part, put on a perfect act. It was his way of getting endless quality hours in private with Netanyahu, and with the Americans. "Which is why," said Yadlin in private conversations, "I was relatively cool." Yadlin tried to reassure the people around him. He argued with Dagan, Ashkenazi, and even with Yuval Diskin, the Shabak chief. Once, at the end of a meeting of the Knesset foreign affairs and security committee at which he presented an intelligence review, Yadlin was approached by opposition leader Tzipi Livni. She, too, was deeply concerned by the possibility of an attack on Iran, and dragged Yadlin aside for a private conversation. "You've no need to worry," Yadlin told her. "It's not going to happen."

According to American sources, the major debate surrounding an attack on Iran consisted of coordination with the Americans. Israeli security heads made it clear that a possible Israeli attack would not be effective without strategic cooperation with the United States and with other countries in the region. In his meetings with Netanyahu, Yadlin explained: "There is no need to ask for permission from the Americans, but they are sitting in Iraq. They are able to launch their fighter jets against you, they can intercept us; we are dependent on them and on what they will do the day after. We'll need the backing of the UN Security Council, we'll need to place a marine and air closure on Iran, and America must be behind us. We don't actually need a green light from Washington; we won't get it. What we do need is a yellow light. A tacit agreement. Background cooperation. An Israeli attack vis-à-vis a red light from America is tantamount to an act of insanity."

Netanyahu was unconvinced. On American issues, he was unprepared to accept advice or to listen to criticism. "Amos, when you talk to me about Syria, Hezbollah, or Hamas, I listen very carefully. But when it comes to America, it's different. After all, we haven't been collecting intelligence from the Americans [after Pollard, Israel committed itself to refrain from spying on U.S. soil]; you have no material that I haven't. And I know the Americans better than you do. I grew up there, I lived there, I am half American myself. I think like an American." Not to be outdone, Yadlin replied, "It's true that we are not collecting intelligence in America, but I don't agree with the other half of what you are saying. The America you were raised in was completely different. It's changed: with regard to Israel and in many other ways, too. It's more Hispanic, black, colored, and more liberal. It's an America I am not sure you are familiar with." These conversations between the prime minister and the Military Intelligence chief (who is the formal "national intelligence analyst," lasted many hours and included many disagreements. Yadlin resented Netanyahu's use of Holocaust terminology in connection with Iran. "Come on, Bibi," he said, "we're not in the Warsaw Ghetto, we're in the strongest country in the Middle East, why are you comparing it with the Holocaust? It's a strategic threat and a security challenge, but it is nothing like the Holocaust." Netanyahu listened, but didn't really hear.

As time passed, so did the tension increase between Netanyahu and Barak and their security chiefs. A serious incident took place at a meeting attended by the chief of staff; Mossad chief; Military Intelligence chief; air force commander; and IDF Planning Department chief, General Amir Eshel. Eshel asked for permission to speak, but Barak and Ashkenazi denied him this. Netanyahu sent a note to his military secretary, General Califi, in which he asked: "What's that about?" Califi exited the meeting with the prime minister and explained, "He wants to report on the IDF's current capabilities, so you'll understand that it's impossible at the moment to carry out an attack."

Califi and Ashkenazi spoke a couple of days later. Califi, the prime minister's military secretary, was in a delicate position. His direct commander was Chief of Staff Ashkenazi. The military secretary was a member of the forum, headed by the chief of staff, but he works for the prime minister.

Torn between these loyalties, Califi, an officer who is as straight as an arrow, tried to maneuver while sticking to the truth. "You are making a mistake," he said to Ashkenazi. "It would be best if the prime minister were to know the truth." Ashkenazi disliked the comment; he didn't want to be the one to break it to Bibi that the Iran attack plan was unfeasible. As he saw it, this was the defense minister's job. "You are mistaken," Califi said. "In the end, it's you who'll have to manage the war. You are giving the prime minister the impression that it's possible and not telling him that, at the moment, it isn't. You need to tell him everything, with an emphasis on what is missing. He needs to know this." Ashkenazi asked what he thought was the best way to do it. Califi suggested he should write the prime minister a letter detailing preparedness. Ashkenazi did so. In the course of a forum meeting a few days later, Ashkenazi passed to Califi a draft copy of the letter. Califi noted down some comments. Ashkenazi completed the letter and sent it to Netanyahu, who read it and was horrified. He still hadn't comprehended that Barak had been taking him on a wild-goose chase.

During that period, the international media tied Israel to covert operations around the nuclear program. According to reports in *The Wall Street Journal*, Israel was working undercover in Iran, executing several covert and extremely dangerous operations that, had they been revealed, could have started a war between Israel and Iran.

At one point, IDF chief of staff Ashkenazi discovered that Netanyahu and Barak had established their own secret channel for discussions that bypassed the security system. The two had made a habit of meeting almost every Friday, sometimes on Saturday, too, at Netanyahu's residence in Caesarea, smoking expensive cigars, sipping whiskey or cognac and wine, and making plans. Ashkenazi, Dagan, and their friends suspected that at those meetings, Barak was loading Bibi up with false representations and giving him information that didn't match reality. This became obvious later at the debates in security forums. Netanyahu was clearly surprised to hear some of the information presented. Contrary to protocol, the military secretary was not present during those Friday meetings between Barak and Netanyahu, and no notes or minutes were recorded. Barak exercised all his charm and magnetism, as well as his past authority over Bibi, to capture his imagination and present him with the plethora of possibilities for the Iranian nuclear program. For Barak, this was one more element in a sophisticated campaign of fraud. Barak, too, believed he was working for Israel's security. He was thoroughly familiar with Netanyahu and knew that the greater Bibi's conviction in the possibility of an attack, the stronger his message, which meant the West would take the matter more seriously. The only problem was that Netanyahu wasn't in on these secrets. To him, an attack on Iran was the only option.

One of the outstanding points of contention at that time was the question of what the Americans would do if Israel attacked, what they do the day after, and if there was any chance of dragging them into a conflict with Iran. Ehud Barak believed the United States might join the effort under certain circumstances. Meir Dagan and Gabi Ashkenazi firmly rejected the idea. Netanyahu was torn. He wanted to believe his minister of defense. During this period, Barak and Dagan both visited Washington to discuss security questions. In conversation with Jim Jones and Leon Panetta, Dagan was told in plain English that the United States wanted Israel to coordinate any consideration of attack in Iran, and firmly opposed an independent Israeli military action. Dagan returned to Israel with the message: There was no chance of dragging the Americans into war.

The forum convened shortly after this. When the issue came up again, Dagan was surprised to hear Barak declare that following his own visit to Washington, he believed the Americans were "flexible" regarding an attack. Could it be that Leon Panetta had said things to Barak that contradicted what he'd been told? The Mossad chief decided to check it out, and called Panetta, describing Barak's presentation to the forum. Panetta was as surprised as Dagan, and a week later an American representative arrived with a transcript of his meeting with Barak. Panetta had told Barak the same things he'd told Dagan, and there was no mention of "American flexibility." The Mossad chief reported his findings to the prime minister, who didn't seem to be on board with them, so keen was he to believe the minister of defense.

68

Unlawful Alert

2010

The tension reached an all-time high at a meeting of the forum a few days before the eve of the Jewish New Year in September 2010. The prime minister was stressing the importance of a genuine military option, reiterating that it was important Israel's enemies knew this. The importance of American backing for a military move had also already been raised, as was the need for international support. By that stage, Ashkenazi, Dagan, and the other officers were aware that Netanyahu and Barak had a private communications channel shrouded in fragrant cigar smoke and alcohol fumes. By then, the atmosphere between the political side of things and the military was murky. The debate itself dealt with several marginal issues that were not directly connected with Iran. As the meeting reached its conclusion, Netanyahu made an unplanned announcement. "Friends, the minister of defense and I wish to instruct the system to prepare for a C Alert." Silence fell on the room. It took the military personnel several seconds to take in what had been said. Arming the system for an attack on Iran was a strategic order. "C" signifies preparation for an attack shortly after the command is given. The first outburst came from Mossad chief Meir Dagan. "Gentlemen," he said, "this decision is unlawful. Its significance is the recruitment of reserve divisions. This requires a government decision, or a government-authorized cabinet decision." Barak asked Dagan what the problem was. Dagan continued: "You have obviously forgotten the meaning of 'C,'" Dagan shot back. "It is a recruitment of reserves, the air force, intelligence, calling back all the repaired aircraft from the hangars; it goes out with little notice, and deteriorates very quickly into full-scale war. Within one, maximum two weeks, the other side identifies what you are doing and prepares in turn." Ashkenazi joined in: "Your decision is tantamount to a decision to go to war. It's not a decision on a defense-minister or chief-of-staff level. The army is not an accordion that can be easily stretched and then shrunk back. This is a decision that can create an escalation. We'll carry out whatever the political level instructs us, but in a lawful way. Only Cabinet can give the army this kind of order. We can't spend months in such a state of alert." Ashkenazi was a former chief of operations and he, too, understood the significance of the order. After his two colleagues had spoken, Yuval Diskin joined the minirevolt in the room. The atmosphere became heated, the debate loud and strident. The loudest voice belonged to Meir Dagan. He shouted and banged on the table. Netanyahu and Barak panicked. The first to recover was Barak. Netanyahu accepted the verdict slightly differently. They withdrew the order; afterward Barak was overheard saying, "With a general headquarters like this one, we would never have gone to war in 1967." It was a sharp, searing, and unprecedented thing to say, and it reverberated for a long time to come. It was difficult to return to normal after pressing for a C Alert. The national security advisor, Uzi Arad, who had heard of the intention to place the system on alert, was quick to send Netanyahu a letter in which he presented some aspects of such an order prior to going into operation. Netanyahu's response was laconic: "The time will come for it." The cabinet was never convened in order to approve the alert, which faded from the agenda, but Netanyahu's relationship with the most senior levels of the Israeli military establishment would never be the same again. The opening four, Gabi Ashkenazi, Meir Dagan, Yuval Diskin, and Amos Yadlin—the chief of staff, the Mossad and Shabak chiefs, and the head of Military Intelligence—were due to retire in less than a year. Dagan would become one of Netanyahu's bitterest enemies. Yadlin would run against him in the 2015 elections on the Zionist Camp Party lists as candidate for minister of defense. Diskin would voice his opinion on Netanyahu in a series of interviews and Facebook posts and become one of the prime minister's sharpest critics. Ashkenazi, who is considered Israeli politics' next great hope, would be entangled by Ehud Barak in a smear campaign that would keep him out of action for four long years. Barak and Netanyahu teamed up to keep Ashkenazi away from the possibility of entering politics and damaging his image.

A large part of the Forum of Seven's security debates at that time took place in Mossad headquarters in the Tel Aviv area. Ostensibly this was due to security considerations. Netanyahu liked the place, in no small measure because of the pampering elements (a private kitchen and a well-stocked bar), but also because it was considered absolutely safe from spying. When it comes to eavesdropping, Netanyahu is very paranoid. In an attempt to reduce his cell phone use, every call he receives opens with the question, "Are you on a landline or a cellular?" He is convinced that he is constantly under surveillance, even in the prime minister's office. Some of his political rivals have wondered where this fear comes from, and about the source of Netanyahu's knowledge of listening devices. At that time Netanyahu might have suspected that he was being listened to by enemies of Israel or political rivals; he was suspicious of the Americans' mighty National Security Agency. Once he even asked the Shabak to check the garden of his private Caesarea residence. Some of the security chiefs were convinced that his insistence on holding meetings in Mossad headquarters was not due to his paranoia of being eavesdropped on, but because of his and his security minister's hedonistic tendencies, and the isolated compound was far away from the public and the news media. During his first term in office, Netanyahu used to spend weekends at the compound, which boasted a luxury private swimming pool and an excellent chef—until the media found out. Unlike the ministry of defense or the prime minister's office, Mossad provided the means for real pampering without anyone knowing about it. Bibi and Barak were able to sit there, enjoying a glass of whiskey or wine and leisurely smoking their cigars. According to one of the generals present, the atmosphere was more reminiscent of a scene from an Italian Mafia movie than a serious debate on a civilized country's security issues. On several occasions officers or government ministers complained to Netanyahu about the strong cigar smell. Eventually he stopped smoking during meetings. Barak found the separation from his glass of whiskey hard to bear.

69

His Honor the President

2007–2012

The balance of power involved in the passionate struggle for an Israeli attack on Iran included yet another player: Israel's president, Shimon Peres. He objected with all his being to the military adventure into which Netanyahu and Barak were trying to drag the country. In Israel, the president has no authority in operational or national defense issues. His role is mainly symbolic. But the fact that Peres had served as prime minister, minister of defense, and had shared the country's secrets for decades meant he had full access to ongoing reports on matters of security. Peres had a military secretary, an efficient and well-run office, much spare time, and a fully formed worldview. The president maintained regular private audiences with all the heads of the armed forces, from the chief of staff via the Mossad chief, Shabak chief, head of Military Intelligence, COGAT (Coordinator of Government Activities in the Territories), and other relevant people. They all briefed him on a weekly basis. When Netanyahu became prime minister in 2009, Peres had already been president for nearly two years. He had another five years to serve. From the first moment, he began to suspect Bibi's adventurousness. At first, he hoped that Barak's presence alongside Bibi would help restrain the prime minister, but he soon realized that he was gravely mistaken. Peres kept a close eye on his two younger colleagues and understood that they were preparing an escapade. He was terrified.

Shimon Peres and Gabi Ashkenazi took up their positions in 2007, Ashkenazi in February and Peres in July. The elderly president liked the vigorous yet taciturn chief of staff almost at first sight. For the deeply concerned Peres, who was losing sleep over the situation, their regular meetings became something of an emotional prop. The more he understood the dangers embodied in Netanyahu and Barak, the stronger became his relationship with Ashkenazi. Peres exerted all influential weight in persuading Ashkenazi of the dangers of a military attack on Iran. Ashkenazi, who did not support an attack from the onset, shared Peres's concerns, so they racked up many hours of conversation in meetings, telephone calls, and in consultation. Peres had a similar, albeit less intense, relationship with the heads of the other armed forces. In 2010, *Ma'ariv* printed an exposé of the gargantuan struggle over the possibility of an attack on Iran going on between the president and the chief of staff, on the one hand, and the prime minister and minister of defense on the other. The exposé caused an uproar. Netanyahu and Barak were furious. They demanded that everyone who could have been involved be made to undergo a polygraph to reveal the source of the leak. *At one point, Barak demanded that Ashkenazi undergo the polygraph test himself.* Their fury did not subside. Netanyahu and Barak believed that Peres was turning the IDF senior commanders against them and their plans. As far as they were concerned, this was treason.

Peres didn't give in. Experienced in years and in struggles, he forged forward energetically. The president maintained a close relationship with the various security heads, lecturing them at length on the insanity of an Israeli attack on Iran. He met with politicians from all sides and implored them; he met with world leaders and shared secrets with the Americans. Even with the "stars" themselves he had frequent meetings: There was a weekly meeting with Netanyahu as well as regular and frequent meetings with Barak. The two usually avoided references to Iran. When they didn't, they only increased his concern. Peres's relationship with Netanyahu and Barak was complex and multifaceted. They had both, in turn, beaten him. Bibi beat him in the elections following the Rabin assassination, and Barak pushed him out of the Labor Party leadership after those same elections. Peres doesn't take these things to heart. He makes sure that if he loses all the battles, he wins the wars. For three years Peres stood firmly against Netanyahu and Barak's effort to launch an attack on Iran, and conducted a worldwide campaign of pressure, working all his connections, to kill it. Peres never was the kind of person to let things play out and hope for the best. He was familiar with some of Ehud Barak's past campaigns of deception that ended in tragedy. During the tensest years, between 2010 and 2012, Peres was one side of a triangle that included Chief of Staff Ashkenazi and Mossad chief Dagan, a triangle that dealt with horrifying scenarios and profound concerns. When Netanyahu and Barak discovered this triangle, they saw in it an attempted putsch against elected leaders and against democracy, a claim that had some substance. An Israeli president is a symbolic figure who is not supposed to intervene in military affairs. The chief of staff and Mossad chief are supposed to be subject to the political system: the prime minister, the minister of defense, and the government. Whereas Ashkenazi and Dagan made sure not to cross any red lines and considered their relationship with Peres, including updating him, to be a part of their duty, Peres disregarded any such distinctions. He was approaching ninety years of age, he'd already seen everything, he had opposed the successful attack on the Iraqi nuclear reactor in 1981, he was considered the father of Israel's nuclear capabilities; he saw himself as the responsible adult. He was convinced, as Netanyahu and Barak were, too, that the very existence of the state of Israel was at stake, the future of the Jewish nation. Those were two years of war, Peres and the heads of the armed forces together with the U.S. administration against Israel's prime minister and minister of defense. Both sides were capable of anything.

Bibi and Barak fumed. They threatened Peres. At first, this took the form of hints and, as the campaign advanced, it became more detailed. However, protocol reigned in the president's conversations with the prime minister and minister of defense. The threats were obscure. Strong language was reserved for conversations between the advisors and office staff.

According to *The Wall Street Journal*, the situation peaked in August 2012. At the beginning of the month, Israel received a visit from U.S. secretary of defense Leon Panetta. Israel's window of opportunity for an attack on Iran was about to close. Netanyahu and Barak's threats had reached new heights. The Americans had obtained worrying intelligence on Israel's intention to carry out a ground offensive in Iran that would break the paradigm everyone was expecting, and could drag the entire region to war. Israel's security chiefs were replaced in the course of 2011: Ashkenazi, Dagan, Yadlin, and Diskin giving way to Chief of Staff Benny Gantz, Mossad chief Tamir Pardo, Military Intelligence chief General Aviv Kochavi, and Shabak chief Yoram Cohen. It was a new team lacking self-confidence and devoid of any significant specific gravity. It was the definitive moment of truth for the entire Iran business. The "zone of immunity" that Ehud Barak spoke of was about to come into effect. The Iranians were on the verge of launching nuclear installations that were impenetrable to aerial attack. For Israel, it was now or never. That year, Chief of Staff Gantz established new action teams to deal with the Iran issue. In an attempt to think outside the box, he included two retired reserve generals. The plans in the IDF headquarters in the Kirya base in Tel Aviv were altogether different. In October 2015, *The Wall Street Journal* reported that an Israeli military plane had entered Iranian airspace in 2012 and returned unharmed. American intelligence intercepted this penetration. According to this information source, Israel had planned a ground offensive in Iran, consisting of elite forces that would penetrate the Shi'ite country, take control of the nuclear installation in Fordow, destroy it, and be rescued while the IAF attacked other targets as a diversion. The Americans were well aware of the significance of this operation. Panetta had arrived to lift— physically, if necessary—Netanyahu's finger from the trigger and to assure the world that the United States was committed and determined to prevent a nuclear Iran. The only man to welcome him wholeheartedly to Jerusalem was President Shimon Peres. At their much publicized and photographed meeting, Peres said that Israel was unable to attack Iran on its own, and that he had complete faith in President Obama and his commitment to prevent a nuclear Iran. Following this event, Shimon Peres and his people experienced a wave of threats from Netanyahu's people. "We can destroy Peres easily," his people were told. "We'll tar and feather him, and we'll expose his private parts to the public. He is causing untold strategic damage to the country."

On August 2, Peres was supposed to celebrate his eighty-ninth birthday. That day he was on a tour of the southern Israel town of Yeruham. Tension surrounding the Iran issue increased. Peres continued to receive fresh intelligence, in real time, on occurrences in the security system and developments in the plans. Worry caused him to lose sleep. Loud headlines in the local media pumped up the sense of urgency. At the same time, a briefing was published in the United States, stressing that Israel was incapable of destroying Iran's nuclear infrastructure on its own. The briefing came in the wake of an interview that Ehud Barak gave to *Ha'aretz* columnist Ari Shavit. Barak was interviewed anonymously, and referred to in the article as a "decision maker." He was described as a master pianist. Little imagination was required to identify the interviewee, who specifically stated that an Israeli attack on Iran topped the country's agenda and would most probably take place. This interview was supposed to be Israel's statement before the court of history when it attacked Iran. In the course of that year, the Americans began to gradually understand the way various political factions in Israel had been deceiving them. The warning bells began to subside. It was known that the armed forces in Israel opposed an operation, and it became more and more clear that Netanyahu and Barak's intimidation tactics were merely idle threats. Then came the interview with the "decision maker," in the wake of which Panetta and Dempsey declared that Israel had no real ability to destroy or block Iran's nuclear program. Among the Forum of Seven, the American briefing set off a storm. "Look what you've done," said Dan Meridor to Barak. "You've harmed our deterrence; now Iran knows we are incapable of stopping them." The objections among the seven, which had in the meantime become eight, to an offensive in Iran remained firm. Bibi and Barak did not achieve a majority. But President Peres refused to rely on this and decided to take advantage of his eighty-ninth birthday by granting brief interviews to the TV channels, in which he would refer to the Iran issue and warn against an Israeli military campaign. Some of the people around him objected, but Peres was determined. He was aware of the fact that he was celebrating his birthday in the remote southern town of Yeruham, and invited all three television channels to join him there. One after the other he granted them taped interviews for broadcast on the evening news. The day continued pleasantly. Netanyahu called to wish him a happy birthday, oblivious of the trouble about to befall him that evening on television. In the interviews, Peres stressed his trust in President Obama and his determination to prevent a nuclear Iran: "It is clear to us that we cannot do this by ourselves and we have to go with America," he said. The president's stance clashed head-on with Netanyahu and Barak's, and took the wind out of their sails. They were furious with Peres. That evening the threats against him were especially fierce, with the brunt of it coming from Ron Dermer. "Beware of us, Peres will pay dearly for this. We know exactly who he's talking to and what he's aiming for, he's crossing all the lines, we'll make sure to publicly destroy him, his popularity is only because Netanyahu hasn't attacked him"; these were a small part of what Peres's horrified followers heard. One of Peres's team who received a threatening message of this kind on his car phone called his partner into the car so she could hear it firsthand; he was sure she wouldn't believe him otherwise.

President Peres was flying in a helicopter to Jerusalem while all the TV channels aired the interviews and wasn't available by phone. As soon as he landed and climbed into his official car, he was attacked by a barrage of phone calls. Peres's feelings were mixed. On the one hand, he had received a report on the threats against him. On the other hand, countless calls flowed in from senior IDF officers, armed forces commanders, and others who praised him. Some even went so far as to say, "You've saved Israel." Peres was pleased with himself. For years afterward, he was convinced that he had played a key role in blocking an Israeli attack on Iran.

A similar saga took place at around that time before one of Peres's flights to the United States. In those years, Peres made frequent trips to the United States, and for good reason. The timing of this particular trip was sensitive, when tensions were at their height. Netanyahu and Barak tried to take preemptive action and invited Peres to a meeting before leaving for Washington. At the meeting they demanded he refrain from speaking publicly about the nuclear issue, and not to pull the rug from under their joint venture. It was a difficult meeting; voices were raised. From there, Peres left straight for the airport. His face was drawn, but his determination remained firm. "They won't shut me up," he told his aides. Peres belongs to the generation that established the state of Israel. He established the nuclear reactor in Dimona; he sent the IDF to Entebbe; he removed Israel from Lebanon; he built the Israeli aircraft industries; he had no intention of bowing down and giving in. Peres feared his two enemies were capable of carrying out their threats, and he swore an oath that he would do anything to thwart them.

In the struggle between the upper echelons of the IDF military establishment and Netanyahu and Barak, Peres was the tiebreaker. He provided a wailing wall for the Americans; he was the attending psychological prop of the military establishment and the responsible adult for the political system. He also exerted pressure on cabinet ministers and members of the Forum of Seven. To his opinion, he fully deserved the medals granted him by President Obama and Congress. As he saw it, he was acting on behalf of the state of Israel and not the United States of America. Netanyahu and Barak thought differently. To them he was a kind of traitor on a mission against the country's vital strategic interests, and the leader of a gang of collaborators within the system.

70

Dialogue de Sourds

2009–2012

Relations between Israel and America, which had been improving until mid-2009, began to decline shortly after Netanyahu took office on March 31, 2009. The intimacy that Ariel Sharon and Ehud Olmert shared with Washington disappeared, replaced by the bitterness and suspicion that arose from mutual resentment between Obama and Netanyahu. Dissent over the Palestinian issue did nothing to lighten the atmosphere and, once the Israeli push to attack Iran started to heat up, it worsened already deteriorating relations. Throughout Netanyahu's first two years in office (2009–2011) the Obama administration took Bibi's threats about Iran seriously. During the worst tensions, Obama resorted to access dumping, sending an endless stream of top-ranking security personnel to Israel. Each was tasked with reassuring the crazies in Jerusalem and Tel Aviv that Iran would be contained. Secretaries of state and defense, their deputies and assistants; senior members of staff in the Pentagon, the White House, including the National Security Council. All made the trip to Israel. That a week went by without a high-ranking American visitor in Tel Aviv's general staff headquarters or the prime minister's office in Jerusalem was rare. It was a planned march, the objective being to maintain constant contact with a troublesome ally. At the same time, the offices of the prime minister and, especially, the minister of defense and military chiefs were bombarded with telephone calls.

Another cold war between Washington and Jerusalem was being waged in the media. Those years saw a battle of tendentious leaks, with Israel suspecting that the Americans were repeatedly leaking information on the Israeli concept of an attack on Iran, while the Americans knew Israel was deliberately misleading the Western media with false intelligence on Iran's nuclear program, information that made the United States and the West look ridiculous. Every time something happened in Iran and the media went looking for the culprit, sources in the United States pointed the reporters to Israel. Again Netanyahu was annoyed. He knew the Americans were not buying the propaganda war, were isolating him, trying to set him apart. At the same time, according to *The Wall Street Journal*, the United States was escalating efforts to gather information in Israel. The NSA placed top priority on Israel. The CIA greatly increased its efforts. Satellites and radar devices deployed in and above the region increased their output, with Israel in its crosshairs. They were determined that their out-of-order ally did not surprise them. Every time an Israeli fighter jet was sent for maintenance repairs it got recorded; each training sortie was observed. U.S. ambassador Dan Shapiro worked overtime trying to uncover Israel's real intention. During those years he turned into an amateur psychologist, digging into the souls of Netanyahu and Barak to uncover their intentions. It has to be said to Bibi's credit that during those two years he managed to dupe the entire world when it came to Israel's actions/intentions with Iran. Israel's activity in those years greatly increased pressure on the United States, which passed it on to the other superpowers, which increased sanctions on Iran.

The thing that caused the loss of faith between the Israeli establishment and the Obama administration was the president's change in policy once he took office in 2009. Until then, there had been an agreement between Israel and the United States over a joint policy. The agreement had been negotiated by Mossad chief Meir Dagan and his American counterpart back in the time of Bush and Olmert. It was an unwritten but detailed agreement. At first, it was Dagan who formulated the concept and presented it to Bill Barnes at a meeting in Tel Aviv. Later he discussed it with his counterpart in the CIA, and it was subsequently approved by national security advisor Stephen Hadley. George Bush and Ariel Sharon sealed the deal. The United States would place sanctions on Iran, which would become more severe with time, until they became crippling. The idea was to exert ever-increasing pressure on Iran. During the early stages, the United States would recruit the rest of the world, including Europe, Russia, and China, and paralyze Iran's economy to such an extent that it undermined the ayatollahs' regime. The objective was to force Iran to stop its nuclear program. Israel and the United States would not initiate negotiations with the Iranians, and would forge no ties with the country until Iran asked to enter negotiations. Israel and the United States agreed to coordinate and report to each other on their various findings. According to reports, Hezbollah military commander Imad Mughniyah was assassinated in Damascus in a joint Mossad/CIA operation.

When he replaced Bush, Obama made a twofold decision: to downgrade coordination with Israel on everything connected to Iran's nuclear program, and to increase intelligence cooperation and the pace at which sanctions were imposed. This was the core of Obama's policies, which consisted of exerting soft force. In Israel they didn't like the restrictions imposed on them with regard to operations. Senior officers in Israel's security establishment recalled that their counterparts in Washington shared this feeling. The Pentagon believed this coordination was vital and important, but accepted the president's decision with reserve. This move set off the first warning lights within the political establishment in Israel. Obama appeared weak. At that stage no one believed sanctions would go as far as they did.

According to Meir Dagan, blame for the flawed nuclear agreement between Iran and the world powers rests with Benjamin Netanyahu. The sanctions had begun during the Bush administration, orchestrated by then deputy treasury secretary Richard Levi and Phil Rosenberg, who oversaw staff work. In accordance with the initial plan, Iran was supposed to capitulate in 2015, which is why Dagan pledged that it would not achieve nuclear capabilities until then. The American operation was built secretly, in full cooperation with the Gulf states and Sunni countries, who were also panicked by the possibility of a nuclear Iran. As Dagan saw the Netanyahu and Barak government's insistence on galloping ahead with a military option, the speeches, the warnings, the plans, and the warning signs all drove the United States to initiate negotiations with Iran much earlier than originally planned. This was the reason that instead of Iran arriving to the negotiations from a position of inferiority, it was the United States that had been weakened. In 2013, Iran wasn't sufficiently "cooked" to enter into negotiations. The timetable was moved forward because of the panic aroused by Netanyahu and Obama. A second-rate agreement with Iran was, however, preferable to an all-out regional war. By the time the United States understood Israel was bluffing, it was too late and the secret negotiations had already begun in Oman.

On this point, Dagan was in the minority position. Most of his colleagues, senior officers in the security establishment at that time, were giving Barak and Netanyahu credit for recruiting the rest of the world in favor of the harsh sanctions imposed on Iran. Obama and his people used Israel's threats to persuade Russia, China, and Europe to join the sanctions based on the bluff that Netanyahu and Barak might launch a unilateral attack against Iran, resulting in catastrophe for Israel. This fear vanished in late 2012.

The problem with the U.S. policy was that a real military option wasn't on the table. Time after time, Netanyahu and Barak, as well as senior members of the security establishment, heard well-placed Americans refer to the military option in a way that ridiculed and belittled it. A classic example took place at the Saban Forum in December 2011, when Secretary of Defense Leon Panetta explained the futility of a military option, infuriating General Amos Yadlin, who had retired from his post a few months earlier. Yadlin's mood reflected the general opinion in Israel that the Americans were dragging their heels and not being firm enough with Iran. The Israelis reminded their American counterparts repeatedly that the only time Iran initiated a freeze of its military nuclear program was in 2003, during the American invasion of Iraq. It achieved nothing; senior American officers and diplomats continued to dismiss the threat, and no one was convinced by the Obama administration's military option. Typically, Netanyahu went overboard. Obama was a collaborator with Iran. He was hell-bent on abandoning America's traditional allies in the region, Israel and Saudi Arabia, to establish a new alliance with Iran. Netanyahu believed that Obama saw Iran not as the problem, but rather as the solution. This belief was propped up by his political confidant Ron Dermer during his stint as Israel's ambassador in Washington. Netanyahu believed that Obama will reach an agreement with Iran that will lift the sanctions and give Iran the status of a nuclear threshold state, and with that recognition as a regional superpower.

At around the same time, Israel managed to antagonize Washington, especially officials in the Pentagon. According to one American involved, "The Israelis were trying to pull the wool over our eyes. They were making sounds of a pending attack and, when we showed interest and tried to get information, they shut us down. All those years we had shared a 'no surprises' agreement and they were suddenly playing dumb. They were telling us that they couldn't provide us with too much detail, so that later we wouldn't look like collaborators with Israel in the eyes of the world.' They were actually trying to compartmentalize us in order to 'defend' us. We knew it was a load of nonsense. We told them that if they attacked, America would be seen as 'collaborators' in any case. You are not revealing anything, we told them, so we won't block you. You prefer to say sorry at the end, instead of asking permission at the beginning."

A special team in the Pentagon was established to deal with what would happen if the United States found itself in the middle of an unwanted military conflict with Iran. America's fears regarding the possibility of Israel dragging the United States to a war were very strong in 2009, Bibi's first year in office. In June 2010, the UN passed a resolution calling for especially harsh sanctions against Iran. The Americans breathed a certain sigh of relief, in the belief that this would reassure Israel. In the meantime, the Stuxnet computer worm—a collaboration between American and Israeli intelligence that attacked the Iranian nuclear infrastructure—and the "Olympic Games" scheme were revealed by the international media. The United States blamed Israel, fearing an Iranian response and the possibility of serious financial damage in a counter-cyberattack, which led the U.S. to shut down all covert activity and focus on political efforts and sanctions. According to the editorial "Spy vs Spy," which was published by *The New York Times* in October 2015, it was at this stage that Netanyahu decided the only option was a military offensive. The fear level in the Pentagon had risen, and in the White House a presentation was prepared for Israeli officials proving Israel did not possess the military wherewithal to cause real damage and halt the Iran nuclear program for more than a year or two. According to the *Times*, the Israelis presented their secret plan to take control of the Fordow installation and blow it up from inside. The Americans saw this as a suicide mission, and expressed their objections. They demanded forewarning. Israel would not promise to provide it.

In the meantime, the United States hinted at its partial responsibility for Stuxnet. Gary Samore, Obama's former top Iranian nuclear advisor, said in a television interview, "We are very happy that Iran is having problems with their centrifuges and we, the U.S., and its allies will continue to do all we can to complicate things for them." The United States believed the worst was behind them, but summer 2011 was worse on the Israeli front. During a White House debate that dealt with Israel's intentions, an intelligence officer entered suddenly with fresh information. "OK, ladies and gentlemen," he began, "we think it might happen." He was referring to an Israeli attack on Iran. It was worrisome, particularly for Hillary Clinton and Robert Gates. A list was drafted of fourteen to twenty measures the United States could use to try to persuade Israel not to attack. Most of them were implemented during the year to come.

To its credit, the United States admitted that Obama's decision to scale back on military operations had no effect on the struggle against the Iran nuclear program. "Cooperation with Israel had three aspects," explained a former Pentagon official. "Sanctions against Iran, the intelligence cooperation, and activity coordination. We were afraid that he was going to allow Israel to accumulate intelligence and attack. Intelligence cooperation, on the other hand, was upgraded and highly developed. The policy we decided on against Israel was 'reassurance and dissuasion.'" The idea was to reassure that America was serious in its determination to prevent Iran from developing nuclear capabilities, and to dissuade Israel from launching a military offensive on its own.

America's reassurance included, among other things, the provision of another aircraft carrier in the Persian Gulf; escalated development of sophisticated bunker-busters that were tested on models specially built to resemble

Iran's nuclear installations; intensifying political cooperation; and briefing Israeli officials, including demonstrating new bombs. "We can do it better and more effectively than you can," the United States told the Israelis. "But this is not the time. We'll do it only as a last resort. We have to first try the sanctions and political negotiations. We are serious, we mean it."

Netanyahu was unconvinced. His disdain for Obama only increased. To defray messages passed on through clandestine channels, American officials would occasionally speak publicly in ways that increased Israel's doubts. In November 2010, Netanyahu said, "If the U.S. wants to stop Iran's nuclear aspirations without using military force, it should persuade Iran that we shall not hesitate to use it." Secretary of Defense Robert Gates responded with a declaration that was welcomed neither in the Pentagon nor the White House. The military option, he said, was less effective. This reignited Israel's doubts. After Gates came Panetta with a declaration at the Saban Forum, and there were others, too. Any good faith accorded the United States in Jerusalem via the secret channels faded after those public declarations. Netanyahu, Barak, and Ya'alon, as well as other Israeli officials, were furious. "This is how they want to place pressure on Iran?" the Israelis lamented. "It's a naïve and weak approach, tantamount to turning out the lights; it's an eclipse. The only thing Iran understands is force, and America is coming to these negotiations as if it's Iran that is the superpower and not America."

In January 2012, Israel suddenly informed the United States that it was canceling the large joint military exercise scheduled for that summer in Israel. The exercise, a defense scenario against ballistic rockets, had been planned long before. Ehud Barak called Panetta and asked for a postponement. When Panetta insisted on knowing the reason, Barak mumbled something about Israel not wishing to embarrass the United States, that it was a bad time for United States forces to be in Israel. Panetta repeated the United States' position: You are not allowed to attack; we alone can do that. You don't have the ability to do it, and now is not the right time. Trust us. Barak disagreed. The postponement of the exercise was, in retrospect, a desperate Israeli attempt to stoke the fading American fear of an attack.

In hindsight, former Pentagon officials admit that America's double message, initiated by Gates, Panetta, and other officials, was damaging. The undertone of appeasement muddled the message that the West was trying to pass on to Iran, undoing much of the pressure from it. Today, Pentagon officials have excuses, retrospective analyses, for how it happened: Gates was the secretary of defense in the Bush administration and his job description consisted of broadcasting appeasement and moderation. Surrounded by Bush's neocons, he was obliged to break to the left to become the cooling agent. Later, when the White House changed hands, Gates didn't adjust fast enough. It took him a while to understand that he needed to be a right-winger. The Obama administration wanted to send an aggressive message to Iran, but there was no one around who could do it. By the time Robert Gates understood his new job, he was replaced. Leon Panetta, they say in the Pentagon, made his big mistake by stating that the military option was not relevant. He should have been firmer, according to some of the people who were around him at the time. Yes, they admit, we could have done a better job of sending Iran a threatening message. The frustration is especially deep because the Obama administration actually prepared the where-withal for a real military option and invested considerably in it. The problem was in getting the message across to Iran.

Earlier, in 2011, the United States believed that if Israel were to attack Iran, there would be no more than a few hours' warning, maybe less. That would be the only way to prevent the United States from thwarting the operation. On one of his visits to the United States, Barak was given a realistic demonstration of the ability of the new bunker-busting bombs that were being developed by the Americans. The Israeli minister of defense's interlocutors proved to him that the new bombs were built especially to split open the layers of mountain and concrete that protect Iran's nuclear sites in Qom and Fordow. Behind closed doors and in deep secret, the United States continued to argue over the question of Bibi. Among the president's advisors, Pentagon officials, and State Department personnel there was a strong sentiment that Netanyahu was "chickenshit," and there was no way he could carry out his threats. Others took the threats seriously. Former ambassador Martin Indyk said he overheard Barak saying that "Israel's threats are meant to cause you to take action." What did he mean by action?

"To increase pressure on Iran, to attack Iran, or to join the 'second wave' of an Israeli attack." The United States refused to so much as contemplate such a thing. On the matter of sanctions, there was an organized program. On the matter of attack, it was a nonstarter. "There's no way we'll participate in such a move," the United States told Israel. "Forget it." Sometime in 2012, they figured out that Barak and Netanyahu had pulled one over on them. "We understood that the new military top brass were opposed to an attack," say sources in Washington. "We stopped being upset by Israel's threats. The chickenshit concept outweighed the alarmism. We're cool." The Americans understood that even in Iran they weren't overwhelmed by Netanyahu's threats. "Bibi has completely lost his credibility, against us and against the Iranians, too," said a Pentagon source. "Until then we handled the Israeli threat successfully, but in 2012 it all ended. No one was bothered. Even the jaded trick of telling the Europeans 'it's impossible to control Israel' no longer worked. Europe was no longer concerned. Netanyahu's balloon had burst, and it cost Israel dearly. According to assessments, by that time the Americans pulled back from the sanctions. It was clear the solution would have to be diplomatic.

"At that time we were the only ones with a reliable deterence vis-à-vis Iran," recalls an American political source. "They took us seriously. When Iran started carrying out maneuvers in the Strait of Hormuz in early 2012, we drew a red line and sent them a clear message, and they blinked. Similar exercises in Iraq were dealt with in the same way. The bottom line was clear: Israel had no deterrence against Iran, and we did. They knew all about our capabilities and were taking no chances," said the source.

That same year the underground facility in Qom became operational and Iran started focusing on the "zone of immunity" as defined two years earlier by Ehud Barak. Israel's military option gradually dissolved.

Israel did what it always does under desperate circumstances: it tried to resurrect the threat. According to various media outlets (*The Wall Street Journal*, *The New York Times*), Israel began to formulate a plan of action for a large ground offensive in Iran, in which an Israeli elite force would take control of the big underground installation in Fordow and blow it up. This program was included in a new series of things on which Israel was laboring that included the postponement of the joint exercise with the United States, talk of a ground offensive, and Barak's *Ha'aretz* interview in which he donned the image of a "decision maker" in an attempt to reaffirm the credibility of the Israeli threat. Netanyahu and Barak knew that it was show time and reckoned that Obama was moving toward negotiations with Iran, and they aspired to thwart him. In Washington, concern was mild. It's possible that Israel found out about the secret negotiations with Iran in Oman and was trying to sabotage them through war mongering. "In retrospect," says a Pentagon official, "we were wrong to hide these negotiations from Israel. We had good reasons, but when Israel discovered these negotiations on its own, the damage was considerable. The Israelis have this strange personality, that they need to know everything. They are incredibly anxious. In all truth it's hard to blame them. It's what helped them survive in that difficult neighborhood of theirs."

According to the source, "Israelis will always take into account the worst-case scenario. It's part of their everyday lives. Thus in all our negotiations with them, they always demanded answers, even to the worst possible thing that could happen to them. We used to present them with solutions and replied to every scenario, and then they'd come back with an especially bad one that we hadn't even thought of, and we would ask for more time to come back with a solution to this or that scenario. The truth is that the Israelis like this approach and kind of dialogue. The problem after 2012, as suspicion increased between the two countries and the intimacy disappeared, that dialogue ended. The Israelis remained alone with their phobias."

71

The "Decision Maker" Bolted

2012–2013

Throughout 2012, Netanyahu continued to toy with the possibility of launching a last-minute attack on Iran, both in the form of a ground offensive and a combined ground and air attack. Ehud Barak still stood by him, but the trust between them had begun to crack. In the summer of 2012, Netanyahu held a series of secret one-on-one meetings with people from Israel's security establishment: former Mossad chiefs and generals. He sought legitimacy, a moral prop, an operational tip. One of these people, a retired general, was summoned to the prime minister's residence on Balfour Street in September. "We sat together for three hours," he recalls. "Bibi was tense and agitated. He delivered a long and detailed speech on why Israel had to attack Iran on its own. He included an improvised simulation of various scenarios." The questions arose as to how Iran would respond. Bibi believed the response would be minor, because a response would drag in the Americans. "You have to understand," Bibi went on, "it's not that we have a choice. They are about to enter the zone of immunity, they are violating agreements and will continue to violate agreements in the future, and the sanctions are not serious enough. America is busy with elections; it's now or never." The feeling among the people he spoke to was that Bibi was capable of carrying it out.

In December 2011, Ehud Barak visited the United States and had an informal meeting with President Obama on the sidelines of a congress of Jewish organizations, where they were both speakers. Netanyahu was not informed. Recognizing the sensitiveness vis-à-vis Netanyahu, the Americans rejected Barak's request for a formal meeting. Bibi was very suspicious of the independent channel of communications between his defense minister and the president. He was familiar enough with Barak to know that it was better not to turn one's back on him. Barak's meeting with Obama was short and went down in a way that made it appear improvised. The two were pictured sitting on mustard-colored plastic chairs on the edge of a conference hall, facing each other. Netanyahu was furious. He was afraid Obama would get Barak on his side and persuade him against the plans to attack Iran.

This time, Netanyahu's fears had substance. As Israel was continuing with its plans to attack Iran, Barak was secretly planning the amazing U-turn he would make toward the end of the year. That didn't stop him having that interview with Ari Shavit on August 10, 2012. Although he maintained his anonymity, most of the readers knew whom the piano-playing "decision maker" was. In the interview, Barak gave a brilliant analysis of the dangers of a nuclear Iran to the rest of the world, to the Sunni states, to the Middle East, and to Israel. He went on to explain why Israel's time was running out, because it didn't have the same capabilities as the United States, and very soon Iran would be fortified and virtually invincible against an Israeli attack. The piano player explained that if Israel didn't attack now, it would soon come to pass that the only one able to do so would be America. After a series of well-presented arguments, the interview reached to its unequivocal solution, that Israel had to attack. He explained that Israel was a one-bomb state and wouldn't be able to sustain a nuclear attack and survive, like World War II Japan. "There are moments in the life of a nation when the demand to live is the demand to act. It was thus on the eve of the Six-Day War. And it could well be this time, too."

One month after the piano man speech, Barak changed direction. In closed conversations that were leaked to the media, he clarified that despite the differences of concept between Israel and the United States, it was imperative to remember the importance of Israel's relationship with the United States, one that had to remain unharmed. Barak had very quickly climbed down from the mountain he had been on only a month earlier, and prepared the field for the real thing. Ten days later he was flying to Chicago, where he was scheduled to meet Chicago mayor Rahm Emanuel. Although Emanuel was no longer chief of staff at the White House, he was still considered a close confidant of President Obama. He was also one of the Americans who was pure anathema to Netanyahu and his people. In Bibi's eyes, Emanuel symbolized the extreme left and one of his greatest foes who had the president's ear. It would have been more forgivable for Barak to meet Mahmoud Ahmadinejad—and behind Netanyahu's back, no less.

Emanuel and Barak had an intimate lunch, and the meeting was leaked to the media. Netanyahu knew nothing of the meeting and hadn't approved it. Pandemonium broke out between the prime minister and the defense minister. Close associates of the two exchanged public barbs, and smoke rose from Netanyahu's office. It didn't take the prime minister long to understand that Barak had defected. Just before zero hour, the historic moment of truth for which Netanyahu had prepared himself all his life, Barak resigned and left him alone in the battlefield. From that day on, Barak changed his rhetoric, stopped hinting at an unavoidable Israeli attack, and replaced it with the importance of coordination with the United States, and the historical alliance Israel shared with that great nation.

It is not known to this day what Barak's agreement was with the Obama administration, and why he made it. Israel was approaching a general election, although no date had been set. Barak was planning to stand for election at the head of an independent party established by himself and desperately sought to distance himself from Netanyahu. He had chosen the moment to desert meticulously. He had never intended to stay with Netanyahu to the end.

One month after Barak's U-turn, the Knesset brought forward the elections and a date was set for January 2013. A month later, on November 26,

2012, Barak dropped another bombshell by resigning from politics. His partners in the Independence Party who had left the Labor Party several months earlier with the promise to run together were left by the roadside. Barak didn't look back. He was done, Israel's military option a thing of the past; Bibi was on his own. Along with the expired military option was Israel's relationship with the United States. Netanyahu had lost what little credibility he'd enjoyed in the White House. In March 2013, Obama would establish the secret communication channel with Iran in Oman, and Washington and Jerusalem would part ways forever. Netanyahu had even lost the option to threaten.

72

Defeat in Jerusalem

2013–2015

At the height of Israel's fervor over a possible attack on Iran, the Obama administration came to the conclusion that conditions were ripe for negotiations with the Iranians. According to Meir Dagan, it was too early. Regardless, the foreplay between the United States and Iran commenced in 2013 in the form of secret negotiations in Oman, under the auspices of Sultan Qaboos. After some deliberation, it was decided not to inform Israel. "We thought about it and said it was too dangerous," admits a former Pentagon official. "The Israelis would have leaked it, or used the information to undermine negotiations. They were doing everything they could at that time to raise the pressure and tension. Quite simply, we no longer trusted them."

But the Americans underestimated Mossad. According to foreign reports, Israel's national security advisor Ya'akov Amidror informed his American counterparts that Israel knew American aircraft were landing in Oman. Netanyahu was furious when he discovered that America was conducting negotiations behind his back. As far as he was concerned, the secret negotiations between what he described as "thieves in the night" confirmed his opinion of Obama from the very beginning. Among Netanyahu's circle, much use was made of the president's middle name, Hussein. By that time, Netanyahu was convinced that Obama's objective was to lend legitimacy to Iran's nuclear program and grant the ayatollahs admission to the nuclear club. The United States knew there was no chance of Netanyahu revealing so much as a spark of pragmatism. "All he wants is to get us involved in another war," they said in the White House and in Washington. A former Pentagon official added, "Relations by then were so shattered, that there was no mutual attention. It was a situation that Netanyahu had earned honestly. He thought he could manipulate Obama on the Palestinian issue and get a foot in the door and control of the nuclear negotiations, as well. He was mistaken."

"In retrospect, if we are to analyze Netanyahu," said an American who worked against him, "what we have here is a stock market investor who loathes taking risks. As conservative as it gets. He'd prefer a small, regular, risk-free profit to a large high-risk profit. That's the reason we managed to persuade him not to attack Iran, something that holds a huge risk factor, and we didn't succeed to go for an agreement with the Palestinians. In both cases, he did exactly what is expected of someone who loathes risk. He simply chooses the least dangerous option."

Netanyahu has a completely different analysis. From his point of view, it was a foretold chronicle of surrender. Instead of bringing Iran to its knees, Obama went down on his own knees. It was a direct continuation, according to Netanyahu, of the disastrous Cairo speech, the degrading head-bowing to the king of Saudi Arabia, and the last-minute cop-out from the attack on Assad's chemical weapons. "That event in Syria, when the Americans had already announced that they would attack and backed down at the last moment, was definitive," says a Netanyahu associate. "If the Iranians weren't convinced by then that Obama was a coward, then they knew now that they had no reason to blink during nuclear negotiations."

Moreover, Netanyahu believes that Obama made a series of grave mistakes that brought about this result. Some of his claims are accurate. The United States, says Netanyahu, entered the negotiations needing to achieve results at all costs. This was repeated and stressed on many occasions, whereas the Iranians appeared indifferent. It should have been the other way around. Netanyahu also claims that Obama did not create any real military option or present a tangible argument regarding Iran. It's not sufficient to develop sophisticated weapons; you also need to have the determination to use them. In 2012, Obama folded up Israel's military option and did everything he could to neutralize and block Israel. And having done that, he moved Israel from the front seat to the back and from there to the trunk, so it wouldn't have a toehold in the diplomatic negotiations. The Americans did all this—as Netanyahu saw it—while continuing to swear they were on the same page as Israel, declaring that they would demand the absolute suspension of Iran's uranium enrichment program and promising there was no danger of a nuclear Iran. "They violated each of those promises," says Netanyahu, "and threw Israel under the bus as part of the policy of a president who believes Iran is a stabilizing force, and tries to buy quiet at any price without the risk of exerting force. America has agreed to recognize Iran as a nuclear threshold state, while at the same time allowing it to continue to spread terror and violence throughout the Middle East, whether directly or via emissaries. The damage thus caused will last for generations to come."

Not everyone agrees with Netanyahu, not even in his inner circle. One Israeli security official who was closely involved in the process says, "Netanyahu identified the Iranian threat early on, placed it on the agenda, forced the international system to deal it, and led the sanctions. The bottom line is that he failed both militarily and politically. He should have understood from the start that Israel lacks the ability to stop Iran on its own. The only possible conclusion was that it should have invested in the United States, building trust and affinity with Obama. He had to create fraternity over the Iran issue and compromise on other fronts."

To the question of whether such behavior would have allowed Netanyahu to reach a different result on Iran, the source says, it would have improved his ability to influence the president. He wouldn't have changed Obama's world view, but he would have been given a toehold inside the process. The moment Tom Donilon, the former U.S. national security advisor, and Ya'akov Amidror, the former Israeli national security advisor, left, everything collapsed. It was a crucial moment when the negotiations began. It was a time when there was absolutely no dialogue between Obama and Netanyahu. For the first time in history, there was no direct back channel with the White House. There was no precedent for that. Fareed Zakaria once wrote in *Newsweek* that Bibi often compares himself to Winston Churchill. The trouble is that Churchill understood back in the 1930s that he had to reinforce Britain's alliance with America. It was his obsession, and he was prepared to pay the price because it was worth it. Netanyahu turned America into an enemy. "So no," the source concluded, "I am not convinced that Netanyahu could have succeeded in fitting Obama with a pair of balls, or turning him into a Republican, but he could have been able to influence the final configuration of the agreement with Iran."

In Washington, too, the resignations of Amidror and Donilon were seen as the final burial of the intimate channel between Netanyahu and Obama. Donilon left in June 2013 and Amidror in November of that year. That same year, too, Iran arrived at the historic interim agreement with the superpowers, heading toward final negotiations. For Israel, this was the most fateful hour, and it was then that the break was absolute between the administration and the Israeli establishment. The relationship between Amidror and Donilon was close, intimate, and based on high professionalism. It was a relationship of mutual trust and, together, they reinforced the sensitive, essential, and problematic communication channel between their respective bosses. The Americans had great respect for Amidror's professionalism, pragmatism, and businesslike approach. Yossi Cohen, who replaced him, was unable to fill his predecessor's big shoes. Cohen was a Mossad professional accustomed to seeing things in minimal resolution and unused to operating large systems. Facing off against him was Susan Rice, Donilon's successor, who was already full of revulsion for everything that Netanyahu symbolized. There was no longer intimacy between the White House and Israel's prime minister's office. Cooperation was severely weakened. Meetings between Cohen and Rice were held mainly for protocol. Obama is a realistic, analytic president; he needs someone to explain to him Israel's sensitivities, Netanyahu's phobias, so as to translate them into the proper acts and words. "Obama needs analytical reasoning," says an American official. "He just needs to be able to understand." The dismantling of the axis between Amidror and Donilon was seen by many in Washington as a major game changer that ultimately led to the absolute break between Jerusalem and Washington, the seeds of which were sown during Obama's 2012 campaign when Netanyahu adopted Romney. Those seeds sprouted when Netanyahu sent Ron Dermer, a close associate of Sheldon Adelson, to be Israel's ambassador in Washington. It all peaked after the exposure of the secret negotiations in Oman, the signing of the interim agreement in Geneva, and the resignation of the two national security advisors. It went on for almost two years, until the president's success in Congress on the way to approving the final agreement with Iran.

"When it comes to two opposites like Obama and Netanyahu, the key to a successful relationship lies in the hands of their close associates," explains a former White House official. It is necessary to soften, explain, and maneuver, to "sell" the other leader to their own boss in order to maintain an open line of communication and useful discourse. They have to emphasize points of agreement and understate differences. Donilon and Amidror focused on this mission and fulfilled it. They were devoid of personal ideology and interests, and understood that the good of both countries required proper working relations. "A classic example of this," according to the American source, "is the serious crisis that erupted after it became clear that the agreement with Iran granted Iran a twenty-four-hour warning before they have to open suspicious installations to IAEA inspectors. As far as Netanyahu was concerned, this revelation proved his thesis: that the agreement was bad. According to the American official, if Amidror and Donilon were still in office, Amidror would have received a sufficiently detailed professional explanation, understood it himself, and been able to persuade Netanyahu that there was no story. But by this time the break in relations was already a done deal, Susan Rice did not have the energy to explain anything to Yossi Cohen, who made no effort to understand. Even a *dialogue de sourds* (dialogue of the deaf) no longer existed between the sides, at this point.

73

Postmortem

2002

The best way to understand the way Netanyahu's head works is to speak to Elliott Abrams, the former American official who reflects Bibi's approach better than anyone else besides Adelson. According to him, the agreement with Iran is a bad one, just as Bibi says, for the simple reason that they were never afraid of Israel attacking them, so they didn't make the necessary concessions. "I really don't understand what the Obama administration is afraid of," Abrams said. "And who invented the illusion that an American attack on Iran constitutes a Middle Eastern Armageddon? What harm can Iran cause the United States? They'll close the Straits of Hormuz? So we'll open them. They can't reach us, they are deeply in Syria, embroiled in Lebanon, stuck in Yemen, and that's a partial list. They've been pumping terror in Lebanon for years already. A conflict between the United States and Iran is not the end of the world, it's a local and passing conflict because the balance of power is obvious, especially in light of the fact that neither side intends to get involved on the ground. Since America openly admitted that there is no chance of an attack, the deal is a bad one. When Obama hesitated and was afraid of bombing Syria, Khamenei felt he had the upper hand. The deal is bad because in ten years' time Iran will be the same Iran, with a big and legitimate nuclear program. Whoever says it was impossible to destroy the Iranian nuclear program militarily is mistaken and is misleading people. What would have happened if they'd rebuilt it? We'd destroy it again. It's not complicated. During the Bush administration, the president used to ask what would be the effect of an American attack on Iran on its internal political map. The experts said that an attack would unite the nation around the ayatollahs. Today, some of the experts are convinced otherwise. They believe that the Iranian nation would rise up. It's already ripe for it. I remember Netanyahu saying to President Bush in 2008 that he didn't agree with the assumption that an American attack on Iran would strengthen the regime. They had met during a presidential visit in Israel in May 2008 and Bibi said that an American attack would actually weaken the Iranian regime, because no regime likes to lose, and no nation supports a losing regime."

The only problem with this thesis is that in 2002, Netanyahu explained to Congress that an attack on Iraq would topple Saddam Hussein's regime and reinforce stability in the Middle East. This prophecy was wrong. During that self-confident performance in Congress prior to the invasion of Iraq, Bibi sowed wind, and now it was time to reap a storm.

One of Netanyahu's closest and longest-standing advisors, who also accompanied the efforts on the Iran issue, sums it up: "History will not forgive Netanyahu for the Iran failure. He built a power of the void. He wasted billions, but instead of harnessing all his energies in the supreme interest of creating a tight strategic partnership with the United States, he invested his energy in undermining the basis on which such a relationship rests. He caused allies of Israel, such as Biden, Ross, Hillary Clinton, and others, to deal ad nauseam with the West Bank settlements, the first freeze, efforts to achieve a second freeze, the ineffectual negotiations with the Palestinians, and so on. He exhausted the Americans to an extent that they no longer wanted to see him again. It's a fiasco of historic proportions. In the judgment of history, Netanyahu won't be able to claim that he did everything possible to avoid Iran's invasion of the nuclear threshold space. It happened on his watch. He has recited repeatedly that if Israel reaches the day of reckoning, it would take its fate in its hands and defend itself. He did reach the day of reckoning, and he chickened out. He is fully responsible for the strategic collapse of the core issue that constitutes the very justification of his existence as a leader. It is he, after all, who took this mission on his shoulders and declared that he could bear it. He spared no resources, he neglected every other sphere; he lived, breathed, and thought only of this, and at the end of the day, Iran has come within a hairbreadth of having a nuclear bomb in spite of him."

74

"Burn Down the Clubhouse"

2013

When the interim agreement was reached between Iran and the superpowers in December 2013, Netanyahu had to make an important strategic decision. Should he continue to function as the world's "bad boy," ranting and raving about the agreement and the negotiations and presenting an alternative from the outside, or should he accept the verdict, come to terms with the new reality, and try to make it work for him? The main negotiations hadn't begun yet, so it was still possible to attempt to influence the powers, under American leadership, regarding objectives and the best way to realize them. But Netanyahu was already in an awkward position. He was furious at what he saw as Obama's betrayal and America's shunning of responsibility for world peace. Scenes of catastrophe wandered around his brain and he became a knight of agony, a biblical tragedy, the little boy trying to plug a hole in the dike with his finger.

Following his efforts to overthrow Obama during the previous year, Netanyahu was virtually an outcast in the White House. He was no longer driven to reinvent himself, to swallow his pride and start anew. He preferred to declare all-out war and adopt a scorched-earth policy.

It was a big mistake. Israel's isolation reached new heights. Netanyahu's claims and speeches impressed no one. The ensuing duel between him and President Obama did not help him and did nothing to harm Obama. Everyone disrespected him: President Obama, the foreign ministers of the European Union and, of course, the Iranians. His prophecies of doom continued at full steam, but the world ignored him. One day, Bibi was urged by several high-ranking security officials to shift gears. It's better to influence from within, they told him. He wouldn't listen. He was convinced that Obama was heading for complete surrender in any case, so there was no point in trying to influence him. Preferring to fight an external, Don Quixote–like war to the end, he decided to present a "moral stance." At this stage, Netanyahu returned to basics: The thing that interested him was not how he would succeed in influencing the details of the negotiations, but rather how his current behavior would appear from a historical perspective. Every word he said, during those long months in which negotiations were conducted for a final agreement, was said to be included in historical records to prove, when the day came, that the prime minister of Israel was not only the "first to identify" the danger posed by Iran, but also the "only one to sound the alarm," who had no part in the abomination that legitimized Iran as a nuclear threshold state.

"The watershed," explains an Israeli general who was involved in the affair, was President Obama's realization that it is Iran's right to enrich uranium to a limited extent. "Until then," he explains, "Bibi and Obama were on the same page and both agreed that enrichment was the key and had to be denied from Iran. At some stage, Obama changed his mind and said in his own voice that Iran had the right to enrich uranium. That was when Netanyahu broke off relations and started to go haywire. He should have swallowed it to remain inside the tent. Instead of disqualifying in advance any agreement that might include the ability to certain enrichment, Netanyahu should have understood the limitations and accepted the ruling in return for a seat at the table in secret negotiations, even as a back-bencher, with the ability to influence throughout the debates certain critical points."

Netanyahu met John Kerry for a three-day marathon in early November 2013, in a final effort to prevent the Americans from signing the interim agreement with Iran, which he coined "bad for the world and bad for

Israel." Those meetings were extremely tense. At the end of them, Kerry, who wanted to avoid a public confrontation in front of the cameras, refused to appear in a photo op with Netanyahu. Several days later, Under Secretary of State Wendy Sherman arrived in Israel on a "softening" visit. Her attempts to change Netanyahu's mind failed completely. Behind his back, she held a lengthy meeting with six Israelis, carefully picked retired members of the security establishment, including former generals, all authorities in the nuclear field. One by one Sherman refuted Netanyahu's claims against the agreement. The economic incentives granted to Iran in the first stage were fewer than Netanyahu claimed. She tried to prove that Netanyahu was not conversant with the details, and that the agreement was much better than the one presented in Israel.

One of the Israelis, a reserve army officer, asked, "Supposing Israel agrees to Iran's right to enrich uranium, what next? Where was the red line from which there is no turning back? Do you accept the necessity to insist that all enriched uranium is moved from Iran to a third country, such as Russia? If the answer is yes, then to me the agreement is reasonable and I say this despite the official stance of Israel's security establishment."

Had Netanyahu acted like this reserve general, he might have been able to influence matters. He could have said to the Americans, "Gentlemen, you are mistaken and I want this on record, but I agree to work with you. Let's decide together on the next demarcation line. Don't abandon Israel. We have much knowledge and intelligence on the subject; we are familiar with the Iranians and have studied them for years." According to the security establishment, in this manner Netanyahu could have prevented or greatly reduced some of the damage caused by the final agreement. But he preferred to quarrel.

As soon as Netanyahu disqualified the interim agreement signed in December 2013, Israel was given a restraining order from the negotiations. Not only did it affect Israel's relations with the White House, it also influenced the professional working relations between the two sides. "Professional elements," explains a senior Israeli security official, "were affected by the situation. It was impossible to continue as usual. The intimacy was damaged; the level of cooperation had dropped drastically." The matter was even raised at a conference in Tel Aviv attended by a large number of American embassy personnel. Two Israeli reserve generals, Amos Yadlin and Giora Eiland, were completely open about it. An American representative responded angrily that "all the meetings are continuing as usual," to which Eiland replied that it was "not the number of meetings, it was their quality. It was the depth, the frequency, the seriousness, the openness, and the attentiveness. The two sides are now reciting to each other. The dialogue is no longer there."

PART FOUR

✡

THE PALESTINE ISSUE

75

Bibi A or Bibi B?

W ho is the real Benjamin Netanyahu? Is he an idealist or a pragmatist? There is no disputing the fact that Netanyahu was brought up a Revisionist Zionist. However, the Revisionism of the Netanyahu family was theoretical, not practical. Netanyahu's ancestors were primarily theoreticians who mostly talked. Netanyahu spent most of his childhood in the United States. When he was in Israel, he was mostly in Jerusalem. He is not moved by Rachel's Tomb or the Cave of the Patriarchs; he is indifferent to the settlements. Nor is Netanyahu's ideology rooted in the Divine Promise or the sanctity of God. It is a result of the inherent pessimism typical of the Netanyahu clan: Their grasp of Jewish history is as a series of inevitable catastrophes; Israel must exist within closed walls, ready to battle for its existence at any given moment. The Jews are destined to prepare for the next Holocaust—always. This is the core of Netanyahu's ideology.

Netanyahu can appreciate the advantages of peace. No ideology bars him from surrendering "pieces of the homeland." His barrier is different: Due to his basic skepticism, he cannot believe there exists a partner for peace. He is a self-appointed "guardian of Israel's security." Therefore, to agree on peace, he must be persuaded there will be no harm to its security. But his inherent pessimism obstructs him from seeing things this way. This is Netanyahu's catch-22: He's willing to make painful concessions for peace, if only a partner existed. The problem is he will never believe there is one.

Over the years Netanyahu has convinced himself that he is the only leader capable of standing at Israel's helm in these times. Any other leader will immediately place Israel and its Jews in jeopardy. As time went by, this feeling of exclusivity grew stronger, until it became the Netanyahu family's black magic, reaching the realm of the messianic. Bibi is the "chosen one," and his wife Sara is his counterpart. In recent years, there has been talk of Yair Netanyahu, his elder son, as heir apparent of the Netanyahu dynasty.

"Without Bibi, Israel is doomed," Sara would repeat to her interlocutors in the years when her husband was pushed into political exile, and even subsequently upon his return to government. He himself would say that he had to come back "to save the country." A short while after being voted out of office, Netanyahu met with Yair Lapid, then a popular newspaper columnist. They sat in a restaurant on the Tel Aviv shoreline, and Netanyahu said to Lapid: "I'll be back as prime minister." Lapid scoffed. How will you come back? he asked. The people have just kicked you out. Netanyahu was unfazed. "My return is a certainty," he told Lapid. "Some people have it, and some people don't. Those who do—there aren't many of them." Netanyahu then adjusted his chair to face the sea. "When I was prime minister, I used to miss the sea. I like looking at it," he said. "I'm racking up beach hours now because when I get back they're going to shut me up in a security cage again."

This messianic conception is what drives the couple's desperate need to hold on to power at any cost. They are firmly persuaded that their struggle is not for their own benefit; it's for the sake of the people and the state. They are amazed by criticism of trivialities like the massive expenses incurred by the prime minister's residence, their luxurious lifestyle, and their hedonistic extravagances. Netanyahu believes that had he not chosen to devote his life to his country, he would have been an American billionaire, living like his rich friends. But he has sacrificed himself for the people of Israel, and anyone criticizing his behavior is ungrateful.

Therefore, the two descriptions of Netanyahu—pragmatist or idealist—

may indeed coexist despite their intrinsic contradiction. For if remaining in office is the true ideology, the frequent flip-flops in policy are justified, along with the many concessions (the Hebron Agreement, the Bar-Ilan speech) and the tough stances (stopping the Oslo Accords, freezing the peace process). Netanyahu manipulates and maneuvers to stay in power, which is what Israelis need.

A high-ranking American who worked closely with Netanyahu for years describes it thus: "When Netanyahu gets up in the morning and looks in the mirror, he sees two little Bibis—one on each shoulder. The first is Netanyahu the bold political leader, the only one capable of making peace and preventing Iran from becoming a nuclear power; that one has the courage and the ability to make grand historical change. The second is the cowardly politician unwilling to take any risk, who clings to his seat at any price, even when national interests are sacrificed." This American claims that Netanyahu is wired so that the second Bibi—the wary politician incapable of decisions or risk—will always have the final word.

In 2001, Netanyahu paid a condolence visit to a woman named Geula Hershkowitz in the settlement of Ofra. Geula's husband had been killed in a terrorist attack, and her son suffered a similar fate several months later. Ariel Sharon's premiership was in its infancy, the second intifada was accelerating toward its bloody climax, and Bibi was playing the role of "concerned citizen." On this visit he was accompanied by Shlomo "Momo" Filber, his loyal longtime aide. The family taped the visit. At a certain point Bibi asked them to turn the camera off, which they did, but a few minutes later, someone turned it back on. They said they were afraid to drive on the roads, and Netanyahu asked, "Were you afraid when I was prime minister?" It was a clumsily veiled critique of Prime Minister Sharon. He then proceeded to outline his political theories, including the steps that should be taken to end the intifada. "We should launch an overall attack on the Palestinian Authority," he said. The Hershkowitzes asked if he wasn't afraid of global condemnation. "The world may condemn us," Netanyahu said. "The world doesn't scare me, especially today, with America at its center. I know America. America can easily be moved—moved in the right direction." One of the sons asked him whether America would interfere with the Israeli war on terrorism. Netanyahu replied, "They won't. Let's suppose they say something. So they say it. Eighty percent of Americans support us. It's absurd. The Clinton administration was pro-Palestinian. I was not afraid of maneuvering them, or to confront Clinton." Another of the sons asked Netanyahu why he had supported the Oslo Accords and continued to implement it as prime minister. The Oslo Accords were a disaster, Geula added. Netanyahu: "You know that, and I know it—we need the people to know it too." And then he elaborated his method: "Before the elections I was asked if I would adhere to the Oslo Accord. I said I would, subject to mutuality and a reduction of our withdrawals. I would grant the Accords a reductionist interpretation that would allow me to stop this blind rush toward the 1967 borders. The Accords defined three stages of land transfer from Israel to the Palestinians. At the end we should give them back all the land, except settlements or military sites. But no one said what those military sites were. I said they were security zones—take the Jordan Valley, for instance. But then there was the question of who would define military sites? There was a letter from Warren Christopher, addressed to me and to Arafat, stating that Israel alone would define the location and size of its military sites. But they did not want to hand over the letter, so I refused to sign the Hebron agreement. I stopped the cabinet meeting and said I wasn't going to sign it. Only after the letter came, during that meeting, did I sign and approve the Hebron agreement. Why is that important? Because that was the moment I stopped the Oslo Accords."

This is the "Bibi technique." He screws the system by adding an asterisk to the Oslo Accords, and then buries it. Continually maneuvering from one dead end to another, busting out with a Bar-Ilan speech or a Wye River Memorandum, during times of crisis only to create a new dead end, and so on.

The paradox becomes even more complex when we realize that as Netanyahu sees it, the Bar-Ilan speech was not a speech but an important, historic concession. Netanyahu conceives speeches as the truest form of action, as history defining. To him the Bar-Ilan speech is a historic move more significant than Ariel Sharon's disengagement. This is why he's always surprised anew whenever the world refuses to be bowled over by his speeches, waiting for action. In the meantime he buys time. The Bar-Ilan speech bought him five years.

Still there remains no finite solution to the Netanyahu riddle. As leader of Likud he acknowledged the Oslo Accords, handed Hebron back to the Palestinians; he signed the Wye Memorandum and gave the Bar-Ilan speech, but he also demolished the Oslo Accords and buried the peace process.

76

Bibi, Make History

In 1996, Benjamin Netanyahu was elected prime minister, defeating Shimon Peres. When Netanyahu returned to the premiership in 2009, Peres was president of the state. In Israel, the president is practically devoid of authority; it's largely a symbolic title. But Netanyahu was respectful toward Peres. After the Entebbe operation, Peres, then defense minister, gave a eulogy for Yonatan Netanyahu that was highly praised by Bibi's father, Professor Benzion Netanyahu. Peres also approved naming the operation after Yoni Netanyahu: Operation Jonathan. Peres was subsequently instrumental in establishing the International Institute for Counter-Terrorism, and even recommended Bibi for the role of deputy foreign minister. Also, Peres is the forefather of the Jewish people's life-insurance policy in Dimona; and in Netanyahu's eyes, he is a prime example of modern Jewish existence. Despite the clear ideological differences, the elderly Peres played the role of mentor to the young Netanyahu.

After Netanyahu overcame Peres by a margin to win the premiership in 1996, their relationship began to blossom. Bibi was a rookie; Peres an elderly statesman with no intention of departing from political life. He was happy to share his experience with Netanyahu. The young prime minister conducted an ongoing secret relationship with the older politician, who sat on the sidelines of the opposition. They would hold long heart-to-heart talks throughout Bibi's entire traumatic first term. "I have a plan without a party; you have a party without a plan," Peres would say to Bibi, thus managing to sell the latter on his plan for "economic peace." Netanyahu has taken tremendous credit for it up to this very day.

Netanyahu was sixty when he returned to office. President Peres was eighty-six, and as vigorous as ever. The affair resumed in full force. They both had vested interests: Peres wanted to harness Netanyahu to the peace process. Bibi wanted Peres content and busy. The president was very popular, and Bibi needed that. They had long face-to-face meetings at the president's residence at Peres's invitation. In terms of personality, they are complete opposites: Peres is a sworn optimist who can find hope even in genocide. He lectured Netanyahu about Israel's existential need for a diplomatic breakthrough, about the historic opportunity that must not be missed, about the perils of the status quo to which Israel was so addicted, etc. Netanyahu listened and heaped lavish praise on Peres, in person, in writing, and in public. He knew that Peres took pleasure in being honored, so he sent him on frequent missions, consulted with him, shared his qualms, and generally kept him close.

President Peres knew that it was possible Bibi would take him for a ride, but Peres is the kind of person who doesn't overthink things. He's always confident that he can outmanipulate his partner. In the past, Peres had been a full partner to the manipulation that took place at Ambassador Mohammed Bassiouni's villa, which had forced Netanyahu to go to Wye River. Peres was hoping to re-create this success. He met Netanyahu at least once a week to discuss diplomacy. Peres did his homework and studied Netanyahu, realizing that Sara's influence was crucial: Bibi wouldn't budge without her. He even read the book by Bibi's father on the inquisition of the Spanish Jewry. "A terribly boring read," Peres used to say behind closed doors, "but I wanted to get into the father's mind to learn about the son."

At some point these meetings turned into a long series of dinners at the president's home with Bibi and Sara, with Peres on his own or with his close personal aide Yona Bartal. Peres knew that Sara was Netanyahu's gatekeeper.

By winning Sara's trust, Peres thought, he would catch Bibi, too. Thus began a long series of pseudoromantic meetings where Peres spoke to the Netanyahus at great length about the need to make history, about the benefits of peace and the glory Bibi would gain for his courage, of how the people would applaud him, about the perils of the dead end, the binational state evolving around Israel, and many other topics.

Peres found a willing audience in Sara, of all people. She listened closely, occasionally praising his analyses and prodding Netanyahu to do something. Eventually Peres got what he wanted: carte blanche from Bibi to conduct confidential negotiations with Mahmoud Abbas on a framework that would be the foundation for any permanent agreement with the Palestinians. It would be something similar to the agreement he had formed with Abu Alaa under Prime Minister Sharon. However, Netanyahu looked at it differently: He had given Peres permission to talk to Abbas, period. Everything else was Peres's responsibility. He did not feel obligated to endorse whatever Peres came up with.

Peres and Abbas held at least five secret meetings—in London, Italy, Amman, and other places. These were not improvised meetings. Peres did careful groundwork, and kept Netanyahu informed. He was assisted by his former chief of staff Avi Gil; along with Dan Rothem, senior policy consultant for the S. Daniel Abraham Center for Middle East Peace; and the map expert Shaul Arieli. Netanyahu informed national security advisor Ya'akov Amidror, Yitzhak Molcho, and Ron Dermer.

Peres and his people swear that the negotiations with Abbas were serious, elaborate, and authorized. Colonel Shaul Arieli, one of the spearheads of the Geneva Initiative, played an important role. Arieli has a computer application containing a database of all demographic and geographic data, which can within seconds create a map separating Israel from the Palestinians that is tailor-made to any scenario or requirement. Netanyahu, wary of Arieli, who is identified with the left, called in Colonel Danny Tirza, who participated in the administrative committee on the security fence, the barrier Israel had to build after the eruption of the second Intifada, in order to stop the suicide bombers. Tirza was proficient in the territorial issues based on the layout of the fence. Arieli, not allowed to participate in meetings held at the prime minister's office, was practically a back channel. In reality, Peres's people discussed the maps, while Netanyahu's camp, headed by Amidror, remained elegantly oblivious to them. In one of the meetings attended by Amidror, a map was pulled out. Amidror declared, "We do not look at maps," as he picked up and examined a map. Peres, for his part, took the length of rope Netanyahu gave him, and stretched it to its limit and beyond. He overstepped by far the boundaries Bibi had granted him, and agreed with Abbas on a framework on which to base the detailed negotiations.

This was Netanyahu's regular modus operandi: He would send Peres, but leave himself wiggle room for denial. If the matter leaked, Netanyahu would claim that Peres had no executive authority and that the discussions were purely theoretical. Peres's people swear that they were witness to conversations, communications, and lengthy phone calls between the prime minister and the president, before and after every meeting Peres held with Abbas. "It was very serious and advanced," Peres's people say. "They worked on drafts, clauses, maps—everything. Bibi knew everything—he was informed of every step, voiced his opinion, argued, approved, or rejected every detail." This continued for nearly ten months, with intense communication between Peres and Netanyahu, even while the president was on official visits to various world capitals. "They exchanged documents and even maps via classified transmissions that traveled the world," says one of Peres's close associates. "Some of the meetings took place at the prime minister's office. You cannot deny they happened, or erase them from history."

Peres agreed with Abbas on the territorial issue: The Palestinians would receive exactly 6,205 square kilometers—an area equal to the size of the West Bank, including the Gaza Strip and East Jerusalem prior to 1967. Some of this territory would be transferred via land exchange, and in return Israel would keep the three large settlement blocs. Netanyahu demanded the Peres team leave 90 percent of the settlers on their land. Arieli said this was impossible. Under Clinton and Barak, the talk was of 80 percent of the settlers. Olmert had raised it to 85 percent; now Bibi wanted to leave 90 percent. "Impossible," said Arieli. "In order to leave 90 percent of the settlers on their land we would have to annex 6 percent of the West Bank, and no Palestinian will agree to that. The Palestinian state will be lined with dozens of Israeli offshoots crisscrossing the West Bank to include the settlements. We cannot exchange land at this rate; we don't have the land to give."

In summer 2011, negotiations between Peres and Abu Alaa had matured to a stage where the draft was vague enough for both to sign. They decided to schedule a meeting, at the end of which they were to reach conclusions and Peres was to present Netanyahu with a finished document. The meeting was set for July 28, 2011. But then Netanyahu began to hem and haw. Abu Mazen had already driven off from Ramallah to Amman; Peres was also about to approach the bridge over the Jordan when Netanyahu called.

"Shimon, I know you're supposed to meet Mahmoud Abbas today. I'd like to ask you to postpone the meeting by two or three days," the prime minister told the president.

"Why?" Peres asked.

"I'm waiting for Tony Blair," said Netanyahu. "He's supposed to bring a better deal."

Peres was angry. "There is no better deal," he said, "Mahmoud Abbas will never give Blair what he is willing to give me. Besides, I know you and your 'three days.' It will turn into three months, and then into three years." Netanyahu mumbled something, but Peres continued, "I don't want to deceive Mahmoud Abbas. I'm no bluffer. I'm willing to cancel everything, but I'm not going to start postponing it." Bibi cleared his throat, and then said, "Fine, then cancel it."

"All right," Peres said, "I'll call him right away. I'm pulling the plug on the negotiations. But Bibi, remember, you and I are finished."

It was an empty threat. You can finish *with* Bibi, but you can't finish Bibi. He'll always be back, stoically ignoring the fact that it's over. He's extraordinarily thick-skinned, taking offense at nothing. Politics is a career, and when he needs someone or something he'll do anything to get it while ignoring any residue of the past. In the meantime, Peres called Abbas and told him the truth: "I'm not coming to Amman, we have to call it off. I apologize but I cannot supply what I promised." Abbas told Peres that he appreciated his candor. Peres realized that Bibi had taken him for a ride, making a fool out of him. He was furious, but contained his rage. Although he had threatened to do so, he had no intention of declaring war on Netanyahu. After endless years of humiliation, defamation, and attacks from the right, in his golden age Peres was the beneficiary of unexpected glory. He was a well-liked and popular president—a real consensus man. Enthralled with this new status and the generous polls showing that the people of Israel embraced him warmly, Peres did not want to return to the days of rotten tomatoes. (During the 1981 elections, many of Peres's campaign rallies were disrupted by Begin's supporters, who would throw rotten tomatoes at the candidate.)

In truth, Netanyahu was not deceiving Peres entirely. For at the time, another confidential back channel was at play, led by King Abdullah of Jordan. The second senior partner was Tony Blair, former prime minister of the United Kingdom and the EU's Middle Eastern emissary. Confidential talks were held for a while, with Yitzhak Molcho representing Netanyahu, occasionally accompanied by military secretary Major General Yohanan Locker. The Americans were also privy to these discussions. At a certain point, the parties were supposed to draft a final formula to allow for the beginning of negotiations in Amman, the capital of Jordan. But at the crucial moment Abbas failed to appear. "It was incredible," says an Israeli source who participated in the talks. "We waited at Abdullah's office for the final handshake, but he disappeared. Apparently Mahmoud Abbas had secretly flown to the Emirates, and went off the grid. King Abdullah was furious. I saw him yelling and cursing. We could not even get Mahmoud Abbas on the phone. He simply evaporated."

Peres did not know any of this. He was severely disappointed by Netanyahu. "I had several meaningful conversations with Bibi," said the president in a private conversation. "He was willing to go far and showed flexibility. He made it a point not to evacuate more than eighty thousand settlers. He asked for a map. I gave him a map. He asked me to leave it for him. I did. Incidentally, I've written this all down and kept it, in case anyone denies it." When asked if Netanyahu had approved the map, Peres said, "He asked to keep it. Later he suddenly said that eighty thousand was too much. It would be hard to move them. I told him, 'Bibi, you know what, forget it. Go to the settlers and give them three options: evacuation/compensation where they can leave; they can move into the large settlement blocs; or anyone wishing to stay under any circumstances can stay in his home under the Palestinian Authority.'"

Peres indeed convinced Bibi to go for the option of leaving Israeli settlements within Palestinian jurisdiction. "Why not?" Peres asked, "There are two million Arabs in Israel, why can't there be two hundred thousand Jews in Palestine?" But then Bibi asked what Israel would do about security for those settlements left in Palestine. "I told him," Peres recalls, "that he had nothing to fear. Palestine would be free of arms. We have helicopters; we can be anywhere in five minutes. He liked that. 'Talk to Mahmoud Abbas and convince him,' he told me."

Peres persuaded Abbas. Then, when the agreement was within reach, Bibi flipped. In hindsight, this may have been because at that time the confidential London back channel (where Netanyahu was negotiating through Yitzhak Molcho with Abbas's associate Hussein Agha) was beginning to develop. But Bibi wasn't really serious about London either. He was simply switching one false channel (Peres) with another (London), until the third empty channel (John Kerry) arrived. Like a fake relay race. In the meantime, he kept Peres quiet and occupied for two years.

"He is devoid of kindness or generosity," Peres grumbled, "Jabotinsky spoke of a race that was brilliant, kind, and cruel; in Netanyahu there is only cruelty. His power is in his words. His most important organ is his tongue. Throughout the entire process, he knew he'd stop me at the last moment. He planned it carefully. As he sees it, it's never too late to change your mind and stop. He wanted glory from all directions: He moves towards peace, but also he doesn't. He's what the Americans call a 'mermaid.' When you want to eat, she's a woman. When you want love, she's a fish. Bibi forever conducts himself under this inner contradiction, certain that he'll always find a way out."

Historically speaking, Peres is right. He always finds a way out.

77

London Calling

2010–2013

In 2010 Israel floundered around the freeze on building in the occupied territories. The Palestinians were adamant in their refusal of everything, and George Mitchell was trying to break the glass ceiling with his futile "alliance talks." In London, the secret back channel was established between the Israelis and Palestinians, with American mediation. Benjamin Netanyahu was represented by Yitzhak Molcho, who was usually accompanied by Brigadier General Mike Herzog (Yitzhak "Bougie" Herzog's brother and the government official most proficient in all Israeli peace processes throughout history). The Americans sent their perpetual envoy, Dennis Ross. Mahmoud Abbas was represented by Hussein Agha, a Lebanese academic who had been allied with him for ages and had represented him in the 1990s in negotiations with Yossi Beilin after pushing through the Oslo Accords (that negotiation brought about the Beilin–Mahmoud Abbas Agreement). Although a Shi'ite, Agha had joined Fatah in Beirut and was a member of the national Palestinian movement. His relationship with Abbas spanned decades. In certain ways, Agha was to Abbas what Molcho was to Netanyahu, but more distant and not as total.

In London, the three parties drafted a framework agreement. The principle was simple: The draft was defined "the American document," and was
arrived at through negotiations with both parties. Dennis Ross guaranteed
the parties would be able to "make accomplishments" after the document
was completed. The negotiations were intense at times and dormant at
others, but continued for over three years, with Ross driving the work. Agha
kept total secrecy. Even his partner at the London research institute knew
nothing of the discussions with Molcho. Revolutionary, historic progress
was made. Although the parties tried to deny the importance of the London
channel, reality shows otherwise: President Obama received individual
confirmations from both leaders—Abbas and Netanyahu—of their commitment to the London channel. According to American sources, Abbas confirmed the London conclusions to Obama no fewer than three times: at the
beginning, the middle, and toward the end, in a meeting held in Ramallah
in March of 2013, during the president's visit to Israel and the Palestinian
Authority. This was also true of Netanyahu. Obama received the prime
minister's official confirmation verbally and in person. Moreover, Netanyahu held a confidential individual meeting with Hussein Agha within the
framework of the negotiations. That meeting has remained under strict media blackout to this day. Thus it is clear that both Netanyahu and Abbas
kept close watch over the development of talks. For a while, President Obama
relied heavily on the London channel, calling it "the only game in town."
The problem was the asymmetry of the envoys: If Abbas could keep his distance from London somehow by claiming that Agha was not an official
Palestinian representative (and wasn't even Palestinian), Netanyahu was represented by his closest and most loyal associate, his personal envoy Yitzhak
Molcho. Abbas used the London channel to finally get the words "1967
lines" out of Netanyahu; this was Agha's mission. The means Agha used to
get Netanyahu to this Promised Land were of less importance to Abbas, who
didn't care about the details.

The London channel led to incredible results, a real earthquake in terms
of Middle Eastern policy. Netanyahu supplied the "1967 lines" and showed
unprecedented flexibility on the refugee issue. Agha, for his part, was sur-
prisingly adaptable on behalf of the Palestinians. But how closely coordi-

nated was Agha with Abbas in the concessions he made? A million possible answers exist. The fact is, however, that Abbas prepared himself for immediate disengagement from the London talks. In this way he was no different from Netanyahu. They were both weak leaders incapable of making a historic decision or of committing to it once it was made. Although the writing was on the London wall in broad daylight, the Americans could not (or would not) see it. The president believed both leaders, who promised him their commitment to their emissarie's negotiating in London. It was a mistake.

"Many of us felt that London was unreal, that Mahmoud Abbas would disown it at the crucial point," recalls one of the Americans, "but we had nothing better." Molcho was obsessive about London. Molcho had created the London document and was infatuated with it. He had given life to Netanyahu's concept of handing over the 1967 borders with exchanges of land, and receiving in return everything else: Jerusalem, refugees, security, a Jewish state. It was the Israelis' trade-off in London. They liked the channel and they liked the document.

"Agha is a brilliant man," attests a senior American official who was privy to negotiations. "He's a back-channel genius. It's a shame he's not at the head of the Palestinian Authority instead of Mahmoud Abbas. He could have reached an agreement with Bibi. Agha was the one to get Bibi to agree to the 1967 lines as a basis for negotiation with an exchange of lands. He brought this achievement, one the Palestinians had been waiting generations for. He wore Bibi down. He did to Molcho what Molcho was used to doing to others."

What Agha accomplished no one else has been able to achieve before or since. He managed to obtain Israeli agreement to the term "1967 lines" and exchange of land as a foundation for peace negotiations, signed by Molcho, Netanyahu's personal envoy. On the issue of refugees Netanyahu was flexible. He agreed to establish a system for rehabilitating refugees, with voluntary intake of a restricted number of refugees into Israel, on humanitarian grounds, and subject to Israel's discretion. The system was supposed to contain six cumulative conditions for accepting refugees, and provide Israel with final discretion. If these two concessions had been advertised in real time, Israel would have been shaken to its foundation. But the negotiations were confidential, from 2010 until November of 2014, when their very existence was first reported by journalist Amir Tibon in *The New Republic*. In early March 2015, Nahum Barnea of *Yediot Ahronot* published parts of the agreements that were completed in London up to August 2015. Netanyahu denied having anything to do with it. "It's an American document," he said. "I never agreed to withdraw to the 1967 lines, I had reservations." Dennis Ross, as agreed in advance, substantiated Netanyahu's account. Ross supports, Netanyahu escapes. The Bibi method at work.

Barnea's story was published less than a week before elections in Israel, and the Israeli public was not convinced. It seemed like political spin. Netanyahu sent Benny Begin into the ring to deny any and all concessions. Simultaneously, Netanyahu lashed out at Barnea's newspaper and its publisher Arnon "Noni" Mozes. But this was all irrelevant. The document published by Barnea was true, albeit partial. Netanyahu's Houdini escape had succeeded. The right considered the London document a media conspiracy to defeat Netanyahu. The prime minister managed to have his cake and eat it, too. He won the elections by a landslide, and nobody remembers the London channel, which gave him five precious years of breathing space. London's historic achievement—the agreement to the 1967 lines—has also faded into oblivion. After the dust settled, Netanyahu won another term in office, and the peace process froze to death.

Back to 2013: Netanyahu established his third cabinet in March and granted Justice Minister Tzipi Livni responsibility for negotiations with the Palestinians. Simultaneously, American Secretary of State John Kerry formed a peace task force headed by Ambassador Martin Indyk, and efforts commenced to renew negotiations. Naturally, Livni was unaware of the secret channel in London. Only in August 2013 was she updated, a month after official negotiations; the Kerry channel began in July. What really floored Livni was Netanyahu's attitude toward the refugee issue—he had circumvented her from the left. She was indignant, but not to the point of crisis. She subsequently made some adjustments on the refugee issues. Receiving only partial information from Molcho, Livni asked Kerry to test the waters with Abbas over how committed the Palestinian leader was to London. Kerry met with Abbas, but according to Livni, he did not perform due diligence. Apparently Kerry was hesitant to present Abbas with a dilemma. Livni was worried. Some of her people, including Gadi Baltiansky, who was very proficient and had played a key role in the Geneva Initiative, said, "There's no way Mahmoud Abbas will agree to this document." The London document included wording that was biased in Israel's favor, particularly in acknowledging a Jewish nation and security arrangements. Livni pestered the Americans incessantly: Is the London channel real? Does Abbas know? Does he approve? The Americans responded positively. After all, President Obama himself had heard the Abbas confirmation.

But one person didn't appreciate being kept in the dark about London: Saeb Erekat. When he discovered that a secret channel of negotiation had been operating behind his back in London, Erekat was incandescent with rage. He had been the regular Palestinian negotiator for decades, and this sudden revelation that the real thing was happening behind his back infuriated him. Unlike Livni, he had been there at Abbas's side all along, knowing nothing, out of the loop.

Toward the end of 2013, the fate of the London channel seemed to be sealed. With adversaries like Livni, Erekat, and Martin Indyk (who considered the secret channel a kind of "mutant son" competing with the primary channel he conducted), it seemed that the glory days of London were over. On the other side were Hussein Agha and Dennis Ross, who had nurtured London and considered it a real chance at a historic breakthrough. Only their Israeli counterpart, Yitzhak Molcho, was complacent. He had managed to get through three more years in London, and had no problem wasting further time on alternative channels.

Some tried to persuade John Kerry to continue the London negotiations. An Israeli source claims that he told Kerry, "You mustn't create competition between the two channels; it will harm both. In London you achieved 90 percent of your goal, and anything left should be resolved with the leaders. Give London time and it will blossom." But Kerry wouldn't listen. London was not his toy; he didn't mind it breaking. "London was the real thing, a genuine brainstorming process that brought us closer on many issues, but required incubation that takes time. The efforts in London were real on behalf of both parties, and lasted over three years in complete earnestness and secrecy." But Kerry had no time. He pressured Obama to abandon London and begin open negotiations. Obama deliberated. Many of his advisors recommended continuing London. "Your chances of getting hurt in the London channel are low," the president's advisors said, "if you replace it with open negotiations you will be the one targeted if it fails." According to the London people, Obama's surrender to Kerry ruined their odds of success. According to an Israeli official, "It was stupidity of the first order. They haven't been able to reach an agreement in twenty years, and now they're going to do it in nine months because John Kerry said so? It had no chance, and only caused damage. Instead of letting the London channel mature and bear fruit, they caved in to Kerry's obsession, bringing the channels together crudely, casting London's content onto Kerry's team unprofessionally, and ruining everything."

78

Joining Forces

2013–2015

John Kerry stormed the barren Israeli-Palestinian front like Don Quixote tipping at windmills. He was determined, zealous, and certain of success despite his predecessors' grim results. As an old friend of Netanyahu, he was sure this approach would suffice. Having been a senior Democratic senator, a veteran supporter of Israel, and a seasoned politician, he believed that he could square the circle and break through the impasse, and was sincerely passionate about it. After all, as an avid supporter of Israel, Kerry was also worried about its fate and believed wholeheartedly in the two-state solution as the only option for security and prosperity. All that remained was to convince Bibi. His passion and belief, dubbed "obsessive and messianic" by Defense Minister Ya'alon, helped him recruit President Obama to this lost cause, and the latter gave him room to work. Early in his term as secretary of state, Kerry sounded like an evangelical about brokering a historic agreement between Israel and the Palestinians. His eyes would glow; his conviction would burn in his heart. Behind his back Netanyahu and Ya'alon looked upon him with pity. They considered his naïveté to be borderline stupidity, that he was completely detached from reality.

Kerry formed his task force, headed by Martin Indyk, one of America's highest-ranking diplomats and a two-term U.S. ambassador to Israel. This appointment was met with some criticism from Jerusalem. On the positive side, Indyk needed no guidance or time to study the issue. He hit the ground running. After all, he was one of those most proficient in the history of the conflict, had been accompanying it for at least two decades, and was well aware of the parties, their weaknesses, the issues at play, and the mutual history. Indyk's most prominent disadvantage was his problematic relationship with Netanyahu. Indyk had been ambassador during Bibi's first term as prime minister, a time of which neither had fond memories. Netanyahu saw Indyk as a cunning adversary out to entangle him with the right and topple his government; but then this is Netanyahu's opinion of virtually any Democratic official—especially the Jewish ones. Indyk ignored this background noise. A professional, he believed in making an attempt to lead Netanyahu and Abbas to an agreement that was not too specific in order to improve the situation. Indyk, a veteran soldier for peace, believed that Israel, no less than the Palestinians, needed an agreement; somewhat like Kerry, only less messianic, more realistic, and perhaps somewhat cynical.

Kerry began his effort to renew negotiations immediately after Obama's visit to Israel and the Palestinian Authority in March 2013. It took almost five months; six trips from Jerusalem to Ramallah; dozens of meetings and phone calls; countless offers, arbitrations, and crises. Eventually, on July 18, 2014, the declaration came: a launching of nine months of negotiations between Israel and the Palestinian Authority (negotiations commenced officially in Washington ten days later). Even before they began the parties loathed each other; Kerry was already exhausted.

The negotiations were bad from the onset. And this continued to be the case until their ugly demise nine months later. What happened to the Americans in this round is exactly what had happened with the freeze on building in the West Bank during the previous term: In both cases, they devoted all of their energy to the process itself, then could extend it no longer. To agree to negotiations, the Palestinians demanded that Israel fulfill one of three conditions: acknowledge the 1967 borders as a base for negotiations, freeze building in the West Bank, or release "pre-Oslo" prisoners—i.e., Palestinians in Israeli jails from before 1993. These demands caused political uproar in Israel. Livni supported a building freeze as a reversible move with little damage. Lapid preferred acknowledging the 1967 lines as grounds for negotiation, and was willing to support a freeze or prisoner release. Naftali Bennett's Jewish Home, whose electorate consists primarily of settlers, strongly opposed all of the conditions.

On July 15, 2013, Kerry presented Abbas with a package that seemed to contain "a little of everything," one he had put together with Netanyahu. Bibi would not commit to any of the conditions in full but rather a bit of each. On July 18, the Palestinian Authority rejected the offer, as expected. According to an American source, "Bibi handed them various toys, construction permits in Area C, economic perks, things like that." The prime minister hoped he could seduce the Palestinians with second-rate benefits to avoid the political obstacles entailed in a building freeze, acknowledging the 1967 borders, or releasing prisoners. The Palestinians had learned their lesson and did not bite. Abbas wasn't sure whether he should embark on another wild-goose chase. To him, only Israel's agreement to one of the conditions would prove there was a real Israeli partner. His basic question was whether Kerry could deliver Bibi.

Netanyahu toyed with the idea of acknowledging the 1967 lines with exchange of land as grounds for negotiation, provided it would be confidential. He had already agreed to this principle in London. This option was examined in his talks with Kerry. Netanyahu led Kerry to believe that he was in. On July 18, 2013, one day before Kerry was about to leave the region, someone leaked to Reuters that Netanyahu had acknowledged the 1967 lines as grounds for negotiations.

The leak had a factual basis. A month earlier, Netanyahu had brought Kerry into a private room at the prime minister's office, without any witnesses, and said he would consider acknowledging the 1967 lines with exchange of land as grounds for negotiation. Kerry lit up. He realized he had a live negotiation. This is why he gave Abbas an American letter guaranteeing that negotiations would be based on the 1967 lines with exchange of land. To this day, the Americans swear that Netanyahu agreed to 1967. In any case, the leak quickly ignited the Israeli political world. Naftali Bennett threatened, Lieberman squirmed uncomfortably, the Likud hawks aligned.

Within hours, Netanyahu's spokesman denied everything. The 1967 option was off the table. John Kerry began losing his famous patience; his nerves were racked. The secretary of state looked desperate that morning, and told Minister Livni that he'd had it. He had built mountains upon the possibility of renewing negotiations with a "quiet" acknowledgment of the 1967 lines, but suddenly everything was gone. His countless hops from Jerusalem to Ramallah in recent months had made him a laughingstock. In Washington he was looked upon with compassion. He intended to leave the next day and announce his failure to renew negotiations. "Get along without me," he said to his Israeli counterparts. "I'd like to see you do it." Livni would not give up. Let's make one last bid, she said; call Bibi again. Kerry agreed. "Bibi," said Kerry, "I need an answer today. Tomorrow I'm flying back and I won't return. It's now or never. Prisoners, 1967, or freeze. That's the deal. Take it or leave it."

Israeli deliberations continued for the entire day into the next, July 19. Everyone knew that at the end of the day Kerry, who was in Amman, would board his plane and return to the United States. In the afternoon, Defense Minister Ya'alon and Minister Yuval Steinitz met with Netanyahu. Livni joined them. Also present were national security advisor Amidror and Ron Dermer. The latter convinced Netanyahu to go for the prisoners. "It's the only thing the cabinet and the public will accept," he said. "We have no choice but to swallow this bitter pill." Netanyahu decided to agree to release prisoners in four stages spread over the entire negotiation period, to avoid a situation in which all prisoners were released and the Palestinians stopped negotiations. Ya'alon and Steinitz were in favor of releasing prisoners. Livni preferred a building freeze, but agreed to support the prisoner release. Amidror called Minister Yair Lapid, who also agreed. Another phone call obtained the consent of Minister Avigdor Lieberman. The toughest remained: Minister Naftali Bennett. Although the Sabbath was nigh, Bennett rushed to the prime minister's office. It was an emergency, which overrides Sabbath observance. To Bennett, a freezing on building, or the 1967 lines, were both unacceptable. Only the prisoners remained. Bennett tried to prevent renewed negotiations but realized that the entire cabinet, including Netanyahu, was united. He was the only holdout. Realizing he could not stop the move, he consented. On his way home, he started to hear the wrath of his party and changed his mind. He urgently called the prime minister's office to recant his consent, but Netanyahu was no longer listening. As far as Bibi was concerned, Bennett was in favor. Meanwhile, John Kerry got the green light and announced the renewal of talks in Amman, in an announcement devoid of ceremony; it was sour, urgent, and almost angry. Kerry looked stressed out, Abbas was ashen and, in Jerusalem, the prime minister's office was locked tight. The first meeting was scheduled in ten days, July 29, 2013.

On July 19, a gun was placed on the table, one that would kill negotiations nine months later. The Palestinians' list of pre-Oslo prisoners consisted of 104 names, 85 Palestinians and 19 Israeli Arabs. In Israel opposition is traditionally fierce on the release of Israeli Arabs as part of negotiations. These are considered Israeli citizens and subject to Israeli law, and many Israelis consider their inclusion in foreign-prisoner-exchange transactions a severe undermining of Israeli sovereignty. Justice Minister Tzipi Livni is one of those people. When she discovered that John Kerry's list included nineteen Israeli Arabs, she protested. On the afternoon before announcing the renewal of negotiations, Livni had an angry phone conversation with Kerry while sitting in her car in the parking lot of the prime minister's office. Kerry was in Amman. There were harsh words, and Livni raised her voice. "Where did you get that number?" she roared. "We don't have one hundred and four pre-Oslo Palestinian prisoners, only eighty-five." Kerry said it was the number the Palestinians gave him. "That includes Israeli Arabs," said Livni, "and it's not going to happen." "Why?" asked Kerry, adding, "Bibi already released Israeli prisoners in the Shalit deal." Kerry was right, but Livni would not budge. "I don't care what Bibi already did," she told Kerry, "I won't have it." "Why?" asked Kerry again, stunned. "Because I'm their justice minister and Shimon Peres is their president, not Mahmoud Abbas. The Palestinians will not intervene in the affairs of the state of Israel. The whole concept of establishing a Palestinian state is that they deal with their issues and we with ours. Keep them out of our affairs!" Livni was practically screaming. She felt uncomfortable with the driver present, so she stepped out of the car, talking as she paced back and forth outside the prime minister's office. It was an unforeseen problem caused by bad preparation and misunderstanding of the issue by Kerry's team. They were completely unaware of the potential problem, and they should have known. Indyk's task force had not yet been assembled; Kerry was almost alone.

Eventually an improvised solution was put together, but it didn't last. "We'll try to replace the Israeli prisoners with Palestinians whose crimes were not security-related," said Livni to Kerry, whose jet was already warming its engines in Amman. The American secretary of state was under terrible pressure—he had to bring the plane back at the end of the day because Vice President Biden needed it, he was a nervous wreck from dealing with all these Middle Eastern loonies, and negotiations hadn't even begun. "Sometimes there's a vague line between a security prisoner and an ordinary one," said Livni, and he hoped for the best. The Israelis would find some Palestinian pre-Oslo criminals, and everything would be fine. In any case the release of prisoners was to be carried out in four stages, with Israeli Arabs scheduled for the fourth. There would be time to find a creative solution. In the meantime, Kerry asked the Israelis not to divulge the dispute. It could spur the Israeli right and provoke the Palestinians. He had enough trouble.

During that day, Kerry heard hints that if President Obama were willing to release the spy Jonathan Pollard, the Israeli cabinet might achieve a majority vote for releasing Israeli Arabs. Kerry was hopeful about this option. "I'll discuss it with the president," he said. He realized that Pollard would bring him the fourth stage. All that remained was to convince Obama. It was not impossible. Kerry's renowned optimism enabled him to push aside the obstacles and move on. "It'll be OK," he said, getting on the plane, "we'll cross that bridge when we come to it."

A senior member of the American task force recalls, "You can't blame Kerry. For six months, all he heard from Bibi was 'no, no, no,' and suddenly for five hours on July 19 he was hearing 'yes.' He was in Amman, and Saeb Erekat came to his hotel, with Bibi on the line from Jerusalem. The three worked at it, with Frank Lowenstein the only one there to help Kerry. The Israelis and Palestinians played hardball; nobody was there to check everything they were selling Kerry or to go into details, they had to settle things and within that chaos there was the gaffe on prisoners."

Unfortunately, that was not the only gaffe. "We also blundered on the issue of settlements," an American source admits. The Israelis promised that throughout negotiations they would show "restraint" in everything related to construction in the West Bank. "In reality," the American source recalls, "Bibi tricked us. There was no restraint. Every time prisoners were released, the Israelis came forth with bids and construction announcements that drove the other side crazy. I think at this point Mahmoud Abbas realized that Kerry could not 'deliver' Bibi. It was an illusion."

Kerry's road to hell was paved with good intentions. Upon returning to the United States, when he realized the blunder with the prisoners, Kerry set March 2014 as the new deadline for the aspired framework agreement. The fourth stages of prisoner release were due in April; Kerry wanted to reach the finish line beforehand. In the meantime, he formed a peace task force headed by Martin Indyk. Indyk's role was coined "facilitator," not mediator or negotiator. The point was to give both parties the feeling they controlled their destinies and were responsible for overseeing progress. Indyk formed an efficient and homogenous team comprising experienced professionals: Frank Lowenstein, David Makovsky, Ilan Goldenberg, spokeswoman Laura Blumenfeld, etc. Most members were Jewish, which made them suspicious to both sides. To Abbas they were pro-Israel; to Netanyahu they were liberals trying to bring him down. "Whenever we handed over the list of staff names to organize talks," one of the Americans jokes, "it read like a list of guests to a Brooklyn bar mitzvah." In Ramallah and Jerusalem nobody was laughing. Abbas's skepticism increased and Netanyahu's people said, "These are the kind of Jews who hate Bibi. Liberals, left-wingers, Obama's Jews."

Shortly after his appointment, Indyk came for a first series of talks in Jerusalem and Ramallah. He sat with Netanyahu for a first meeting at the prime minister's office in Jerusalem. Bibi arrived worried. He was afraid of excessive assertiveness. His nightmare was that the Americans would lay upon him a draft of parameters for negotiation and begin discussing issues like borders, Jerusalem, and the settlements. But he left the meeting encouraged. Indyk clarified that negotiations would begin with talks between the parties, and "in six months the administration would reevaluate what had been achieved and decide how to continue." To Netanyahu this was wonderful news. Negotiations would be within his comfort zone; he would be able to dissolve them easily.

This is precisely what happened in the first few months. Netanyahu assigned Molcho to Tzipi Livni. She was not allowed to make a move without him. Molcho was the official babysitter who insisted on attending every meeting and supervising every statement. Even photos weren't taken without him. An amusing incident occurred at the first Jerusalem meeting when Molcho pushed into every frame so that no photo would feature Livni alone with the Palestinians. Netanyahu thought such a photo would provoke the settlers. Livni did not even create a logistic or professional "backup team" for negotiations. The reason was simple: There were no real negotiations. Livni had two excellent secret advisors in Gadi Baltiansky and Avi Gil. She realized she did not really have carte blanche from the prime minister. Moreover, Molcho preferred London. Every time the issue of refugees arose, Molcho would mention his aunt Rosa, who had escaped Egypt penniless. "She's a refugee, too," he claimed. Molcho repeated the Aunt Rosa story until it became a joke among the negotiators. "It's all because of Aunt Rosa," they would say each time they hit a stalemate, but it wasn't really funny. Molcho was Bibi's gatekeeper; his role was to impose the "Bibi method" on Livni, too.

Netanyahu was also concerned about the military and security command. He realized that among his generals there were several who believed that peace was an existential need for Israel, and who were, to him, exceedingly respectful of the American stance. In previous cabinet terms, Israeli officers had played significant roles in negotiations. Senior officers had enjoyed direct contact with American mediators and Palestinian interlocutors alike. Chiefs of staff such as Ehud Barak and Amnon Lipkin-Shahak; generals such as Uri Sagi, Oren Shachor, Uzi Dayan, Udi Dekel, and many others had taken active roles in diplomatic negotiations, with authority and permission.

This was also true of Netanyahu's first cabinet (1996–1999), until the coordinator of government activities in the territories, Major General Oren Shachor, was caught providing progress reports to opposition members Shimon Peres and Yossi Beilin behind Netanyahu's back. When Netanyahu returned to office in 2009, he decided to put an end to this. Scorched by the mixing of executive and military command, Ya'alon shared Netanyahu's belief that there should be an impermeable barrier between IDF officers and the diplomatic process. Netanyahu forbade the Americans from making any contact with senior IDF command, unless it was arranged through him. Later this demand was extended to include reserve officers. IDF officers were permitted to present the Israeli opinion at General John Allen's staff meetings on security, but were forbidden from any further dialogue with the Americans. Israeli security was represented solely by Defense Minister Ya'alon. Bibi and Ya'alon knew what they were doing. Part of the Israeli defense institution believed that Allen's security proposition was not as bad as Ya'alon and Netanyahu thought it was. But they did not have the chance to make their case. The executive administration built a firewall separating them from the media and from the Americans.

Netanyahu tried to build a similar wall between the American staff and his cabinet ministers. Bibi asked Kerry not to meet or talk with Israeli ministers without his permission; this instruction reached Martin Indyk and his staff. He did not want the American team unsettling his team. He had learned the bitter lesson from his previous term, when he had been reluctantly dragged to Wye, and swore that this time he would control the process, and not vice versa.

The Americans, not fully accepting this, found detours to the people they wanted to talk to. A prime example is the former minister of science, space, and technology, Yaakov Peri, from the Yesh Atid party. As former head of the Shabak, Peri had a productive working relationship with then ambassador Indyk. Peri is well versed on the security and diplomatic aspects of the Palestinian issues, and closely associated with his party's chairman, Yair Lapid. Indyk was not going to pass on the chance to communicate with him. They came up with a system of creating social events—dinners and cocktails—to which senior Israeli executives were invited, and at which Americans were present. Through these frequent social events, the Americans managed to circumvent the wall that Netanyahu had constructed around his officers and ministers. Such is the privilege of a superpower. The other way around and Israel may have found itself accused of espionage.

David Makovsky was the secret weapon: a shrewd Jewish American who had lived in Israel for a long time, spoke Hebrew, and was the former editor of the *Jerusalem Post* and an esteemed columnist for *Ha'aretz* (he is currently a senior member of the Washington Institute for Near East Policy). Makovsky is a walking encyclopedia of all peace process–related issues, well versed in Israeli customs, has a good sense of humor, and is also well connected with the Palestinians. He maintains a complex network of connections within Israel's political-diplomatic-security elite. Some of those involved in the negotiations called Makovsky a double agent, in the positive sense of the term. Actually, he was a triple agent. He moved constantly between Washington, Jerusalem, and Ramallah in a continuous effort to generate new ideas. His brilliant mind and journalistic instincts guided him through this impossible labyrinth, while his connections in Israel helped him work around restrictions and make contact with former defense system senior officials. He paved detours that allowed him to remain updated at all times, and all behind the backs of Netanyahu and Ya'alon.

On the security level, the Americans managed to create indirect channels with retired officers and defense system executives. In Israel, retired officials are still kept posted and remain well connected at any given moment. It's a small country and the security world there is intimate; everyone knows everyone and all are connected. Makovsky and his staff managed to meet with retired officers including Gadi Shamni and Avi Mizrahi (former heads of Central Command); Brigadier General Udi Dekel; and head of the peace administration under Olmert, Shlomo Brom (formerly of the IDF's planning division); Ephraim Lavie (former Israeli intelligence officer) and many others at cafés, restaurants, and various offices. The isolation Netanyahu tried to impose on Indyk and his people was futile.

The Americans also used the services of Israeli specialists, members of the "peace industry." The most prominent of these was Gadi Baltiansky, the director-general of the Geneva Initiative, who tried to infuse the process with new ideas. Another special consultant was the maps specialist Brigadier General Shaul Arieli. At one point, Arieli simultaneously advised all three parties—the Americans, the Israelis, and the Palestinians—on topographic issues. Arieli met Indyk in Jerusalem's King David Hotel; he met his staff in cafés and restaurants as well as his Tel Aviv office. He was also summoned to the State Department and the NSC in Washington, and had never stopped meeting with the Palestinians. This was also true of Avi Gil, a veteran diplomat and the protégé of billionaire Dan Abraham, who is chairman of the S. Daniel Abraham Center for Middle East Peace in Israel. Gil is relentless in his campaign for peace and is well connected with the Palestinian regime. Ultimately, despite Netanyahu and Ya'alon's attempts at stonewalling, everyone was talking to everyone, all the time.

But no real progress was made. Molcho, dubbed "Doctor No," would not allow any progress; he stuck to Livni and curbed any attempt at a breakthrough. He blocked any discussion of sensitive core issues, including the examination of maps. Once, when he stepped out of the room, a map appeared on the table. When he returned, he saw Livni and Erekat leaning over the map. "What is this supposed to mean," Molcho asked. Erekat tried to explain that they were checking something specific and Livni suggested that he pretend what he was seeing was science fiction. Molcho immediately pointed out that the prime minister did not permit maps. When Livni asked for permission to show a map, Netanyahu demanded it be a map that left 95 percent of settlers in their homes. He knew perfectly well that such a map was impossible.

Twenty-five futile meetings were reported. Meanwhile, Israel executed the first three stages of the pre-Oslo prisoner release. Each of these stages was accompanied by loud declarations of new building and bids in the territories. The Americans were asking what had happened to the promised "restraint," and the Palestinians were furious. Criticism of Abbas increased. The negotiations were beginning to look like a disaster.

Only one way existed out of the dead end: appropriating the London channel and merging it with Kerry and Indyk's formal efforts. Netanyahu preferred London, as it was confidential and therefore deniable. It did not include any official Palestinian representation. The official channel led by the American secretary of state was far more dangerous. But the official channel had reached a stalemate, and in December 2013, after heavy pressure, President Obama made the decision: London had been exhausted; Kerry would take over the London document and run with it through official channels. Obama took over London. At the same time, he also raised his personal bet on the entire process.

"It was inevitable," a senior American staff member recalls. "We had promised to end negotiations by the end of April; it was December and we had made no progress. We could not meet the April deadline. If there was a document in London, we had to take it and continue from there, as long as we reached an agreement." In those months there was ongoing tension between Martin Indyk and Netanyahu's envoy, Yitzhak Molcho. Indyk feared Molcho wanted to sabotage the front channel in order to promote the back channel. "The dynamic was lethal," recalls an American source. "They also developed personal antagonism. Martin was convinced that Molcho wanted to stall the whole deal, and Molcho saw Martin the way Bibi saw him: an agent of Peace Now who wanted to drag Israel into an agreement." They loathed each other and did not bother to hide it.

Indyk was in a delicate spot. He realized that Netanyahu was citing official negotiations to alleviate international pressure on Israel but had no real intention of making progress. But Indyk had no intention of deflecting the birds of prey from Netanyahu. Indyk was also aware of the London mechanism. Hussein Agha was actually the bait used by Abbas to extract the words "1967 lines" from Netanyahu. Once Netanyahu had said it through Molcho it was irreversible. Abbas, on the other hand, could distance himself from what Agha had promised. The asymmetry was worrying.

Tzipi Livni was also antagonized. She had been sure she was center stage, but had found herself off-off-Broadway. Netanyahu tried to appease her. An amateur illustrator, he drew Livni a picture of two parallel lines. One was London, the other the front channel in which she participated. "The London line is moving forward," Bibi said, "and yours is stuck for now. When the London line matures into an agreement, we'll unite both lines and your time will come." Livni very much wanted to believe him.

It was national security advisor Susan Rice, an Obama pick, who helped "unite the channels." Rice considered the London channel to be her predecessor Tom Donilon's "baby" and had no interest in promoting it. She did not bother to tap Dennis Ross, and accepted Indyk's position: If London matured they should go with London. If it didn't, the channels should be united. "There's no time," Indyk said. "We have to seal the deal and it's the only way." He was right.

The London people—especially Agha—were furious. They had extracted Netanyahu's historic concession (1967 lines) and now they were being pushed aside. "Agha was not a crook," an American source says. "He had the full authority and permission, and Mahmoud Abbas confirmed three times that Agha was working on his behalf." It was useless now. The London channel was officially closed. A large puddle of bad blood spread between London, Ramallah, and Jerusalem. Agha was offended and Dennis Ross was not happy. He was a London man. Martin Indyk did not trouble himself with personal issues. He had a mission he was trying to fulfill.

In retrospect, it is clear that with the London channel shut, the Palestinian leader lost hope and interest in talks. Indyk defines what happened to Abbas as a "complete shutdown." He realized that neither Kerry nor Indyk could "deliver" Bibi. When Indyk suggested discussing the core issues with the Palestinians, Abbas replied, "First finish with the Israelis." In the end, he complained that the Americans had invested all their efforts in the Israelis, forgetting that from the start he had taken no interest.

Despite its premature demise, the London channel went down in history. Netanyahu had made unprecedented diplomatic mileage. He had agreed to the 1967 lines as a basis for negotiations (with exchange of land) and to establishing a mechanism, with Israeli participation, for rehabilitating Palestinian refugees. "We managed to achieve breakthroughs in two of five core issues," an American source says. "Borders and refugees were allegedly agreed upon; what remained was Jerusalem, security arrangements, and acknowledgment of a Jewish state." For the first time the Americans felt the agreement was within reach. If Bibi had come through on two so very sensitive matters, there was reason for further discussion.

In January, John Kerry and his staff began their primary efforts. The

Americans decided to develop the London document into a framework agreement. The method: a concentrated marathon negotiation between the Kerry team and the Bibi team. Kerry and Bibi supervised the talks. The Palestinians were completely ignored. The U.S. strategy was to seal the deal with Bibi and then show it to the Palestinians. In hindsight this was a mistake that allowed the Palestinians to play their traditional role of victim and claim that the Americans were only in agreement with one party, while conveniently ignoring Abbas's refusal to conduct a similar process with Kerry's team. The Palestinians simply did not believe that the Americans would get any real concessions from the Israelis.

For almost six weeks, from late January to early March 2014, real drama unfolded in these marathon talks between Kerry's and Bibi's teams. It was an unprecedented, intense, ongoing, and concentrated process. Most of the meetings were held through a sophisticated satellite video system. Four three-hour sessions a week, a total of more than twenty marathon videoconferences, over almost one hundred net hours. Kerry, who oversaw the meetings from all corners of the world, invested tremendous effort in the project. The assiduous secretary of state continued to work his job full-time while combing the world with his senior assistants and staff, dragging along the video system, which allowed him to set up a negotiating room at any given moment from anywhere on earth and connect with a similar room in Netanyahu's office. "There were some bizarre moments," an Israeli participant recalls. "Once Kerry sat in Indonesia under a decorative mosquito net; then he was in a fancy tent in the UAE, and another time he was in a five-star hotel in China. The meetings continued worldwide, his patience endless, handling constant crises and numerous disputes." Another participant says, "Kerry's ability to drop everything and focus on the minute details was superhuman."

The marathon was nerve-racking, and sometimes hostile to the point of shouting. Occasionally tempers were lost. There were "incidents of elbows being poked around the table, especially on the Israeli side," recalls an Israeli participant, "and several times the atmosphere was tense, with yelling and even screaming on both sides," an American participant adds. When the issues were important to him, Netanyahu's anxiety rose. He would sweat, and sometimes even yell. "Tempers flared," says an American participant. "Bibi was on the verge of mental collapse. He was discussing things he had never dreamed he'd discuss: Jerusalem, refugees, the 1967 lines. He was shaken, sometimes leaving the meeting, only to return later. It was clearly very difficult for him."

Netanyahu would show up for these marathon video meetings with an English dictionary in hand to choose the most precise word for each issue. He badgered the Americans with endless bickering and arguments over mundane issues and cumbersome phrasing. As the negotiations were coming to a close, the Americans applied unprecedented pressure on Netanyahu to seal the deal. They were discussing the Palestinian refugees. Kerry was in Paris, and the videoconference was tense and brusque. Netanyahu raised his voice. A recess was declared. The meeting was supposed to resume later, but then Netanyahu failed to show up. The Americans were sure he was having a nervous breakdown. "He was falling apart," says a senior American participant. "He was clearly breaking down and couldn't handle it." Molcho appeared without Netanyahu, and Justice Minister Livni apologized to the Americans for the prime minister's absence. Netanyahu had escaped at the crucial moment when the teams were discussing how he would sell his agreement to create a mechanism for rehabilitating refugees to the Israeli public. Liran Dan, Bibi's media advisor, warned him, "You will not be able to get this past the Israeli public. People will say that we don't help Holocaust survivors, but we help Palestinian refugees." Netanyahu bailed, and the discussion continued without him.

When Netanyahu is under excessive pressure, he has been known to catch a bad cold. Headaches, inflamed sinuses, a runny nose, and red eyes are all tools of Bibi's trade. Israel's first prime minister, David Ben-Gurion, suffered from similar symptoms during Israel's infancy.

Few understand the depth and nature of the relationship between Netanyahu and Kerry. "They have a very special intimacy," says an American participant in the talks. "Sometimes they seem like a married couple. They are very fond of each other, yet are capable of reaching pinnacles of hostility and anger." Another American who knows them well adds, "Perhaps the fact that they are both married to domineering women—perhaps too domineering—has brought them closer over the years. They share a very special camaraderie. They can talk ten times a day and never tire of each other. In terms of their ability to wear a person down verbally, they are well matched. Netanyahu is known for his ability to exhaust his interlocutor and dispirit him or her. John Kerry is equally capable."

"It was very strange," says a third American who was there. "They had the craziest conversations. Sometimes we thought Bibi was paranoid or suffered from schizophrenia, and we wondered how Kerry could take such abuse from him. The prime minister would call and yell at Kerry, and a few minutes later they would be conversing warmly as friends. [. . .] Bibi is one of the only people who can out-argue Kerry, and their conversations would last forever. At that point, Kerry believed he needed to listen to Bibi, to let him vent, because that was the only way to 'deliver' him." He wanted to give Bibi the feeling he was on his side. He conveyed proposals from Bibi to Abbas although he knew that Abbas would reject them. The point was to make Bibi feel he was representing him. Kerry believed that was the way to win Bibi's trust and then press him to move forward."

According to an Israeli participant in the negotiations, Kerry's intentions were pure. "He is an old-school Democrat with an inherent sympathy for Israel. He has a problem with execution. What's weird about him is that the more you spit on him, the more he begs to be in your proximity. Bibi quickly caught on to that. They had terrible fights, pounding their fists on the table and yelling to high heaven. Kerry can yell, often saying things like 'Bibi, that's bullshit!' but Netanyahu has endless restraint and a thick skin. He would just move on."

After the worst conflagrations between them, Kerry and Netanyahu would angrily disengage. "When Kerry didn't return his call, Bibi would go crazy, and vice versa," says an Israeli participant. "When Bibi wouldn't accept a call from Kerry, the secretary of state would become anxious." An Israeli who knows their relationship says, "Bibi and Kerry share a type of hubris. They are both bad at teamwork; they would sit in a room together and come up with something that surprised everyone. They are not always in touch with reality. Sometimes they just live in a fantasy. That's how the idea for a framework agreement was born. They are both very self-assured, certain of their abilities and their advantages. They have cooked up many things together. Sometimes it worked; other times it failed."

Kerry had a worrying tendency to make a slip of tongue each time the tension on both sides came to a peak. It caused public outrage, political crisis and sharp criticism on the Israeli and Palestinian sides. During those crucial days Bibi asked Kerry not to visit the region, and to spare both parties the pressure of his physical presence. Kerry was also in a complex situation: Many at the White House thought he was pro-Israel; Netanyahu's yes-man. In order to prove he was an honest broker, he occasionally said things that Jerusalem perceived as anti-Israeli, which inflamed things in Israel. In January 2014, Netanyahu met Kerry at Davos and they agreed that the latter would not visit the Middle East for the next few weeks. The marathon talks continued via satellite, as usual.

As time passed, internal White House criticism increased that Kerry was not working closely enough with the Palestinians. Not everyone was convinced that Abbas wanted Kerry to figure things out with Netanyahu first.

"We should have worked with Ramallah simultaneously," one of the Americans admits in hindsight. "We devoted all our energy on dragging Netanyahu to reasonability, and left Mahmoud Abbas barricaded in his own polarity. Ultimately, we paid a steep price for that."

Another source of opposition was Tzipi Livni. She didn't like the wording Netanyahu approved for the refugee issue. He had circumvented her from the left. She had put great effort into blocking and then adjusting the refugee issue in London. Phrases like "restoring the refugees' dignity" were unacceptable to her. She demanded the inclusion of President Bush's letters in the framework agreement as well as the declaration that the very establishment of the Palestinian state was the primary solution for the refugee issue. Livni also inserted the matter of Jewish refugees from Arab countries and demanded that they, too, be addressed within the rehabilitation mechanism. These amendments were not in the original London document negotiated by Molcho with Agha and Ross. Livni added them later. Nevertheless, the refugee item within the Netanyahu-Kerry framework agreement was dramatic.

The framework agreement opens with a declaration of intent: "The two-state solution shall be implemented; each nation realizing its national aspirations in its own country. As part of this arrangement, both parties confirm that the Jewish people and the Palestinian people will acknowledge each other's right to self-definition within its own state." This is how the principle of two nations is phrased—a state for the Palestinian people and a state for the Jewish people (Livni considered this the Palestinians' recognition of Israel as a Jewish state). The item on refugees declares that an international foundation will be established to compensate refugees, and Israel would be one of the contributors. The full solution for the Palestinian refugee issue would be the establishment of a Palestinian state. Refugees would be able to return to Palestine, to remain where they were, or to legally emigrate to a third country. Regarding the return to Israel, the item asserted that Israel would have the authority to determine a limited number of refugees on humanitarian grounds (e.g., reuniting family). It subsequently states that the parties would establish an international mechanism for rehabilitating refugees. Israel committed to contributing funds to this mechanism, along with the international community, and to absorbing Palestinian refugees under certain conditions. There would be six cumulative criteria enabling refugees to apply for naturalization in Israel, but Israel would have final discretion. No numbers were discussed. Clearly Netanyahu would not be able to match the numbers mentioned by his predecessors (under Olmert the figure was five thousand a year for ten years).

Regarding territories, the framework agreement included a full and final withdrawal from the occupied territories. There was no timeline for this withdrawal and it was not subject to the execution of the agreement; nor was it performance-based. It included the exchange of land with the Palestinian Authority. The Jordan River Valley was declared a special military zone, along the river border with Jordan. The article did not state how long Israeli military presence would continue along the river. There were great discrepancies between Israeli and Palestinian perceptions of this presence. Netanyahu demanded forty years. Abbas agreed to three years, and then went up to five. The Americans said seven to ten years. Netanyahu refused. They decided to leave the scheduling clause open. "Duration will be discussed later," the draft said. Abbas was not very happy about this. We will not accept the absence of a deadline for ending the occupation, he said.

A "Trojan horse" that was inserted to the agreement, stated that the Palestinian state would be established only after there was "one authority, one law, and one weapon." The meaning behind this clause was to force the Palestinians to unite Gaza and the West Bank and not allow the establishment of a state containing an entity within the Authority. The agreement also included an option for Jewish settlers to remain in their homes under Palestinian jurisdiction. Netanyahu voiced this idea publicly at the Davos conference in January. Peres had spoken of it much earlier with Abbas. Leaving the settlers in place should have made it easier for Netanyahu to win approval for the agreement. Regarding Jerusalem, Kerry could not drag Netanyahu into making concessions. The framework agreement contained a vague reference to the fact that each party was aware of the other's aspirations vis-à-vis Jerusalem, and that no permanent arrangement could be achieved without resolving this matter. Under no circumstance would Netanyahu agree to a declaration of "two capitals in Jerusalem." Netanyahu knew the Shuafat refugee camp could not be within the boundaries of Israel's capital, but the sensitivity regarding Jerusalem did not permit any flexibility. Whenever he seemed to be softening, his advisors, headed by Liran Dan, calmed him; there was no way of selling that to the Israeli public.

Throughout this time, Abbas sat in Ramallah, stewing, his frustration growing. He, like Netanyahu, was trying to hold on to both ends of the stick. He did not want to discuss the details with the Israelis before the deal was closed, but felt hurt and neglected when he realized the Americans were only talking to the Israelis. On one of his Middle East visits Kerry was scheduled to meet Abbas in Ramallah for a briefing. However, his earlier meeting with Netanyahu ran longer than planned, and Kerry canceled at the last moment. Abbas was angry. Kerry suggested that Erekat come by his hotel for a late-night update. The Palestinians were both offended and dangerously frustrated.

On February 19, 2014, John Kerry met Mahmoud Abbas in Paris and showed him the framework agreement with the Israelis. Kerry arrived at the meeting like a groom on his wedding day. He had been through an exhausting battle with Bibi, but had managed to achieve some important concessions. He was sure Abbas would be excited, which only serves to illustrate Kerry's naïveté. Not only was Abbas not excited, he nearly turned the table over on Kerry. As he saw it, he had been abandoned in the corner and was now being presented with an agreement as a fait accompli. Moreover, there was no mention of any Palestinian presence in Jerusalem. He considered Kerry's document incomplete and insufficient, and that was before Kerry stressed that Netanyahu had reservations. Even Abbas's London achievements were in doubt. When Abbas asked how the document was crafted and Kerry responded that it was based on the London document, Mahmoud Abbas developed instant amnesia.

The Americans should have known this would happen. After all, virtually the same thing had happened with the Beilin–Mahmoud Abbas Agreement in 1995. Then, too, Abbas's representative had been Hussein Agha. A draft had been created, and Abbas had wriggled out of it at the last moment. Kerry was now faced with the reality that the paper was a nonstarter. The absence of any mention of two capitals in Jerusalem was simply unacceptable to the Palestinians. He offered Abbas a side letter from the Americans guaranteeing that the permanent agreement would express the Palestinians' aspiration to have a capital in Jerusalem. Abbas flatly refused. To him, the framework agreement was not worth the paper it was written on.

"Mahmoud Abbas's rejection of the document was predictable," says an American who participated in the talks. "We spent all those weeks with Bibi trying to make him feel good. The axiom is that if Bibi feels good, Abbas will feel bad. We devoted all our energy to the Israelis; Bibi micromanaged every word and comma. After presenting the document to Mahmoud Abbas in Paris and it was turned down, we went back to the Israelis and explained that we had done our best but there was no deal. What should we do now? To our surprise, the Israelis were indifferent. They were expecting that result. As far as we are concerned, they said, you can put anything you like in the document, as long as it's fair, since the Palestinians will refuse anything submitted to them."

In the meantime, drama was unfolding at the White House. National security advisor Susan Rice also insisted on the framework document drafted with Netanyahu being "pro-Israeli." She assigned Prem Kumar, a highly esteemed specialist on the NSC, to a special project comparing the framework agreement negotiated by Kerry to the parameters set by Clinton in 2000. The comparison was informative: Clinton declared that in Jerusalem "what was Israeli would be Israeli, and what was Palestinian would be under Palestinian control." He had gone into details, addressed the issue of the Old City, dividing it between parties. None of this thinking had found its way into the framework agreement save for a vague acknowledgment of the parties' mutual aspirations for Jerusalem. Kerry offered Abbas a capital in the Biet Hanina neighborhood with limited territory. Rice found other issues advantageous to Israel.

The Americans decided to make one final effort. They would improve the document to appease Abbas and try again, just as the Israelis had suggested. The week before Abbas's arrival in Washington to review the new document, the Americans briefed Molcho. To their surprise, the Israeli position remained: "Write whatever you like, it doesn't really matter, Mahmoud Abbas will never say yes. He will never agree."

The Americans convinced themselves they had Netanyahu's approval through Molcho. This was not unfounded, although Molcho would later explain that he was speaking only theoretically. In any case, the Americans improved the framework document drafted with Netanyahu, and included the sensitive phrase according to which there would be "two capitals for two states in Jerusalem." They were hoping to get Abbas's general consent, and then to return to Netanyahu and bulldoze him into "doing Jerusalem." But Abbas failed to realize the weight of the moment. His meeting with Obama took place on July 17, 2014. He was polite but refused to provide an official response. "Give me time, I'll discuss it with the cabinet and get back to you," he told the president. Obama insisted on resolving the matter. "I need an answer within eight days," he said. The number was not random. The deadline for the fourth stage of the agreed prisoner release was April 29. Obama wanted Abbas's reply by March 25, to leave the American staff a month to prepare for the critical release date.

Susan Rice was furious. She had been sure the Palestinians would cooperate. She had invested a great deal of effort on their behalf in order to balance the draft, and once again they were backing out. "You have to be complete idiots to reject this offer," she told the Palestinians. A heated argument erupted between Rice and Erekat. "They almost came to blows," says one of the participants. Later Martin Indyk sat with Saeb Erekat and explained the document in detail, including the historic reference to "two capitals in Jerusalem." It was all in vain. "We'll think it over for a few days and get back to you after we get our prisoners," the Palestinians said. To this day, they are still thinking. Netanyahu and Molcho were right. "Mahmoud Abbas just wasn't there," says an American source. "He never engaged."

Tzipi Livni says Abbas just walked away. Most of the Americans believe he made a mistake, although some understand it. "Bibi's behavior wore him down," one American says. "He completely lost faith. He was exhausted by all the declarations about building in the settlements; his public lost its patience, and he lost interest."

At this stage, with only five weeks remaining until the scheduled end of negotiations (the April 29 date was exactly nine months after the first meeting in Washington), the United States moved to plan B. Understanding that Abbas could not accept the framework agreement as it was, their efforts now focused on extending negotiations by another nine months. They still believed they could make progress, improve the agreement, and eventually force both sides to accept it. The only problem was how to disarm the gun placed on the table in the first act: The fourth stage of prisoner release was imminent, and the ticking time bomb activated by Kerry's early blunder was about to explode. The Palestinians had received a promise to release Arab Israeli prisoners, but the Israelis had never made that promise. The Americans were somehow supposed to circle the square, and shove Abbas and Netanyahu into it. But Abbas and Netanyahu did not want to be shoved.

Netanyahu said he would not release Israeli prisoners without a dramatic gesture like the release of Jonathan Pollard. The Palestinians simultaneously made it clear that Abbas was ready to walk away. He was fed up and planning to sign a series of requests to add the Palestinian Authority to UN institutes. Such a gesture would set off a diplomatic war against the Israelis and put an end to negotiations. Two days before the deadline, President

Obama agreed to release Pollard. Israel and the United States began to con-
solidate the terms of release. In the meantime, however, Bibi got cold feet.
He worried that he would release the prisoners but the Palestinians would
not agree to extend negotiations. In his Jerusalem office, he deliberated. He
was supposed to announce a special cabinet meeting to approve the release,
but was incapable of doing so. He was torn between the settlers, who were
applying tremendous pressure, and Tzipi Livni, who was running franti-
cally around him. She could see Netanyahu talking to right-wing leaders
like Uri Ariel, Ze'ev "Zambish" Hever, and others, and begged him to at
least issue a press release announcing that a cabinet meeting was imminent.
She knew that Abbas's people were waiting in Ramallah, while his patience
was wearing thin.

It was the perfect trap. Each side of this impossible triangle was afraid
of drawing the short straw. The Palestinians claimed, rightfully, that they
should receive the prisoners of the fourth stage with no strings attached,
because that was the basis for their agreement to resume negotiations. They
would not pay for it again. Israel claimed it had never agreed to free Israeli
prisoners and would do so only in exchange for Pollard's release. Israel, too,
was right. Obama agreed to release Pollard, but realized he might be doing
so for nothing; the Palestinians would not even return to the table. So,
Obama was right, too. And when everyone is right, it means someone is very
wrong.

There is nothing Netanyahu hates more than being a sucker. It was he
who coined the expression "If they give they'll get, if they don't, they won't"
during the Wye River talks. He was traumatized by the early promise at
Wye to release Pollard. He was afraid the Americans would cheat him again,
leaving him with nothing. Only Livni believed it. She stormed into Netanyahu's office and found him, again, with settlement leaders and Minister Uri
Ariel. "Bibi, it's going to end, at least say you're convening the cabinet;
they're waiting in Ramallah." Netanyahu looked at her, and did nothing.
"There are moments in life," Livni said to Netanyahu, "when everything
changes. Such a moment is approaching, Bibi." The prime minister did not
respond. Maybe he hoped to get to that moment.

A senior American official who had been privy to the talks recalls, "At the height of suspense, just as Tzipi was begging Netanyahu to at least announce a cabinet meeting, and Abbas was preparing to sign the documents for joining the UN and thus drawing the curtain on diplomatic efforts, Netanyahu called Kerry. Bibi was in the car with Molcho and other advisors, and said that the formula for extending negotiations was acceptable; he just wanted to add or remove a comma or so in the phrasing. Kerry did not know what to think. Either someone here was crazy, or Bibi was intentionally sabotaging the deal."

Then, as the drama peaked, Abbas suddenly appeared on television. Everyone watched—in Washington, Jerusalem, and Ramallah. It was over. On live television, Abbas signed official applications to UN institutions, thus marking the end of negotiations. Livni called Erekat and tried to stop the last-minute collapse, but in vain. She vented her frustration on the Americans: "You could have guaranteed that the prisoners would be released and they would have been appeased," she said in despair. But the Americans were completely drained. They had had enough. The process exhausted them. The next day, Livni met the Palestinian staff in a final effort to salvage the situation. They considered substituting the release of prisoners with a three-month freeze on building. Then, the following day, Abbas delivered another surprise by signing a historic truce between Fatah and Hamas. The peace process had died an ugly death. "A tragedy," wrote Livni's advisor Tal Becker in a note. "I will remember this day until I die," she wrote back. To the very last minute, she believed that it would be possible to extend negotiations and make progress later. But she was the only believer. The truce between Fatah and Hamas has not been realized to this day, just like peace between Israel and the Palestinians.

79

Mr. Security

2014

John Kerry believed security to be the cornerstone of any Israeli-Palestinian agreement. He knew Netanyahu was the self-appointed "guardian of Israel's security" with absolute belief in this role. In State Department discussions prior to negotiations, the concept was that if the United States and Israel managed to put together a plan providing sufficient security arrangements in case of withdrawal from the West Bank, the road to an agreement would be smooth, and vice versa. In the absence of such a breakthrough, the odds of an agreement were zero. Kerry decided to invest heavily in security. He recruited General John Allen, a highly esteemed U.S. military officer, placing all necessary means at his disposal. Allen brought in over one hundred American security specialists from all fields and began working on an American-Israeli "security plan" that would provide Israel with the "security package" it needed in case an agreement was reached with the Palestinians causing the withdrawal of the IDF from the West Bank.

The American team went all out trying to satisfy the Israeli generals. The problem was not with the officers themselves but rather their superior, Defense Minister Moshe "Bogie" Ya'alon, who looked upon the entire process skeptically. According to the negotiators, Ya'alon's stubbornness on security issues left the American team no chance of success. "You under-stand the significance of an American security plan that is acceptable to us?" Netanyahu asked Ya'alon once, adding, "At that moment we'll have to start talking borders." Ya'alon understood perfectly. "I won't let it come to that," he said.

Ya'alon was not acting in bad faith. Born into the left of the Labor Party, he had been a kibbutz member, but his world view changed after being appointed commander of Military Intelligence where he was exposed to clas-sified material on the Palestinians' true intentions. He believed there was no way of resolving the conflict as things stood, preferring to manage it while promoting projects from the bottom up. He respected the United States but believed they were naïve and out of touch with reality in the Middle East. While the Americans decorated their plan with impressive technol-ogy, including satellites, infrared detectors, drones, and innovative cyber- and nanotechnology, Ya'alon and Netanyahu insisted on physical presence. "At the end of the day," Ya'alon said, "the explosives lab in Qalqilya will not be deactivated by sensors but by the IDF and the Shabak." Molcho sup-ported Ya'alon and made clear in all security-related meetings that no technology in the world could replace boots on the ground. The Ameri-cans offered a special Israeli outpost in the West Bank when a special Israeli force for rapid intervention will be stationed, with helicopters. "In case of an emergency you will be able to act", they told the Israelis, but Ya'alon & Netanyahu were not impressed.

"What would you do," Molcho asked, "if Jordan suddenly collapsed and there were thousands of ISIS militants on the other side of the river?" The Americans had a response: "In such a case, Yitzhak, do you think that any-one would stop Israel from immediately invading and recapturing the West Bank? That's exactly what happened in Operation Defensive Shield, isn't it? The Palestinians won't accept an Israeli presence for forty years, but if something happens, the world will understand and accept reoccupation of the area."

The Israelis were not convinced. General Allen put his soul into the se-curity plan. The Palestinians showed some flexibility. The goal was to find a formula where the Palestinians would feel autonomous, even if it was an illusion only, and the Israelis would feel safe. Under American pressure, the Palestinians agreed to the military presence of a "third party" on the Jordan River. The identity of this third party was to be determined. King Abdullah of Jordan contributed his share by agreeing to build a Palestinian airport, the lion's share of which would be on the Jordanian side with its west end on Palestinian territory. Thus the Palestinians would have autonomy over their airport, while terminals would be on the Jordanian side and Israel could be involved in security checks. There were also optional solutions for the issues of airspace and cyberspace. The Americans presented an elaborate security program that included an unprecedented package of technology. Ya'alon was not impressed. "All these toys and gadgets are not worth much," he said. "Until Palestinian nature changes, we cannot surrender physical presence on the Jordan River." When shown the special means of securing the border between Palestine and Jordan, what he wanted to know about was the border between Jordan and Iraq, as that was, to his opinion, the source of evil.

The Americans were deeply offended by the Israeli attitude to their plan. They had the somewhat justified impression that some of Israel's security institutions saw positive elements and grounds for progress in the plan. But Ya'alon would not let the Israeli generals speak their minds. His fist was closed. In meetings with General Allen's staff, IDF officers were not allowed to voice opinions or ask questions; they were only permitted to respond and refer to purely security-related issues. Nonetheless, the Americans got a positive impression from their Israeli counterparts. General Allen and his people were convinced that they could reach a formula if it depended on the Israeli command. In the Americans' quiet talks with their Israeli counterparts, Allen's people understood that among IDF command there was significant support for the plan. But the final word in Israeli security matters belongs to the defense minister, with the prime minister above him. They sent Allen for another round of discussions, and then another, until it collapsed.

David Makovsky had high hopes for the success of the security plan. At a certain point Makovsky talked to his friend, reserve Major General Amos Yadlin, former head of Military Intelligence, who now headed the Institute for National Security Studies (INSS) in Tel Aviv. According to Makovsky, the Israeli security institution is of great importance. Israel's retired generals and commanders are a strong, well-connected guild committed to Israel's security. Makovsky tried to get Yadlin to declare his support for the plan on behalf of the INSS. "If I can't convince you, it's a waste of time," he said. He did not succeed. Shortly after the process collapsed in mid-2014, Netanyahu made a strategic decision that in light of events in the Middle East, Israel must not surrender physical presence and military freedom in the West Bank, and it must not withdraw its presence along the Jordan Valley. No technology in the world could substitute or compensate for physical presence.

80

The Blame Game

A senior American participant of the talks was recently asked where they'd gone wrong. "We were aiming at the grand prize," he explained. "We wanted a home run instead of starting with a single, moving on to a double, and so on." When asked who was to blame, he answered, "Everyone. We were playing baseball, the Israelis were playing football, and the Palestinians were sitting on the fence. We were speaking different languages. There were huge gaps in our perspectives, our points of view. In retrospect, these may have been unbridgeable."

Who is more to blame for the collapse of negotiations, the Israelis or the Palestinians? Here, too, it depends on whom you ask. The Obama administration did not confront the Palestinians throughout the entire negotiation. Obama began with a conception that the Palestinians were weak; they were the ones who needed help, and therefore there was nothing to demand of them. The Americans devoted all their energy to the Israeli side. "That's a misguided approach," one American admits. "It just immortalizes Palestinian weakness and victimhood. They have grown accustomed to just sitting there without having to decide or make concessions, waiting for us to do the work for them."

The United States did not confront the Palestinians after Abbas failed to give the president his response, or after he signed the truce with Hamas. "How could we lead them to an agreement without confronting them?" asked a senior American official. "Pressure should be applied in both directions."

Another American official has an alternative explanation: "There's no matchup between the Israelis and Palestinians in Washington. That causes an imbalance. We had Makovsky on our staff, and he worked wonders for the Israelis, but we didn't have a Makovsky on the Palestinian side. Our relationship with the Israelis is deep and long-standing, while we have practically nothing with the Palestinians except negotiations. There's also the matter of logistics. Kerry and Netanyahu could talk for hours. Bibi's English is perfect. Kerry could not talk to Abbas like that. Where there's no language, there's no connection. A disproportion of relations is created. Besides, we knew the Israelis could hear every word the Palestinians said and were listening to everything. If we wanted to say something to the Palestinians without Israeli interception, we had to invite them to the White House. That weakens your ability to conduct equal negotiations and be a fair mediator. It puts you on the defensive. You're constantly afraid the Israelis will find out you said this or agreed on that."

The Israelis are also at fault. "Bibi put the Americans through hell on every comma and word," an Israeli participant says. "He allegedly delivered the goods when agreeing in principle to the 1967 lines and the refugee rehabilitation mechanism, but constantly left himself some wiggle room. He made concessions, but actually didn't. At the moment of truth, he wasn't there." An American official adds, "The process Bibi puts you through is so crazy you lose the will to continue. Every time you think there's progress, he releases some more building permits or announces tenders in the West Bank, driving the Palestinians crazy. As he sees it he's made a concession, but in reality he hasn't. He's a master at these manipulations and tricks. He did not make a single real historic decision—to choose the path of peace. He stayed close to his base in the settlements, feeding the monster throughout the entire process, knowing it was sabotage."

However, there are other opinions. "Bibi wasn't bluffing," says one of his close advisors. "When he went into negotiations, he was earnest. His problem is different: There's a discrepancy between what happens in his head and his ability to translate it into action. The political considerations win over. If he had been working in a politics-free environment, he would have reached an agreement. The process built was supposed to allow Bibi to overcome the political obstacles along the way, and come out of the closet only at the very end, when everything was in place. But there was no chance and he simply could not come out. He has no ability to cross the Rubicon. It's a psychological matter. Netanyahu is the opposite of Sharon. Sharon would first decide where he was going and then bulldoze his way to get there. Netanyahu needed someone to pave his way and arrange his coalition, and then he would try to make it. I maintain that throughout all the years and in all of the discussion I attended, there was never the feeling of idle talk. Netanyahu behaves as if it is real, and believes in it." The problem is, it isn't real.

According to Tzipi Livni, "Conflicting internal forces are at play within Netanyahu's soul. On the one hand, there's the understanding of the situation and the need to change it; on the other, there are his perpetual Holocaust survivor feelings and political cynicism. He's turned Israel from an autonomous nation into a Jewish ghetto. The only thing he cares about is whether or not his base will accept his dealings. Instead of leading, he's being led. His head is constantly in the settlements, in the Holocaust, in the next catastrophe. Whenever we agreed on something, he would later deny it. Why do you say we agreed, he would ask me, and I would say 'Because I was in the room when we agreed, and you were there too.' Yes, he would say, but I had reservations. He would leave himself room for leverage at any given moment. Even Dennis Ross, in London, later said it wasn't Bibi, it was him."

Netanyahu and Kerry are two gifted marketers whose encounter resulted in failure. Kerry is an optimistic, naïve, and enthused Democrat. Bibi is a pessimistic, skeptical, and suspicious Republican. Netanyahu's working assumption is that Obama's America is out to get him. He and Kerry wore each other out in vain. There was no consolidation into agreement. Netanyahu cannot separate the wheat from the chaff; the principle of standing your ground on important issues and making concessions where you can is beyond him. When he is flexible on something, he builds a wall separating him from that flexibility. And at the very last moment, fear and insecurity always conquer courage and hope. He has a mystical belief that any time he departs from his mythological base, he is defeated. That's what happened in 1999 after the Wye River accords, and Bibi swore it would never happen again. He has neither the ability nor the leadership to stand up and walk in the right direction, sweeping the people behind him. Instead of leading the base, the base leads him.

In mid-May 2014, *The New York Times* reported that Obama had told Kerry to abandon negotiations in the Middle East. This was not news to Tzipi Livni. On May 15, 2014, the justice minister was in London. Mahmoud Abbas was there, too. Prime Minister Netanyahu was on an official visit to Japan. Netanyahu discovered that Livni's people were trying to set up a meeting with Abbas's people. He was furious. He called Livni to ask whether there were such talks. "It's true," Livni confirmed. "I was going to inform you once we had scheduled the meeting." Bibi was not convinced. After Abbas's truce with Hamas in March, the prime minister had ordered everyone to stop talking to or meeting with the Palestinian leadership. Livni was disobeying orders. Her meeting with Abbas took place; she had to reach closure. "Why didn't you answer the Americans?" Livni asked the Palestinian leader. "I don't believe Netanyahu, that's why," he answered. "You don't have to believe Bibi," Livni said. "The Americans presented you with the document, you have to believe them. Let's put Bibi to the test. Say yes, and we can move forward with this." Livni knew her battle was doomed. The horses had already bolted. But she could not bear the terrible sense of missed opportunity. "The Americans worked with Bibi on every sentence and every word to lead him to a result they thought would really please you," she told Abbas. But what was done could not be undone.

After Netanyahu discovered that his minister of justice had met with Abbas despite his explicit order, he considered firing her. When Finance Minister Yair Lapid got wind of it, however, he told Bibi that firing Livni would be grounds for dissolution of the government. Lieberman was also opposed to firing her. Netanyahu clenched his teeth. He was not ready to dissolve the government, but he'd made his decision. He would dissolve it and fire Livni, and fire Lapid, too. He would not fire his electoral base—the purpose of his existence.

One question remains, and it was aimed at the United States: What would be done with the draft framework agreement? There were, in fact, two: the one drafted by Kerry and Netanyahu, and the version improved at Israel's expense and presented to Abbas. The Americans involved were practically unanimous: President Obama should publish the document, even as an American initiative. "It's a historic paper, arrived at through negotiations between the U.S. and Netanyahu, and it should enter collective history," said an American staffer in a private discussion. Indyk, Makovsky, Ilan Goldenberg, and other staff members wanted very much to publish the document; so did John Kerry. But President Obama vetoed it. The staff was angry. "Even if we've given up on Netanyahu, why not put the principles on the table, for them to take it or leave it?" they asked. A considerable number of Israelis, especially on the left, berated the Americans. "You're irresponsible. Negotiations lead to hopes and expectations, and that's dangerous. When hopes are high and results are zero, explosive energy is created," they said. These prophecies materialized in October 2015, with the outbreak of a wave of individual terrorist attacks throughout Israel, on both sides of the Green Line. "This is a result of hopelessness," said an external Israeli advisor to the negotiations. "Nothing is more dangerous than raising hopes and expectations and then dashing them."

"The perfect time for the Americans to present the document," said an American source, "was in the fifteen days between Abbas's receipt of the document on March 17, 2014, and the day he signed the UN applications, killing the process. It was a window of opportunity. Members of the peace task force tried to get the president and his staff to present the document to the world, but the president was not convinced. Kerry sat with Obama for one last attempt. Obama pointed out the advantages and disadvantages of such a move, and concluded, "John, it's not worth it. Both parties will refuse." Obama was influenced primarily by his chief of staff Denis McDonough and NSA advisor Susan Rice, who warned him of further entanglements. Members of the American staff believe this was a mistake.

"I blame us most of all," says one. "In late March we could have presented the document and it would have changed everything. But we were no longer capable or perhaps not fully committed. Then Abbas signed the resolutions and went into a unity cabinet with Hamas, which gave Bibi the ultimate excuse for shutting everything down."

Eventually, it was a chronicle of predetermined failure. Netanyahu and Abbas are weak leaders. Not only do they lack the courage to make historic decisions, they do not trust each other, and each is convinced the other will betray trust at the last moment. "The tragedy," says an American source, "is that in Abbas's case it's true. He really is unable to deliver the goods. But Netanyahu can. The Israelis would have supported any agreement Bibi made. Netanyahu, unlike Abbas, has unlimited diplomatic credit among his people. He had a chance to make history, and he missed it."

When John Kerry went to the Jordanians and convinced them to support a Palestinian recognition of Israel as a Jewish state, the American continues, "Abbas panicked, and went to the Arab League and made them pass a resolution never to recognize Israel as a Jewish state. We called Mahmoud Abbas and asked why he had done so, and he said it was just for protocol. But the decision was accepted by a large majority; Egypt and Jordan also voted in favor, and everything was over."

Abbas and Netanyahu tried to have their cake and eat it, too. They lied to themselves and tried to hold on to both ends of the stick. Neither had the real ability to deliver the goods. The Israeli-Palestinian conflict is a struggle between two demands, each justified in its own perspective. These legally grounded mutual demands contradict each other. Chaim Weizmann, a founding father of Zionism and first president of Israel, coined it "justice and justice alike." To resolve the conflict, each party will have to understand the other's narrative and make a leap of faith. Benjamin Netanyahu is miles away from such a leap. He once said, "My father taught me to surrender a little to achieve a lot." Netanyahu is enamored of his role as "guardian of Israel's security." That's his image, his legacy; he wholeheartedly believes in the righteousness of the Zionist enterprise, and has no intention or desire to understand the other side. He's not willing to accept a Palestinian state nine miles from the Tel Aviv shore, and his tactic is simply to manage the conflict and keep things stalled in order to somehow maintain an alliance with America while maintaining the status quo. Netanyahu believes time favors the Jewish people. Kerry tried to explain that quite the opposite was true, but Netanyahu was unconvinced. Kerry once tried to compare the hatred of Palestinians for Israelis to the hatred he had seen in the eyes of the Vietnamese during the Vietnam War. Netanyahu dismissed the comparison, appalled. The West Bank is not Vietnam, he said. It's the birthright of the people of Israel. Only a few minutes separate Tel Aviv and Jerusalem from the West Bank. We're protecting our home, not fighting thousands of miles away.

Netanyahu's inner struggle will eventually result in a lean to the right. To break through this paradigm, the Americans will have to become more proficient at using sticks and carrots. Meanwhile, Netanyahu has won. History's verdict will be handed down later.

Epilogue

Netanyahu's against-all-odds landslide victory in the 2015 elections toppled the last remaining walls of caution in the prime minister's official residence on Jerusalem's Balfour Street. Sara and Benjamin Netanyahu became convinced that they were immortal. In contrast to his predecessor, Netanyahu, and his wife, perceived *their* victory as a personal one; a national vote of confidence for *them*. They had faced down all the others and won.

Sara and Benjamin Netanyahu stopped being the elected prime minister and his wife and established themselves as the first Israeli royal family of the modern age. This included all the honors and graces, all the pomp and circumstance. Netanyahu, who, all his life had exercised caution, consideration, and hesitance, now shed all the checks and balances. He intensified his attacks on the media and insisted on personally holding five ministerial positions, in addition to being prime minister. He stopped consulting, stopped considering rules and regulations, stopped being afraid. He looked to the right and to the left and concluded that he had no substitute. Gulliver in Lilliput. Even President Barak Obama ate his dust, until he despaired. There was no one except Netanyahu.

On February 1, 2016, the tenure of Attorney General Yehuda Weinstein came to an end. He was replaced by Maj. Gen. (res.) Avichai Mandelblit, formerly Netanyahu's Cabinet Secretary. Netanyahu believed that what was is what will continue to be: after all, Mandelblit had for close to four years been a part of his bureau. There was no way he'd bite the hand that had fed him.

In November 2016, Donald Trump—against all odds—won the presidency of the Unites State. For the first time since coming into power in 1996, Benjamin Netanyahu will have the good fortune of serving opposite a Republican President of America. No more will he have to deal with Barak Obama or the hated Clintons. No more Liberals and Lefties; long live the new era. From now on it's him and his old friend Donald Trump. No one can stop them. Netanyahu's lifelong dream has come true. Salvation is nigh.

In early 2016, parallel to the changing of the guard in the office of the attorney general, members of the elite police investigating unit, Lahav 433, began checking scraps of information that arrived at Police Intelligence regarding the Netanyahu administration. It began with the allegedly illegal funding of Netanyahu's personal expenses by foreign NGOs and went on to his extensive connections to the large group of Jewish billionaires that had formed around him. The police conducted secret interrogations of dozens of witnesses and collected large quantities of evidence before Attorney General Mandelblit did what his predecessor did not agree to do during his six years in office: He authorized the police to open a broad criminal investigation against Benjamin Netanyahu, with regard to various scandals.

The arrest of Ari Harow, Netanyahu's former chief of staff and CEO of American Friends of the Likud, led the investigators to a hidden treasure: the two lengthy meetings with Bibi's nemesis, *Yediot Ahronot* publisher Arnon (Noni) Mozes, which had been secretly recorded and kept on Harow's cell phone. The investigators, who downloaded the contents of the cell phone, found that Netanyahu and Mozes conducted negotiations to curb the influence of *Israel Today*, the freebie daily funded by billionaire Sheldon Adelson, in return for a change in attitude on the part of *Yediot Ahronot* toward Netanyahu. The affair was reported widely in Israel and cracks started to appear in the fortified defense wall that Netanyahu had built around himself. In addition, news of Netanyahu's personal attorney David Shimron started to appear with regard to a submarine deal with Germany worth billions of dollars, which did nothing to enhance the prime minister's image. Simultaneously, the police began building the "gifts file," with its focus on Israeli/American millionaire, Arnon Milchan, a top Hollywood producer who for many years came and went in the bureau of various Israeli leaders. It would appear that for decades Milchan had been supplying the Netanyahus with a constant flow of expensive cigars and pink champagne among other benefits, in response to their demands. He wasn't alone. The couple's ties with other billionaires were investigated. The prime minister's throne began to wobble.

What remains, as this book goes to press, is how the investigation will pan out. Benjamin Netanyahu has already announced the he has no intention to step down, even if the attorney general decides to indict him. The law does not require him to resign, until or unless he is judged guilty of a criminal offense. The fact that former PM Ehud Olmert stepped down in 2008 even before being indicted neither adds nor subtracts from Netanyahu's current case. He has made it clear that he'll fight to the end, from the prime minister's throne. The "Bibi Spirit" mentioned in the first chapter of this book had become a perfect storm. Bibi will fight to his last drop of blood. He knows that a voluntary "abdication" on his part will open the gates of hell and could spur all those who kept quiet until now to start talking. He's not going anywhere without a fight.

Whichever way it goes, Netanyahu's story is one of miserably missed opportunity. Ever since David Ben-Gurion, in the earliest days of the state, Israel has never had a leader with the kind of unlimited credit given to Netanyahu. For many years, Netanyahu has enjoyed absolute exclusivity over the power and consciousness of the state of Israel. There has never been any real competition; he could have done anything he wanted. Israel would have followed him, had he only chosen to lead. But Netanyahu chose to stick to the here and now, to become addicted to a misleading status quo, caught in the Likud's endless dilemmas, and to do everything it takes to preserve his seat.

As time went by, the real objective of the Netanyahu regime was molded: to remain in power. He failed to block Iran, he destroyed the peace process, contributed to the growing process of delegitimizing Israel in the world, and was forever striving further to the right, in a never-ending chase after the mythical electoral "base" that will enable him to remain in power one more term, another year, longer and longer. He became addicted to leadership and made it the be all and end all, without which Israel will be lost.

Benjamin Netanyahu is a highly talented man. He is perceptive, intellectual, and charismatic, with incomparable verbal abilities and the properties of a superlative politician. Ultimately, all these were wasted by his propensity for treading water. During his first term in office, he introduced some important reforms, and during the last decade he managed to preserve Israel's economy and maintain a reasonable security situation on the borders. As of now, these are his only achievements. It could have been very different. Netanyahu could have gone down in history as a leader who influenced the future of his people, who brought Israel to a new place and burst through the cul-de-sac into which the Jewish state was forced in the seventh decade of its life. Instead, he made a stamp on the seventh decade of his own life, a decade which he spent in power, but left behind nothing at all.

Acknowledgments

This book took more than three years of work and included interviews with 168 various sources, in three languages, spread over three continents and five countries. My sources consisted of Israelis (112), Americans (26), Europeans (11), and people from the Middle East (19). The heroes of this book are those sources who agreed, at times after serious misgivings, to help in the preparation of a biography of an incumbent prime minister, as powerful and predominant, as was Benjamin Netanyahu during the last decade. Some of the sources provided their testimony in secret meeting with me in safe houses, remote hotel rooms and out-of-the-way gas stations. My thanks go to all the anonymous heroes of this book, who stepped up to tell their tales, to speak the truth and to make a contribution to drawing the extremely complex character of one of the most fascinating leaders in the history of the modern state of Israel.

In reality, this book took much longer to compile: I have been following Benjamin Netanyahu since 1988, when he first burst into Israel's political arena. At that time, I was already an active journalist, looking on in wonder at the young political meteor, fluent of speech and dripping with charisma, who stormed his way to the leadership of the Likud party and became Prime Minister of Israel at age forty seven, eight years after entering politics. It seemed at the time that, to Benjamin Netanyahu, even the sky was not the limit.

The first part of this book is based on my earlier biography of Netanyahu (which I wrote with Ilan Kfir) in 1997 (*Netanyahu: The Road to Power*) and includes new revelations, fresh research, and many new insights. 20 years later, some of the events appear differently, their significance has changed; history is beginning to have its own say. Netanyahu's life is spread out the length and breadth of this book from various angles: the story of his grandfather, Nathan Mileikowski, who was active in the early 20th Century and whose similarity to his famous grandson is extraordinary; the enormous influence of his father, Professor Benzion Netanyahu, who died in 2012, at the age of 102, the young Netanyahu's military service in the prestigious Sayeret Matcal, his studies in the US and of course, the icon, whose painful death launched the rise of his younger brother, Col. Yoni Netanyahu.

This book would never have come to be were it not for the patience and support of my family, especially my wife, Hila and my children, Itai, Alona and Avigail. The book would not happened without Ora Cummings, my translator, who pointed out that "it was time for a comprehensive biography of Bibi Netanyahu to be published in English." I thank her and my agent, Lynne Rabinoff, as well as my publisher, Thomas Dunne, and his professional, efficient and devoted team at St. Martin's Press, who together made this book possible.

Thanks to my researcher, Ofri Eliyahu, my extraordinarily efficient transcriber Michal Weizman and everyone else who had faith in this complicated project and survived to see it completed.

As this book is going to press, Benjamin Netanyahu is conducting a rear-guard battle for his political survival, vis-a-vis a big wave of criminal investigations. If he does indeed step down from the political stage, he will have been the personification of the biggest missed opportunity in Israel's history. The man, who could have achieved almost everything, but did practically nothing. If he survives, we'll meet in the next biography.

Ben Caspit, 2017

Index

Index